Motherhood Lost

Motherhood Lost

*A Feminist Account
of Pregnancy Loss
in America*

LINDA L. LAYNE

ROUTLEDGE
New York & London

Published in 2003 by
Routledge
29 West 35th Street
New York, NY 10001
www.routledge-ny.com

Published in Great Britain by
Routledge
11 New Fetter Lane
London EC4P 4EE
www.routledge.co.uk

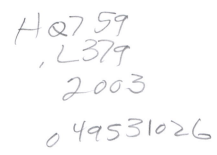

10 9 8 7 6 5 4 3 2 1

Library of Congress Cataloging in publication data

Layne, Linda L.
    Motherhood lost : a feminist account of pregnancy loss in America /
by Linda L. Layne.
        p. cm.
    Includes bibliographical references and index.
    ISBN 0-415-91149-4—ISBN 0-415-91148-6 (pbk.)
    1. Motherhood—United States. 2. Pregnancy—Complications—
United States. 3. Fetal death—United States. I. Title.

HQ759.L379 2002
306.874'3—dc21
                                              2002021336

For Beth Layne, my mother

Contents

Acknowledgments

The process of researching and writing this book has been complexly interwoven with the lengthy and arduous process of forming my family. It began on the day that I had my first miscarriage, and continued through four more miscarriages, the adoption of our eldest son, the traumatic birth of our youngest, through two more miscarriages, and then, finally, the decision to call our family complete.

During the fourteen years of these interrelated projects, I have been fortunate to have had the support of numerous institutions, colleagues, and friends. Just as members of pregnancy-loss support groups fear the effects of the passage of time on memory, I am afraid that time has obscured my memory and that, in the future, some incident will trigger my memory of others whose help I ought to have publicly acknowledged. If you are among those I have failed to recognize here, please trust that your help was appreciated and will be remembered.

Let me begin by acknowledging the members and leaders of the pregnancy-loss support groups who are the subject of this book. Those I had the privilege of meeting were exceptionally kind and giving. *Thank you* for sharing your stories with me, supporting my work, and providing such a warm and welcoming community. The leaders and members of UNITE, SHARE, and the New York Section of the National Council for Jewish Women welcomed me warmly as a parent and later as a professional. It has been wonderful working in such a supportive environment, and I am deeply appreciative of both the work they are doing and the assistance they extended to me.

My research was funded by a grant-in-aid from the Wenner-Gren Foundation for Anthropological Research and a Paul Beer Minigrant Award. Rensselaer Polytechnic Institute provided two semester-long sabbatical leaves, which enabled me to work on the book. In 1997–98 I undertook research on "Environmental Hazards and Pregnancy Loss" sponsored by the

Ethics and Values Studies Program at the National Science Foundation. The research from that project will form the basis of my next book, but the process of doing that research enriched this one as well.

I have also been lucky to have had the help of a series of able research assistants. Deborah Blizzard, James Destro, Heming Jiang, Elizabeth Shea, Jennifer Snediker, and Noel Rosa made sure I got the library materials I needed and used their own initiative to bring me relevant leads. My administrative assistant, Kathie Vumbacco, has enabled my work in countless ways.

I want to thank Bruce Adams who generously shared with me his personal collection of post-mortem photographs, and Harriette Hartigan (www.harriettehartigan.com) who allowed me the use of one of her stunning photographs of homebirth and Robbie Davis-Floyd for her help with this. I'd also like to thank Priti Gress and Paul Johnson at Routledge for their valuable assistance in bringing the book to press and Ben Barker-Benfield for proofing the manuscript for me.

Much of the material in the book was first presented at conferences and in my classes. In addition to regular presentations at the annual meeting of the American Anthropological Association and Society for Social Studies of Science, I also presented papers on pregnancy loss at the annual meetings of the American Ethnological Society; Society for Cultural Anthropology; the Society for Medical Anthropology; the Society on Science and Literature; the Committee on the Anthropology of Science, Technology, and Computing; the International Society for the Comparative Study of Civilizations; at the Conference on Women, Politics, and Change in Twentieth-Century America at The New School for Social Research; the International Conference on Narrative; and as part of the electronic conference "Cultures & Environments" organized by the Washington State University American Studies Department. I profited from the feedback I received on those occasions from the audience and copresenters. I am especially grateful to Gwynne Jenkins, Marcia Inhorn, and Kathleen DeWalt for their invitations to present my research in terms of developments in, and feminist critiques of, medical anthropology.

In addition, I presented work that eventually made its way into this book to the Florida International University School of Nursing; the Department of Anthropology at the State University of New York at Albany; the Department of Anthropology and Program in Women's Studies at Vassar College; the Department of Anthropology and Program in Science and Technology Studies at MIT; the Five Colleges Women's Studies Research Center, the Women's Studies Program and Department of Anthropology at the University of Rochester; and then later as one of the Morgan Lecture

Seminar participants at the University of Rochester. These were particularly congenial and stimulating venues and I am grateful to Anthony Carter, Lisa Cartwright, Colleen Ballerino Cohen, Jean Jackson, Lynn Morgan, Judith Stiehm, and Walter Zenner for these opportunities, and to the coparticipants at these events for such invigorating intellectual exchange. I also want to thank the students in my anthropology of new reproductive technologies seminar who brought me wonderful examples of relevant popular culture.

I have published a number of articles based on this research in journals and collected volumes. Some of the information on the groups found in chapter 3 appears in each of my publications. Part of chapter 5 appeared in 1992 in *Knowledge and Society* 9:29–58. Parts of chapter 6 appeared in 2000 in the *Journal of Material Culture* 5(3):321–345, in a chapter in Ragoné and Twine's *Ideologies and Technologies of Motherhood*, pp. 111–138 (Routledge), and in 1999 in Morgan and Michaels' *Fetal Subjects/Feminist Positions*, pp. 251–278 (University of Pennsylvania Press). A version of chapter 7 appeared in 1999 in my edited collection *Transformative Motherhood*, pp. 167–214 (New York University Press). A version of chapter 8 was published in 1996 in Cecil's collection *Comparative Studies in Pregnancy Loss*, pp. 131–152 (Berg). Part of chapter 10 appeared in 1997 in *Feminist Studies* 23(2): 289–315, and other material from that chapter will appear in the special issue of *Social Science and Medicine* on "Reproduction Gone Awry" edited by Jenkins and Inhorn, 2002. I have benefited from the feedback and suggestions of anonymous reviewers, and from editors including Rosanne Cecil, Ellen Lewin, Daniel Miller, Claire Moses, Lynn Morgan and Meredith Michaels, Helena Ragoné and Frances Winddance Twine, and Rayna Rapp. I also want to thank my co-editors, Danielle Wozniak and Janelle Taylor, as well as the contributors to *Transformative Motherhood* and *Motherhood and Consumption*. They have been a pleasure to work with, and my understanding of pregnancy loss is greater for having thought about it in comparison with these other cases. I'd also like to thank the readers who took the trouble of writing to me to let me know how much they appreciated finding a feminist response to the subject. These letters have meant a great deal to me.

Carol Collatrella, Michael Halloran, Roxanne Mountford, Alan Nadel, and Liz Wright graciously shared their literary expertise with me. Medical historian Andrea Rusnock was always a generous and valuable resource. I also am grateful for the many useful suggestions offered by Joe Brown, Carole Browner, Jennifer Croissant, David Hess, Barbara Katz Rothman, John Schumacher, and Edward Woodhouse.

I owe special thanks to Faye Ginsburg, who encouraged me during the early years of the project while I was a visitor at New York University and then in the final stages, carefully read the book manuscript, and provided exactly the type of suggestions I needed and hoped for.

I might not even have taken up pregnancy loss as a research topic had it not been for Rayna Rapp's example of transforming a painful reproductive experience into a topic for anthropological inquiry. Her groundbreaking work on amniocentesis remains a model for me. In addition, Rayna's generosity is legendary, and I have been privileged to be among the scholars whose research she has supported and whose professional development she has so ably mentored.

I am indebted to Lynn Morgan for providing both the practical and intellectual impetus for articulating my ideas on pregnancy loss with the current feminist debate on fetal personhood. Her invitation to participate in the "fetus seminar" at Mt. Holyoke was a turning point in my work, and two of my subsequent articles were in effect commissioned by her.

I thank Mary Huber for sharing her best ideas so generously with me over the years. Time and time again, right up until the end, I have benefited from her wide-ranging reading, her scholarship, her creative perspective, and astute editorial skills.

I owe special thanks to Shirley Gorenstein. During the six years I overlapped with her at RPI, her exemplary chairing created an ideal intellectual home. In addition, her own work was instrumental in focusing my attention to the material culture dimensions of pregnancy loss.

Mary and Shirley, along with Linda Jacobs and Danny Vecchio, have also graciously served as my children's godparents, supporting not only my efforts to understand and convey the experience of "motherhood lost," but also helping me to celebrate and make the most of the "motherhood" I managed to attain.

Although Gail Landsman was working on the anthropology of reproduction right across the river, we did not get to know one another until after Jasper's birth. Since that time she has spent countless hours apprenticing me as a mother of a child with disabilities, and her research on that topic has provided endless opportunities for stimulating comparison and fruitful discussion.

I am also deeply grateful to Susanne Hand for always being there and for talking me through my own losses, and in the process helping me to better define the problems addressed in this book.

Bernard lived through each of the ups and downs of these two long-term enterprises. Where his impulse was to put our reproductive hardships behind us, I felt compelled to probe and probe again the contours, meanings, and ramifications of disrupted reproduction. Bernard hoped, year after year, that I would stop working on "dead babies" and choose a more cheerful topic. Now, at last, both book and family are complete, and I am finally, with a certain relief, ready to move on.

I also want to thank my children, Fletcher and Jasper. This book was fueled by my deep desire to become a mother. Though the book focuses on motherhood lost, they are living testament to motherhood gained, and words cannot convey the profound joy and satisfaction they give me.

Finally, I would like to thank my own mother, Beth Layne. Throughout my childhood I was aware of how much she loved being a mother. Motherhood was something she was, and still is, extremely good at and thoroughly enjoyed. Although my reproductive difficulties were hard for her, perhaps stirring up memories and feelings of her own reproductive past, she still provides a model of mothering to which I aspire. I hope I can be as good a mother to my children as she has been to me.

CHAPTER 1

My Miscarriage Years

When I married in February 1986, my husband extracted from me the promise that I would finish my dissertation before getting pregnant. So full of joyful anticipation and confidence were we that when the date of my oral was set, we announced our intention to start a baby.[1] I defended my dissertation on October 15 and conceived on the 31st. Fifteen days later a home pregnancy test gave us the wished-for confirmation and we immediately called our parents to announce the imminent arrival of what would be the first grandchild on both sides of the family. I also went to the local knit shop, bought a teach-yourself-to-knit book, a pair of number one needles, and some pastel-yellow baby-weight yarn and started knitting. The next three months were very happy ones indeed. I spent hours comparing notes with friends who were or had been pregnant on the minutest bodily transformations, each and every one of which I relished as a sign of my new state of being. I remember one morning sitting by the front window of a café, basking in the sun, drinking a decaf and enjoying some extra calories, and having a profound and exhilarating sense of myself as being like the trees out front, *alive* and *growing*!

Then, on the evening of Friday, January 16, 1987, in the thirteenth week of my pregnancy, I started cramping and spotting. I called the birthing center where I was a patient, and they reassured me that many women spot during their pregnancies and that it might not mean anything. I was instructed to rest and to call again if it got worse. All through that night, while my husband lay beside me sleeping, I kept a worried vigil. By six the next morning I was bleeding profusely. I woke my husband and called the birthing center. This time the midwife told me to go to the emergency room, suggesting that we call there first to let them know we were coming. By this time I was terrified and was horrified to learn that no one from the birthing center would accompany me. During my initial visit at the center they had stressed that if anything went wrong during labor and I had to be transferred to a hospital to deliver, they would be by my side. I hadn't contemplated anything going wrong earlier in the pregnancy, but now that it was I found that I had wrongly assumed their principle of care would apply to these circumstances too. My husband called the hospital and a nurse asked him how much I was bleeding. When he hesitated, puzzled at how to answer such a question, she prompted, "Is she having to change a pad every hour or so?" By that time I was soaking bath towels at a rapid rate and our panic increased precipitously as we followed her instructions to come to the hospital *immediately*. Upon our arrival the nurses were kind and counseled me not to give up hope yet. After what seemed an eternity, a doctor came in and did a pelvic exam, then gruffly announced that there was placental tissue protruding from the cervix. He asked Bernard when I had last eaten and then left the room without ever having addressed a word to me. Still unclear as to whether all hope was lost, we did not know for sure that I was miscarrying until a nurse came in to tell us that I was being transferred to a ward to wait until my stomach was clear of food and a dilation and curettage (D&C) could safely be done. By the time we made it upstairs to the room, I was in full labor, panting instinctually with each contraction and in no condition to answer, for the second time that morning, all the bureaucratic questions required for admission.[2] At four that afternoon they wheeled me on a stretcher down the corridors, hair in cap, IV in arm, just like on TV, to the glare of lights in the operating room where I was put under and my precious pregnancy finally and officially ended.

I spent that night in the hospital, and was happy to be there in that unreal world, as I tried to come to grips with this sudden, horrible turn of events; not yet ready to go back through the door of my house from which I had left, only the day before, a pregnant woman and expectant mother.

That miscarriage was not only one of the worst experiences of my life, it was also one of the most confusing. Although I had never had a miscarriage before, nor realized that I even knew anyone who had, I found that I had certain expectations about what constituted reasonable behavior in such a situation on the part of the birthing center I had been going to, the doctor who attended me, my family, my coworkers, and my friends. And although some people did act in ways I felt were appropriate for the occasion, more commonly I found that people's reactions were not at all what I expected. While some friends phoned to say they were sorry or came by the house to keep me company as I lay on the living room couch recuperating the day after, others acted as if nothing had happened. One particularly memorable occasion was when my mother called while I was in the hospital and talked about the weather. Others minimized my loss by comparing it to what were, at least to their minds, worse hardships, such as being unable to conceive. And although many of the nurses who cared for me were wonderful (several came and shared their own experience/s of miscarriage), the attitudes of both the male, allopathic doctor who performed the surgery and the female, self-avowed alternative women's healthcare providers at the birthing center expressed a shared, culturally dominant view concerning such events.

Pregnancy losses are very common. The most frequently cited figure is 15 to 20 percent of all pregnancies.[3] This ratio is much higher if one in-cludes pregnancies that end during the first two weeks after conception, that is, usually before a woman is aware of the pregnancy.[4]

Despite their frequency, these events are taboo in our society. The fact that so many different people (doctors, midwives, relatives, and friends) seemed so uncomfortable and at a loss as to how to appropriately respond to pregnancy loss alerted me to the fact that something important was going on culturally. I realized that the tools of anthropology might help illuminate the cultural confusion surrounding pregnancy loss.

A short time earlier I had heard Rayna Rapp present her research proposal for a multisited investigation of the then-still-relatively-new re-productive technology amniocentesis. Her model gave me the intellectual permission I felt I needed to study a topic that touched me so personally. I started attending the Princeton branch of UNITE, a pregnancy-loss sup-port group, as participant and observer, and thenceforth shifted my re-search focus from Jordan to the United States, from collective to individual identity-making processes.

As I undertook this research it never occurred to me that I would con-tinue to explore this topic in such an actively participatory way, but as Bernard and I pursued our quest for a family, pregnancy after pregnancy ended in loss. Ultimately I had seven miscarriages—five before our sons and two after. (Fletcher is adopted and Jasper was born to me at thirty weeks gestation). I turned out to be what is medically termed a "habitual aborter," and, despite years of testing and experimental treatments, no com-pelling medical explanation was ever found.

Despite the still-vivid horror of my first loss, and the particular agonies of each subsequent loss, when I sat down to write this chapter I found that my memory had failed me, much as the members of pregnancy-loss support groups I describe in this book fear. I still remember certain details, of course, such as the time I had the D&C at an abortion clinic in New York City and was heckled by protesters on my way in, and then flew to Jordan the next day as a scholar escort for a group of university professors and I was horrified to discover that one of my wards was quite visibly pregnant. Or the time I had the D&C at New York University Medical Center and had to spend two needless nights in the hospital being awakened repeatedly for the cardiogram, chest X-ray, and complete family medical history that were required of all patients undergoing surgery there. Or the time my doctor's office called, just as we were headed out the door to drive to Pennsylvania for the funeral of Bernard's grandmother, to tell me my progesterone level was low and that I needed to boost it with progesterone suppositories immediately or risk losing the pregnancy. We got a cousin who worked at a pharmaceutical company to help us get the drug, but I miscarried anyway. I also remember the time I tried to give myself a progesterone shot in my thigh and then couldn't walk for days. Or the time I learned that the baby had died right before I was scheduled to speak at a conference and I talked my doctor into prescribing progesterone to sustain the pregnancy long enough for me to go, so my personal loss would not be compounded by a professional loss. Then, once I got there, how weird I felt acting as if nothing was wrong; carrying a dead baby inside me that no one could see and feeling unable to broach the subject in that setting even with my closest colleagues. What could I say, standing there looking/feeling physically fine? "I am in the middle of having a miscarriage"? And what would the appropriate response be in that context?

I also remember going to a clinic on the Lower East Side of Manhattan but can't remember now whether that was for the chromosomal testing or for the first of several excruciating endometrial biopsies. I do remember that my hysterosalpingogram (a test where dye is injected into the uterus then X-rayed to identify structural abnormalities) was done while we were still living in Princeton, and I remember that Bernard and I traveled from Hoboken to Philadelphia to take part in a clinical trial where I was immunized with his white cells, but I can't recall which pregnancy that was. I also remember the first time that I had a miscarriage without having a D&C. It was after we had moved to Troy. Because my fertility specialist's clinic was set up to do daily lab work on female hormones for IVF patients, I had the option of having him surgically end the pregnancy or letting my body do it. Weekly monitoring of HCG, the pregnancy hormone, until it dropped back to zero would assure that all tissue had indeed expelled. I don't know what I was expecting, but I remember how shocked I was when days after I had stopped bleeding, I discovered the embryo. It looked just like the pictures in the pregnancy books, and I was confused about what to do with it. I called my husband, but he would not look at it; in the end I flushed it down the toilet, then regretted having done so.[5]

In pulling out my yearly agendas to try to reconstruct a chronological narrative of what Mary Atkinson,[6] one of my Woburn informants, calls the "miscarriage years," I found there were many details that I had either forgotten or misremembered. For instance, my memory was that we got our dog Jessie between pregnancies, after I decided that I could not undertake another anxiety-ridden pregnancy, or face another loss without the comfort and companionship of a dog. But apparently I was already well into my third pregnancy when I brought Jessie home from the Jersey City pound.[7] I have also rediscovered things I cannot believe I ever forgot. Such as the four months I tried unsuccessfully to get pregnant using the fertility drug Clomid on the theory that perhaps if I conceived at the beginning of ovulation when the egg was fresher, I might have a better outcome. Unaccountably, I seem not to have recorded the time we used artificial insemination (in order to see whether using only the fittest sperm made a difference and because we just couldn't bear to copulate on command any longer), but seeing the record of those Clomid trials brought back that memory. I had also forgotten the fact that it was on the day my Grandma died that I discovered I was pregnant for the second time. I was shocked to find the words "Baby, Baby, Baby" inscribed there on the page next to the words "Grandma dies." I now recall being sad that she would never get to see her great-grandchild but also feeling some comforting rhythm to the cycle of life and death. I am surprised now, and touched, to see that at that point, even though I was certainly by then aware and vigilant against the possibility of loss, that I could still embrace a pregnancy with such innocence and hope.

Of course, I remember many more details about the two more recent losses, for instance how I arranged to have a friend who is a nurse give me my daily progesterone shots because Bernard had reached his limit, and the combination of shame and girlish giddiness we felt when we would meet at the day care center when we picked up our children and commandeer a bathroom stall for the shot. And how a month after the D&C I suffered acute abdominal pain but when I called my doctor's office the nurse decided that I was probably just having ovulation pain and suggested I take aspirin and rest. When this terrible pain recurred a month later and I insisted on seeing the doctor, he confirmed my suspicion that my cervix was blocked by scar tissue from the last D&C and that I needed to be redilated in order to be able to menstruate. I also remember how this medical mishap convinced me to forgo a D&C for my subsequent miscarriage and how much blood there was when I finally began to expel the pregnancy in the middle of the night in a stranger's house while "in the field" in Oregon. By afternoon the bleeding had slowed but I was too afraid to drive alone through the only partially paved winding mountain roads to my scheduled interview in that condition, so I substituted an urban informant and by the next day was well enough to make it to the village of Alsea to interview a woman who had had even more pregnancy losses than I. Then, under the guise of research, I listened to her story and set about, once again, revising my own.

In addition to these kinds of memories, I also remember how with each new pregnancy, each subsequent miscarriage, I came to feel increasingly ashamed of both my inability to carry a child and my determination to keep trying. What would my friends think when they learned I was pregnant *again*? Would they admire my perseverance or think I must be crazy and obsessed to keep hitting my head against this brick wall? Would they have faith that one of these times it would work, or did they think I was just stupidly setting myself up again for failure and disappointment? Shouldn't I just accept this shortcoming and get on with my life, put my energies into projects that promised more success?

Like many pregnancy-loss support group members I have studied, I experienced these losses as an assault on my sense of self. The losses forced me to revise the story of my life and my account of myself. What kind of person, what kind of woman, was I after all? How was it that this person who was a college athlete and had a body that could always be counted on to perform could fail so miserably at this most important bodily task? How was it that this person who had always managed to overcome challenges through tenacity and hard work could not get this right, no matter how hard she tried?

I also found that the experience challenged my tacit understanding of the world, of how things are and the way life works. I had grown up with the nickname "Lucky Louie" but had never articulated, let alone questioned, how the notion of "luck" fit into my worldview.[8] Many people find comfort in an "it's all meant to be" theory of the world; others find that the experience of loss challenges those cherished beliefs. Lacking such a belief system, how could I best theorize misfortune?

Although over the years I had kept track of the number of losses and periodically revised my articles to reflect the current total, I never produced a single, cumulative narrative account of my losses. How can this be? How is it that when I thought perhaps I should give a brief accounting of my losses for this text, I found I had lost track of them? How can it be that with all the writing I did on the subject, I was not prompted to write my own story? How is it that an anonymous reviewer of the proposal for this book had to draw my attention to the fact that given the extremely personal nature of this research topic, I was strangely absent from the text? I have written about and publicly presented the story of Jasper's traumatic birth and his two-month stay in the Neonatal Intensive Care Unit on several occasions

(Layne 1996a).[9] What accounts for my willingness to narrativize that event and reluctance or inability to do the same for the miscarriages?

The answer lies, I suspect, in the fact that through all those child-bearing/child-losing years, I felt the jury was still out. Each new loss provided new data to be taken into account. Instead of a single narrative I produced many stories, each one replacing the one before it, each one tentative, provisional.

Each of the first five losses added to the growing evidence that I might never be able to bear a child. Then when Jasper was born I had to revise my story again. Perhaps the immunological theory was true after all; perhaps Bernard's and my genes were so similar that my body didn't recognize his cells as different soon enough to start the immunological response to protect the "foreign bodies" that fetuses are.[10] Perhaps all those losses had been a learning process and perhaps my body had finally figured this out and would be able to handle it even better the next time, perhaps even making it all the way through a pregnancy to an idyllic "natural" birth of an idyllic healthy baby.[11] Then came the sixth miscarriage. So invested was I in the story that I was getting better at pregnancy through dint of effort that I rationalized—perhaps this one was "a normal miscarriage," just the odd bad egg, or sperm, or cell division that accounts for most people's miscarriages. But then, with the seventh loss, I had to abandon the "It took a long time but I finally learned how to carry a pregnancy" story about myself. After that loss I asked my fertility specialist about the latest experimental treatments for suspected immunologically based habitual abortion. The picture he drew was daunting: before conception a slew of blood tests, then multiple immunizations, and then more tests. Once pregnant, I could look forward to a daily regimen of baby aspirin, progesterone shots in the bum, and heparin shots in the stomach, as well as periodic afternoons hooked up to an IV drip of something he described as "chicken soup for the immune system." I then asked the chief perinatologist at the medical center whether, if I was willing to undergo these intense immunotherapies, and I did manage to carry a pregnancy, I would get toxemia again. Even though she thought these therapies did reduce the chance for toxemia, she concluded that, given my history, chances were good that I'd get it again. To her mind, this was not a major concern, but since I had lived through it once, toxemia constituted a *very* large concern for us. Given all this and the fact that we had two young children to raise, I finally agreed to consider our family complete.

This, then, is my story. The book, though obviously grounded and informed by these experiences, is not based on my story but on the narratives of pregnancy-loss support-group members. Though I rarely return to my

personal experience in the text, the reader will recognize a number of similarities between my story and the others I relate.[12]

But there are several important ways in which my narrative differs from
those of most pregnancy-loss support-group members. For instance, during
each of my pregnancies I thought of myself as "with child" and I have been
changed by the grief I felt each time I lost a "baby"; unlike many members
of pregnancy-loss support groups, however, I did not name them, and do
not think of them as "members of my family." At times, in fact, I had the
sense that they were not separate individuals, but more like a Trobriand Island spirit baby, a single spirit who kept trying to enter the world (Malinowski 1987).

In the end, though, my own narrative has inevitably been changed
through years of listening to, reading, and reciting other's narratives of loss.
I began this research with the conviction that the tools of anthropology
would be helpful to Americans who had suffered a pregnancy loss. Over the
years I have analyzed the cultural resources that women and their networks
draw upon to make sense of their loss and have written this book in the hope
of adding some lesser-known resources to the available repertoire. Ultimately, as is so often the case, the exchange went both ways, and I have
found the images and symbolic vocabulary of pregnancy-loss support
groups working their way into my personal narrative of loss.

On a shelf in my office I keep a crêpe-paper butterfly from one of
UNITE's conferences. At that conference, bereaved parents were invited to
write the name of their dead "baby" or "babies" on the butterflies and then
hang them on a felt tree to commemorate their loss/es.[13] I remember how
awkward I felt on that occasion, wanting to participate, to share in the healing power of ritual, but being unable to do so, never having attributed full-
fledged individual personhood to my losses. But years later, in a moment of
anguish, this metaphor of the child as butterfly came to me unbidden. In
1997, as I lay alone on the table in the examination room at my doctor's office where I had just had the D&C for my sixth miscarriage, with lights off
and blinds drawn, resting in the cool, dim light until I felt well enough to
get up and drive myself home, I had a vision of a butterfly leaving my body,
fluttering off, out the window, toward the light

good-bye Baby,

good-bye. . .

CHAPTER 2

Caught in the Middle: Pregnancy Loss at the Turn of the Century

"Pregnancy Loss"

Over the years, as I continued to add to my direct, personal knowledge of pregnancy loss, I focused my scholarship on the experience of pregnancy-loss support-group members. I discovered that the first pregnancy-loss support groups had been established in the United States in the mid-1970s and that during the 1980s such groups spread quickly throughout the country. By 1993 there were over nine hundred pregnancy-loss support groups, and similar groups had been established in Canada, Australia, Israel, Italy, England, West Germany, South Africa, and the Virgin Islands (SHARE 1993).

By 2000 the number of pregnancy-loss support groups had dropped to 709 and of those approximately thirty to forty did not offer peer support. The drop in numbers is due in part to the fact that one large organization that had offered peer support changed its policy and now offers only one-on-one support (Cathi Lammert, personal communication, July 16, 2000). Another reason may be that people are getting better support in hospitals at the time of their loss, and this care often includes a one-on-one follow-up session (Lammert, personal communication, 2000). The advent of pregnancy-loss support websites may also be a factor (see chapter 10).

The concept of "pregnancy loss" itself most probably emerged simultaneously with the groups. It is a lay term which encompasses multiple terms from the somewhat overlapping languages of demography ("fetal wastage," "intrauterine mortality," "fetal loss," "wasted pregnancies") and biomedicine ("spontaneous abortion," "stillbirth," "perinatal" and "neonatal death").

"Spontaneous abortion," the medical term for "miscarriage," is defined as the involuntary termination of pregnancy "before the fetus is sufficiently developed to survive" (Cunningham et al. 2001:856). "Stillbirth" is used to designate any fetal demise after that point.[1]

Many members of pregnancy-loss support groups express discomfort with the use of these terms. "Spontaneous abortion" is disliked because of the primary association of the term "abortion" with "elective abortions" (cf. Reinharz 1987: 238). Some also express dislike for the word "miscarriage" because it implies some negligence on the part of the mother. For instance, Angie Farrell (1992), who miscarried at 11 weeks, writes seven years later, "I do not like the word miscarried. It implies that I did not know how to carry my baby in my womb. . . . So I prefer to call it my missed baby. Oh, how I miss her!" (cf. also Hoch 1988b). Others express similar feelings about the word "stillborn." For example, in her piece entitled "He Was Still Born," Janet Jones (1991) writes, "STILLBORN—how I have come to hate that word. . . . STILLBORN—It shouldn't be used. It should be two words, giving it a true meaning. "Still Born" is to be "Still delivered" or "still Brought into this World". . . .On June 14, 1990, my son was *still* born, two words, NOT one! I *still* pushed, I *still* had labor and he was *still* born. . . ."

Over the past twenty-five years, as advances in neonatal medicine have pushed back the date at which a fetus has any possibility of surviving ex utero, the boundary separating miscarriage from stillbirth has changed. The latest edition of *Williams Obstetrics* sets the boundary at "20 weeks based upon the date of the first day of the last normal menses." Because birth weight is considered to be more accurate than gestational dating, the trend is moving toward reliance on birth weight. *Williams* now suggests 500g as the cutting off point (Cunningham et al. 2001:856).

"Perinatal mortality," a term coined in the late 1940s to highlight the commonalities between late fetal deaths and early infant deaths, has multiple definitions. The most restrictive includes deaths that occur between twenty-eight weeks gestation and the seventh day after birth (Hoyert 1995, MacFarlane and Mugford 1984:34). The more inclusive definition, recommended by the National Center for Health Statistics, suggests using the birth weight of 500g (or twenty weeks gestation) and includes death occurring up to twenty-eight days after birth (Cunningham et al. 2001:856). A "neonatal death" is one that occurs during the first twenty-eight days after birth. In other words, this category overlaps with perinatal death, but includes only those perinatal deaths that occur after birth.

There were an estimated 890,000 spontaneous fetal losses in the United States in 1992 (Ventura et al. 1995:12), and the most recent National Vital Statistics report shows this number as having grown to 983,000 (Ventura et al. 2001:1). Miscarriages represent the vast majority of pregnancy losses. For approximately every four live births in the United States, one pregnancy now ends in elective abortion and one in "spontaneous fetal loss" (Ventura et al. 2001:1). More than 80 percent of these spontaneous losses occur during the first trimester (Cunningham 2001:856). The rate decreases rapidly thereafter; only about 3% of all intrauterine deaths take place after sixteen weeks gestation (Bongaarts and Potter 1983:39, Cunningham et al. 2001:1073-1074). There were a reported 35,926 perinatal deaths in 1991 and 18,520 neonatal deaths in 1999 (U.S. Dept. of Health and Human Services 1999:22).

Changes in reproductive medicine and demographic trends in the United States during the last twenty years have resulted in new patterns of pregnancy loss, with an overall increase in the number of pregnancy losses but with some types of loss increasing while other types have decreased. One explanation for the overall increase is found in the changing distribution of women of childbearing age. The rate of pregnancy loss generally increases as women age. The rate for women under 20 years is 12 percent and 26 percent for women over 40 (Cunningham 2001: 856).[2] During the 1990s pregnancy rates declined for women under the age of 30 and rose for women over 30 (Ventura et al. 1995:1).

Another source is found with the dramatic increase in ectopic pregnancies during the past twenty years. According to the latest edition of *Williams Obstetrics*, "there has been a marked increase in both the absolute number and rate of ectopic pregnancies in the United States" and these figures are "out of proportion to population growth" (Cunningham et al. 2001:885). The rate of ectopic pregnancy "increased fourfold from 1970 to 1992" bringing the rate up to almost 2 percent of all pregnancies by 1992. This increase is attributed in part to the use of assistive reproductive technologies such as in vitro fertilization (IVF) and gamete intrafallopian transfer (GIFT). An earlier reproductive innovation, the administration of Diethylstilbestrol (DES) to over three million women in the United States between 1938 and 1975 as a preventative for miscarriage, also accounts in part for this increase. DES daughters have "between 8.6 and 13.5 times more ectopic pregnancies than normal" (Dumit and Sensiper 1998: 218). They also have a higher risk of miscarriage and "between 4.7–9.6 times more premature births" (Dumit and Sensiper 1998: 218).

At the same time, a number of factors have led to an overall decrease in the number of late losses (Tangir 2001).[3] Although malaria is believed to affect "reproductive health at each stage" including "increased likelihood of miscarriage and stillbirth" (Townsend and McElroy 1992:23 quoted in Bledsoe 1999:63), many infectious diseases, including venereal diseases, are particularly associated with late pregnancy loss. Perinatal rates have also been reduced by prenatal diagnosis. According to one study "the fetal death rate due to lethal anomalies declined by almost half between the 1970s and 1980s" because of early terminations for these pregnancies (Cunningham 2001:1074).[4]

Some types of perinatal death have become more common, however. For example, the frequency of multiple gestations has significantly increased because of the advent of fertility drugs and due to a later age of childbearing—women over thirty-four years of age being more likely to spontaneously conceive multiples. Research indicates that about "10% of all perinatal deaths are multiple birth babies" (Launslager 1994:120).

Studies show "real interpopulation variation in risk of pregnancy loss" (DeLuca and Leslie 1996). DeLuca and Leslie (1996:126) note that third-trimester pregnancy loss has decreased in Western countries during this century but point out that the rate within Western countries varies with ethnicity and education (1996:126).

The United States continues to rank far behind other industrialized countries in terms of fetal, perinatal, and neonatal mortality rates (Hoyert 1995:1). In all three of these categories black women are significantly over-represented. The estimated rate of pregnancy loss is nearly double for women of color—21.3 percent for blacks and 23.2 percent for Hispanics, in contrast with 12.9 percent for non-Hispanic white women (Ventura et al. 1995:18). Black women continue to be about three times as likely to give birth to "very low birth weight" babies (i.e., less than 1,500 grams or 3.3 pounds), and these babies "account for up to half of the deaths of newborns" (U.S. Dept. of Health and Human Services 1999:19).[5] "Nonwhite women" also have a higher incidence of ectopic pregnancy in every age category and "this disparity increases with age" (Cunningham et al. 2001:885).

In medical textbooks like *Williams Obstetrics*, information on all of these events can be found under the large categories of "pathology of pregnancy" and "pathology of labor." Many of the pathologies described in these sections would almost certainly result in a pregnancy loss, for example, extrauterine pregnancy or diseases and abnormalities of the ovum, while others could, but might not necessarily, result in a loss, for example, prolapse of the umbilical cord, preterm rupture of membranes, or infectious diseases. In other words, medical knowledge is organized around different principles than those that inform pregnancy-loss support.

These diverse etiologies mark an important way in which pregnancy-loss support groups differ from many other patient support groups (Heath 1998, Rapp, Heath, Taussig 2000, Taussig, Heath, Rapp 1999), in that they are not organized around a particular medical disease or syndrome. The specific medical cause of the loss is not the organizing principle for pregnancy-loss support. Indeed, in many if not most cases, the actual cause of the demise is not known. Instead, it is the shared experience of not having a baby to take home at the end of a desired pregnancy that unites members of pregnancy-loss support groups.

Pregnancy Loss and Mutual-Aid Groups

What accounts for the rapid spread of pregnancy-loss support groups? One answer is that they might simply be part of the proliferation in the United States of support groups for all manner of medical or psychological ills. The rise and spread of pregnancy-loss support groups during the 1980s and 1990s are clearly part of a larger cultural trend. Pregnancy-loss support groups, like other contemporary mutual-help groups, are testament to "the evolution of a social milieu conducive to the public airing of intimate problems" (Sandelowski 1993:9).

A critical component of this trend is the rise in the twentieth century of "psychoanalysis and the talking cure" (Cartwright 1995:47). Prior to Freud, psychiatry had privileged "sight and the body's surface appearance." Freud's "techniques based in speech and hearing" represented a radical innovation (Cartwright 1995:50). At the time of Freud's historic visit to the United States in 1909, "talking cures" were little known and looked on with suspicion by the medical community (Caplan 1998). By the end of the century there were "tens of thousands of licensed psychotherapists" and "perhaps an equal, if not greater number, of unlicensed practitioners" of over a hundred "recognizable varieties of 'psychosocial' therapies" (Caplan 1998:2, 152). Pregnancy-loss support, in fact, emerged following one of the most significant periods of growth in psychology, the number of doctorates conferred in that field having "nearly doubled between 1971–1987" (Irvine 1999:37).[6]

Mutual-aid groups also grew in number during those years. Histories of mutual-help groups[7] in the United States normally begin with the establish-

ment of Alcoholics Anonymous (AA) in 1935. Scholars frequently make a
distinction between groups, such as AA, which follow a twelve-step program (approximately one-third of mutual-aid groups according to Wuthnow 1994:71), and those that do not; pregnancy-loss support being of this
latter type.

According to Katz (1993), among the earliest and still among the most
important of the non-twelve-step-type groups are groups for parents of sick
children. By the early 1950s there were organizations to help people care for
children with mental retardation, cerebral palsy, hemophilia, and muscular
dystrophy. In addition to helping parents cope with particularly challenging
parenting experiences, these organizations publicized the problems, got
professionals to pay more attention to them, and influenced the government
(Katz 1993:87).

The populist movement of the 1960s brought forth new sites and forms
of mutual-help groups. Pregnancy-loss support groups are clearly part of
the proliferation that started in the 1970s and continued through the '80s
and '90s of new "voluntary organizations." These local groups, many of
which were initiated by "graduates of the New Left," make up what Boyte
(1980) has dubbed a "Backyard Revolution." An important subtype of these
"local groups" is "self-help" or "mutual aid" groups. By 1982, Frank Riessman, the director of the New York–based National Self-Help Clearing-
house, estimated that in North America there were fifteen million people
involved in self-help groups of one kind or another (Reissman 1982:42), up
from "an estimated 5–8 million people in 1976" (Brown 1988).[8] A self-help
group is defined as "one in which people who face a common concern or
condition come together voluntarily for emotional support and practical assistance. They generally meet without professional supervision, though
they may draw upon professional expertise" (Brown 1988). Although such
groups are found in many other countries, the United States has "the highest concentration of these groups" (Katz quoted in Brown 1988). Their
popularity here has been linked to "the decline of neighborhoods, increased
mobility, and the breakdown of family relationships,"[9] which has resulted in
people being now more often "linked by special rather than community interests," as well as "Americans' historic penchant for joining" (Katz quoted
in Brown 1988). Some see this movement as an important component of
progressive politics, with its "ethos" of "antiexpertism" and "irritability
with bigness" and value of knowledge that "is experiential, indigenous, and
rooted in wisdom, which comes from struggling with problems in concrete
shared ways" (Reissman 1982:42). Others see it as "simply an extension of

the self-absorption of the seventies" (and one could add, of the eighties and nineties) and of a "retreat to individual solutions and a ploy to keep people from demanding what they need from the state" (Withorn 1986:416).

These two views are not mutually exclusive, and they point to changes that occurred during the twentieth century in dominant cultural under-standings about the proper relationship between self and society. Mutual-aid organizations established at the end of the twentieth century, like preg-nancy-loss support groups, share a very different understanding of the relationship between self and society than that of organizations like AA. As Irvine observed, AA was established during an era when "norms and insti-tutions" were viewed as "essentially good and psychological health involved fitting in and conforming" (Irvine 1999:22). In contrast, pregnancy-loss support groups were established in the context of a new "therapeutic ethos," which understands the self to be "innately good, with 'needs' that deserve priority over conforming to society's norms" (Irvine 1999:22).[10] In addition, pregnancy-loss support groups are well described by Irvine's con-cept of a "lite" institution, a new form of institution that provides "the ben-efits of enduring structure without the burden of rules, assigned roles, and onerous obligations" (1999:83, see also Wuthnow 1994). These new institu-tions, Irvine (1999:67) argues, offer "anchors for selfhood," which in the past had typically been provided by the institutions of family, religion, edu-cation, that is, those institutions traditionally studied by sociologists. These new "lite" institutions, she suggests, are more suitable and acceptable "to a generation of free agents" (1999:83).

While it is clear that the advent of pregnancy-loss support groups were part of a larger late-twentieth-century movement toward mutual help in North America,[11] there are a number of factors that help explain the emer-gence of this particular type of mutual-help group at this time. Simonds and Rothman (1992) attribute the emergence and spread of pregnancy-loss support groups to the empowerment of upper- and middle-class women in the public world. "As women gain power, the concerns of women are in-creasingly seen as matters of public concern" (Simonds and Rothman 1992:4). They explicitly argue against the theory that contemporary upper-and middle-class women grieve more than did their counterparts one hun-dred years ago or their less-fortunate sisters today. "It is not the experience that changes: it is our power to make our experiences heard and to have them credited that varies" (Simonds and Rothman 1992:6). But rather than positing a universal, historically constant experience of maternal grief that is simply expressed more publicly now, my analysis stresses the cultural and historical particularities of the experience of pregnancy loss during these years.

The Argument

I argue that since the 1980s middle-class women in the United States who experienced a pregnancy loss were caught in the middle of two contradictory sets of powerful cultural forces, and that this location exacerbated their experience of loss and explains in part the rapid growth of the pregnancy-loss support movement.

The first set of forces concerns the increasingly important role in the public imaginary that fetuses have come to occupy (Morgan 1996a, 1996b, 2002, Michaels and Morgan 1999). A number of sociopolitical, demographic, and medical developments since the mid-1970s have contributed to this trend. The legalization of abortion in 1973 and the trenchant and ongoing debate over the legality and morality of abortion are both cause and sign of the American collective preoccupation with the physiological capacities and existential status of fetuses (Luker 1984, Ginsburg 1989). The demographic shift toward a smaller family size and the related, though not identical change toward a later age for women to have their first child, has resulted in less shared common knowledge among women about the frequency of pregnancy loss. This has led to unrealistic expectations about pregnancy outcomes (see chapter 5).

These same demographic changes precipitated changes in the medical management of reproduction, which in turn contributed to the emergence of an increasingly prominent fetal patient (Harrison 1982).[12] Sandelowski (1993:7) attributes the greater demand for effective infertility treatments in the 1980s in large part to the experience of members of the baby-boom generation who postponed childbearing, then were confronted with the effects of age on their fecundity.[13] In response to this new demand, and the fact that the demand for regular obstetrical services had declined between 1965 and 1975 with the decline in fertility rates, many doctors began to specialize in reproductive endocrinology/infertility, board certification having become available for this subfield in 1974 (Sandelowski 1993:9). Research in these and other areas, such as neonatology, resulted in the development of a host of new reproductive technologies—technologies that contributed, in both direct and indirect ways, to the construction of fetal patienthood and personhood and had a number of unintended consequences for the experience of pregnancy loss (see chapter 5).

Together, new reproductive technologies, particularly home pregnancy tests and ultrasound imaging, as well as a related movement toward medically managing pregnancy at ever earlier stages, and the media campaigns of pro-life activists, have moved up the time and pace with which many American women begin to socially construct the personhood of a wished-for child.

Many women now begin this process from the moment they do a home pregnancy test. Each cup of coffee or glass of wine abstained from and each person informed of the impending birth add to the "realness" of the baby they are growing within. They may follow the weekly physiological development of their "baby" with a home pregnancy manual, and each prenatal visit contributes to and confirms the growing sense of the baby's realness and their growing sense of themselves as "mothers." This may be especially true of those visits at which one hears the heartbeat, sees the baby moving on the sonogram screen, or is informed of the baby's sex. They may start making or acquiring things for the baby, preparing a place for it in their homes and in their lives. They may have quit their jobs, or taken maternity leave, or bought a new house. They may have given the baby a name or nickname and have started talking to it, or trying to influence its personality by playing it special music. Friends, neighbors, or colleagues may have feted the anticipated child and new mother with a baby shower.

Once a pregnancy loss occurs, however, would-be mothers are confronted with the second set of cultural forces. A deeply rooted cultural taboo still limits the social acknowledgement and support that bereaved parents are given and the incipient personhood of the wished-for child is often revoked (chapter 4). When the pregnancy ends without a baby to bring home, the very people who have encouraged the mother-in-the-making to take on this role and may have participated with her in the social construction of her "baby" often withdraw their support for these interrelated projects and act as if nothing of any significance took place.[14] The cultural denial of pregnancy loss challenges the validity of the social and biological work already undertaken in constructing that child and belittles the importance of the loss.

These contradictory forces create a number of special problems for women who undergo a pregnancy loss. The first of these problems is what I call "the realness problem of pregnancy loss." The realness of the baby, the mother, the event, and the legitimacy of grief are simultaneously challenged. A number of women describe this problem in their narratives of loss published in pregnancy-loss support group newsletters. For example, in a

piece by Anne Ciany of Arundel, Maryland, entitled "I'm a Mother Too,"
published in the Mother's/Father's Day issue of a support group newsletter, Anne describes how after her first child was born prematurely and died
after eighteen hours she sometimes finds herself asking, "Am I a mother?"
In an interesting reversal of the primacy of biological relatedness for forming kinship bonds, she explains that family members tell her "that I am not
really a mother because I have never experienced raising a child and all the
work that is involved." [15] But despite her occasional doubts, Anne maintains
that she does feel like a parent because "we have/had a son, we didn't give
birth to an 'it.' Collin was real; he existed. If we have/had a son, then we
must be parents. If not, what are we? Give us a title if we aren't parents. . . .
We've lost so much. Don't deprive us of our motherhood too" (1999). Lisa
Jeffries, a support group facilitator, describes the realness problem her loss
created for her, both in terms of knowing how to mourn and getting others
to participate in this process. In a piece addressed to a "baby" miscarried at
eleven weeks, Lisa writes, "I will remember you in so few ways it hurts. Because I never knew you. And yet you were real and alive in me. I wish I
could hold on to something about you. I wish I could show everyone how
real you were to me. So then you would be real to them. And then they
would know, As I do, That we've all lost someone special in you" (Jeffries
1998).

A related set of problems also illustrated by this piece clusters around issues of trauma and memory. Many experience pregnancy loss as traumatic,
and as one finds with other types of trauma, pregnancy loss creates a number of problems for memory. Like others who undergo trauma, in order to
heal, bereaved parents need to be able to remember and in order to do this
they must share their stories with empathetic listeners. Yet, because their
stories contradict cherished cultural scripts regarding linear progress, they
appear to be "too corrosive to the moral order" and those who suffer these
events are put in what Langer refers to as a "moral quarantine" (Langer
quoted in Kirmayer 1996:189). This makes "the management of memory"
more difficult (Kirmayer 1996:189). In addition to these problems, which
are shared by others whose lives are disrupted (Becker 1997), pregnancy loss
creates a number of unique problems of memory stemming in part from ambiguity about the nature of that which is to be remembered. If one understands pregnancy loss to be a biological mishap like an illness or injury, then
one should welcome recovery and make an effort to "get over it." [16] However, if one understands pregnancy loss to be the death of a member of immediate family, then the language of recovery is not appropriate. Instead
one is morally charged to remember, especially perhaps if there is social

pressure to forget. Yet this charge is hindered by the fact that the "person" being remembered was so little known, known indirectly, and by so few.

Another distinct set of problems affecting women experiencing pregnancy loss at this historical juncture has to do with moral judgments of failure and blame. Since in the United States we tend to understand moral stature and worldly success to be the result of purposeful, individual effort, a reproductive "failure" like pregnancy loss is often understood by women to be somehow their fault. Although physicians routinely reassure women post facto that there was nothing they could have done to cause their loss, this message contradicts all of the morally laden messages they have received throughout the pregnancy regarding their personal responsibility for the well-being of their child. The women's-health movement has also contributed to the belief that women can and should control the outcome of their pregnancies. The doctrine of individual responsibility and culture of meritocracy that so infuses our society (chapter 7), including orthodox and alternative obstetrics, exacerbates the experience of pregnancy loss by creating a double bind. Either women accept responsibility for the pregnancy loss and blame themselves for the death of their "baby," or they must admit that the loss was a bodily event over which they had no control. This alternative is nearly as damning as self-blame. In fact, many North American women who experience pregnancy losses judge themselves on both of these counts—they tell of how upsetting it was to be "out of control" and at the same time list ways that they may have been responsible.

In this book I explore the contours and import of these historically and culturally specific problems, map out the cultural resources that members of pregnancy-loss support groups routinely use to make sense of and deal with their loss in this context, and begin the work of forging a feminist framework for understanding and responding to pregnancy loss.

A Feminist Anthropological Approach

Motherhood Lost is the first full-length study of pregnancy loss that adopts a feminist anthropological approach. Throughout my years of study on this topic I have written for educated lay readers and interdisciplinary scholars. Although I believe I have been successful in making my work accessible to a wide readership, I have found that anthropological methods and presentation conventions are sometimes misunderstood by those not familiar with them. One of the maxims used to describe anthropological scholarship is that we seek to make the strange familiar and the familiar strange.[17] Traditionally anthropologists conducted their research by going to live for an ex-

tended period of time (at least one and often many years) among people who
understood the world and organized their social lives in ways dramatically
different from the way we do. The goal of anthropological research was to
learn enough about that other way of life that one could understand the
sense and logic of it and be able to convey this to people of one's own culture. A classic example of this was Malinowski's study of the reproductive
beliefs and practices of the Trobriand Islanders. He found that they believed intercourse played only a minor role in reproduction; it opened the
way for a matrilineal spirit baby to enter a woman's womb (cf. chapter 1).
Rather than presenting these beliefs and practices as proof that Trobriand
Islanders were "mistaken, confused, immoral, or less intelligent than Euro-
peans," Malinowski showed how this system made perfect sense in the context of their matrilineal system of descent, and futhermore exposed "the
ethnocentrism of previous assumptions that paternity could only be defined
biologically" (Franklin 1997:22).

In order to convey "the native's point of view," anthropologists use "declarative" writing conventions (Csordas 1997) that may seem strange to
those unacquainted with them. For example, Weiner, who also worked in
the Trobriand Islands, reports that fetuses "are formed by the combination
of a woman's blood and an ancestral spirit" (Weiner 1988:54). Similarly, in
describing "how babies are made" among the Wari' of Amazonia, Conklin
and Morgan write, "Flesh and bones—the solid parts of the fetal body—are
literally created out of semen and nourished by it. . . . Wari' babies can have
multiple fathers; any man who has sex with a pregnant woman contributes
semen to form the fetus's body and has a claim to biological paternity"
(1996:671).

Comparable examples from my study might be things like the beliefs
that dead fetuses become guardian angels of family members left on earth,
or new stars in the sky, or immanent in more mundane aspects of nature
such as little blue spruces. These beliefs are just as foreign to me as many of
the beliefs of the 'Abbadi tribespeople with whom I lived while conducting
anthropological research in Jordan. In both cases, my disciplinary training
leads me to present such beliefs with respect.

This anthropological stance, however, may be easier to accept in the
context of "exotic" peoples like the Trobriand Islanders, the Wari', or 'Ab-
badis. As Csordas (1997:xii) learned while studying Catholic Charismatics
in the United States, when this "relativizing style" is "applied to cultural
phenomena that is close to home and yet puzzling within the cultural context of academics," this "straightforward declarative language" can "suddenly seem strange (and the ethnographer along with it)," *even* to other

anthropologists. Csordas found that when he "adopted this declarative convention in writing and speaking about Charismatics," people frequently "suspected" him of being a "believer" (1997:xii).

I have met similar challenges. Like Csordas, I have found that the apparent religiosity expressed in so many narratives of loss published in the newsletters may provoke feelings of discomfort among secular academics.[18] Furthermore, because I am working within my own culture and on a subject with which I have such a clear personal involvement, I am routinely asked to declare my own beliefs and distinguish my position from my ethnographic subjects in ways that would be inconceivable if I were presenting ethnographic material from Jordan. When simply reporting the ethnographic practices of my "natives," such as their use of the rhetoric of the gift, I have been accused of "condoning" these practices (McLeod 2001:70).[19]

Despite our declarative conventions, however, anthropology is not simply descriptive. Geertz depicts anthropological understanding as contingent on the ability "to grasp concepts that, for another people, are experience-near, and to do so well enough to place them in illuminating connection with experience-distant concepts theorists have fashioned" (1983:58). Like all of those trained in this tradition, in my research I tack dialectically back and forth between "local" ethnographic detail and social theory.

Nor does the "declarative" and "relativizing style" of ethnographic presentation preclude critical engagement. My goals in writing this book have been to provide a fuller understanding of the experience of loss for contemporary middle-class United States women and their social networks and to seek ways in which this experience could be ameliorated. In other words, my research has been of the kind sometimes referred to as feminist participatory or action research (Reinharz 1992:175, Reason 1994). According to Reinharz (1992:175), "feminist scholarship is inherently linked to action." In her view, "the purpose of feminist research must be to create new relationships, better laws, and improved institutions." I would also add the creation of new frames of understanding and responding.

My first miscarriage was a shattering, life-changing experience. Writing this book has helped me to understand more fully why this was so. Gaining a better appreciation of the contradictory cultural forces that shaped the experience of that miscarriage and my subsequent ones helped me come to terms with those losses. I hope this book will help others who have been confused by the experience of pregnancy loss (whether their own or that of their associates) by illuminating some of the sources of that confusion and expanding the repertoire of options for understanding and dealing with such misfortunes.[20]

This action-oriented approach is also part of a trend in Science and Technology Studies. In their introduction to the collection *Cyborgs and Citadels: Anthropological Interventions in Emerging Sciences and Technologies*, Downey and Dumit describe a "diverse and rapidly expanding set of anthropological projects that are seeking new ways of . . . intervening in emerging sciences, technologies, and medicines" (1997:5). They situate these studies as part of a "growing desire among academic scholars . . . to use analytic tools . . . to both analyze and participate" and suggest that this may "mark a generational shift from forms of critical analysis to forms of critical participation" (1997:10).

I have actively and critically participated in the pregnancy-loss support movement. I shared "an affinity" and a "recognition of a common predicament" (Marcus 1998:122) with the members and leaders of pregnancy-loss support groups I studied, and we mutually supported each other in our distinct but complementary efforts to deal with this predicament.[21]

In the concluding chapter to this book I suggest a number of things that could be done to make pregnancy loss less painful. Some of these things, such as changes in ob/gyn office protocols, can be relatively easily accomplished. Other things, such as the American ethic of meritocracy, overblown expectations of technomedical competence, and a preference for narratives of linear progress, each of which makes the experience of pregnancy loss more difficult, will be more difficult to change. One aspect of my experience that I found most problematic was the lack of evident feminist ways of understanding, talking about, sharing, and ritually commemorating these important events in my life. It is also the area where I felt most confident in my ability to intervene. This study is, in large part, an effort to help begin filling this gap.

Situating Motherhood Lost

A feminist, anthropological approach makes a unique contribution to the emerging scholarship on pregnancy loss. As pregnancy-loss support groups proliferated, the topic of pregnancy loss became a new subject for scholarly attention. In the 1980s and 1990s, numerous research projects in sociology, psychology, nursing, and social work investigated the experience of pregnancy loss in the United States.[22] Many of these social scientific studies were quantitative and used various instruments to measure grief, depression, and social support, and often they were "action-oriented" toward caregiving goals. On the whole, these studies focused on the individual and while several attempted to correlate social differences (level of education, marital status, etc.) with reactions to a loss, they have not analyzed pregnancy loss from a cultural point of view. Even those that are qualitative, as a rule, have not situated the experience of loss historically or culturally.

These dimensions have been the focus of other studies, however. Historians of childbearing almost inevitably dealt with the issue of death.[23] The first half of Slater's 1977 book *Children in the New England Mind* is devoted to "the dead child" and the issue of infant damnation. Hoffert's 1989 study *American Attitudes toward Childbearing and Infant Nurture in the Urban North 1800–1860* and McMillen's (1990) book on motherhood in the South during the same era each devotes its last chapter to infant death.

European historians Jacques Gelis (1991 [1984]) and Barbara Duden (1991 [1987], 1993 [1991]) have described the medical categories, treatment practices, and lay vocabularies for pregnancies, including those that ended in loss in early modern France and eighteenth-century Germany, respectively. Duden uses this material to show how recent and radical is the belief that a woman of childbearing age whose menses have stopped is "pregnant," which in turn means that she is carrying within her an "unborn child." Cross-cultural and historical differences are also the focus of Janet Sha's (1990) compendium of "customs and rituals of infertility and miscarriage"[24] and sociologist Shulamait Reinharz's (1988a) review of customs and beliefs regarding the prevention of miscarriage. She shows how in many cases these beliefs add "burdens to a woman's self-care," restrict women's activity, and may encourage shame and guilt for those who have such losses.[25]

In recent years, a number of Japan scholars (Smith 1988, 1992, LaFleur 1992, Hardacre 1997, Schattschneider 2001) have published analyses of the increasingly popular Buddhist shrines and rituals used to commemorate miscarried, stillborn, or aborted fetuses, and dead infants or children. Most of this work focuses on abortion, the most common type of loss commemorated at these shrines today, but their analyses of the forces shaping contemporary Japanese understandings of the status and meaning of dead fetuses and the proper way to treat them provides valuable cross-cultural alternative models for ways of dealing with pregnancy loss (Orenstein 2002). Rosanne Cecil's 1996 collection on the anthropology of pregnancy loss includes essays covering rural north India, rural Jamaica, Papua New Guinea, Tanzania, Cameroon, South Africa, Northern Ireland, eighteenth-century England, as well as a comparative piece on variation in risk for pregnancy loss and a chapter of my own on the United States.[26]

In the mid-1980s, cultural anthropologist Nancy Scheper-Hughes published a series of articles leading up to her book *Death without Weeping: The Violence of Everyday Life in Brazil* (1992). She describes how mothers living in a shantytown in northeast Brazil, under conditions of extreme scarcity and high infant mortality, "delayed attachment" and neglected infants that they believed were not destined to survive. Weak or sick infants were thought of as "temporary household visitors," "angels" who would soon return to whence they came. Although she acknowledges that these mothers' neglect was often in fact "mortal neglect," that is, causal, she argues that this does not mean that the mothers should be blamed given the "pernicious social and economic relations" that shape these maternal practices. She reminds us that poverty, then and now, remains the greatest threat to child survival (Scheper-Hughes 1992:354, 356).

Ellen Ross's historical account *Love and Toil: Motherhood in Outcast London, 1870–1918* (1993) addresses similar issues. She describes "the tentative attachment" that women formed with their newborns during this period of high infant mortality.[27] Mothers and neighbors would speculate whether a baby had "come to stay" (1993:184).[28] While during their first few weeks of life babies "were not officially viewed as persons and were not always loved as children" (1993:184), older infants were and the frequency of infant and child deaths among the poor did not make "them less painful" (1993:190). A notable difference between these women and late-twentieth-century United States women appears to be the fact that their "grief was seldom . . . mixed with self-blame" (1993:192).

The work closest to my own both topically and in terms of approach has been done by feminist sociologists. For example, Alice Lovell's study (1983:755) focused on "the identity construction and deconstruction of the baby and the mother" in hospital settings. Her study was based on in-depth interviews with twenty-two British women who had late miscarriages, stillbirths, or perinatal losses.

Following a miscarriage while doing research in Israel in 1973, Reinharz wrote a series of important articles on "the sociology of knowledge concerning miscarriages" (1988b:84). In "What's Missing in Miscarriage?" (Reinharz 1988b), she examines the way miscarriage is understood and defined from medical, feminist, psychoanalytic, and community psychological perspectives and uses her own loss to show how each of these perspectives is inadequate. In "The Social Psychology of a Miscarriage" (1987), she applied symbolic interaction theory to the topic. She used W. I. Thomas's notion of "the definition of the situation" to analyze one "American middle-class married mother's" narrative of loss, a woman who happens to be one of the authors of a popular book on miscarriage (Pizer and Palinski 1980). Reinharz uses this case to show how "contradictory definitions may coexist within a single person, and that definitions may be temporarily dropped and then revived." She also shows how such definitions are "negotiated with others," for example, how they are "constructed in relation to the expert definitions of medical caregivers," and also "with oneself in self-conversation and reflection" (1987:247). In another piece (1988a), Reinharz uses "interpretative content analysis" to examine published miscarriage accounts of a number of American and British women.

Simonds and Rothman published *Centuries of Solace: Expressions of Maternal Grief in Popular Literature* in 1992. In it they compare first-person accounts of loss published in nineteenth-century women's magazines, early-twentieth-century confessional magazines, and current forms of popular maternal consolation literature in the United States. Whereas Reinharz, writing in the 1980s and informed by her personal experience in the 1970s, seeks to explain why pregnancy loss has been neglected as a topic, and attributes this neglect in part to the lack of importance credited to women's lives, Simonds and Rothman seek to explain why the subject "[came] out of the closet" since the 1970s. They argue that the current interest in the topic is "based not on changes in the meaning of babies for women but on changes in the meaning of women's lives for society" (1992:4). In contrast to Reinharz (1988a), Scheper-Hughes (1992), and Cecil (1996), each of whom stresses the ways cultural and historical differences shape the experience of pregnancy loss, Simonds and Rothman stress the commonalities. They believe that "maternal grief is timeless . . . [that] the sense of pain and loss when nurturance is untimely ended is universal, extending beyond the boundaries of culture" (1992:2). In fact, they suggest that this experience extends to all mothers regardless of whether their babies die. "There is a sense in which all of motherhood is loss, an ongoing continual separation, an unending grieving" (1992:9, cf. chapter 6).[29]

Simonds and Rothman provide a valuable critique of several aspects of the pregnancy-loss support movement; for example, they note how profoundly apolitical the current institutionalization of grief is and how the popular psychological notion of "grief-as-stages" (following Kubler-Ross) "reduces women's experience." They are particularly concerned with the way that this model treats anger and guilt "not in substantive ways but only as transient feeling states—to be experienced and then surpassed" (1992:161). They also challenge the implicit and often explicit assertion in pregnancy-loss literature that all such losses were unavoidable, noting that sometimes pregnancy losses are "caused" (e.g., by car accidents or domestic violence) in which cases the assigning of blame and feelings of anger and/or guilt may be appropriate (cf. chapter 10).

Although in many ways my approach is similar to that of Simonds and Rothman, my findings regarding contemporary narratives of loss differ from theirs in substantial ways. In their comparison of nineteenth- and late-twentieth-century maternal consolation literature, Simonds and Rothman list a number of differences, including "the move from traditional religion to a secular view (or to a looser spiritualism); . . . the move from poetry to social science or self-help; . . . a transition from the more flowery language of nineteenth-century women writers to the almost stark language of the current era" (1992:22). In studying narratives of pregnancy loss that support-group members published in the 1980s, '90s and '00s, I have been struck more by the continuities than the differences. Pregnancy-loss support newsletters are filled with poetry and replete with metaphoric, "flowery" language. Poetry continues to be, as Faulkner said, "one of the props, the pillars" to help people "endure and prevail" (Morris 1997:31). As Schwarcz (1997:119) observes, "a cold, calculating intelligence cannot grasp the rough contours of grief" (see also Berman 2001).

I have been particularly struck by the prevalence of Christian imagery and language. Indeed, as I explained in my article "Of Fetuses and Angels," when I read the newsletters looking for mention of new reproductive technologies, as often as not I found angels. In addition, Simonds and Rothman note that in both the nineteenth century and late twentieth century, "writers seek to teach readers to turn the loss around, to use their experience for personal growth." They maintain that in the earlier era "this meant growth toward God, and often growth toward being a better wife and mother" but in the current era, the mourner is asked to use the loss "to strengthen herself" (Simonds and Rothman 1992:159). In contrast, the narratives of loss analyzed here indicate that contemporary mourners often combine these goals and see them as complementary (see chapter 7).

Through the Lens of Pregnancy Loss

I knew when I decided on pregnancy loss as a research topic that its location at the intersection of life and death would provide an ideal vantage point for examining the complex and dynamic relationship between birth, death, personhood, and parenthood. I had not anticipated, however, what a powerful lens pregnancy loss would be for illuminating many other important dimensions of contemporary culture. Pregnancy loss has proven to be very good to think with.[30] In the course of writing this book I have found that because the subject of pregnancy loss is a site of struggle over the construction of identity it offers a unique and valuable perspective on issues of current concern to a number of interdisciplinary areas of inquiry. In the following sections I situate this study in several of these literatures and show how pregnancy loss enriches the dialogue in each case.[31]

Interdisciplinary Studies of Reproduction.   In addition to the specialized literature on pregnancy loss, this book addresses a number of issues of
more general concern in recent interdisciplinary scholarship on reproduction. In tracing the major feminist trends in the study of motherhood, Taylor (1996:14–15) notes "early feminist writings accentuated the oppressive
aspects" of mothering but "the 1980s saw an about-face, with feminists cel-
ebrating and valorizing motherhood." As I discuss in the final chapter (see
also Layne 2002), this trend in feminist scholarship and activism, manifested in the natural childbirth movement, which celebrated women's in-
nate abilities to bear children, created additional burdens for women whose
pregnancies end badly.

In the 1990s feminist studies of motherhood "expanded to emphasize
the varied practices of mothering" (Taylor 1996:15) with studies of postpartum depression (Taylor 1996), lesbian motherhood (Lewin 1993, Dalton
2000), homeless mothers (Connolly 2000), foster mothering (Wozniak in
prep, 1999, Modell 1999), adoption (Modell 1994, 1999), surrogacy
(Ragoné 1994, 1999, Dalton 2000), and mothering children with disabilities
(Landsman 1999, 2000, Lock 1998, Rapp 1999, and Ginsburg and Rapp
1999), or biracial children (Ragoné 2000, Twine 2000) and collections of
feminist analyses and personal narratives of "mothers and children" (Chase
and Rogers 2001, Reddy, Roth, and Sheldon 1994). *Motherhood Lost* contributes to this growing understanding of those whose mothering experience, whether by choice or by chance, does not conform to the norm.

Motherhood Lost also articulates issues concerning mother love with discussions of fetal personhood most commonly addressed in terms of the
abortion debate. Since the 1970s, the question of whether or not women are
naturally endowed with mothering instincts has been debated by historians,
sociologists, and anthropologists, and has also been a topic of interest to
physicians and psychologists (see chapter 5). Lawrence Stone's (1979) study
documenting "massive shifts" in the family in England between 1500 and
1800 was one of the first to put forward the argument that "the omnipres-
ence of death colored affective relations" including those between mothers
and children "by reducing the amount of emotional capital available for
prudent investment in any single individual, especially in such ephemeral
creatures as infants" (1979:407). Stone (1979), Scheper-Hughes (1992),
Ross (1993), Tsing (1990), and Taylor (1996) show that "mother love is
anything *other* than natural and instead presents a matrix of images, meanings, sentiments, and practices that are . . . socially and culturally produced"
(Scheper-Hughes 1992:341).

These studies each attempt to explain why something one expects to
find is absent. The absence of maternal love represents "a discrepancy be-

tween private emotions and the emotional states perceived as 'normative'"
(Taylor 1996:35). Writing as they were during decades when a whole host of
new types of "bad mothers" (Ladd-Taylor and Umansky 1998) (e.g., alcohol, illegal drug, and tobacco users, or overly busy professional women)
(McDonnell 2001, Campbell 2000) were being vilified in the press and public-health discourse (Boling 1995, Oaks 2001), several authors take a defen-
sive tone, putting forward extenuating circumstances to defend women and
to explain their socially aberrant behavior.

The case of pregnancy loss offers a counterexample at the opposite end
of the spectrum. In this case mothers violate a different set of "feeling
norms" and "expression rules" (Hochschild quoted in Taylor 1996:35). Bereaved mothers risk criticism and even ostracism for exhibiting too much
mother love,[32] or more accurately, for being indiscriminate in their mother
love, for showering this love on inappropriate/inadequate objects of love.
Landsman (in press) has observed a similar phenomenon with regard to
mothers of children with disabilities, who are judged for unwisely expend-
ing their love and labor nurturing hopeless cases. Women who do their best
for children with disabilities are open to criticism because they don't have
sense enough to recognize that they "got a lemon" and should cut their
losses and save their love for children who are more worthy of their maternal investment (Landsman in press).

These concerns speak to the issue of personhood so central to arguments
about women's right to terminate pregnancies. On the whole, feminist
scholars have been careful to avoid the topic of pregnancy loss. Yet because
the ambiguous status of fetuses is central to both pregnancy loss and abortion, pregnancy loss provides an ideal arena from which to explore alternative ways to conceptualize maternal/fetal relations. *Motherhood Lost* provides an empirical study of person-making practices in our culture. It
documents a social constructivist (Layne 1999) or "processual-relational"
(Conklin and Morgan 1996) approach that coexists as an alternative to the
essentialist, biologically based model of personhood that is thought to characterize contemporary Euro-American views of personhood (Conklin and
Morgan 1996, Franklin 1991) and is apparent in anti-abortion rhetoric.[33]

It also is centrally positioned among new studies that focus on reproductive "mishaps" or "disruptions" (Bledsoe 2002, Becker 1997, Boddy 1998,
Ginsburg and Rapp 1995, Jenkins and Inhorn in press, Davis-Floyd in
press). These studies, in turn, are part of a larger trend to attend to disruptions, misfortunes, and suffering more broadly (Newman 1988, Becker
1997, Irvine 1999, Riessman 1990, Kleinman, Das, and Lock 1997), including those resulting from technological failures or disasters.

Cultural, Gender, and Social Studies of Science, Technology, and Medicine. *Motherhood Lost* engages and expands Science and Technology Studies (STS), or what some are now more accurately calling Cultural, Gender, and Social Studies of Science, Technology, and Medicine (Traweek 1993), in several ways. Since the 1980s STS scholars have been concerned with the unintended or unanticipated consequences of technological innovations (e.g., Perrow 1984, Tenner 1996, Rochlin 1997). *Motherhood Lost* exposes a number of unintended consequences of the new reproductive technologies and developments in reproductive science (Clarke 1998, Oudshoorn 1994, Pfeffer 1993). The intention of these biomedical developments was to improve pregnancy outcomes. It is unclear whether on balance they have been successful,[34] but the physical, emotional, financial, and societal costs of developments in reproductive medicine have been extensively documented. *Motherhood Lost* exposes other as yet unexamined consequences of these new reproductive technologies. I show how the earlier and more intensive medical management of pregnancy is implicated in the earlier and more intensive social construction of fetal personhood, and how this makes pregnancy loss more difficult. I also show how the trope of "revolution" in reproductive medicine leads to unrealistic expectations about what biomedicine can actually deliver.

In the 1990s, partially due to the infusion of anthropology into the field, STS scholars moved away from a focus on the production of scientific knowledge by experts in laboratories to a much broader understanding of where and how scientific knowledge is produced (e.g., Hess and Layne 1992; Hess 1992, 1995, 1997, Layne 1998, Downey and Dumit 1997). For instance, Epstein's study of AIDS activists showed how this grassroots social movement changed the way AIDS research is conducted. The women's health movement had similar effects on reproductive medicine—influencing both basic research and clinical practice. One of the primary thrusts of the women's health movement was to resist the increasingly invasive medical management of birth. Feminist scholars and health activists focused on the negative consequences of these "innovations and improvements" in obstetrical care. Yet, ironically, as *Motherhood Lost* shows, this well-meaning and in many ways positive reformist movement has had unintended consequences for would-be mothers. These consequences include "revenge effects," effects that result when an intervention meant to reduce a negative effect actually produces another of the very type of problem it was meant to solve (Tenner 1996:7).[35] The women's health movement, in seeking to improve the experience of pregnant women by insisting on how natural it is for women to make babies (if they so desire), emphasized individual choice, autonomy, and empowerment, and thereby inadvertently made the experience worse for women whose efforts to reproduce were thwarted by infertility or pregnancy loss (see chapter 10).

In the 1990s Science and Technology Studies scholars began to borrow the concept of "negative externalities" from Economics to describe negative, large-scale consequences of certain technologies or technological systems (e.g., Mesthene 1997, Volti 1995, Callon 1998). *Motherhood Lost* illustrates a number of negative externalities deriving from narratives of linear progress—a preferred narrative genre intricately and intimately tied to our assumptions about technoscientific progress. Individuals who suffer pregnancy loss (like those who suffer job loss and downward mobility, premature birth, or other misfortunes that challenge narratives of linear progress) tend to be ill prepared for these eventualities, as are members of their social networks. Narratives of linear progress add unnecessary angst to those involved and hamper the enactment of a host of sociotechnical aids for these problems. (See chapter 10.)

Scholars of "high risk technologies" (Perrow 1984, Marone and Woodhouse 1986, 1989, Winner 1977, 1986, Perin 1998) concern themselves with human-made "catastrophes," "disasters," and "failures." In doing so, they work against the grain. As engineer and essayist Samuel Florman discovered, it is not easy to tell these types of stories. In his article "Technology and the Tragic View" (1997), Florman tells of how, when doing the research for a piece he had been asked to write for the bicentennial issue of *House & Garden* on "American Know-How," he unearthed, in addition to information on Benjamin Franklin's "inventions and successful experiments," "a record of calamities caused by the technological advances of his day" (1997:95). As a result, instead of writing a "cheerfully optimistic" piece, he focused on how "our forebears" constructively confronted "the adverse consequences of their own inventiveness" (Florman 1997:96). The editor of the magazine was dismayed—"We like the part about tenacity and ingenuity, . . . but, oh dear, all those disasters—they are so depressing." Through a lengthy process of negotiation and revision, Florman gradually eliminated the accidents and casualty statistics and changed the emphasis until the piece was deemed "suitably upbeat." The experience taught him that "there is no room in [the pages of magazines like this one] for failure, or even for struggle," and he concludes that *House & Garden* "speaks for many Americans, perhaps a majority" (1997:97) in this regard.

Similar tensions can be found in medicine. In Paget's phenomenological study of clinical medicine, she characterizes medical practice as an "error-ridden activity." Because "medical work is inaccurate and practiced with considerable unpredictability and risk" (1988:20), mistakes are inevitable. These are what Perrow (1984) refers to as "normal accidents," an ironic term meant to convey the inevitability of failures in complex systems, particularly ones with "interactive complexity and tight coupling." Yet "a clinician's description of medical work does not emphasize the error-ridden nature of the diagnostic and therapeutic process; instead, it stresses the progressive refinement and modification of the process" (Paget 1988: 20–21).

Motherhood Lost illustrates homologous tensions and demonstrates some of the ways the stories we like to tell about science, technology, and medicine inform and are informed by those we like to tell about ourselves. In each case, similar social mechanisms work to silence accounts that do not conform. It thus points to some similarities between technology critics and members of pregnancy-loss support groups, both of whom are struggling to find airspace for this inevitable aspect of human experience.

Since 1966, when physicist Alvin Weinberg introduced the term "technological fix," STS scholars have used the distinction between technological and social fixes. Research on pregnancy loss led me to develop the concept of a "cultural fix," which I see as a distinctively, though not exclusively, anthropological addition to the STS theoretical tool kit. I recognize that the very notion of "fix" is problematic, given the fact that people may not agree on what needs fixing and premised, as it is, on a mechanical model of social life. Furthermore, just as the distinction between social and technical fixes is not easily sustainable on close scrutiny, I recognize that if one adopts, as I do, a broad understanding of technoscience, all interventions are bound to be simultaneously social, cultural, and technical. Nevertheless, given the durability of the social/technical fix distinction in Science and Technology Studies and popular literature, it seems worthwhile to highlight the importance of interventions of a broader cultural nature as well.

In dealing with the negative externalities of narratives of linear progress, a cultural fix would involve enriching our discursive repertoire by lifting taboos and expanding the range of acceptable story lines. It would also entail creating rituals that would acknowledge these unfortunate events and support those who suffer these misfortunes. Such cultural fixes would also facilitate sociotechnical fixes. Cultural fixes are thus necessary prerequisites, or at least necessary accompaniments, for enabling us to do a better job as a society to plan for these occurrences.[36] (See chapter 10.)

A final contribution to STS stems from the scope of this research. Writing in the late 1980s, Pinch and Bijker (1989:17) observed, "one of the most striking features of the growth of 'science studies' in recent years has been

the separation of science from technology." In the ensuing decade anthropology became a powerful voice in STS, and anthropology's holistic approach has made the division between science and technology appear less
important, less absolute, and at least in some contexts, less meaningful.
Motherhood Lost is a case in point, since it is hard to imagine how one could
study the changing experience of pregnancy loss without taking into account developments in reproductive science, such as the discovery of hormones that made early pregnancy-testing a possibility (Clarke 1998), *and*
the advent of new reproductive technologies, such as sonograms.

What is more, technoscience is just one among several interpretive systems that bereaved parents routinely employ in making sense of their loss.
In other words, *Motherhood Lost* provides an example of an anthropological
approach that calls into question not only the separation of science from
technology but also that of technoscience from the larger cultural system of
which it is a part. For example, narratives of pregnancy loss provide a compelling portrait of the ways in which ordinary people weave together the discourses of science and religion. Like the members of the African revitaliza-
tion cult studied by Fernandez (1986b), who restore a sense of wholeness by
iconically linking images from diverse domains in their rituals, members of
pregnancy-loss support groups struggle with feelings of incompleteness by
culturally constructing their loss in ways that suggest "a larger integration
of things, a larger whole" (Fernandez 1986a:178).[37] In addition to constructing or reconstructing a sense of personal and familial wholeness, contributors to pregnancy-loss support newsletters deploy a variety of tropes that
build a bridge between the normally separate discursive spaces of biomedicine, religion, and everyday life. This has important implications for understanding the place of technoscience in our culture.

Another important nexus is found in the relation between biology and
consumer culture. Narratives of loss suggest that in the United States, in
addition to the sharing of genes and blood, those most culturally privileged
bodily substances, the sharing of commodities also plays a critical role in
"impart[ing] qualities of identity" to those to whom they are given, including fetuses. This is one of the contributions *Motherhood Lost* makes to interdisciplinary studies of consumer culture.

Studies of Consumption, Consumer Culture, and Gift Exchange.
During the 1980s scholars of reproduction often analyzed the ways in which
the ideology of capitalist production informed the ideology of reproduction.
Martin (1987) focused on relations of production in her discussion of the
ways in which capitalist ideology influences women's views of their bodies

as objects and informs the dominant cultural understanding of childbirth. Rothman (1989) describes how the "sweat labor" involved in gestating and giving birth to a baby is undervalued in our society and how pregnant women are systematically alienated from the products of their labor. Pregnant women are seen as "raw material" from which the baby/product "has to be produced according to exact specifications" of which mothers are ignorant and must be instructed by experts (Rothman 1989:19).

After a decade of fruitful research on the influence of production metaphors, a number of feminist scholars have begun to explore the role of consumer culture in shaping the experience of childbearing and motherhood (Anagnost 1995, 1997; Layne in press, 1999b,c,d; Markens, Browner, and Press 1997, Taylor in prep, 2000a,b, 1998, 1992; Wozniak 1999; Taylor, Wozniak, and Layne nd). In 1992 Taylor published an analysis of a Volvo advertisement featuring an ultrasound image of a fetus, showing how fetal images were being "hitched to the imperative to consume." In a more recent piece (2000a), Taylor describes pregnancy as "an all consuming experience," highlighting the ways pregnant women consume on behalf of the fetus during a pregnancy by purchasing mass-produced consumer goods for the anticipated child, altering and monitoring their bodily consumption,[38] and choosing the type of provider and setting for prenatal care, childbirth classes, and birth.

Taylor's work (2000a, 2000b) on the proliferation and meaning of prenatal ultrasound imaging has explored the benefits and limits of both production and consumption analogies. She notes that it is generally assumed that commodification and personification are antithetical, yet her ethnographic study of obstetrical ultrasound challenged this either/or view. She found instead a simultaneous standardization and singularization of the fetuses via ultrasound, with the fetus being constructed "as a commodity at the same time and through the same means that it is also [being] constructed . . . as a person."

Motherhood Lost explores a similar interplay between standardization and singularization. It shows how consumer culture is implicated in the setting of standards for babies and childbearing experiences and the consequences of these standards for women whose pregnancies and babies do not measure up to the norm. In the face of their apparent failure, bereaved parents sometimes reject or adapt these standards. For example, members of pregnancy-loss support groups frequently reject the principle of consumer culture that more is better. They argue that size and amount, whether it be of the body, length of a lifetime, or number of memories, are irrelevant as markers of value. They turn this on its head, in fact, and stress the merits of the small, in the spirit of the natural theologians who found the miraculous in the ordinary, the infinite in the small (Cooksey 1992). They also reject a definition of babies as replaceable and interchangeable. Many use consumer goods to continue the processes of singularization that were begun during a pregnancy loss but were interrupted and put at risk by the loss. These practices provide a new dimension to studies of consumption that highlight the creative, often hidden, work of consumers (de Certeau 1984, Miller 1998). The case of pregnancy loss offers a new range of ethnographic examples of the "arts of making" and "acts of everyday creativity" that consumers engage in (de Certeau 1984:xiv). In addition, bereaved parents embrace and sometimes extend the principles of possessive individualism by preserving a baby's personal possessions, and in some cases in continuing to acquire "baby things" for a baby after a demise. Yet this case also points to limits in the trope of ownership that obscure the ongoing and collaborative dimensions of the constitution of personhood evident in the accounts of pregnancy-loss support members.

Consumer culture also proves to be one of the primary cultural resources members of pregnancy-loss support groups use in making claims that their baby not only existed but was worthy of memory. Consumer goods are routinely employed as technologies of memory by pregnancy-loss support-group leaders and members to combat the effects of time on memory and social pressure to forget, and to compensate for the fact that there are so few memories in the first place. One of the most interesting findings of this study was the discovery that, like anthropologists and historians, members of pregnancy-loss support groups understand memory as something created.

Motherhood Lost also engages in current interdisciplinary studies of gift exchange. A staple of anthropological theory, "the gift" is enjoying renewed scholarly interest. "Philosophers, literary critics, and literary theorists [are] with increasing frequency joining anthropologists . . . in their attempt to theorize gift exchange" (Schrift 1997).[39] *Motherhood Lost* contributes to these current interdisciplinary discussions of "the gift" and at the same time represents a new direction in anthropological studies of gifts and giving.

Although Mauss begins his book *The Gift* with a discussion of childbirth and the rituals that accompany it (1969:6–7), classical anthropological theories of the gift, as well as more contemporary theories of consumption, have focused primarily on the giving and consuming of things (Layne 1999), and in particular on the ways that the exchange of material objects forges and maintains social relationships. (See chapter 6.) In comparison with goods, much less attention has been given to other types of gifts. Despite their pervasiveness in popular culture, the notions explored in chapter 7 of the child as gift and the giving and receiving of intangibles like "love," "hope," and "enlightenment" have been neglected in studies of Euro-American gift exchange. *Motherhood Lost* highlights the "spiritual" and/or "religious" dimensions of "giving" in Euro-American culture. It also contributes to a renewed interest in inalienable possessions and what Weiner (1992) calls "the paradox of keeping-while-giving." As Godelier (1999:8) remarks, this leads one to contemplation of "the sacred" and, as he concludes in the final lines of his book *The Enigma of the Gift*, back to the "first bond between humans, that of birth" (1999:210). As I argue in the introduction to my edited volume on the child as gift (1999), to fully appreciate the meaning and import of giving, whether it be in "archaic" or "contemporary" societies, the realm of childbirth remains an important site. A greater comprehension of giving and gifting in this context will enrich our understanding of the burdens and pleasures of mothering and the tension-fraught and generative dynamics of consumer culture alike.

American Deathways. Death, like other rites of passage, has been of abiding interest to anthropologists. Traditionally anthropological studies focused on the ritual management of death (e.g., Weiner 1976, 1988, Huntington and Metcalf 1979). In 1984, after his wife's tragic death in the field in the Philippines, Rosaldo called for anthropology to move away from the study of death rituals to the study of bereavement and to focus on emotions and the way grief is experienced not only in ritual settings but also "the informal settings of everyday life" ([1984] 1993:15). The narratives of pregnancy-loss support-group members provide a particularly rich source for understanding bereavement in such settings. They also point to the importance of formal rituals. In its focus on the experience of death in the United States, *Motherhood Lost* joins interdisciplinary scholars and social critics exploring "American Deathways" (e.g., Mitford 1963, Glaser and Strauss 1965, 1968, Sudnow 1967, Stannard 1975, Aries 1975, Jackson 1977, Huntington and Metcalf 1979, Charmaz 1980, Laderman 1996, Regis 2001, cf. Seale 1998). Of particular relevance are those who examine the ways that new medical technologies, such as those for organ transplanation, are changing the definition, meaning, and management of death (e.g., Lock 1997, 2002, Sharp 2001, Ohnuki-Tierney 1994, Squire 2001) and at the same time bringing into question taken-for-granted assumptions about personhood. Because of the continuingly central role that religion plays for many during life crises, especially perhaps those involving death, *Motherhood Lost* also contributes to studies of "lived religion" in the United States (Csordas 1997, Hall 1997, Rapp 2001). In particular, the narratives of loss analyzed here may be of special interest to those studying the "Americanization of Christianity" and emergent "religions of the self" (Csordas 1997:43, 53).

Memory and Commemoration. During the same period when pregnancy-loss support groups were proliferating, memory became a compelling topic for scholars in history, philosophy, psychology, anthropology, literature, film, media, and cultural studies.[40] As Antze and Lambek (1996:vii) note in the introduction to their edited collection on memory, "Memory . . . has become a major idiom in the construction of identity, both individual and collective, and a site of struggle as well as identification."

One stream of this research has focused on traumatic individual memories. For example, Antze 1996, Brison 1997, Hacking 1996, and Young 1996 have explored post-traumatic stress syndrome,[41] and multiple personality and other ailments believed to come from suppressed memory of childhood sexual abuse, as well as nineteenth-century ailments linked to suppressed traumatic memories, such as railway spine, shell shock, and hysteria. This research documents changing scientific understandings of such memories and probes current understandings of the relationship between memory and identity.

Another major stream of research has focused on collective, or social, memory (and forgetting). Much of this has examined traumatic collective experiences such as the two World Wars and the Holocaust and strategies used by nations, localities, and other groups to commemorate these events (e.g., Arad 1997, Fussel 1975, Gillis 1994, Nora 1989, Sherman 1999, Young 1993, see also Feuchtwang 2000). These scholars have documented "the historical metamorphosis of memory" (Nora 1989:15) during the twentieth century and describe "the construction of commemorative culture itself" in postwar Europe and North America (see also Hass 1998 and Muschamp 1995).

My work on pregnancy-loss support is informed by and contributes to both of these streams (see especially chapters 9 and 6). Many members of pregnancy-loss support groups experience their loss as "traumatic."[42] The post-Freudian belief that it is therapeutic to give voice to such experiences, and the related idea that suppressed emotions and memories are damaging, clearly informs the whole support-group enterprise; and the first-person accounts produced at support-group meetings and in the newsletters provide an excellent source for studying the therapeutic aspects of "narrative memory."[43]

But whereas in research on traumatic memory it is access to memory that is problematic because the experience was so painful that the memory was buried, at pregnancy-loss support groups painful memories are still vivid and fresh. The problem in this context is the risk of losing these memories gradually over time. As the executive director of SHARE writes in a recent issue of its newsletter, "Many of us struggle with the overwhelming question, 'Will I forget my baby over time?'" (Lammert 1999a). In a social setting that does not reinforce these memories, but quite the contrary, encourages people to put the experience "behind them" and "get on with their lives," bereaved parents fear that the passage of time will wear away the memory of their wished-for child.

One of the three key aspects of the transformation of memory during the last century delineated by Nora (1989) is the extent to which the responsibility for memory has shifted away from the social to the individual. "The atomization of a general memory into a private one has given . . . everyone the necessity to remember and to protect the trappings of identity: when memory is no longer everywhere, it will not be anywhere unless one takes the responsibility to recapture it through individual means" (Nora 1989:16). *Motherhood Lost* provides a compelling example of the ways in which memory has come to be seen and experienced as an individual achievement. In the rhetoric of pregnancy loss, memory is consistently presented as the result of deliberate, individual choice. What is more, the decision to remember is clearly understood as a moral act (Lambek 1996). Narratives of loss routinely conclude with pledges that the author will "never forget" and acts of remembrance are understood and presented as acts of resistance in the face of social pressure to forget. These pressures are part and parcel of a larger social phenomenon. As Brison observed, "As a society we live with the unbearable by pressuring those who have been traumatized to forget" (Brison 1997:26).

In their vows to remember, and through their use of other conventions such as the symbol of the "eternal flame," members of pregnancy-loss support groups draw on the edifying idiom of public postwar commemorative culture. This provides a suitably public and valorizing rhetoric to support their claims that they have suffered a socially significant loss that deserves recognition. In illuminating how these acts of remembrance operate "within a charged field of contested moral and political claims" (Antze and Lambek 1996:vii), *Motherhood Lost* contributes to our understanding of contemporary "memoro-politics" (Hacking 1996). This, in turn, suggests another dimension for the study of the new social movements.

New Social Movements. In recent years anthropologists have critiqued older anthropological theories of social and religious movements that treated "movements as discrete entities rather than as phenomena characteristic or diagnostic of the cultures in which they are spawned" (Csordas 1997:4). Newer treatments focus more on meaning and less narrowly on cause, and now understand movements to be made up not so much of "social types," but of "indeterminant selves in the process of reorientation and transformation" (Csordas 1997:4).

During these same years political scientists began to develop theories to account for "the new social movements." Up until then the prototypical social movement had been "a worker's movement—a class-based movement developed to change society in the interest of its members' class" (Makela et al. 1996:9). The new social movement theorists have focused on movements like the ecology movement and the peace movement, based on "'conscience' constituencies" rather than class identity. More recently, scholars of organizations like Alcoholics Anonymous (AA) (Makela et al. 1996) and postpartum depression (Taylor 1996), have argued that mutual-aid organizations like these should also be considered as new social movements, noting the extent to which the new social movements focus "on self-transformation and problems of self-definition" (Diani 1992 quoted in Makela et al. 1996:9). The crux of the debate regarding the suitability of considering mutual-aid organizations like those offering pregnancy-loss support as a new social movement concerns the extent to which these organizations are aimed at changing society. Critics of mutual-aid groups argue that they do not qualify as social movements because their agendas are personal, rather than political. For example, feminist critics of women's self-help argue that such groups represent "an apolitical variety of cultural feminism, of identity politics" (Taylor 1996:7). Similarly, critics of codependency support groups argue that such groups offer "a false sense of empowerment while taking energy away from political solutions to political problems" (Lodl quoted in Irvine 1999:130).[44] *Motherhood Lost* provides a case study of mutual-aid organizations that are "consciously struggl[ing] over the power to socially construct new identities, . . . *and* to reinterpret norms and reshape institutions" (Cohen 1985 quoted in Makela et al. 1996:9, emphasis added). Although the primary emphasis of organizations like SHARE and UNITE is to provide emotional support to participants, these organizations also work for institutional changes in law, public policy, and medicine and challenge societal norms. (See chapter 4.)

Studies like this one of pregnancy-loss support organizations will facilitate current efforts to investigate new social movements comparatively. In particular, pregnancy-loss support offers a useful case for thinking about the relationship between women, self-help, and feminism (Taylor 1996, Simonds 1992). (See chapter 3.) In addition, in its focus on "cultural fixes" (as well as social and technical ones), *Motherhood Lost* adds a new perspective on the relation between the politics of contested identities, identity formation, and new social movements (cf. Mellucci 1989, 1996).

What Lies Ahead

In the chapters that follow I describe the pregnancy-loss support groups, discuss the contradictory forces that exacerbate the experience of pregnancy loss, and then describe the creative ways in which members of pregnancy-loss support groups appropriate a variety of cultural resources to deal with their losses.

Chapter 3 provides an introduction to the pregnancy-loss support organizations that I worked with, including a description of their missions, leaders, members, support-group meetings, newsletters, and other services.

In chapter 4 I explore pregnancy loss as an incomplete rite of passage for would-be mothers, fathers, and babies. I discuss the ways dead embryos/fetuses/neonates are doubly and sometimes (if they are malformed) triply liminal. I also explore the ways in which pregnancy loss challenges the contemporary interdiction on death and the related primacy of narratives of linear progress and describe how all of these factors help explain the ongoing taboo surrounding pregnancy loss. I sketch out the many silences that surround pregnancy loss in our culture, including those in popular culture, medicine, civil records, epidemiology, demography, and feminism. I then describe some of the many ways that pregnancy-loss support organizations are contriving to break this silence.

In chapter 5 I describe some of the ways that changes in the medical management of pregnancy (including the use of new reproductive technologies) are affecting the experience of pregnancy loss. This discussion centers around four themes: biomedical definitions of life and death, ultrasound and prenatal bonding, changing expectations of biomedicine's abilities to guarantee a live birth, and the use of biomedical technologies by bereaved parents to deal with the "realness" problem of pregnancy loss.

In chapter 6 I focus on the ways that bereaved parents use the "realness" of material things to assert their claim that a "real baby" existed and is worthy of memory, and to simultaneously construct themselves as "real" parents deserving the social recognition this role entails.

In the next chapter I show how bereaved parents use a spiritually in-fused rhetoric of the gift to deal with the fact that pregnancy loss represents serious deviations from important moral mandates in contemporary North American culture: the mandate to always be in control of one's body/one's self, the mandate to be successful, and the related mandate to always be happy. I discuss how the paradoxical dimensions of gift-exchange and Christianity help bereaved parents negotiate the discrepancy between the experience of loss and these moral mandates, and to address the problem of self-blame without jeopardizing the treasured notion of control.

In chapter 8 I explore the nexus of irony, innocence, and loss. I give an account of the ways in which bereaved parents use "ironies of circum-stance" to help recall and give shape to their experience. I draw some com-parisons with the World War I soldiers, described by Paul Fussell, who also used irony to mark the vast gap between the way things were expected to turn out and what transpired instead. I also show how nature is used by con-tributors to pregnancy-loss support newsletters to accentuate the "freakish-ness" of their experience and as a source for, and model of, redemption. I conclude by exploring the politics of irony in such cases.

In chapter 9 I delineate six problems of memory that pregnancy loss can pose and describe the ways in which bereaved parents embrace a moral mandate to remember and use consumer goods and postwar commemora-tive culture to honor their babies' lives. In the final chapter I look toward the future and set an agenda for a feminist response to pregnancy loss, sug-gesting social and cultural "fixes" that could improve the experience of pregnancy loss.

CHAPTER 3

Pregnancy-Loss Support

Pregnancy-Loss Support Organizations

My research on pregnancy-loss support involved participant observation with three pregnancy-loss support organizations in New Jersey and New York: UNITE, SHARE, and the New York Section of the National Council of Jewish Women's (NCJW) support group in New York City between 1987 and 1989. In addition to attending support-group meetings, I participated first as a "parent" and later as a "professional" at several of UNITE's annual conferences, and attended other special seminars and events sponsored by UNITE and SHARE. I also completed UNITE's training program for support counselors, participated in the New York Section of the National Council of Jewish Women's telephone counseling program, and interviewed some of the founding members of these and other groups.

SHARE is the nation's largest pregnancy-loss support organization, with, as of 1995, ninety-seven groups throughout the United States. Its founder, Sister Jane Marie Lamb, became involved in the issue when in 1974 she was called upon as "an unprepared chaplain" to help a bereaved couple (Lamb 1997). Although Lamb never had a pregnancy loss, she often explained how the untimely death of her brother helped her empathize with the parents she helped (personal communication 1989). SHARE was established in 1977 at St. John's Hospital in Springfield, Illinois, and Lamb recalls knowing of only two other such groups at that time. Lamb's initial concern, and one that she maintained throughout her years of direct involvement with SHARE (1977–1992), was "the education of all staff who might encounter these families" (Lamb 1997). The national SHARE office relocated to St. Elizabeth Hospital in Belleville, Illinois, in 1988. In 1992 the organization moved to its current home at St. Joseph Health Center in St.

41

Charles, Missouri. At that time it changed its name from SHARE (Source of Help in Airing and Resolving Experiences) to SHARE Pregnancy and Infant Loss Support, Inc. in order to better express its mission, which it defines as serving "those who are troubled by the tragic death of a baby through miscarriage, stillbirth or newborn death." In addition to the newsletter, SHARE has a website, which, as of fall 1999, was "averaging 75–100 hits a day" (Lammert 1999a:3) and a chat room, which runs every Monday evening and usually hosts two to three people (Lammert 1999b:3).

UNITE is a regional organization with, as of 1999, twelve support groups serving over one thousand bereaved families each year in Pennsylvania and New Jersey (Keyser, personal communication 1999). Established in 1974/75 "at Jeanes Hospital by several nursery nurses who saw [an] important need" (*UNITE Notes* 1(1):1), it was one of the first pregnancy-loss support groups in the country. One of the founding members was Janis L. Keyser (formerly Heil). Janis explains her involvement with the group: "I became involved with UNITE in January 1980 when my daughter Jessica Brooke (my second child) was stillborn. Well familiar with the value of support groups through my work as a nursing mothers counselor, I attended my first meeting three weeks after Jessica died, just to 'check it out.' I didn't think I really needed a group; I would be fine. . . . But when I was at that first meeting, I immediately felt at home. . . . I didn't say a word. Yet I could identify with all the things which the other parents were sharing. They were putting into words the feelings I was having but was unable to identify and articulate. Attending was the beginning of healing for me" (Keyser 1999, personal communication.)

Although UNITE initially stood for Understanding Newborns in Traumatic Experiences and was designed to help "parents of children who had birth defects or who were at high-risk due to prematurity, as well as for parents whose babies had died," by the early '80s it had come to focus on pregnancy loss. By the time Janis (who in the meantime had delivered a healthy son), and her coeditor, Kris Ingle, published the first issue of *UNITE Notes* in 1981, UNITE defined itself as a "support group for parents who have experienced miscarriage, stillbirth or infant death" and addressed its newsletter to "all individuals dealing either personally or professionally with infant or neonatal death" (*UNITE Notes* 1(1):1).[1] In addition to support groups, UNITE offers a telephone-support network with trained parent counselors, a quarterly newsletter, hospital inservices, community education programs, and training workshops for bereavement counselors, caregivers, parent-support counselors, and group facilitators; since 2000 they have also run a website, sponsored by Philadelphia Newspapers.

Janis had a major role in the development of each of these components of the organization. She cofacilitated the UNITE group at Jeanes Hospital in Philadelphia from 1981 until 1997; she was a coeditor and major contributor to the newsletter from 1981 to 1986, and she has served as executive director of UNITE Inc. since it incorporated in 1985. She recalls, "Within a few months [after starting to attend UNITE support group meetings], I began co-presenting inservice programs to hospital staff to sensitize them to the needs of parents whose babies had died" (personal communication 1999). In 1985 she and John Murray developed the UNITE Grief Support Counselor and Support Group Facilitator Training Course, and they have offered this five-day course each year "to bereaved parents who wish to grow into a helping role, as well as professional caregivers who want to further develop their grief support skills" (Keyser, personal communication 1999).

Pregnancy-loss support-group members often say that their loss changed their life. This is certainly apparent in the life of Janis Keyser. As she puts it, "My stillborn baby daughter, Jessica Brooke, has given direction to my path over the past 20 years and for that I am grateful." In addition to her extensive volunteer work with UNITE, this experience guided her graduate education—an M.Ed. (1986) and Ph.D. (1992) in Psychoeducational Processes (applied social psychology) from Temple University. Her doctoral dissertation, "The Grief Recovery Process after the Death of a Baby: Inner Experiences and Personal Meanings," is a qualitative/humanistic study of the loss experiences of seven families and she has published a number of articles in this area (Keyser 1999, 2000).[2] Bereavement is now the focus of her professional life. Janis now works as bereavement coordinator at St. Christopher's Hospital for Children in Philadelphia, where she established and serves as director of The Center for Grieving Children, Teens & Families, "helping young people and their families grow through loss."

The support group of the National Council of Jewish Women (NCJW) in Manhattan was established in 1982/83 by Nina Cardin and Ingrid Kohn. Nina was employed as the director of the National Council's Jewish Research Center when she had her miscarriages in 1979 and 1982. When I interviewed her in 1989 she was a rabbinical student at the Jewish Theological Seminary. Nina recalls being dismayed at how little information she was able to find in bookstores and at women's resource centers in the city. When she met Ingrid, an obstetrical social worker at Mt. Sinai Hospital who was married to a fellow rabbinical student, she discussed the need for a support group for women who miscarry, and they agreed to organize one. Around the time of their first training session of peer counselors, Ingrid had a pregnancy loss too. In the beginning they planned to include "any spontaneous or required, or medically recommended loss. It could be you went into the hospital for an abortion but if it was because the baby would not have survived anyway, we considered that a miscarriage. That's why we called it the pregnancy-loss group, so that we could accommodate them." They did not plan on including women who had "abortions by choice," thinking that "it would be easy to define the abortions that were in our category and abortions that were beyond," but found that "it's not always easy to define . . . it's very hard, there's a hazy line there" (personal communication 1989). Although the groups had initially been for miscarriage, they soon expanded to include stillbirth and eventually newborn death as well.

In addition to the support groups, they put together materials to give to women when they left the hospital. Nina explained, "I remember in the hospital, when I had a baby, I was given a little care package to take home. . . . Now I leave as a miscarriage patient, I don't have anything" (personal communication 1989).[3] She reasoned, with our materials, at least when they got home "if they want to turn to us" they could.

The final component of their program, and the one Nina was most involved in, was their phone-counseling program. Even though she was instrumental in setting up their support group, she recognized that groups are not for everybody. Indeed, she was certain that she would not have attended a support group even if there had been one available at the time of her loss. "I know I wouldn't have gone to a group, to tell you the truth. I didn't have the time. I didn't know who those other people were. I'm not a group person. But just someone to talk to . . . , I would have loved. I figured . . . if it was important to me, maybe somebody else would like a phone call too." Ingrid estimated that a little more than twice the number of people who attend their groups made use of the phone-counseling service with many group members using the counseling service while waiting for space to become available in a support group. By 1989 they had started limiting the number of phone-counseling sessions to three calls unless there were special circumstances, since they had found that when volunteers asked people if they wanted to be called again, no one wanted to offend them by saying no. Today the National Council of Jewish Women also provides support services for couples who are pregnant after a loss and referrals for physicians and psychotherapists who specialize in this area. Ingrid, along with one of the group's first members, Perry-Lynn Moffitt, published *A Silent Sorrow* (2000), a widely praised guidebook on pregnancy loss for women and their families.

Both UNITE and SHARE hold regular monthly or bimonthly support groups, which individuals may attend as they please. The New York Section of the National Council of Jewish Women's support group was more structured. Their program consisted of six consecutive two-hour weekly meetings, each week being devoted to a particular topic.[4] Space was limited at these meetings to six couples, and in order to attend one had to go through an intake interview with one of the phone counselors. From their point of view, the ideal time for a couple to join a group was two to three months after a loss but on one occasion they had accepted a person whose loss had occurred six years earlier. The NCJW group also differed in that it suggested a set voluntary contribution to attend. UNITE and SHARE do not charge for their meetings but cover some of their expenses for meetings and their newsletter through membership dues. (One is not required to become a member to attend meetings; and copies of past newsletters are distributed free at meetings.) UNITE and SHARE are also supported by tax deductible donations from businesses and not-for-profits and from individuals, the latter often being made in the memory of a child (see chapter 6).[5]

Rana Limbo[6] and Sara Wheeler, leaders of the pregnancy-loss support organization Resolve through Sharing, whom I interviewed in 1989 during the Pregnancy and Infant Loss Awareness Weekend in Washington, D.C., provide a broader picture of the "pregnancy loss support movement" and some of the tensions within it. Limbo and Wheeler credit the beginnings of their organization to the work of two maternal nurse-practitioners in Madison, Wisconsin, Carolyn and Cathy, who in 1979 became interested in perinatal bereavement. Together they had put together some photocopied materials to hand out to their high-risk patients who were having losses. Apparently, "word gets around, and when you are kind of interested in bereavement, people are delighted. News travels fast, because they don't want to do it, and if they think you're interested, they'll back away." So these two nurses started seeing patients from other departments as well. Around that time they started communicating with SHARE, and there were some attempts to start a support group since "they felt like, when they got real busy . . . the first thing that would go was the follow-up." Apparently the committee that had been formed to start a support group had "many false starts" and in the meantime another hospital in Madison started one. Limbo and Wheeler described what it took to start such a group. "They had finally gotten the right combination. If you don't have the right kind of people on a committee, people who are willing to work, people who are willing to get rid of the political stuff, and people who have the administrative power to be able to implement something. . . . So they got the right jell of a committee in February of 1981." But the committee also agreed that they needed to continue the type of "one to one helping relationship of a health care professional" that Cathy and Carolyn had started. With that "resolve through sharing" counselors were formally instituted, with the plan that they would "take care of families at the time of their loss, wherever they would be in the hospital, and provide them with the opportunities to make some choices about how that experience was going to be for them." As Limbo and Wheeler stressed, one of the reasons this type of care is so important is that only a fraction of those who experience a loss will attend support groups. They mentioned a national study that suggested that of any given eligible population only about 10 percent would make use of support groups. They felt that, while members of support groups are "the most visible," it is important to remember the other parents, and "what happens to them when they're in the clinic, when they're in the hospital." They also described their unpublished study based on questionnaires with eighty-seven women called "Miscarriage and Women's Responses," the most important finding of which was that "people don't feel the same about miscarriages." Women's responses varied from "it's no big deal" to "it's the worst thing that ever happened to our family." They noted that the key to whether there was grief was whether people felt as if they had lost a "baby." In their study and a similar study they knew of, about 75 percent of the women were sad and 25 percent weren't. They worried about pregnancy-loss support groups in this regard. "The problem in perinatal bereavement is that for a very long time the pendulum was over here, and that was, you know, nobody grieved, and it wasn't that big of a deal. Pull yourself up by your bootstraps. Well, the pendulum is swinging, and it can't get over here, because then it'll be that everybody grieves, and see, we know that that's not true." They went on to describe what they saw as "a healthcare professional's responsibility. It isn't just being sympathetic to the person who's sad. It's being equally understanding of the person who isn't and not making any judgment of that; but simply being where they are" (Limbo and Wheeler, personal communication 1989).

Support-Group Meetings

At UNITE and SHARE, some people come to only one meeting and decide for whatever reason not to attend again; others attend on and off for years. At any given meeting there will be people for whom this is the first meeting, or the second, third, or fourth, and others who have been attending for years. There will also be a mix of people who have had only one pregnancy loss and those who have had multiple losses; those who got pregnant after a long struggle with infertility and the use of assistive conceptive technologies and those who got pregnant easily; those who have living children at home and those who do not.

Sometimes women, and occasionally a man, attend on their own, but most support group meetings are attended by couples and at the NCJW group, this was a requirement. When the NCJW group first started they accepted only women but then as Ingrid recalls, "we thought men are feeling this too so we should really include them somehow. So we invited them to the fourth session of the six and then realized it's really awkward for them to be kind of plunked down in the middle of a very intensive, sort of cohesive group and so we tried" meeting together. They found that "this was absolutely crucial" because what emerged was that one of the most "difficult things they faced was the stresses that occurred between them as a couple" and so we found that "their issues became a primary focus of the whole group and then they added, at the suggestion of one of the participants, having the women and men meet separately for one of the six meetings (Kohn, personal communication 1989).

As with other self-help groups, pregnancy-loss support group members are "a story telling population" (Irvine 1999:2). One of the primary benefits of group meetings is the way they help people deal with what Irvine calls "narrative wreckage." Pregnancy loss "disrupt[s] the continuity" of would-be parents' "existing stock of stories, . . . derail[s] the plots . . . remove[s] key characters, . . . [and] ma[kes] future chapters or episodes unimaginable" (Irvine 1999:46). The new stories that members craft at support group meetings are "simultaneously individual and social" (Irvine 1999:3), drawing on a shared set of cultural resources and stock of "narrative formulas" (Irvine 1999:5).

Most people who attend meetings talk, but this is not mandatory, and sometimes one person acts as a kind of spokesperson for the couple. In my own case, during the first several meetings I found myself unable to speak, and I listened in fascination as my husband spoke, saying things in this setting about his own experience of the loss that he had not expressed privately to me.

Normally a session begins with opening comments from the facilitator who welcomes people and lays out the ground rules, for example, about confidentiality, being respectful of other's feelings, and not using full names of people being talked about.[7] Then participants go around the room and introduce themselves, giving accounts of what brings them there. Sometimes these are brief. More often, especially for those who are first-time attendees, the accounts involve a heart-wrenching blow-by-blow account. In addition to a description of events leading up to the loss, these accounts may include a description of the mother's physical symptoms (such as swollen, leaking breasts), details of the funeral or memorial service, how the loss was handled by others, and their own feelings of shock, disbelief, anger, and grief. As people told these stories, I would often find myself thinking, "Well that is the *worst*, the absolute *worst* possible thing that could happen," only to have the next person tell an equally or even more anguished tale.

Once the meeting is in full swing, a theme-centered pattern to the story-telling often emerges. For instance, someone might tell a horror story about the way she or he was treated by their mother or brother-in law, and so on. Then others in the room will chime in with similar stories about bad experiences they had with relatives or give contrasting stories indicating that they were lucky to have had supportive relatives but sharing a similar tale of denial or disrespect from some other party. Or someone might describe their feelings about being invited to a good friend's baby shower and then others will share how they dealt with such events or tell of how difficult it is for them to be around a good friend or relative who is pregnant, or who was pregnant at the same time and whose baby lived.

The most enduring memory I have from the years I attended support-group meetings is the feeling, by the end of the evening, of overwhelming, cumulative, raw, tangible pain that seemed to fill the room. After several years I found that I could no longer deal with the intense, compounded collective pain of support-group meetings. Instead, I came to prefer working alone in the privacy of my office, where I could pace and limit my exposure to this pain. Pregnancy-loss support-group activists report similar feelings. For instance, in her letter announcing that she had decided, after five years, to take a break from serving as a group facilitator, Bambi Warren (2001) tells how she explained to her daughter why she was crying after counseling a newly bereaved family. "Each time a new family begins that struggle through their sadness, [I feel] sure that now my heart is full, and I cannot fit another sorrow." In my case, I had also grown uncomfortable with the "old-timer" status I was acquiring in the groups.

Support-Group Members

The membership of all three of the organizations I studied is predominately white and middle class.[8] Like other pregnancy outcomes, the frequency of pregnancy loss appears to be linked to socioeconomic factors (MacFarlane and Mugford 1984).[9] According to MacFarlane and Mugford (1984), pregnancy loss varies dramatically from country to country and "within the UK, regional variations in perinatal and infant mortality have a broadly similar pattern to regional variations in mortality in adults both of which are statistically associated with measures . . . such as the state of the housing stock and consumption of food, alcohol and tobacco" (MacFarlane and Mugford 1984:113–114).

As far as I know, there are no studies available that compare the experience of pregnancy loss for women from different class backgrounds. Because of the profound impact that race and class have on the experience of pregnancy and motherhood in the United States, one must not assume that the experience of members of pregnancy-loss support groups is representative. Perhaps, like the infertile women in Sandelowski's study, socioeconomically advantaged women are more likely "to place their faith in physicians sometimes likening them to 'God almighty,'" while less advantaged women may be more likely to believe that reproductive outcomes are "in 'God's hands' (1993:92–93, Rapp 1999). Or it may be that for women living in poverty the import of pregnancy loss is muted by a whole host of other troubles (Rapp 1999). It is also possible that the greater frequency of these losses among less-advantaged women means that women have more shared knowledge about pregnancy loss and alternative forms of social and institutional support.

However, while it is reasonable to assume that women from different socioeconomic backgrounds draw on different cultural resources in making sense of a pregnancy loss, it may also be true that, like the mothers of young children with disabilities that Landsman (2000) studied, class is not a major factor in how mothers experience this unplanned and unwanted reproductive experience. One of Landsman's explanations for this unexpected research finding is the fact that the "illusion of control and of the potential for 'perfect' babies [is shared by] mothers of all socioeconomic classes who have access to and utilize the medical system." As I describe in chapter 5, the problem of expectations of medical omnipotence also frames the experience of pregnancy loss.[10]

All three groups are ecumenical and include Jewish, Catholic, and Protestant members. Testimony of participants at UNITE and SHARE meetings and the personal narratives published in the newsletters of those two groups indicate that many members of pregnancy-loss support groups turn to religion in their search for answers.[11] To judge from these sources, participants vary in the strength of their religious commitment. Some held deep religious convictions prior to the loss, and for many of these individuals their faith provided an important source of solace; for others, their con-

victions were severely challenged by the loss. Some who normally led relatively secular lives turned to religion in their efforts to deal with this life crisis. For some, the idea of an afterlife and/or a master plan proved to be of
comfort while others found such beliefs wanting.

The January/February 1997 issue of the SHARE newsletter is devoted
to this topic, and provides a good representation of different responses. For
example, the piece featured on the first page by Karen W. Burton, "When
God Is Silent . . . ," describes the crisis of faith that this United Methodist
pastor experienced following her son's death nine days after birth from a
heart defect. This issue also includes a piece by Jean Kollantai, the founder
of the Center for Loss in Multiple Birth (CLIMB), on the importance of
recognizing and accepting the fact that not everyone has spiritual beliefs.

In addition to providing a rich rhetorical resource for making sense of a
loss once it occurs, there are many ways in which religion may affect expectations and practices during the pregnancy. Rapp has noted that religion
(for example, Christian Science) may affect individuals' choice of whether
or not to use new reproductive technologies and also may affect their experience of these technologies if they do choose to use them. Rapp (1997:48)
found that the Jews in her study, whether ultra-orthodox or very secular,
"expressed an unambivalent relationship to technology in general, in
marked contrast to those drawn from other religious groups." Religion can
also influence the construction of fetal personhood in a number of ways,
such as traditions about when one should buy things for an expected child
(see chapter 6), and often influences mourning practices after a loss.

Some founders and leaders of pregnancy-loss groups are supporters of
women's right to choose, while others clearly feel that their work in pregnancy loss support complements their anti-abortion stand. It is not safe to
assume that individuals who participate in groups share or even know the
position of their group's leaders on abortion.

Luker (1984:151–153, 284) found that one-third of the pro-life activists
she studied reported some form of "parental loss," such as infertility, a miscarriage, or the death of an infant or child, whereas only 6 percent of the
pro-choice activists reported such a loss. This difference is accounted for, in
part, by the fact that pro-life activists have more children (that is, get pregnant more often) than their pro-choice counterparts (1984:196–197) since a
larger number of pregnancies means a greater chance of having a pregnancy
loss. Luker found that the experience of a pregnancy loss was important in
the decision of some to become active in the pro-life movement.

Although people join support groups to mourn losses ranging from very
early miscarriages to deaths that occur during the first year after birth, a dis-

proportionate number of members have had later losses. Given the relatively small incidence of second and third trimester and neonatal losses, observations at support group meetings suggest that such losses are much more often represented than one would expect based on frequency alone.

Certain types of pregnancy loss are less likely to be dealt with at generic "pregnancy-loss support groups." A number of other organizations specialize in these types of losses. For example, the Center for Loss in Multiple Birth, Inc. (CLIMB) and the Twin to Twin Transfusion Syndrome Foundation (1994) help women who lose part of a multiple conception, for example, one twin. As discussed in the previous chapter, losses involving multiple conceptions are increasingly common. According to one of their spokespersons, women who have experienced such a loss and attend a pregnancy-loss support group may feel "different" and guilty for their grief because they still have a healthy baby at home (1988:38). Another type of loss that one occasionally finds at UNITE or SHARE support-group meetings, but more commonly would find at a special support group is that due to Sudden Infant Death Syndrome (SIDS). Notwithstanding the early intentions of the NCJW's group, pregnancy-loss support groups do not ordinarily include would-be mothers who terminate a wished-for pregnancy because of negative results of prenatal testing or other reasons.[12]

In addition to the regular support-group meetings, UNITE has periodically offered a support group to help women and their partners deal with the stresses and fears of going through a pregnancy after a loss, known in the language of pregnancy loss support as a "subsequent pregnancy." In 1995, UNITE also held a meeting for "those of us 'down the road' . . . in grief recovery," that is, for "anyone at least three years past their loss experience."

The Newsletters

Both UNITE and SHARE also produce newsletters. *UNITE Notes* has appeared four times per year since 1981; the *SHARE Newsletter* (renamed *SHARING* in March of 1997) comes out six times per year.[13] UNITE mails their newsletter to about 250 dues-paying members. An additional fifty to one hundred copies are distributed quarterly to parents who request them (personal communication, Nuccitelli 2000). *SHARING* is sent to between 1,800 and 2,000 individuals. A grant enables SHARE to give parents a one-year subscription free of charge, and they mail between five and ten copies to each group leader to distribute at support-group meetings. A number of professionals also subscribe, and SHARE produces a special newsletter,

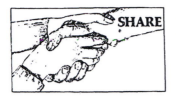 **SHARE**

newsletter

. . . a Source of Help in Airing
and Resolving Experiences

St. John's Hospital - Springfield, Illinois

| Volume 10 - No. 2 | March - April 1987 | Editor: Jeanette C. Colburn |

UNTITLED
Brenda Terneus
Macon; IL

[Matthew David Terneus was born November 19, 1985 and died December 3, 1985.]

To the baby boy
whose voice
would now have
been gurgling,
laughing and cooing,
perhaps by now
saying "da-da"
maybe even "ma-ma"
this poem is dedicated.

I miss you so:
this aching
hole in my heart
throbs terribly
at times---
here for so short
a time,
and yet here
forever, too.

By now I thought
it would be
better, somehow.
The other day
I realized
I've been waiting--
waiting for
"things to get back to
"normal."
But they never will.
Nothing can be
as it once was again.
I hope others
will understand--
as it took me
so long for the
realization, perhaps
they never will.

But I have--
and that step
is what matters.

DEAR KEVIN
Tony and Sandy Goetsch
Sheboygan, WI

[Kevin Michael was born September 30, 1984 at 9:15 AM and died at 10:30 Am due to extreme prematurity.]

Mommy and Daddy wanted you so much.
Happily looking forward to your birth,
To your precious smile and to your soft touch.
Everything about you - a treasure's worth.

Ending our glow,
Such deadly woe,
Why did you go?

In Mommy for just a twenty week stay.
Born in the bathroom so fragile and small,
You stayed around not even a full day,
And from our heavenly God came your call.

You are so still.
No, not our will,
What to do 'till...?

Our dreams and our hopes fade into a mist.
Kevin we think of you and we still cry,
the future forever feelings resist,
It's so hard when our love must say goodbye.

Never forget.
Spirit here yet.
Tomorrow's debt?

Oh dear Kevin we love you and miss you.
We all hope to see you again someday,
So please pray for us back here on earth too,
And guide us everyday to come your way.

SHARE Newsletter.

Caring Notes, specifically for caregivers (personal communication, National SHARE office staff, 2000).

The newsletters feature poems, narrative accounts, excerpts from personal journals, and letters of bereaved parents describing their experience. SHARE announces the upcoming themes for its newsletters, and members are encouraged to "share thoughts, feelings, ideas, poems or stories . . . on these topics." Some topics include the following: "Surviving the Holidays," "Lessons We've Learned from Our Babies," "Grandparents' Grief," "Mother's Day/Father's Day," "Subsequent Pregnancy(ies)," "Recurrent

Losses." The newsletters also include a letter from the editor; articles by professionals on topics of interest such as "research on treatment of repeated miscarriage" or "father's grief"; reviews of new publications and films on pregnancy loss; announcement of upcoming bereavement conferences; acknowledgment of donations; announcement of successful births and adoptions by members; and advertisements for special pregnancy-loss products (see chapter 6), as well as patterns and directions for making pregnancy-loss memorial goods. SHARE has a section called "Parent Connection," where members request correspondence from others who have had experiences similar to their own. Short self-descriptions in this section typically include a specific medical condition or circumstance associated with the loss, for example, arterial venous malformation of the brain, hypoplastic left heart syndrome, nonimmune hydrops fetalis, Turner's syndrome, incompetent cervix, cord accident, but sometimes are as general as "anyone whose first pregnancy ended in miscarriage."

There is some overlap between the newsletters; each sometimes reprinting pieces from the other. Pieces are also sometimes reprinted from other bereavement magazines. Pieces from earlier issues are also often reprinted, especially if they deal with the theme or seasonal holidays covered by that issue.[14]

The SHARE newsletter typically provides at the end of each entry some background information on the contributor, such as where s/he is from, the date of the loss, the medical reason for the loss if known, how far along in the pregnancy the loss took place, previous losses, and if there are surviving children. I include this information when available. Although UNITE does not publish comparable information, through e-mail correspondence I have been able to attain some additional background information on a number of UNITE's contributors.

In selecting which pieces to include in my analysis, I have tried to convey the full range of responses represented in the newsletters on a given issue. I have also consciously included pieces that represented both ends of the continuum of practices and beliefs conveyed, not only to give readers a sense of the full range of responses, but also because I have found that identifying what is striking and sometimes unsettling about these cases helps provide a better understanding of the key issues at stake.

As at support-group meetings, later losses are proportionately much more frequently represented in the UNITE and SHARE newsletters. Of the 447 losses reported in the newsletters (UNITE 1981–1994/SHARE 1984–1994), 197 referred to a miscarriage; 113 to stillbirth; 80 to a newborn death following a full-term pregnancy and 57 to a newborn death after premature birth.

Women, mostly bereaved mothers but also sometimes other female relatives, friends, and nurses, write the vast majority of the newsletter items.[15] Some women contribute multiple items, and these often span a period of years, allowing the reader to piece together a fuller account of their loss and to see how the experience of loss changes over time. This includes the editors, who contribute some of their own poems and narrative accounts and also publish a regular column in which they draw on their personal experience. Men (again, mostly bereaved fathers but also occasionally grandfathers or brothers) contribute more regularly to the SHARE newsletter (about 12 percent of the personal items) than they do to the UNITE newsletter (about 4 percent).[16] Men write a somewhat larger portion of the professional items (16.13 percent for SHARE and 17.02 percent for UNITE) but even for this type of contribution women write the lion's share (45.16 percent for SHARE and 63.8 percent for UNITE). A large number of the professional pieces written by women are by the editors of the newsletters. An additional 38.7 percent of such items in SHARE and 19 percent in UNITE are unsigned. Pieces that take a minority position on an issue (for example, express anger, or doubt about the ultimate meaning of a loss) are more likely to be published anonymously.

Pro-life discourse and symbols appear more regularly in the SHARE newsletter than in that of UNITE. For instance, SHARE periodically provides a cross-stitch pattern for a "precious" footprint in its newsletter. In 1984 the editor of the SHARE newsletter included the following discussion of SHARE's policy of providing women who had pregnancy losses with "precious feet" pins.

> Some of you have asked about the Precious Feet [pins] we give to parents who have experienced a miscarriage or ectopic pregnancy. They are a Pro-Life symbol. In giving them to the parents, we remove the portion of the card that indicates that they are Pro-Life. As a group we do not take a stand on controversial issues. Individual members have their own views. Should a parent be asked if it is a Pro-Life symbol, they can answer simply that they wear it in memory of their baby who died early in pregnancy. I do not see that it needs to cause conflict (Colburn 1984).

In the next issue SHARE's founder, Sister Lamb, published an item in the section "Notes from Sister Jane Marie" retracting this rather veiled pro-life position and embracing an unambiguous pro-life stance. "We would like to clarify any confusion resulting from the last Newsletter commenting on the Precious Feet. We value every life and mourn the death of every baby, regardless of the gestational age or the cause of early demise" (Lamb 1984).

More recently, a piece in the SHARE newsletter discussing the fact that October is Pregnancy and Infant Loss Awareness Month offers a number of answers to the question "Why Have an Awareness month?," the final one being "because society needs to be reminded that each baby, even the tiniest life: was wanted, was real, is loved" (1998 7(5):10).

Yet the current director of SHARE, Cathi Lammert RN, is aware of the risk of imputing meaning to a loss that is not there, and of imposing practices that are not desired. After having read a draft of the first chapter to this book, she told me that "it's OK when people choose not to name their babies. . . . That's something I really struggle with when caregivers feel, you know, this would really help you. Well, do we really know that? It may help someone, but it may not help you." She went on to explain, sometimes people "contact me who feel violated from the other aspect. 'I didn't want to see my baby,' 'I didn't want to know the sex of my baby, and the nurse made me do that.'" She has lectured caregivers on this issue in an address entitled "Rights of Parents When a Baby Dies: Choices or Mandates?" Despite her personal commitment to individual choice and tolerance of differences in the ways people respond to their losses, there is a remarkable consistency in the attitudes expressed in the newsletters.

Since very few of the pieces published in the newsletters are written by "experts," but instead tend to be by others like the reader, the "respect for the printed word" found among readers of self-help literature noted by Simonds (1992) does not operate the same way. Contributors whose work is published in a newsletter may find seeing themselves "in print" a validating experience, but readers of the newsletters are not likely to think of the information found there as "disembodied, unconnected with any creator" (Simonds 1992:28). Another difference between such newsletters and self-help books is that the primary purpose of the newsletters is to offer comfort rather than provide a guide for self-improvement. Many members of pregnancy-loss support groups report personal growth as a result of their loss. These changes, however welcome, were not sought after, and, although the personal accounts published in the newsletters may serve as models for how to turn hardship into a source of personal growth, credit for this self-improvement is typically given to the baby or the experience, rather than to personal effort and/or advice literature.

Pregnancy-Loss Support, Women's Self-Help, and Feminism

Pregnancy-loss support groups provide a valuable case with which to refine understandings of the relationship between "women's self-help" and feminism. It seems appropriate to consider pregnancy-loss support as "women's self-help." Taylor defines women's self-help as "women joining together to solve common problems not being addressed by existing organizations and social practices" (Taylor 1996:7), and pregnancy-loss support clearly fits this description. Although pregnancy-loss support organizations work hard to make visible and legitimate men's grief,[17] the movement is clearly women-initiated, organized, and led.[18] All the founders I know of are women, and although UNITE's facilitator-training program is run by a man and a woman (psychologist John Murray and executive director Janis Keyser), of the approximately twenty past and current UNITE facilitators recognized at their twenty-fifth anniversary event, all were women. The various UNITE support groups are referred to as "sister groups" in the organization's newsletter (UNITE 2000). In addition, as mentioned above, the vast majority of pieces published in the newsletters are authored by women, and although support-group meetings are frequently attended by couples, at any given meeting there is likely to be a majority of women in attendance.

But are all women's self-help groups, by definition, feminist? Clearly not. Some of the critics of women's self-help have been concerned that such groups "valorize traditional notions of femininity." On the whole, this seems an apt criticism of pregnancy-loss support. On the other hand, given the fact that pregnancy-loss support challenges dominant understandings of

UNITE facilitators.

what counts as "motherhood," one must acknowledge that there is more to pregnancy-loss support than a simple endorsement of "traditional notions."

Of even greater importance is the fact that an "unequal burden" of the problems of pregnancy loss (for example, medical risk, assault on identity, ascription of blame, and difficulty gaining social recognition of the validity of the experience of loss) clearly falls on women. Yet the rhetoric of pregnancy-loss support does not consider pregnancy loss in terms of "the specific disadvantages of gender" (Taylor 1996:5).[19] Quite the contrary, in an effort to enroll as many allies as possible, the pregnancy-loss support movement plays down the importance of gender.

I support the movement's efforts to define pregnancy loss as an event that affects not just individual women, but also families and broader social networks. At the same time, I believe it is important to acknowledge the ways in which gender operates to shape the experience of pregnancy loss. Moreover, I believe that it is both possible and desirable to transform this women's mutual-aid movement into a feminist one (see chapter 10).

CHAPTER 4

Challenges to Narratives of Linear Progress

Uncompleted Rites of Passage and Liminal Entities

The avoidance behaviors I noticed during and after my first loss can be explained in part by the liminal character of dead embryos/fetuses/neonates and the women who bear them—that is, those two sets of actors stuck in the middle of an uncompleted rite of passage. In many cultures including our own, pregnancy is treated as a rite of passage, especially if it is a first pregnancy (Miller 1997, Laderman 1983).[1] Despite the feminist movement, some Americans still believe that a woman is not a "real" or "complete" woman until she has borne a child (cf. Luker 1975). Hence the transition to the status of "mother" may also entail the assumption of the status of "real woman" and/or "adult" as well. As a condition that marks these transitions, pregnancy has a liminal status and represents a temporary condition that places the woman between two structural states.[2] The pregnant woman, especially in the case of a first child, is "betwixt and between fixed points of classification" temporarily set apart from the structural arrangements of the culture (Turner 1974:232, Davis-Floyd 1992).

Van Gennep observed that the three phases of rites of passage—separation, transition, and incorporation—are not developed to the same extent in every set of ceremonies, and noted that pregnancy is often dominated by rites of transition (1960:11). Several studies have focused on the transitional character of pregnancy in the West and delineated the pollution beliefs and practices of pregnant women that set them off from the routines of everyday life, including food taboos; avoidance of the ugly, sick and deformed; minimizing physical exertion and social activities; avoiding evil thoughts; and pregnancy and postpartum sex taboos (Newman 1969, Comaroff 1977, Paige and Paige 1981, Reinharz 1988a). Comaroff describes the pregnant woman as "interstitial in respect both of her social classification and of her behavior" (1977:116). Others (Stacey 1997) have described pregnancy as a "borderline state." "More than one, but less than two, the reassuring boundaries of self and other are lost" (Stacey 1997:89). As Douglas (1966), Leach (1976), and Turner (1967) have shown, such liminal statuses are typically charged with both "power and danger."

Normally, the liminality of a pregnant woman ends some established time following the birth of her child. In many societies, the woman and her infant are kept in ritual confinement for a period of time during which they are considered to be especially vulnerable and also, in some cases, potentially dangerous to others.[3] Then through a ritual or series of rituals, confinement is ended and mother and child venture out into the world with their new social identities. For example, "among the Ganda, a pregnant woman is . . . considered dangerous and is forbidden to touch any man or his possessions. She is usually segregated in a special house throughout her pregnancy, and she remains in seclusion for nine days after delivery while a series of purification rites is held" (Paige and Paige 1981:186).

In the United States, at the end of a normal pregnancy a woman is gradually reintegrated into society in her new role through rites of incorporation. These may include flowers sent to the hospital, visits, gifts and cards from relatives and friends, the lifting of taboos, and being addressed as "Mom."

When a pregnancy ends without a live birth, there are no rites to reincorporate the woman.[4] My research with members of pregnancy-loss support groups indicates that many participants feel trapped in a liminal social position. One woman reports that after two stillbirths she was told by someone not to worry about "Limbo." Later she says she realized "that there is a Limbo, but it's not for the stillborn babies. It's for their parents," a state which she and her husband felt powerless to escape. "We gave birth—sort of. We had a child—sort of. Our child died—sort of. . . . Soon we learn to speak of things somewhere between birth and death, as we live in our someplace between heaven and hell" (Gana 1986). Another expressed similar feelings in a poem: " . . . a mother without a child. What am I? I had a baby, but she's gone. Am I a mother? What am I?" (Chaidez in Schwiebert and Kirk 1985).

Lovell (1983:757) notes that for losses that end in a hospital women lose their status as "mother" and as "patient" simultaneously. In the British hospitals where she conducted her research the "nursing staff often stopped carrying out routine procedures such as taking [the patients'] pulse and temperature." One medical social worker recalled a case where, "after her baby was born dead" a woman was put in a room alone, not even given a cup of tea, and then not checked on for twelve hours. Lovell (1983:757) concludes, "hospitals seem to have no physical or psychological space for such a person, and the problem of a woman who seemed to have no legitimate role was often 'solved' by sending her home with what felt (to the woman) like indecent haste."

In many societies pregnancy also represents a rite of passage for the father.[5] One of the infertile men in Becker's study describes the series of milestones in life that help people know that "you're finally grown up" and how he realized that for him, and for society, fatherhood was "a mark of an adult." He describes his experience of infertility as "this kind of limbo thing . . . I'm no longer a child nor yet a full-fledged adult" (Becker 2000:69). The ethnographic literature provides documentation of men's observance of food taboos and seclusion during their wives' pregnancies and of the birth process as a rite of passage for both parents in many societies (Paige and Paige 1981; Young 1965). Reed describes the traditional American ritual confinement of fathers to hospital waiting rooms during birth as a rite of passage for men. "Strangers in a strange land, . . . the waiting room was . . . [an] arena for creating a new identity for men as fathers. Separated from partners, . . . and mundane matters, . . . men had the opportunity to focus on their own transformation" (1997:8). Rothman (1982:99–100) has suggested that many of the new roles for American fathers, such as actively preparing for the birth, helping the mother do prenatal exercises, learning breathing techniques, and so on may represent new forms of couvade rituals in which the husband imitates to a certain extent the wife's pregnancy and her birth rituals.

Despite all this, men have largely been ignored by most social and demographic studies of reproduction (Townsend 1988), and the area of pregnancy loss is no exception. Studies of reproductive loss rarely include fathers in their sample. Given the extent to which stillbirth or miscarriage is treated as an illness, it is understandable that the focus of friends and relatives, healthcare practitioners, and social scientists alike tends to be on women and their bodies. But as the rite of passage framework makes clear, pregnancy loss is a social event as well as a biological one, and involves both men and women albeit in different ways.[6]

Like pregnant women, in nearly all cultures embryos and fetuses are considered liminal entities that must be ritually controlled (Van Gennep 1960, Douglas 1966, Leach 1976). In many societies this liminality does not end automatically at birth (Morgan 1996). Newborns are often ritually secluded and not named until a fixed period of time has elapsed. For example, in rural China a "child-reaching-full-month" ceremony is held at which "the child is shaved and given a personal name by his maternal uncle" (Fei 1946:35). Among the Wari' of Amazonia, mothers and their newborns remain in seclusion for six weeks after birth and the baby is referred to during that time by a term which means "still being made." The child is given a personal name once seclusion ends and it begins interacting with the wider community (Conklin and Morgan 1996:672). In the Gambia, a newborn is "ritually carried outdoors, named, and blessed, to establish its place in the paternal family" about one week after birth (Bledsoe 1999:26). Similar practices have been reported in some African-American communities. A lay midwife in Alabama (Smith and Holmes 1996:42, 51) describes the "taking-up" ceremony that takes place a few weeks after birth, during which the mother goes outside carrying the infant and circles the house a set number of times, then drinks a thimbleful of water before reentering.

Corpses, like embryos/fetuses/newborns, represent another border crossing and are the source of both power and danger.[7] Partially still of this world/already part of the next, corpses are universally treated with ritual precautions designed to protect the living and to assist the deceased in completing the transition.

Thus, dead embryos, fetuses, and neonates are liminal in at least two ways. One member of a pregnancy-loss support group describes visiting her son born at twenty-three weeks gestation where he is buried in the infant section of a Jewish cemetery, which is "hidden behind a shroud of hedges because under Jewish law an infant is not recognized as legitimate until a month of age. I cross into this Netherlands . . . " (Di'Saro 1998). Lewis compares "our image of a stillborn" to "a black hole in the mind, full of invisible things and difficult to recall and, therefore, hard to think about" (Lewis quoted in Ruby 1995:183). He tells of one obstetric resident who when instructed to photograph a stillborn baby said, "'What is the point? It will come out fuzzy!'" (Lewis quoted in Ruby 1995:183).

In many cultures the liminality of fetal or newborn corpses is considered to pose significant dangers. According to Rasmussen (1975), among the Igloolik Inuit of the Melville Peninsula and Baffin Island, a miscarriage was so polluting that as soon as a miscarriage occurred everyone living in the house, men and women alike, were required to throw away all of the "soft things," that is, all of the clothes, skins used as bedding, and the sealskin covering used to line the whole interior of a snow hut. If this was not done the sea spirit Takanakapsaluk would bring the family terrible misfortunes.[8]

According to McKinley, people on the Malay Peninsula believe that "a pregnancy can just as easily produce a voracious vampire as a human infant." If the "very delicate process" that "leads from the formless but life-giving power of blood to the organized, soul-bearing and morally aware condition of human being . . . begin[s] but [does] not reach its conclusion, then people must fear that another form of life, perhaps a birth demon, has entered their midst" (McKinley 1981:373).

Miscarried embryos/fetuses are also often considered to be great sources of power. Sha (1990) reports that Hungarian and Romanian Gypsies "attributed great powers to unborn babies, so when a woman miscarried they cut off the little finger of the child's left hand and put it in the foundation of a dwelling to ward off lightning." They also used the baby's blood to increase their efficacy as thieves (1990:66). In Egypt, stillborn infants, dead newborns, and miscarried fetuses are thought to be among the most powerful agents for both causing and overcoming ritually induced infertility, *kabsa* (Inhorn 1994).[9] Because of their potency, "an informal market in miscarried and aborted fetuses and stillborn infants exists among poor urban and rural Egyptian women. Instead of burying or disposing of these infants, women often keep them for ritual use" (Inhorn 1994:145), preserving them by wrapping them in cloth or keeping them in a plastic bag or jar.

Sometimes "dead babies" are liminal in yet a third way. Many pregnancy losses occur because of severe congenital malformations.[10] This is widely believed to be the primary cause of miscarriage and for white women (including Hispanics), congenital anomalies are the leading cause of neonatal mortality (U.S. Dept. of Health and Human Services 1999:22).

Morgan (1996b:25) provides a number of examples of cultures in which people do not assume that the product of a human pregnancy will be human. In many societies premature or malformed fetuses are believed to be ghosts, "malicious bush spirits in human guise," or the young of some other animal and are killed, burned, or thrown into the sea (Morgan 1996b:25). We know from Duden's (1991, 1993) analysis of the German physician's text *Diseases of Women Wherein Primarily Such Mishaps as Concerns Lumps, Womb Growths or Fake Fruits are Discussed Theoretically and Practically* that in eighteenth-century Europe, early pregnancy losses were considered to be losses "not [of] children but other kinds of fruits" variously described as "evil growths," "untoward matter," "burnt stuff," "singed skins," "bubbly lots," "inconsistent beings," and "fleshy morsels" (Duden 1993:64–65). Malformed concepti delivered dead at term or who survived have been known since antiquity as "monsters" (Park and Daston 1981, Paré [1573] 1982, Todd 1995).[11] Many such individuals were considered to be half-human/half-animal, resulting from God's wrath at the copulation of human beings with other species (Davidson 1991:45). Davidson explains, "The issue of monstrous births . . . raised practical problems for priests, since they had to decide whether any particular monstrous child was human, and so whether it should be baptized or not" (1991:48).

Today, such births are still sometimes described in these terms. For example Lovell (1983) reports several instances of health professionals in Britain referring to late malformed pregnancy losses as "disgusting," "terrible," "monsters." They are also now described in terms of disabilities, but as Murphy (1988) observed, persons with physical disabilities are treated in much the same way as initiates during the liminal phases of rites of passage. Disability is also an "in between state," a disabled person's state of being, being "clouded and indeterminate, just as is that of the neither-boy-nor-man initiate" (1988:238). Murphy notes that "one of the peculiar qualities of the disabled is that they so often inspire fear and revulsion."[12] When a pregnancy loss involves a visible malformation, the status of both mother and baby are affected. Lovell (1983:756) found that "when the lost baby had a physical deformity, he or she was not considered to have been a proper baby. In such cases there was a strong likelihood that the perceptions of the people around the mother helped to confer a spoiled identity upon the baby. . . . Thus, the woman who, as well as having a dead baby, had an imperfect baby, seemed to feel that she had been doubly deviant."

Pregnancy Loss—A Tabooed Topic

The liminality of women who do not complete wished-for pregnancies and the superliminality of the dead embryos/fetuses they bear helps to explain why pregnancy loss is a tabooed subject in our society.[13] The silence that surrounds this topic does not result from its lack of consequence; on the contrary, taboo status signals the importance of these events. Taboo is defined as a "prohibition put upon certain people, things, or acts which makes them untouchable, unmentionable, etc." (Webster's 1970). The word comes to English via anthropology from the Polynesian term *tapu*. According to Shore in his review essay on the concept in Polynesia ethnology, the term "seems to combine contradictory properties, suggesting on the one hand sacredness, reverence, and distinctiveness, and, on the other, danger, dread, and pollution" and, he concludes, "nowhere is this conceptual knot more thoroughly tangled than in . . . the relation between tapu and the feminine" (Shore 1989:144). Because of their reproductive powers, Polynesian women represented "a passageway between the godly and human realms of existence (Hanson quoted in Shore 1989:147). Thus "under varying conditions, the vagina could be either a source of pollution or a source of vitalizing potency" (Shore 1989:148). What is of particular importance for our purposes is the way the notion of *tapu* concerns not only "the life-giving powers of the . . . gods [and women] but also the imparting of order . . . without which life-forces become destructive and polluting" (Shore 1989:148).

In the United States, as in Polynesia, dead newborns combine the potency of women's life-giving power with the destructive, polluting power of life-forces gone awry; thus, it is not surprising that such entities should be subject to taboo. Dead embryos or newborns are an unwelcome reminder of the fragility of the boundary between order and chaos, life and death.

Pregnancy Loss as Challenge to the Contemporary "Interdiction on Death"

While the liminality of dead and/or malformed fetuses and of the women who bear them may be issues everywhere, there are a number of cultural particularities that contribute to the way that pregnancy losses are handled in the United States. One such factor is the fact that the feelings of bereavement members of pregnancy-loss support groups feel run counter to what Aries has identified as the modern "interdiction on death" (1974:87). Aries (1974) and Stone (1979) have traced the major changes in Western attitudes toward death and related changes in notions of personhood. In the early Middle Ages when death was accepted as the order of nature, there was a certain sense of interchangeablity of persons. For example, Stone reports the sixteenth-, seventeenth- and early-eighteenth-century practice of giving a child the same name as that of a recently deceased sibling (1979:57). Throughout this period, however, one can observe a gradually increasing recognition of the individuality of each person. This is reflected in the individualization of sepulchres and funeral inscriptions, as well as of many aspects of family life and childhood socialization. Some of the earliest evidence of the greater attention that was paid to children is the representation of them on tombs and the inclusion of children that died shortly after birth in genealogies in order to "register the existence on earth, however brief, of

all infants born" (Stone 1979:257). By the eighteenth and nineteenth centuries in Europe and the United States, death had become dramatic and romantic, and a cult of tombs and cemeteries flourished (Stannard 1975).
However, since the beginning of the twentieth century, starting in the
United States and spreading to industrialized Europe, the cult of the dead
was replaced by an "interdiction on death" (Aries 1974:87). According to
Aries (1975), this interdiction was caused by the combination of several interrelated phenomena—the lack of familiarity with death due to increased
longevity, advances in medicine that have made it increasingly difficult to
be certain that a serious illness will be fatal, and the increasing emotional
centrality of the family. In addition, he asserts, there is a modern "need for
happiness—the moral duty and the social obligation to contribute to the
collective happiness by avoiding any cause for sadness or boredom, by appearing to be always happy, even if in the depths of despair" (1974:93–94).

In his book on "the struggle for self-control in modern America,"
Stearns (1999:175–179) describes a related historical process—a process he
traces from the early years of the twentieth century to attenuate strong emotions including anger, mother love, and grief. He links the attack on Victorian intensity to "increasing pressures of middle-class employment," which
made elaborate mourning impractical, and to the appeal of consumerism.
"Pleasant emotions and enjoyment clearly better fit the new consumerism"
(Stearns 1999:177).

Thus, although "violent death has played an ever growing part in the
fantasies offered to mass audiences," "natural death" has become "more and
more smothered in prudery" (Gorer 1965:197 quoted in Ruby 1995:12).
Despite the death-awareness movement of the 1960s and the growing popularity of hospice care, death is still very much a tabooed topic (Stearns
1999:178). Ruby (1995:2) reports that while conducting his research on
postmortem photography he learned that others found his interest in this
topic "morbid and strange." He notes that one colleague's wife was "uncomfortable at the thought of coming to my home because I have all 'those
pictures of dead babies'" and his efforts to mount an exhibition on the subject "was rejected by several curators as being too 'difficult' for the public"
(Ruby 1995:2). He also reports that two photo-historians who had successfully published other books had "pictorial studies of the social customs of
death" rejected "several times by publishers who thought [them] too depressing to sell well" (1995:2). One of the reasons for this diversion is that
death presents a challenge to our cherished narratives of linear progress.
And if death challenges such narratives, the death of newborns is in some
ways the ultimate such challenge.[14]

Pregnancy Loss as Challenge to Narratives of Linear Progress

The cultural historian Lynn White Jr. has observed how narratives of progress permeate our everyday lives. "Our daily habits of action . . . are dominated by an implicit faith in perpetual progress" (White 1967:346).[15] According to White, this faith in perpetual progress is "rooted in, and is indefensible apart from, Judeo-Christian teleology" being "unknown either to Greco-Roman antiquity or to the Orient" (White 1967:346). Newman (1988:8) has also remarked on this American propensity—"from our earliest beginnings we have cultivated a national faith in progress and achievement."

This faith stems in part from our belief that science and technology "advance" in a linear fashion according to "an inherently dynamic and cumulative process" (Volti 1988:7). (The ways in which pregnancy loss is exacerbated by and poses challenges to our beliefs about the linear progress of biomedicine will be discussed in the following chapter.)

This preferred American narrative structure informs the stories we tell about the proper and expected trajectories of individuals' lives. Becker found in her study of mostly white, middle-class infertile couples that people believed "that their lives should follow predictable, coherent, linear paths" (Becker 1994:390). Newman's (1988) study of unemployed white- and blue-collar workers also illuminates how deeply held and widely shared these beliefs are and, in addition, makes clear the fact that this linear trajectory should be upward. As Stacey observes, even though not everyone's lives are filled with success and progress, "in a society so obsessed with its own progress and improvement it is almost impossible for us to avoid the pull of such narratives" (1997:9).

Popular biomedical accounts of both fetal and child development that now form a mainstay of middle-class Americans' experience of pregnancy and parenthood present a concentrated, telescoped view of these beliefs. Popular guidebooks on pregnancy document the development of one's "baby" from conception to birth—from fertilization to meiosis, the division of the egg into two identical cells "thirty hours after fertilization," and then "some ten hours later" further division into four cells, sixteen cells on day three, sixty-four on day four, "a tube-like heart" on day twenty-two that will begin to beat on the twenty-fourth or twenty-fifth day, a stomach at week six, eyelids in week seven and so on (McClure and Bach 1986:16–17).

Pregnancy books describing fetal development are followed by parenting guides with titles like *The First Twelve Months of Life: Your Baby's*

Growth Month by Month (Caplan 1973). On the front cover, my 1973 edition boasts "over 450,000 copies in print" as well as "monthly growth charts." Some such books describe "slow" and "superior" as well as "normal" development of the baby's visual, auditory, tactile, mobility, language, and manual competence (Doman 1988), but in all cases the developmental tales are linear ones. These parenting manuals are accompanied in many middle-class American homes by baby books and/or first-year calendars for recording and chronologically plotting all the important "firsts"—baby's first tooth, baby's first step, and so on—which chart the dramatic but also incremental development of a normal infant's life. In addition to these unofficial records, most pediatricians provide a pamphlet in which they chart the baby's development (weight, length, head circumference) at regularly scheduled checkups. Although some babies are relatively large and others relatively small (most babies, like adults, being either above or below average in size), the graphs provided by the National Center for Health Statistics show steady, upward, linear development for each of the seven delineated percentiles, and it is in comparison with these norms that each individual child's development is plotted.

Fetuses that don't develop properly and babies that die challenge these cherished narratives about the natural course of individual development and, given its own linear progress, our assumptions about biomedicine's ability to assure that pregnancies and babies stay on this expected path.

A Culture of Silence

All of these factors contribute to the culture of silence that shrouds pregnancy loss in the United States (Layne 1997, 1990). Since the formation of pregnancy-loss support organizations and hospital bereavement teams in the 1980s, the scholarly and popular press have made the subject of pregnancy loss more visible. However, members of pregnancy-loss support groups attest that the suppression and avoidance of these unhappy events remain the norm. As Simonds and Rothman note, "in all of this recent writing and discussion about . . . loss . . . , the most consistent theme is the silence surrounding the actual experience. Bereaved mothers say, again and again, no one wanted to hear, no one let me talk, no one listened, no one said 'I'm sorry.' It happened in silence" (1992:2).

In the following section I sketch the taboos and silences that surround pregnancy loss and explore the ways in which pregnancy-loss support groups are challenging them. As Foucault noted, "there is not one but many silences" (1978:27). At the level of popular culture, one of the clearest indicators of the culturally sanctioned nonexistence of these events is the fact that there are no greeting cards for such occasions. This was brought to my attention during a support-group meeting, and the woman who mentioned it went on to say, "Heck, they even have cards to send to someone when their pet dies."[16] If one is hospitalized, or when a death occurs, there are clear acts by which those who belong to one's social network are expected to acknowledge the event and show support. Depending on the degree of intimacy it is customary to mail a get-well or sympathy card, send flowers, pay a social visit, bring food, and in the case of a death, to attend a ritual ceremony. Even though in the case of pregnancy loss some individuals may show support in these same ways, it is not *customary* to do so when the reason for hospitalization was a pregnancy loss or the death is of a fetus or neonate.[17]

From time to time I give public lectures on my work on pregnancy loss and questions from the audience are frequently from those who know someone who has had a loss and want advice on what to say or do. In these cases, it is clearly not a lack of sympathy or goodwill that is the problem but the absence of accepted cultural scripts for how to behave in such circumstances.

The cultural denial of pregnancy loss clearly has a profound effect on those who experience a loss. One of the most frequent complaints voiced at pregnancy-loss support meetings is that relatives, friends, and coworkers pretend that nothing happened (cf. Reinharz 1988b:85). All evidence that a baby was expected (shower gifts, nursery furnishings) may be hidden away before the woman returns home from the hospital and all topics relating to pregnancy studiously avoided. Alternatively, the details of others' pregnancies may be reported in painful detail. In both cases the experience of loss is denied. Those who do acknowledge the loss often diminish the importance of it, saying, "You can always have another."

Barbara Cuce of Mt. Sinai, New York, tells of how following the death of her infant son she "began to realize that people shied away either because they didn't know what to say or because it could be a reality for them that they couldn't deal with, . . . feelings of loneliness . . . began to sink in. People who know what had happened either ignored me or said something inappropriate" (Cuce 1998).

Perry-Lynn Moffitt (1994) reports that after her first miscarriage "people responded by sending flowers and notes of condolence. Others stopped by for brief, but supportive visits," but when her next pregnancy also ended in miscarriage, "most [of our friends] didn't want to talk about it. There were no notes or flowers this time."

It should also be noted that women who miscarry may inadvertently col-
lude in the silence-making by their decision not to reveal their pregnancy
until after the first trimester (i.e., until after the greatest risk of pregnancy
loss has passed) (cf. Reinharz 1987:234). This practice appears to have been
with us since at least the Victorian era. Reinharz (1988a:27) quotes from the
diary of a Kansas woman who had two miscarriages in the 1890s. She had her
second miscarriage on a Friday and went with her sisters to their parents'
house on Sunday. "I cannot tell them of my disappointment, since I had not
let them know of my expected joy, wishing to keep it for a sweet surprise."

Because of this reticence, many people who have a loss do not realize
that they know others who have had similar experiences. Reinharz
(1987:235) remarks that women frequently mention that they did not know
anyone who had miscarried. In my case, it turns out I did know a great many
women who had miscarried, but I wasn't aware that they had until they
shared their experience with me after my own loss. The same proved true
for my mother. Several weeks after my first loss she called to tell me that,
following my miscarriage, a number of her friends, including one of her
dearest lifelong friends, had shared their own experiences with her for the
very first time.

I have other anecdotal evidence that indicates that the silence surrounding these events (even among close female friends) is not a new phenomenon
but existed in the 1940s and 1950s. In the early 1990s I was invited to discuss my work on a local radio talk show. At the end of the program I gave
out my phone number and asked anyone who was interested in sharing their
story with me to call. One of the women who responded had lost a son more
than twenty years previously. She said that she and her husband had never
discussed it with anyone! This was the first time she had ever told her story.

As my own story illustrates, other silences are located in the medical domain, whether orthodox or alternative. The neglect I experienced from the
physician in emergency is partially explained by the medical unimportance
of such events. Most pregnancy losses are considered evidence not of pathology but of the body operating as it should. "Because it happens so often,
it is considered a normal variation in the pregnancy process" (Pizer and
Palenski 1980:26). "Physicians have considered miscarriages 'humdrum and
dull' because they are rarely life-threatening, require only routine intervention, and generally cannot be reversed" (Reinharz 1988a:4). As mentioned
earlier, Lovell (1983) attributes the poor treatment in hospitals of women
whose babies die to their ambiguous status. In my particular case there were
other factors at work as well. I later learned that the doctor who attended me
resented taking care of patients from the birthing center: in his view, the

birthing center kept patients when everything was going fine but when things went wrong, sent the messes to him to clean up.

Although the effects on the miscarrying woman are the same, in the case of midwives, the lack of support for women who miscarry presumably stems from other sources. In their effort to demedicalize pregnancy, women's health centers have overemphasized happy outcomes (cf. Reinharz 1988b:89, Layne in press). By defining *The* Problem in childbearing as medical intervention into what should be a joyful, natural process, nonmedically caused problems become invisible. In addition, given the underlying premise of alternative women's health centers, the policy of the birthing center I went to was paradoxically fetus- rather than woman-centered. I remember thinking at the time that it wasn't fair that the women who got the babies were also the ones who got all the support and attention.

Despite their differences, both conventional and alternative healthcare providers share a culture that encourages the avoidance of any unpleasant topic. When I questioned the director of the birthing center about why the possibility of miscarriage had never been mentioned to me, she told me, "people don't want to hear about it."

The medical neglect of pregnancy loss is also evident in many of the lay-educational materials available on pregnancy and childbirth, including feminist ones. (See also chapter 10.) Often how-to books of pregnancy take a woman step-by-step through a pregnancy starting with the moment of conception, without making clear that a pregnancy may end at any point along the way. Pregnancies are broken up into a series of stages (trimesters, weeks of gestation) and presented as if one stage *inevitably* follows another. For instance, *Getting Ready for Child Birth: A Guide for Expectant Parents* (1986) devotes one of its 285 pages to the topic of pregnancy loss but not until chapter 7, which is entitled "The Newborn." *The Rodale Book of Pregnancy and Birth* (1986) neither includes figures on the frequency of miscarriage nor explains the normal medical procedures for miscarriage. It does mention miscarriage and stillbirth in its flow charts at the beginning of the book (mostly to warn women who have had a previous miscarriage to be more careful this time), but discussion of these topics is placed incongruously in the section on the third trimester. *Our Bodies, Ourselves*, widely known as "the bible for women's health" (Byllye Avery on the back cover of the 1998 edition), has been, and continues to be, organized in a similar fashion (see chapter 10).

This narrative structure is also powerfully portrayed in the prenatal development exhibit at Chicago's Museum of Science and Industry. Adjacent to this exhibit is the museum's popular baby chicks exhibit where one can

watch chicks hatch. Placards inform museum guests that "the embryo starts
to develop after it has been placed in the incubator . . . The fertile egg develops into a healthy baby chick in 21 days." Here again, the fact that some fertilized eggs will not develop at all, let alone into healthy baby chicks, is
rhetorically negated by a positive, normative assertion of inevitably successful outcomes.

The Emmy Award–winning NOVA documentary *The Miracle of Life*
(1986), featuring Lennart Nilson's photographs, "follows the development
of the single new cell into an embryo, then a fetus, until finally, a baby is
born." Although it does stress obstacles to fertilization, particularly those
that occur during "the perilous journey" of sperm, it suggests that a live
birth is the inevitable outcome once fertilization has taken place.

Nor is the topic a standard part of childbirth classes, even those whose
philosophy is based on the assertion that women have the right to control
their own bodies and that this right can only be actualized if women have
adequate information (Panuthos 1984:157).[18] Kathryn March (2001), a feminist anthropologist who suffered first a tubal pregnancy and then an infant
death, contrasts how negative reproductive experiences are dealt with in
Nepal, where she did her field work, and the United States. Nepalese
women, she reports, talk "easily" and "loudly" about "infertility, repeat
miscarriages, hard births, and deaths in and near birth." In vivid contrast,
we silence these stories and deceive ourselves with a "shared faith that chosen childrearing is always happy" and, according to March, "nowhere are
we so deceived as in . . . childbirth education" (March 2001:171). As Sherokee Ilse, founder of the Pregnancy and Infant Loss Center of Minnesota,
writes after the stillbirth of her son,

> In our childbirth preparation classes we had talked about Cesarean
> birth and the pain of labor. I do not remember any discussions about
> other unexpected outcomes. In fact, the assistant childbirth educa-
> tor's words kept ringing in my ears, "Remember at the end of this
> you will have your prize, your baby. . . . That will help you get
> through the difficult parts of labor" (1989).

After her loss Ilse produced a number of publications on pregnancy loss, including a guide for childbirth educators on "presenting unexpected outcomes." In considering the reasons why such topics are not normally presented
by childbirth educators she mentions the "fear that participants will respond negatively on evaluations," fear that such discussions might provoke
tears that would be uncomfortable for the teacher and other classmates, a

sense that physicians would not like "having their patients exposed to 'fear producing' information," and the broader issue that "in our culture people continually try to protect each other from pain, the truth, or anything that might be difficult to handle" (Ilse 1989:8–9).

Another arena in which silence shrouds these events is that of civil records. Most pregnancy losses are not granted the status of "vital" statistics.[19] The great preponderance of such losses, those which take place during the first trimester, are not reported to the National Health Registry even when they end in a hospital. As a result, unlike most of the figures on pregnancy outcomes compiled by the National Center for Health Statistics, which are actual counts, the figures on "fetal loss" are estimates based on a sample of women who were asked to report retrospectively about their reproductive history for the previous five years (Ventura et al. 1995:2, 2001).

Figures on later losses are also problematic since the gestational age after which a fetal death certificate is required by law varies from state to state.[20] In twenty-eight states the law requires that a fetal death certificate be issued after twenty weeks gestation, "eight states report all products of conception as fetal deaths, still others use birthweights of 350g, 400g, or 500g or greater to identify fetal deaths" (Cunningham et al. 2001:5). Those losses that occur before twenty weeks gestation have typically been recorded along with many other operations as D&Cs or D&Es. The current edition of *Williams* recommends standardization so that regional and international comparisons could be made and recommends that "statistics include all fetuses and infants born weighing at least 500g, whether alive or dead." Those weighing less than 500g are to be "termed abortuses" rather than "births" for "purposes of vital statistics" (Cunningham et al. 2001:5).

Because of the difficulty of reliably documenting the incidence of pregnancy loss, especially spontaneous abortions, it is often avoided in scientific studies.[21] Because toxins, whether in the workplace (Chavkin 1979, 1984, Claybrook 1984, Coleman and Dickinson 1984, Cordes 1993, Daniels 1993, Hamilton 1925, Hemminki et al. 1980, Lindbohm et al. 1991, Markoff 1992) or in the air we breathe (Bertell 1985), the water we drink (Brown 1993, Baker and Woodrow 1984, Wrensch et al. 1992, Deane et al. 1992) or the food we eat (Bertell 1985, Stevens 1994) are particularly hazardous to the unborn, miscarriages, stillbirths, and neonatal deaths loom large in the public-health discourses of environmental disaster or workplace safety. Abnormally high rates of miscarriages are often one of the first and most visible signs of environmental crisis (Layne 2001). However, because miscarriages, the most common type of pregnancy loss, are so hard to reliably document, they are avoided in many epidemiological studies.

This is true not only of epidemiological studies, but of demographic analyses as well. As Bledsoe observes, "Although infant and child mortality is a standard source of demographic data, far less so are non-live births" (1999:63). "The recognition that there are also non-live births, many of them quite traumatic and injurious, has virtually vanished from vision in fertility research" (Bledsoe 1999:62). One consequence of this is that there have been "vast amounts of demographic attention" devoted to "maternal behaviors preceding the deaths of small children . . . but what a mother . . . does after . . . a non-live birth has gone virtually unnoticed" (Bledsoe 1999:62).[22]

Because the issues framing the meaning of miscarriage and stillbirth resonate so strongly with the abortion debate, feminist scholars have on the whole avoided the topic.[23] Here, as in the public eye, the pregnancies that end in this way remain invisible. For example, although feminist scholars have explored the impact of and problems deriving from a wide array of new reproductive and neonatal technologies, this analysis has not been extended to include the impact that these technologies are having on the experience of those whose pregnancies end with a miscarriage or stillbirth. Reinharz (1988a:5) found the subject of miscarriage neglected "in feminist theory about reproduction and in course syllabi on women and health." And while second-wave American feminists created a rich new repertoire of rituals (Broner 1982, Turner 1982) to celebrate birth, menstruation, marriage, as well as seasonal and reformulated religious rites, rites for pregnancy loss are only now beginning to receive attention (cf. Reinharz 1988a:26, 32, Cardin 1999, Dubin 1995–6).

Breaking the Silence

Pregnancy-loss support groups are fundamentally designed to break this silence. Through their meetings they carve out a space in which it is permissible to speak, and with the claim that pregnancy loss is a legitimate source of grief, they define loss as an acceptable topic of conversation outside of support-group meetings.

In many respects their efforts in this regard have been successful. Patterning themselves on the myriad of other self-help groups in our society, participants engage in what Goffman (1963) has called "the management of a spoiled identity," the primary mechanism of which is speech. Most organizations hold regular meetings at which those who have suffered a pregnancy loss meet to share their experiences, to tell their stories.

In addition to these face-to-face encounters, pregnancy loss is discursively produced in pregnancy-loss support group newsletters. These groups are also supporting a booming pregnancy-loss research and publication industry. In the last twenty years, a number of books have been published by pregnancy-loss support organizations and their members.[24] These include collections of poems and testimonials, pregnancy journals, handbooks for planning memorial rituals, as well as more comprehensive books and pamphlets. These publications, written by members, are then reviewed in the newsletters, made available in pregnancy-loss groups' lending libraries, and offered for sale at pregnancy-loss meetings and conferences. Others, like myself, have parlayed a personal loss into a scholarly research topic. Members of pregnancy-loss groups serve both as respondents for these projects and as consumers of the results.

Not all of the discursive productions of pregnancy loss are so inwardly directed, however. Individuals who would like to see greater support for pregnancy loss have had some fair success in making themselves heard by a broader audience. Since the 1980s, articles on grieving a miscarriage or stillbirth have appeared in a variety of wide-circulation publications. *Ms.* magazine published a piece on miscarriage in 1980 (Welch and Herrmann 1980) and on stillbirth in 1982 (Moriarty 1982). Sister Jane Marie Lamb (1997), founder of SHARE, recalls how in 1981 the publication of a piece on pregnancy loss by Ann Landers "brought major changes" to her organization. "Instantaneously, we became internationally known. Correspondence and phone calls increased beyond our comprehension and capabilities." (It is at that time that she was released from her other duties to work full-time with SHARE.) In 1987 articles on grieving miscarriage and/or stillbirth appeared in *Parents, Health,* and *Newsweek,* and in the next few years *Child, Glamour,* and *Reader's Digest* published similar pieces (Atkinson 1987, Moffitt 1987, Wiley 1987, Beck et al. 1988, Van Buren 1999). In 1989 *Parenting* and *Health* (Wiley 1989) both published articles on how a pregnancy loss can strain a close friendship. *Redbook* (1983, 1990) and the *Los Angeles Times* (Roan 1990) published articles on medical research on the topic (Brody 1992a, 1992b). In the last few years pregnancy loss has been the subject of several high-profile pieces in *The New York Times.* In 1997 *The New York Times Sunday Magazine* published a piece entitled "The Ghost Baby" about a woman's experience of finding no heartbeat during a twenty-week exam (Cohen 1997). In January 1998 an article on the front page of the Regional

Sibling participant at the 1989 Pregnancy and Infant Loss Awareness Weekend during visit to the Kennedy grave.

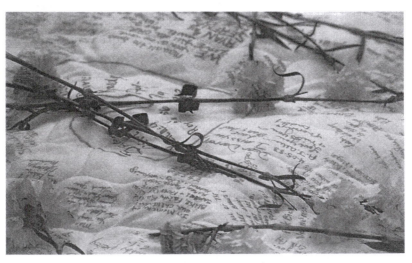

Close-up of memorial quilt and flowers placed on the Kennedy grave.

Baby blankets laid out on Capitol steps.

section of *The New York Times* described some of the "new rites of mourning" for pregnancy loss that members of the clergy and support groups in the New York City area are developing (Fein 1998). Peggy Orenstein's piece describing her experience of a miscarriage while on assignment in Japan appeared in *The New York Times Sunday Magazine* in 2002. In addition, the 1990s saw the establishment of a number of specialized websites and electronic news groups for pregnancy-loss support (see chapter 10). Dr. Michael Berman, the founder of one of these sites and author of a book on pregnancy loss (2001) appeared on the *Today* show and CBS's *The Early Show*, and was interviewed on National Public Radio in 2001.

Many pregnancy-loss support organizations also reach out through training courses and inservice education programs for doctors, nurses, and other interested groups and have been instrumental in changing hospital protocols, especially in the case of stillbirth or neonatal death.

Pregnancy-loss support groups have also garnered governmental recognition for the topic through their efforts to get pregnancy loss on the yearly calendar of public-service-awareness events. In 1984 the Pregnancy and Infant Loss Center of Minnesota secured a Governor's Proclamation declaring October to be Pregnancy and Infant Loss Awareness Month. Since that time other groups have worked to attain similar state and city proclamations. In 1988 President Reagan signed a national proclamation to this effect. In October 1989 pregnancy-loss support groups from around the country met in Washington for a Pregnancy and Infant Loss Awareness Weekend to celebrate this declaration. In addition to a visit to the Kennedy babies' graves, a tree-dedication, a march on the capital carrying baby blankets embroidered with the names of stillborn and miscarried babies, and a service of remembrance, the event also included a legislative briefing. Representatives of a number of groups called on legislators for changes in laws concerning funeral and sick leave in the case of pregnancy loss, health and life insurance coverage, income tax deductions, state laws and Department of Health rulings concerning the "ownership" of the remains, and commitment of research funding.

The following is one example of how pregnancy-loss organizations like SHARE are working to change medical practice and insurance coverage. In a 1995 issue of the SHARE newsletter, one of the coeditors mentioned a pending decision by the Association of Obstetricians and Gynecologists regarding the value of home uterine monitors for prevention of preterm labor and asked "to hear from families that have felt that the home uterine monitor was beneficial for their subsequent pregnancy" (Lammert 1995).

The issue of income tax deductions is still being publicly discussed. In the April 6, 1998 Ann Landers column "IRS doesn't consider the stillborn a person," a bereaved mother, Wendy from Newark, explains that the law required that she and her husband "properly dispose" of the body of their "beautiful, full-term baby girl who died because of a knot in the umbilical cord" and yet the government would not allow them to count her as a family dependent on their income tax. Wendy suggests that "our government ought to allow grieving parents a way to recognize that their stillborn child existed."

As I explained in chapter 2, since the mid-1970s, American women who experience pregnancy loss have found themselves at the nexus of two sets of strong, opposing cultural forces. On the one hand, as discussed in this chapter, they are subject to the double or triple taboo surrounding dead fetuses, and the interdiction on death and any other unpleasant topic that challenges the myth of perpetual linear progress. On the other hand, women's experience of pregnancy and pregnancy loss is influenced by the increasing prominence of the fetal subject in the public imaginary in the last twenty-five years (Conklin and Morgan 1996; Morgan 1996a, 1996b, 2002; Morgan and Michaels 1999). It is to this topic that we now turn.

CHAPTER 5

New Reproductive Technologies
and the Fetal Subject

A wide array of new reproductive technologies became available in the United States in the last twenty-five years. The impact of these technologies on the experience of pregnancy and childbirth, and for the cultural construction of fetal personhood, has been well documented. The import of these developments for the experience of pregnancy loss, however, has not yet been investigated. In this chapter I focus on some of the repercussions of new reproductive technologies on the experience of pregnancy loss.[1]

For a number of reasons, members of pregnancy-loss support groups are especially likely to experience new reproductive technologies. They typically come from class backgrounds that assure good access to reproductive medicine. In addition, women who undergo infertility treatments have a greater-than-average chance of having a pregnancy loss. After a pregnancy loss, women tend to be subject to greater obstetrical scrutiny.

The accounts of members of pregnancy-loss support groups reveal several broad areas in which new reproductive technologies seem to be altering the experience of pregnancy loss: 1) a greater role for biomedicine in defining/confirming both life and death, 2) earlier prenatal bonding, 3) the expectation that advances in biomedicine have eliminated pregnancy loss, 4) the use of biomedical artifacts as evidence that a child existed.

Biomedical Definitions of Life and Death

In the twentieth century, hospitals became the primary sites of both birth and death in the United States.[2] Within these contexts the states of life and death are technologically determined. As Aries (1974:89) observed, "the great dramatic act of death" has been replaced by a series of technologically determined "little silent deaths": the moment consciousness is lost, the moment the heart ceases beating, the moment the person stops breathing, the moment the brain waves cease.[3] In a similar fashion, the beginning of new life has become a matter of science. Since the development of accurate hormonal pregnancy tests in the 1920s (Oakley 1984:95–97, Clarke 1998, Pfeffer 1993, Oudshoorn 1994), women's experiential knowledge of a pregnancy (e.g. missed menses, morning sickness, swollen breasts, fatigue) is no longer credited as definitive of a new life. In recent years these new technological means of determining a pregnancy have been removed from the exclusive control of physicians and made available by pharmaceutical companies to the general public.[4] A pregnancy may now be determined at home with an easy-to-use test, which, with a high degree of accuracy, can establish a pregnancy even before a missed period. In other words, the little pink dot can tell a woman something about her own body before she gains that knowledge experientially.[5]

It is not just a question of one kind of knowledge being more authoritative than another.[6] There are other differences entailed in a technoscientific mode of defining new life. Just as "death has been dissected, cut to bits by a series of little steps, which finally makes it impossible to know which step was the real death" (Aries 1974:88), pregnancy has been broken up into a multiplicity of dimensions. The technological model overturns the old adage that one cannot be a little bit pregnant.[7] The urine or blood test only establishes a chemical pregnancy. A sonogram in the first trimester determines whether there is a physiological pregnancy as well as a chemical one, that is, whether there is actually an embryo or only hormonal changes that usually, but not always, signal a pregnancy. A first trimester sonogram may reveal an embryo that is alive (that is, has a heartbeat), an embryo that is dead (does not have a heartbeat), an empty embryonic sack, or no sack at all.

The scientific determination of pregnancy (hormonally and electronically via electronic stethoscopes and sonograms) before the sensation of fetal movement is undoubtedly changing the experience of those who have early pregnancy losses. Because of the high rate of losses during the first weeks of pregnancy, what in the past might have been experienced as a "late period" is now often experienced as a "pregnancy loss." One man told me of how he and his wife had been unable to have a child until doctors discovered that his wife needed supplemental progesterone in order for a fertilized egg to implant in the walls of her uterus. He explained that they now felt they had been mistaken in thinking of themselves as "infertile"; they now felt they had suffered a series of miscarriages. Because of the earlier establishment of pregnancy with such tests, many women and their social networks are beginning to construct the embryo/fetus as a person at an earlier point in the pregnancy (see chapter 6).

In fact, with fertility treatments like in vitro fertilization some would-be mothers begin the social construction of their "baby" even before implantation (Williams 1987). Becker (2000:121) reports how one couple undergoing IVF said, "We had embryos and we were putting them back, and, you know, you want to name them as they go in." Another couple apparently did name the embryos that were transferred and while waiting to see if any had implanted, took a vacation and sent postcards reporting that "the embryos seem to be enjoying it here" (Becker 2000:156). Couples who use hormonal treatments with artificial insemination and thus witness the follicles growing via repeated ultrasound scans leading up to insemination also sometimes report personifying the follicles and may experience each failed attempt at conception as a pregnancy loss. One Canadian husband describes the experience of attempting to conceive with the use of fertility treatments thus, "Every month for three days it's like a funeral. We've had twenty-four funerals" (quoted in Fillion 1994:50).[8]

Would-be parents are often informed of the sex of their child following ultrasound exams or amniocentesis (Taylor 2000a, Cartwright 1993).[9] This greatly increases the individuation and "realness" of the fetus as a person (see chapter 6). Even if the sex is not known during the pregnancy, the would-be parents sometimes learn the sex after the pregnancy has ended. A pathology exam of the products of conception is often undertaken following a miscarriage in an effort to determine the cause of the loss. The sex of the cultured cells is often conveyed to the parents because it bears on the reliability of the test. If the cells are "male" one can be certain that the cells that were cultured were those of the embryo, whereas if the results are "normal female," the cells may have been those of the mother. It is thus now possible for bereaved parents to know what the sex of their child would have been, even if the demise took place before the sexual organs were physically differentiated.

The determination of a physiological pregnancy with an electronic stethoscope or sonogram also makes the loss seem more concrete. Today, many women have experiences similar to mine. At one prenatal visit they see and/or hear a heartbeat. At the next visit, where there had been a magical tiny flicker of life on the screen, the screen is deadly still; where the room had been filled with the galloping-horse sound of the fast-beating fetal heartbeat, there is thundering silence. For instance, Cari Simons, writing a year after a miscarriage at fifteen weeks gestation remembers, "We saw you

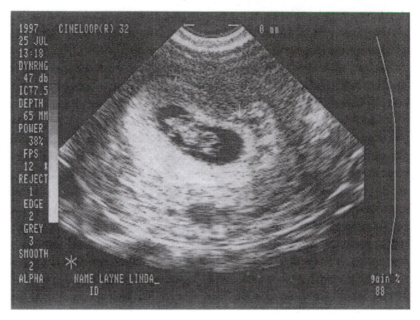

A sonogram photo from one of my miscarriages.

at ultrasound and heard your heart beat. You were absolutely perfect from your head to your feet!" She goes on to describe what one infers took place at a subsequent ultrasound (having had two miscarriages earlier that year, she probably had numerous scans): "Then one day I knew that something was wrong, The wait for the doctor just seemed so long" (Simons 1995).[10]

Pregnancies conceived with in vitro fertilization are monitored even earlier and more frequently with ultrasound and these pregnancies have a significantly higher than average pregnancy-loss rate. Lori Carlin, who was implanted with three eight-cell embryos remembers how, at the first ultrasound at 4.5 weeks gestation, they saw two sacks but at 7.5 weeks, "the ultrasound showed three little babies and we saw your little hearts beating." At five months gestation she delivered, and by the next day all three were dead. In a piece addressed to her children she writes, "I'll always remember seeing you on ultrasound, hearing those strong heartbeats."

While in these cases the technologies are making both the pregnancy and the loss more definitive, more "real," these technologies are also creating situations in which the loss is more ambiguous than it would be without technologically derived information. This can be seen in the case of women who are pregnant for several months, then, following a sonogram, are told that they were never "really pregnant" but had been carrying "a blighted ovum" instead. How is one to experience the loss of a blighted ovum? The same is true in the case of molar pregnancies, where after the demise women learn that instead of a embryo/fetus/baby, they were growing a potentially cancerous grape-like tumor.

As other scholars have noted, ultrasounds are often used by pregnant women to enlist others in the social construction of their "baby" (Rapp 1997, Taylor 1996, 2000a,b, Mitchell 1994). Routine sonograms are now often considered fun family events and accounts of support-group members reveal that women often bring along others who are eager to get a glimpse of the new family member. For example, Rita Fadako, whose pregnancy lasted "twenty weeks, four days," recalls bringing her husband and mother with her for the first sonogram "to have your first pictures taken. . . . They must have taken around a hundred pictures and that is when I knew something must be wrong. The doctor explained that the baby's brain had not and would not fully develop and that there was no hope" (Fadako 1997). Similarly, Anita Horning tells of taking her three-and-a-half-year-old son to the sonogram appointment and telling him he would "see a picture of the baby in Mommy's tummy" but the doctor said "he could not find any 'fetal pull.' I did not understand what he meant. But then he said there was no heartbeat and our baby had died" (Horning 1997).

The technologically derived diagnosis of imminent abortions is also changing the mechanics of pregnancy loss. Whereas in the past a woman would learn that she was "losing the baby" by physiological changes in her body (bleeding and cramping, premature labor, the absence of kicking), now it is frequently through the routine use of devices such as doplers or sonograms that people learn that their fetus has died (or in fact never lived). Because it takes some time before a woman's body begins to expel a nonviable pregnancy, from a scientific point of view "the demise" of the embryo/fetus and its expulsion from the body, "the abortion," are distinct events. From an experiential point of view, however, the two events are often not only synchronic but also synonymous—"a miscarriage." Now, with sonography, one can learn of the demise at a prenatal visit and schedule the surgical removal (via Dilation and Curettage, D&C, or Dilation and Evacuation, D&E) at the doctor's and/or patient's convenience. One doctor explained his procedure for a patient who is spotting:

> Get an ultrasound and see what you are dealing with. Find out whether there is a pregnancy there or not. . . . If you have spotting and you get an ultrasound and you find out that there is no longer a sac and essentially you already have dead products of conception, then there is no sense in sitting around in bed. You can show that

there is a drop in chorionic gonadotropins to convince the woman
that she lost the pregnancy, and you can do a D and C so that you
can study the material so that you can see why (quoted in Pizer and
Palinski 1980:111).

The scientific dis-synchronicity of pregnancy loss is now part of the
woman's experience. Her loss is cut up into discrete moments: the moment
of the demise, the moment of learning of the demise, the moment of surgical
removal. This creates surreal situations in which a woman may still feel
pregnant but for some time has to walk around with the knowledge that she
is carrying a "dead baby" inside of her until the doctor removes it for/from
her. No longer an active agent, a woman who is miscarrying, she becomes
the passive vessel of a corpse. One woman described feeling like "a human
coffin" (Ingle 1981/2a), another like "a living tomb" (Heil 1982).

The surgical removal of sonographically diagnosed imminent abortions
also leads to the disjunction between chemical and physiological pregnancies: when a woman miscarries "naturally" her progesterone and HCG
(Human Chorionic Gonadotropin) levels drop gradually until her cervix di-
lates and the uterus expels its contents; but if the demise is identified by
sonogram and followed by a D&C, a woman remains chemically pregnant
(though no longer physiologically pregnant) for a period of time until her
hormonal levels drop.

In losses that occur later in a pregnancy, after a woman has felt fetal
movement, the impact of some of these technologies is truncated by the
woman's own experiential knowledge of the baby she is carrying. In these
cases the technologies may confirm what a woman already fears:

> When I realized I hadn't felt the baby kick for over 24 hours I got
> really frightened. The next day I went to the doctors. He found no
> fetal heartbeat. I cried. After going to the hospital for x-rays the di-
> agnosis was clear—the baby had died in utero. I cried some more
> (Iacono 1982).

As Julie Gainer (2000) so vividly expresses, even later in pregnancy, the absence of movement for a time can be rationalized, and the ultrasound bring
shocking news. "Then you grew so quiet and your joyous dancing slowed./
I convinced myself you were just sleeping, still warm and safe and hud-
dled./ My strong and healthy Aidan James, just resting peacefully./ Then
your tiny heart screamed its silence across every medical frequency."

Thus, even after quickening, the news these technologies bring may be
totally unexpected. Janis Heil describes the experience of discovering just
before delivery that her second child would be born dead:

I felt sorry for the nurse. She was working hard to find my baby's
heartbeat so that she could replace the fetal monitor belt which she
had removed to prep me. The baby must have moved around a lot,
she said, making it difficult for her to relocate the heartbeat. I
chuckled to myself, amused by the baby's antics, and watched as another nurse attempted to locate the fetal heart tones. Amusement
turned to quiet panic as I realized that the heartbeat I had heard less
than a half hour before could no longer be found. An ultrasound
confirmed the unthinkable (Heil 1981a).[11]

Ultrasound and Prenatal Bonding

Prenatal imaging technologies appear to be changing the establishment and
development of a woman's relationship with her fetus/child during the
course of a pregnancy (see also Taylor 1998). Although the work of Klaus,
Kennell, and their associates (Klaus et al. 1970; Klaus et al. 1972; Klaus and
Kennell 1976) on maternal-infant bonding focused on the "sensitive period"
during the first hour after birth for the attachment of mothers to their infants,
they recognized that maternal attachment usually begins before birth.[12] In
fact, they acknowledge that such attachments may begin well before pregnancy. They mention preschool games in which girls play house as important.

As it happens, the evidence on which they base their belief that women
begin to feel attached during pregnancy comes from a study (Kennell et al.
1970) on women's reactions to the death of their newborns. The study
showed that the length and intensity of mourning after a loss were proportionate to the closeness of the relationship prior to death.

In thinking about prenatal attachment, Klaus and Kennell (1976) followed Caplan (1960) in distinguishing two adaptive tasks that take place
during pregnancy: first, acceptance of the pregnancy, and second, perception of the fetus as a separate individual. They believed that this second task
occurred after a woman first felt fetal movement (1976:41):

> After quickening, a woman will usually begin to have fantasies about
> what the baby will be like, attributing some human personality char-
> acteristics to him and developing feelings of attachment. At this
> time she may further accept her pregnancy and show significant
> changes in attitude toward the fetus. Unplanned, unwanted infants
> may seem more acceptable. Objectively, there will usually be some
> outward evidence of the mother's preparation. She may purchase
> clothes or a crib, select a name, and rearrange her home to accom-
> modate a baby (1976:42).

Since the time of this early work on bonding in the 1970s, when obstetrical ultrasound was "quite rare" and "experimental" (Taylor 1998:17), the use of sonograms during pregnancies has increased dramatically.[13] Estimates vary widely. Petchesky cites a study that estimated ultrasounds were used on at least one-third of all pregnant women in the United States by 1987 (Petchesky 1987:273); Rapp cites a study published in 1993 that gives an estimate of 50 percent of pregnant women in the United States, but she suggests that in urban areas the rate is probably closer to 90 percent (Rapp 1997:31,48); and Taylor (1998:18) cites a national survey that reports that "between 1980 and 1987, the percentage of all pregnancies that were scanned by ultrasound in the United States increased from 35.5 percent to 78.8 percent." Taylor concludes that "it is probably safe to say that in the United States nearly every pregnant woman who has access to any form of health care will have at least one ultrasound scan during pregnancy" (1998:19).[14]

Although the medical consequences of obstetrical sonography are unclear (Petchesky 1987:272, Spallone 1989:39, Taylor 1998), it appears that sonogram images facilitate the perception of the fetus as a separate individual at an earlier stage in the pregnancy, that is, before the woman can feel for herself, without technological intervention, the fetus moving in her body.[15] Fletcher and Evans report "two cases in which women in the late first or early second trimester of pregnancy reported feelings and thoughts clearly indicating a bond of loyalty toward the fetus that we and others had associated only with a later stage of fetal development" (1983:392).[16] They conclude that parents viewing their fetus via ultrasound "will experience a shock of recognition that the fetus belongs to them," that such experiences will result "in an earlier initiation of parental bonding" and are "likely to increase the value of the early fetus for parents who already strongly desire a child" (1983:392).

This phenomenon can even take place before a pregnancy occurs. Sonograms are used in conjunction with ovulation stimulation for a variety of infertility treatments (e.g., in preparation for in vitro fertilization, artificial insemination, or simply, as in my case, to "produce better eggs" and assure that conception took place at the optimum time) and would-be parents are routinely shown the growing follicles on the sonogram screen. Every day or two the would-be mother (and perhaps the would-be father, too) witnesses the gradual growth and development of her egg/s and anticipates the climax of ovulation when the mature egg will be "expelled." Clearly this process can be seen and experienced as analogous to pregnancy and birth. One woman describes how "It really drew me in when I saw those eggs on the surface of my ovary . . . " (quoted in Lasker and Borg 1987:56). Ripening follicles may be counted by would-be parents as the first stage of a pregnancy and sometimes attributed potential or quasi personhood.

Some also view, via microscope, embryos that have been fertilized in vitro, and at some clinics couples are presented with a Polaroid of their embryos before "transfer" (Hopkins cited in Treichler, Cartwright, Penley 1998:17n8). One man tells how, when he told his wife that he wasn't sure what he was seeing, she responded, "What's the matter—don't you even recognize your own kid?" (quoted in Lasker and Borg 1987:67). As one psychologist observed, "Some women become attached to those embryos in a way that's very similar to how attached women get to a pregnancy . . . [and they experience] a failed cycle of in vitro as a miscarriage" (quoted in Lasker and Borg 1987:59).

It is self-evident that the greater the feelings of involvement, attachment, and love for a desired child, the greater the potential sense of loss. Yet given the evidence that viewing sonogram images may encourage the development of would-be parents' attachment to their fetus/baby, it is striking that the impact of sonogram images on those whose pregnancies end without a live birth has either been ignored or viewed as less important than the possible benefits to the would-be child in the literature on bonding. Although Klaus and Kennell (1976) were aware that bonding during pregnancy and birth might result in more pain for would-be parents whose babies died before or shortly after birth, they believed that the risk of increased grief of the parents if the baby died was outweighed by the potential benefit to the baby of parental bonding if it survived. Fletcher and Evans (1983) do not appear to have taken into account the possibility of involuntary pregnancy loss.

As a number of feminist scholars have observed, fetal imaging and other electronic monitoring technologies (for example, dopplers, stress and non-stress tests, and fetal monitors during labor) have contributed to an increasing medicalization of pregnancy, the attendant diminution and devaluation of the mother's role in pregnancy and birth, and an earlier conceptual separation of the fetus from the mother (Oakley 1984, Rothman 1986, Petchesky 1987, Spallone 1989). Several scholars have reported pregnant women's dissatisfaction and resentment with these technologies. For example, Davis-Floyd tells of a woman who said:

As soon as I got hooked up to the monitor, all everyone did was stare at it. The nurses didn't even look at me any more when they came into the room—they went straight to the monitor. I got the weirdest feeling that it was having the baby, not me (quoted in Davis-Floyd 1988:164).

Martin (1987) documents another woman's feelings of resentment toward the technology and the doctor who mediated access to her baby. This woman was not excited the first time she heard her baby's heart and later realized that this was because of the doctor's role.

> It's like he took it away from me because he said, "here's the heartbeat." I mean, he is the one who arranged that I could hear it and I sort of felt like, well, this is my baby's heartbeat but I can't hear it unless he does it for me (1987:72).

But accounts in the newsletters reveal that some people have a very different relation with these technologies. Some become adept at reading and interpreting sonogram screens and fetal monitors. For example, Mickey Hoch writes, "I remember the ultrasound where I could make out the baby's head, but couldn't see the heart beating like I had seen in ultrasounds with my other children" (Hoch 1988b)[17] Another woman reports that her husband noticed that the monitor didn't look right (Heil 1984). In perhaps an extreme case, one couple tells of how they bought their own stethoscope to monitor their baby's heartbeat at home during the pregnancy. In the poem "Intensive Care #1," Marion Cohen reports that after her daughter was born prematurely, her husband felt sure he could recognize his daughter's heartbeat as such on the monitor because of his earlier electronically mediated encounters with her heartbeat via his stethoscope:

> Kerin's Daddy sits, staring,
> "The same," he murmurs, "the exact same."
> Staring, staring, first down at Kerin then
>   up at the screen.
> In particular that top number, the one that shows the heartrate.
> "The same," he tells me. "The same one I heard
>   when she was inside you. I recognize it; it
>   sounds the same. I didn't buy that stethoscope
>   for nothing. That's Kerin's heart, all right.
>   Inside, outside, I'd know it anywhere.
> That's our Kerin Mar; That's Kerin's heart."

According to Starkman's (1976) study of women's responses to the use of fetal monitoring during delivery, women who have had a previous loss were likely to feel positively about the monitor. In fact, a previous pregnancy loss was the most important criterion in determining whether a pregnant woman would welcome or resent the machine. While this may be the case with regard to the use of monitoring devices during labor, the narratives of subsequent pregnancies published in support-group newsletters portray a much more complex reality with regard to monitoring during prenatal visits.

Contrary to Petchetsky's assertion, and Mitchell's findings that these technologies offer women at least the perception of control and predictability, the narratives of these bereaved women indicate that they are well aware that technologies that bring joy on one doctor's visit may bring grief on the next.[18] For example, Marie Keeling (1987) writes:

> "To Laura"
> You were so wanted,
>   trips to the infertility
>   doctor, pergonal shots,
>   estridiol levels, ultrasounds.
> Overwhelming joy when the ultra
>   sound, at six weeks, showed twins!
>   That joy turned to fear, three
>   weeks later—one of the twins
>   had miscarried. . . .
> Weeks later, the same fear
>   struck again—hospitalized
>   with placenta previa: those
>   two words had previously been
>   only words in a nursing text-book.
> Then you were born—too little
>   to live more than a few
>   minutes (Keeling 1987).

The knowledge that there is no guarantee that any given pregnancy will result in a live birth, so vivid for women who have already had one loss, leads women to adopt quite different strategies. Some try to protect themselves emotionally by not getting too attached during a pregnancy.[19] Kelly Gonzalez's (1988b) description of her pregnancy following the loss of her first child at twenty-two weeks gestation is a vivid testimony of the complex feelings that sonogram imaging may evoke:

> At 10 weeks, I had my first prenatal check-up. When the doctor started to listen to the heartbeat, I literally froze. My head was instantly flooded with memories of the last time the doctor was looking for a heartbeat, how she tried for about 10 minutes to find it, how it was never located because Alycia had died.

I remembered the last time I did hear Alycia's heartbeat; only four weeks before she had died, and how thrilled I was when the doctor said everything sounded great, that I had no need to worry about the problems I was experiencing at that time.

I found myself not wanting to hear this new heartbeat. I wanted to shut it out. As the doctor put the stethoscope to my ears, I quickly took it off, after listening for only a few seconds. I realized I was trying to stop myself from getting attached to this new life inside of me, and again I was flooded with guilt. I did not want to punish this baby by not being as excited as I was with Alycia. But I just couldn't allow myself to become attached.

At 12 weeks I had an ultrasound. Once again, I was filled with memories of the last time I was hooked up to an ultrasound machine, when the doctors ultimately learned that Alycia was dead. As the technician started the procedure, I avoided the screen. I did not want to see my little baby moving and kicking, full of life. Curiosity got the better of me and I eventually watched the little gymnast at play. But the moment I realized that I was smiling and laughing, I quickly turned away, trying to stop myself from any attachment.

At 14 weeks, I started spotting. My heart stopped. I just could not go through this again. And while I feared that I was going to lose my baby, I did not find myself relieved that I had not become attached. The truth of the matter was that from the moment I found out I was pregnant, I had become attached to this baby. I was only trying to fool myself.

They performed an ultrasound to see if anything was wrong and I watched every movement, every detail. Everything turned out to be fine . . . (Gonzalez 1988b).

Others, like Kris Ingle, respond to the same knowledge of risk and uncertainty by trying to invest as much as possible during the pregnancy in the belief that their relationship with their embryo/fetus/baby during the pregnancy is an important relationship, one of value in and of itself. Kris, a practicing nurse, was one of the earliest members of UNITE and has remained active in the organization. She did not have sonograms with either of her first two pregnancies (in the late 1970s/early 1980s), but in the pregnancy following her stillbirth her doctor ordered a sonogram at ten weeks gestation. She describes her experience in a poem (1986/87a) by that name:

"10 Weeks Gestation"
I pause to cherish this moment.

Today I saw your heart beat and
   your feet kick as your body
   curled and uncurled.
The doctor tried to measure you
   and you didn't cooperate. Then
   he was finally able to do so.
He called you "my baby," as we
   watched your acrobatics on the
   ultrasound screen. . . .
I'm thankful each hour that my
   body gets to cradle you . . . (Ingle 1986/87a).

Even for women who carry their babies through the second or third trimester and are therefore able to experience the reality of the fetus directly
through its movement, being able to see the fetus via sonogram may add a
welcome, additional dimension to the relationship they are developing with
it while in utero, as it did for Kris. She describes her feelings during a sonogram in the thirty-first week of her subsequent pregnancy:

> I cried when I first saw its small body moving inside me. I marvel
> and cherish each kick and each bump. . . . The day I had a Level II
> ultrasound, the technician told me I'd have to stop crying as my
> stomach jumped up and down, and he needed it to be still. I ex-
> plained that I needed a minute to absorb each limb, each organ, and
> oh, the baby's profile. It might be all I'd have. He looked at me
> funny. I didn't care. This is my child. . . . I will not look back on this
> time with regret as I am already getting to know that little person I
> carry within my body. Already you are my child. You have a person-
> ality and patterns (Ingle 1986/87b).

"Not with Modern Technology"

Another important way that new reproductive technologies appear to be
changing the experience of pregnancy loss is through changing expectations
regarding biomedicine's abilities to guarantee a live birth. Although women
who have had a pregnancy loss are painfully aware that such events can
occur, and experience and respond to subsequent obstetrical care and technologies differently as a result, most women at the beginning of their childbearing careers are ignorant of how common pregnancy losses are (cf. chapters 1 and 4). The silence surrounding pregnancy loss has resulted in

extensive ignorance concerning the frequency of pregnancy loss, and such
ignorance is compounded by the media hype surrounding advances in reproductive and neonatal technologies. (See, for example, the cover story of
the December 1993 issue of *Life*, "Miracles of Birth: The Blessings of a
Medical Revolution, Healthy Babies Who 10 Years Ago Would Never Have
Been Born.")

A central aspect of this faith stems from our ideas about the nature of
science and technology, namely, that they inevitably, cumulatively, and almost automatically, by definition, progress. Winner describes the pervasiveness in our society of the belief that "with the coming of Newtonian science
and the industrial revolution, a pattern of linear growth was established that
continues to the present day" (1977:47).[20]

The "meliorist myth" (Fussell 1975) of unending technoscientific progress is particularly evident in the realm of biomedicine. In the 1970s, a noted
philosopher of medicine asserted that "[n]o disorder, however complex or
intractable, is beyond the possibility of conquest. Man's Promethean hope
of removing the restraints of disease on history seem less illusory than ever
before" (Pellegrino 1976:245), and, by and large, this notion still prevails.
Despite recent public criticism of the costliness of medical care, the increasing dehumanization of patients, and problems of equity, few would doubt
that "medical technology will make possible ever-earlier diagnoses of killer
diseases and provide sufficient back-up spare parts to extend progressively
and perhaps indefinitely the population's life expectancy" (Stell quoted in
Bronzino et al. 1990:519, cf. Poirier et al. 1992:16–19). This faith is expressed by the brother of a UNITE leader on the occasion of a Christmas
memorial donation for his niece who died six days after birth due to a heart
defect. "It is hoped that [this donation] will help build toward that day when
no parent should have to go through what [my sister and her husband] had
to" (Leather 2001).

This vision of the triumphant march of medical progress is especially
clear in "frontier" fields like neonatal medicine. Sociologists of neonatology,
Guillemin and Holmstrom, have remarked on the "conviction" of practitioners in the field "that [its methods] are constantly improving" (1986:26):

> Over the last twenty years, the adaptation of many adult therapies
> to the treatment of full-term infants has been successful. The pre-
> sumption in neonatology is that *progress will continue undiminished at
> the same rate* and prove as equal to the challenge of saving very low
> birth weight neonates as it has to saving more developed newborns
> (Guillemin and Holmstrom 1986:26, emphasis mine).[21]

The overreporting of neonatology's "miracle babies," combined with the underreporting of pregnancy losses (as a result of the taboos regarding this topic), has led to a situation in which expectations concerning reproductive outcomes are higher than the level of medical competence.

In fact, there is no indication that there has been any significant decline in the frequency of miscarriage and stillbirth as a result of medical intervention. As pointed out in chapter 2, because of the increasing rate of first births among women thirty to thirty-nine years of age, there has actually been a net increase in the number of pregnancy losses in recent years.

The experience of loss represents a clash between people's expectations regarding the efficacy of biomedicine and actuality. The gap between faith in technology and the harsh reality of pregnancy loss seems especially great for men.

Jim Friedeck (1984) poignantly expresses the widespread belief that if there is a problem during a pregnancy, doctors will be able to fix it. Even after having gone through one miscarriage, he retained his faith in science's power and described himself as "a joyful, expectant father" during his wife's subsequent pregnancy.

> Things were looking bright. [Until one day late in the pregnancy my wife, Valerie, felt] a series of extremely hard kicks . . . [after which] Val said there was no more movement, and she became very worried. . . . I knew, because I am the eternal optimist, that there was nothing to worry about . . . [The next day she went to the doctor and called, saying,] 'Jim, the doctor said he could not hear a heartbeat.' . . . I met her at the hospital. . . . The dopler was hooked up. Three nurses were checking Valerie and the machine. The electronic wizard would pick up occasional sounds, but nothing definite. . . . 'The baby must have died.' . . . Valerie knew but I didn't want to accept it. Not with modern technology . . . (Friedeck 1984).

Carl Jones describes similar feelings of disbelief: "Surely this cannot be serious. Babies don't die nowadays" (Jones 1987).

Although fathers appear to be especially prone to these feelings, mothers are not immune. For example, Lisa Casimer writes, "We knew instantly that we had created [her] and we were especially careful to ensure that she would be a healthy baby. Naturally, because of our prenatal care, we assumed that we would experience a normal pregnancy" (Casimer 1987). Tami White (2000) tells of how after two miscarriages she and her husband decided to "seek a specialist . . . After many tests and 7 inseminations, I became pregnant again. We believed everything would be okay because we were in the hands of a specialist. Not so . . . " Donna Brunner (1992), a woman who had a C-section for her first child then lost a baby trying what is known as a v-back (a vaginal birth after a C-section) writes, "In our day of advanced technology we seem to believe knowledge will conquer all—even fear, pain, labor, contractions. But it didn't work for me either time."[22]

There is anecdotal evidence that physicians share similar expectations about the power of the new medical technologies and that this faith in medical interventions leads them to feel that it is they (not the technologies) who have failed if a neonate dies (Lovell 1983).[23] The resultant guilt makes physicians less able to offer support to bereaved parents (Klaus and Kennell 1976:214; Down 1986).

Another gap between lay expectations and biomedical reality concerns doctors' ability to explain the cause of death. As Karen Craig (1999) writes in a piece entitled "Why" which describes the death of her older sister's baby, who was born at term but had seizures and died one week later, "Even those who are considered experts, like the neo-neurologist, could not explain what had happened. . . . In this day and age and with all our advanced technology, you would think that someone would be able to explain to me why one tiny baby, who looked so healthy, would just die. I cannot, and will not, accept that things like this just happen" (Craig 1999).

"It Goes to Show That There Was a Child"

Sonogram images and the output from fetal monitors play another very important role in narratives of loss. Several scholars have noted the important role sonogram images play in helping to establish the "reality" of a "baby" during the early stages of pregnancy.[24] Nearly all of the forty-nine Canadian women Mitchell interviewed during their first pregnancies "talked about the fetal image as a form of proof, saying 'Now I know I'm really pregnant!' 'Now I know it's real!' or 'Now I know there's a baby in there.' Having this proof enabled women to talk more confidently about 'the baby' and avoid the term 'fetus' altogether" (Mitchell 1994:153).

Although women may find ultrasound images more "convincing" than hormonal pregnancy tests or hearing the fetal heartbeat (Mitchell 1994:153), seeing such images does not necessarily solve, once and for all, the "reality" question. Oaks cites anthropologist Abu Lughod's description of her own pregnancy, "I was so unsure of my babies that I worried about their having disappeared if I didn't see them every two weeks or so" (Abu Lughod quoted in Oaks 1998:240). Another woman told Oaks that even with the two sonogram images she had, she still doubted the reality of the fetus, "because I didn't see it *all* the time, you know, it wasn't *really* real" (1998:240).

If the "reality" of embryos, and fetuses, especially in the early stages of a pregnancy, is problematic for some women because they cannot be seen or felt, the "reality" or "realness" problem is greatly heightened for women after a pregnancy loss. Because pregnancy loss is a tabooed topic in our society, one of the most frequent complaints voiced at pregnancy-loss support meetings is that relatives, friends, and coworkers pretend that the loss did not take place. For example, Barbara Cuce (1998), in describing the way people responded after the neonatal death of her son, asserts, "It *did* happen and my baby was real, even though perhaps to them he wasn't."

In the face of this cultural denial, parents often appropriate the authority of science to prove their claims. Sonogram photos and scraps from fetal monitors are frequently saved by bereaved parents and utilized as evidence to prove to others that a "baby" existed. Kris Ingle reports, "I told the nurse I needed a piece of each Non-Stress Test reading, proof that the baby is there, heartbeat strong and beating, at least for today. . . ." (Ingle 1986/7b). UNITE member Mickey Hoch writes

> I remember the other ultrasound where the doctor said the aorta was burst and the baby's chest was being crushed. I used to think that was gruesome, but now I think about it and it goes to show that there was a child, a person, even though dead, a baby who once lived (Hoch 1988b).

In 1987 SHARE conducted a "Baby Pictures" Questionnaire and found that, of 438 respondents who reported on losses that occurred between 1966 and 1987, 39 percent had ultrasound pictures; and "93% of these said they were important keepsakes" (Laux 1988a). It is probably safe to say that the number of people with such photos would be significantly greater today given the increased use of routine ultrasound during the past ten years (cf. Rapp 1997:31, 48).

After a loss, sonogram photos are often kept as memorial goods (see chapters 6 and 9).[25] Because they resemble "the person lost through death, [they] serve as a substitute and a reminder of the loss" (Ruby 1995:7). They function iconically in this regard. Shapiro (1988:124) has observed, "of all modes of representation, . . . [photography] is one of the most easily assimilated into the discourses of knowledge and truth, for it is thought to be an unmediated simulacrum, a copy of what we consider the 'real'" (cf. Sontag 1973).[26]

Sonogram images require more interpretive effort, not being as "unproblematically 'real'" (Shapiro 1988:124) as conventional photographs.[27] Newman (1996:108) has commented on "the problem of rendering these new visualizations readable," and Mitchell, writing in the early 1990s of women undergoing routine obstetrical ultrasounds in Canada in about their eighteenth week, quoted one woman as saying, "When I first looked at it, I couldn't see anything. Emptiness, whiteness. She [the sonographer] showed me the head, spine, placenta, arms and the heart. The heart was easy. But if she hadn't said 'here is the baby' I wouldn't have seen it" (quoted in Mitchell 1994:151). Another woman said, "To tell you the truth I couldn't see very much . . . I saw the outline of the baby's body, the head. The best part was the heart beat, finding something that you could really see. You could see it moving. Other than that it was just kind of the outline. . . . I would never have recognized anything if it hadn't been pointed out" (quoted in Mitchell 1994:151).

But by the time one has been given an image to take home, one has been instructed in reading these images by technicians who pointed out the high-lights. Moreover, the images that one is given often include helpful labels indicating, for instance, "the head," "abdomen," and "leg." (The heartbeat, so critical in the case of pregnancy loss, and whose presence or absence is easily recognizable on a live scan, does not appear in the still images most women take home.) Furthermore, I would argue that, by now, for contem-porary American middle-class women, sonogram images have become so pervasive that they require very little reading at all. This is particularly true for the glossy, grainy, black-and-white image given to women to keep fol-lowing a scan (especially those kept as memento mori by women who suffer a pregnancy loss). For these purposes, it is enough to recognize, as middle-class women and men now do at a glance, that this is the picture of a fetus, one's own (or that of a coworker or relative).

Because of their poor visual quality, these images are in some sense in-terchangeable. To a lay observer, one sonogram image looks very much like the next, and, rather than detracting from the reality-making function of these images, this actually serves to increase their iconic power. After a demise, the imprint of medical authority inherent in these images makes them powerful symbols of the reality of that which was lost.[28]

In addition to sonogram images, women whose losses take place in the latter half of their pregnancies are often presented with snapshots by the hospital staff.[29] This practice is a modern variation of a nineteenth-century Euro-American practice.[30] According to Aries, by the second half of the nineteenth century, photographs of the dead, particularly of children, had become very popular: "Few family albums were without their photographs of dead children" (Aries 1985:247). Today, photographs of the dead are no longer considered appropriate; it is photographic remembrances of the per-son in life, not in death, that are socially valued (Ruby 1995).[31] But in the case of pregnancy loss, snapshots of the baby after its birth/death may be the only ones possible.

But whereas in the nineteenth- and early twentieth-century, photographs of dead children were commissioned by the parents, today it is primarily hospitals that take the initiative. The SHARE survey on the importance of photographs after a loss found that of the respondents 63 percent had one or more photograph. Of these, 50 percent were offered pictures by the hospital, and 26 percent had taken pictures themselves (Laux 1988a).

Although at first these snapshots may not seem to qualify as new reproductive technologies, they are clearly part of the new hospital-based system for medically managing pregnancy loss. Much as sonogram use is justified for the "psychological benefits" it provides parents (Taylor 1998:19), these photos are taken by the nursing or social-work staff and offered therapeutically to the parents to aid them in the healing process.[32]

Like sonogram images, these photos play a critical role in establishing the reality of the baby. For example, one of the women in the self-help group featured in the film *Some Babies Die* explains that some of her relatives "took the view that it wasn't really a baby and they were not much support at all. If I'd had photos I could have said, 'Look here, it was a baby. He was a beautiful child'" (Down 1986). And a member of UNITE ends her poem: "One photo. One photo. Our special memory of your birth. A reality. A reality for

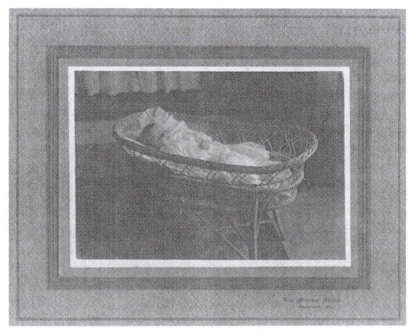

Postmortem photo, circa 1910. Photo by The Morrow Studio of Newport, PA.
Bruce Adams collection.

those who tend to doubt your worth" (Burgan 1988). The respondents to the SHARE survey also testify to the "reality making" function of such photos for both themselves and for others: "We need to remember her as a real person we were holding. This is our proof"; "Although I get no great comfort from her pictures, I do have them put away for when I do feel the need to see she existed"; "on those days when you feel like it really never happened and people are treating you like you never had a child, you do have a picture to remind yourself you did have a child"; another describes having a picture of her twenty-week-gestation baby "hanging on the wall with the rest of the children . . . It is proof she existed" (quoted in Laux 1988b).

In addition to affirming the reality of a baby, such photographs are used by bereaved parents to stress the uniqueness and individuality of their baby while at the same time providing important resources for establishing family ties through the rhetoric of inheritance. They permit bereaved parents to indulge in the postnatal American ritual of attributing family resemblances.[33] Parents who spend time with their child after her/his birth, whether the child is still alive or is dead, engage in this practice. For example, Julie Caiola (2000) writes of her daughter, Angel, who lived 1 hour 20 minutes after her birth at twenty-one weeks gestation, "A mouth like your father's/But you had your mommy's nose." Similarly, the main subject in the film *Some Babies Die*, when presented with her stillborn daughter moments after birth, remarked, "That's me, long toes" (Down 1986). But photos are needed if parents are to convince others who are not present of these kinship relations. The same woman goes on to explain photos are "so essential" because "you can actually say [to others], 'Well, she has got his nose and my lips'" (Down 1986).

But the realist, self-evidence of photographs is not always accepted at face value. For instance, Rita Fadako, who learned at a twenty-week ultrasound that her baby could not live due to a severe brain anomaly, writes in a poem entitled "pictures of an angel," that the "pictures didn't show everything, they missed the halo" (Fadako 1997).

Conclusions

Numerous feminist Euro-American scholars have critiqued visualization technologies like sonograms (Stewart 1986) and fetoscopic imaging technologies for their role in the construction of fetal personhood at the expense of maternal personhood, particularly in the context of abortion politics (Duden 1993, Stabile 1998, Hartouni 1996, Petchesky 1987, Squire 1994). Feminist critics have also questioned the medical necessity, safety, and efficacy of these imaging technologies; have pointed out how they contribute to the further medicalization of pregnancy, and "further deterioration in the sensitive use of hearts and hands" of midwifery (Stewart 1986:41). More recently, these critiques have been linked to broader concerns about prenatal testing and diagnosis, the commodification of life, and disability rights (Rapp 1999).

To date no one has examined the impact that obstetrical imaging technologies have on pregnancies that end without a live birth. Sonograms are routinely offered to women, especially women who have had a pregnancy loss, as a means of reassuring them that everything is all right. But as the narratives of loss cited above show, this reassurance is both fleeting and empty.

One of the most consistent points of concern for feminist critics of fetal-visualizing technologies is the way that these images are used to try to dissuade and/or prohibit women from electively aborting unwanted pregnancies. Little or no thought has been given to the impact that the images have on those whose wanted pregnancies end, despite all their best efforts, in involuntary, spontaneous abortions, even though one of the major medical uses of sonograms is to diagnose and/or confirm fetal demise if a mother has reported bleeding or the absence of fetal movement.

It could certainly be argued that for the nearly one million women in the United States who miscarry each year, it would be better psychologically not to determine their pregnancies so early, not to start investing in the social construction of fetal personhood until a later date, when the chances of ending up with a take-home baby are significantly greater.

As we will see in the next chapter, medical technologies are not the only artifacts implicated in the social construction of fetal personhood.

"He Was a Real Baby with Baby Things": A Material Culture Analysis of Personhood, Parenthood, and Pregnancy Loss

After Hannah Campbell's son was stillborn in 1987, having died in utero at six months gestation from Trisomy 13 (a genetic condition that accounted for his having a cleft palate and six fingers on each hand, and the fact that his intestines were outside his body), she put the I.D. bracelet, picture, and baptismal certificate the hospital had given her, along with his baby blanket, in a picnic basket on the floor of her closet. "Marc's things" stayed there for four years until Hannah decided to follow the example of some of the people she had met at a pregnancy-loss support group and moved his things to the top shelf of her curio cabinet along with her Waterford crystal collection. In addition to the things that she collected at the time of his birth, things that have some direct connection to the child, she has added goods to his memorial collection. "His shelf is acquiring new items to remember him. Family members have given me a Waterford baby block, a Hummel boy called 'I'll protect him' and a Hand of God statue cradling a child" (Campbell 1992). She concludes her account published in a pregnancy-loss support newsletter, "He was a real baby with baby things."

As important as the medical artifacts discussed in the previous chapter may be in establishing the existence of a "real baby," a whole host of other artifacts are also marshaled for this task. Medical artifacts, although no doubt a privileged category in terms of a certain kind of authoritative knowledge, in no way exhaust the range of resources used by bereaved parents to make the claim that a child existed and is worthy of memory.

In the extensive body of anthropological research on reproduction in Britain and North America published in the last twenty years, the greatest emphasis has been on how biomedical models of reproduction and new reproductive technologies affect the experience of women. Paradoxically, in their focus on the "medicalization of pregnancy and birth," anthropologists have contributed to the dominance of the medical model and have been blinded to other interpretative systems with which women understand and experience their pregnancies and other family-making experiences. Likewise, the formidable interdisciplinary feminist critique of the medicalization of pregnancy and childbirth, as valuable as it has been, has in some ways hidden from view equally important cultural domains and practices, such as the role of consumer goods in the constitution of fetal personhood and the importance of gift-giving in the establishment of infants' social identity and community membership.

Of Gifts, Goods, and Persons

In this chapter I show how members of pregnancy-loss support groups use the materiality of bodily traces and artifacts to deal with what I call "the realness problem" of pregnancy loss. As discussed in chapter 4, many factors including the liminal status of pregnancy, embryos/fetuses/newborns, corpses, and the malformed work together to call into question the existential status of baby, parent/s, and event. Gift-giving, a central social practice in the establishment and maintenance of social identities (Mauss 1969, Carrier 1995, Miller 1998, Strathern 1988), is strategically used by bereaved parents to address these problems.

In addition, gift-giving addresses another set of problems discussed more fully in the next chapter, that is, the stigmatizing experience of loss. In the Victorian gift economy, which is still with us today, gift-giving is understood to be, and experienced as, a moral act, an edifying practice. "Gifts were about sentiments, feelings, affinities, connections, memories, and promises. The ability to share in them, to feel others in them and through them, to find presence in absence, was . . . a sacramental sensibility. Giving in this revelatory and integrative sense, 'assimilates us nearer to God than any other' activity," according to Kirkland, one of the nineteenth-century American domestic authors Schmidt identifies as a "consecrator of gifts" (Schmidt 1997:79–80). "Keepsakes," an important Victorian category of gift, and one that features prominently in narratives of pregnancy loss, were and continue to be, particularly charged in these ways.

Through the buying, giving, and arranging of things, American middle-class women and their social networks begin to actively construct babies-to-be as "real," that is, as individuals who count. This process, which typically begins during pregnancy, is often continued by women who join pregnancy-loss support groups after a loss in order to validate the value of the work already done and to claim for themselves the social credit to which they feel entitled as real "mothers."

A number of factors influence these practices, including length of gestation; degree to which the pregnancy was desired; prior reproductive and bereavement experiences; religion, ethnic, and/or family tradition; and class. The moment at which the personhood of the fetus-baby starts to be constructed during a pregnancy, the pace or paces at which it proceeds once it has begun, and the number of people engaged in this process vary. Nevertheless, the later the loss, the more "baby things" (*and* personhood) an embryo/fetus/child is likely to have. It is not surprising, then, that the narratives of loss with the most elaborated accounts of material culture (that is, those on which I focus in this chapter) are those describing losses that occurred either later in a pregnancy or after birth.

Religion also plays a role. For example, according to Jewish religious tradition, one should not buy for an expected child until after its birth. Similarly, beliefs about life after death undoubtedly have an important influence on the ways goods are used following a loss. Members of pregnancy-loss support groups tend to be middle-class, and it is likely that class affects the ways that individuals use consumer goods to construct personhood during a pregnancy and after a loss.

In this chapter I examine five gift-giving trajectories: 1) goods purchased or made for the baby-to-be during the pregnancy; 2) gifts given in the name of the baby-to-be while in utero; 3) gifts given to the 'baby' after its death; 4) gifts given in memory of the 'baby' after its death; 5) goods acquired to memorialize the baby within the family.

I focus on the way meanings are inscribed in the "uses and trajectories" of these things (Appadurai 1986) and describe the cultural and historical context of these "things-in motion" (Appadurai 1986). I also focus on "the things themselves" (Appadurai 1986:5) and examine the categories and physical and symbolic qualities of goods that feature in each of these different contexts.

I am limited in my ability to perform a material-culture analysis because I do not have direct access to the things. The material I examine is more like that used by Barthes (1983) in his analysis of the fashion system, that is, not the objects themselves but the linguistic representation of the objects in a particular narrative genre. The descriptions of baby things in these narratives reveal a pattern to the types of physical qualities thought worth recording in verbal depictions of such goods.[1]

Gorenstein has identified a number of principles that "are of general utility in the interdisciplinary study of material culture" including that "cultural themes" are "expressed in the design and physicality of the object," and this may be done through either a "physical or evocative homology" between the object/s and a theme, and that cultural themes expressed in objects are "sentiently apprehended" (1996:1).

I argue that the objects used to construct the "babyhood" of the embryos/fetuses/neonates that bereaved parents have "lost" do so through use of both physical and evocative homologies. As I will show, babies and their things share several physical characteristics. Baby things embody a number of characteristics thought to be important attributes of babies—being small in size, soft in both color and texture, precious (in both the sense of being cute, and of great value), capable of dramatic transformation, animal-like in some regards, and possessing a gender but being asexual. In addition to these qualities, the predominant quality or theme being communicated by bereaved parents through their baby's things is "realness," to use a native term. The irrefutable "realness" of physical things (even of "fakes") is sentiently apprehended. Things are sentiently apprehended in the same ways that living children are, but that dead children (once they have been buried or disposed of) no longer can be.[2] They can be touched, held, caressed, hugged, and gazed upon. Sometimes they can also be smelled, as in the case of flowers or baby blankets, or heard, as in the case of a musical toy or wind chimes.[3] Like children, they can also be cleaned, protected, and displayed for the admiration of others.

In the face of the denial of pregnancy loss, using things to make the claim that a "real" child existed and is worthy of memory is an example of a de Certeauian "tactic" by which members of subordinated groups use dominant resources for their own interests and desires. As Gorenstein notes, "although most cultural themes embedded in objects are normative and convey and reinforce the generally held cultural themes of a society, the objectification of sentiently-held cultural themes makes objects the perfect vehicles for conveying themes that are not commonly accepted in a community" (1996:8).

Goods Given to the Baby-to-Be during Pregnancy

The bearing and raising of children always involve the acquisition and consumption of material resources. In political economic analyses, this fact is discussed under the rubric of social and cultural reproduction. Gregory, following Marx and Levi-Strauss, discusses the "relations of reproduction necessary to ensure self-replacement." He depicts this process as one of "personification whereby things are converted into people" (1982:35). For Gregory, kinship is "both a method of consumption and a personification process," and he uses the term "consumptive production" to depict the way that children are produced through consumption. Following Levi-Strauss, he focuses on two areas of consumption—food and women.[4] Narratives of pregnancy loss, on the other hand, point to the importance of the consumption of consumer goods in the "productive consumption of children" in contemporary North American culture. Like the Levi-Straussian consumption of food and sex, this other domain of consumption also begins before birth. The authors of a number of poems describe buying and/or receiving gifts for their "baby" during the pregnancy.

According to the marketing director of American Baby Group, the prime period for baby-good purchases is between the sixth month of pregnancy and six months postnatally.

> During the first trimester pregnant women concentrate on themselves. . . . By the second trimester, the baby starts to become a little more real. . . . The excitement is building, but you're still not in a serious acquisition headset. . . . Third trimester, you're down to the wire. That baby's coming. *You go on a buying spree!* . . . "Once the baby arrives, of course, you start massive acquisitions of everything. At about the six-month point, however, the spree begins to subside. All the big stuff's been bought. You're down to routine maintenance: diapers, food, baby wipes (quoted in Larson 1992:87).

While this may accurately portray the aggregate national trend, it masks a wide diversity in individual practices. Some women begin buying things for their baby-to-be well before a pregnancy begins.[5] The "hope chest" in which young women accumulate goods symbolizing their hopes for a future marriage may also include goods for the children they imagine they will someday have. Many start buying or making things early in the pregnancy. For example, Linda Iacono, who began spotting at twelve weeks and whose baby lived for two hours after it was born at six months gestation, remembers how happy she was when she became pregnant shortly after her marriage in 1973. "The idea of having a baby thrilled me. I couldn't wait to start purchasing baby clothes and to set up the nursery" (Iacono 1982).[6]

In my case, I began working on a baby sweater within days of the confirmation of my first desired pregnancy.[7] I had never knit before and I remember that the slow pace with which my sweater progressed felt like an appropriate external replication of the slow, gradual, day-by-day way that I imagined and experienced the baby growing inside me.[8]

Sandelowski (1993) has described the way that couples who are waiting for a baby to adopt try "to pace their activities, especially those involving material preparations for a baby" so that their planned purchases will be complete about the same time that the baby arrives (Sandelowski 1993: 171).[9] Sandelwoski describes a couple who explained how they expected the longest they would have to wait for a baby was twelve months, and how they planned to fill the nursery gradually over that period. When their wait continued after this period they considered painting the nursery again rather than just have it sitting there (Sandelowski 1993:171).

Many postpone shopping until later in the pregnancy (cf. Taylor 2000a:153). For instance, Kristen Ingle, in a piece describing the death of her baby at thirty-three weeks gestation, writes, "I remember the day I shopped for your layette only to learn the next you had died" (Ingle 1981/ 2a). A number of ethnic and religious traditions embrace this practice. Sharon, one of the women I interviewed in my study of loss in toxically assaulted communities, told me how upset her mother was when her friends gave her a shower during the eighth month of her pregnancy. "In my family it is a big deal, you don't do that until after the baby is born and I remember that my mother was all nerved up after my friends had had the shower." Sharon is Catholic and of Irish background. When I asked her if she thought that the prohibition in her family against buying during a pregnancy was part of her Irish heritage, she said "It could be an Irish thing because that's all we are is Irish. There is not another drop of blood in my family and I know this goes back to my grandmother [she told us] no, no, no, you don't ever buy anything [until after the birth].

One woman describes having resisted the urge to buy in advance, perhaps for these types of reasons, yet her precautions did not protect her. In a piece entitled "Tiny Pink Rosebuds," (1981/82) Helen Keener recalls how sometime following her daughter's burial, "my tired young husband and I walked slowly through racks of clothing, baby clothing. I had done this many times before the baby was here, picturing her in these precious little summer things, sunsuits and all. But I never bought ahead."[10]

In subsequent pregnancies after a loss, many women who bought during earlier pregnancies now abstain from shopping for their child-to-be so as not to jinx the pregnancy, or, in the language of popular psychology, so as not to invest emotionally in a pregnancy that might not work, a baby that might not be. One Jewish contributor explains how, following a loss at thirty-three weeks gestation, she postponed arranging the nursery until after the live birth of her subsequent son, and even then left his room unfinished for a month until he was "growing chubby and long on my milk, and . . . graduating out of his infant outfits." With these reassurances of his viability, she "finally ma[de] room for the new baby" in her life/heart/house by organizing and making space for his baby clothes, "separat[ing] the sweaters, pajamas, and shirts into drawers marked 'fall clothing,' 'spring clothing'" (Di'Saro 1998:4).

In addition to purchases made individually by expectant parents, gifts are often given collectively to babies-to-be at baby showers.[11] Baby showers are an example of what Douglas and Isherwood (1979) call a "ritual of consumption."[12] They focus on the role that things play in the constitution of culture and they propose a cumulative model of culture-building. "Each item can . . . be perceived as a mere installment, just part of a flow . . . The stream of consumable goods leaves a sediment that builds up the structure of culture like coral islands" (Douglas and Isherwood 1979:75). Clearly, in addition to the buildup of culture, the social identity of individuals is also being constructed through this process. This is particularly evident when, as in the case of baby showers, rituals of consumption are also rites of passage.[13]

Although part of the ideology of showers (baby and bridal) is the provisioning of a new family with the necessities of life, as anthropologists have long understood, there is no clear distinction between the economic and the symbolic (Lee 1959, Sahlins 1976, Douglas and Isherwood 1979, Appadurai 1986, Fiske 1989a).

In addition to life cycle rituals of consumption, we also celebrate calendric rituals of consumption, Christmas being the most important of these in the United States (Miller 1993, Belk 1993, Schmidt 1995). Christmas is not just the most important ritual of consumption, it is also "the preeminent family occasion" for Christian families in our culture (Aries 1962:359). Aries credits the "extraordinary success enjoyed by Christmas," compared with the other feasts with which it competed under the ancien régime, to the emerging importance of the family and the fact that this holiday, by the seventeenth century, had come to be focused on childhood. Given this focus, it is not surprising that Christmas features so prominently in narratives of loss published in pregnancy-loss support-group newsletters.

These narratives indicate that presents are sometimes given to babies-to-be on that occasion. For example, Paula Baldwin describes how one Christmas, when she was only nine weeks pregnant, she received baby gifts. The pregnancy ended in miscarriage a few weeks later. Writing the following Christmas of her grief for the loss the baby she named Morgan, she tells of how she plans to "look, again, at the gifts that were to have been his" (Baldwin 1994). Lisa Casimer also reports that her daughter Sarah "received many Christmas gifts even though she was not due until late May." The baby was born at the end of January, due to an incompetent cervix and died in the NICU four days later. Lisa says she and her husband are "extremely grateful for those gifts now, because it would be our loved ones' only opportunity to give Sarah something besides prayers and flowers [at the funeral]" (Casimer 1987).

Shopping for one's children is clearly one of the most important acts of parenting in contemporary North American culture. Narratives of loss indicate that for some women this act of parenting begins during a pregnancy. The inability to shop for one's child during the pregnancy or following the birth constitutes a painful deprivation for many. One woman, whose daughter was diagnosed at twenty weeks gestation with anencephaly, describes the torturous process of carrying her baby for four more months, knowing that she would not live. "I remember that the time seemed to crawl by as there was nothing I could buy or do to prepare for this little girl" (Merriott 1995).

The pleasures of shopping, and giving, are often explicitly mourned in narratives of pregnancy loss. For example, Kristen Ingle writes in a piece called "For Elizabeth at Christmas":

> If you were here I'd buy you a red velvet dress with lace and Mary Janes. If you were here, I'd give you dolls and dishes and all the play-house toys I loved as a little girl. . . . You are not here, and I cannot give you any of these things (Ingle 1981/2b).

In another piece, addressed to their stillborn son and signed "mommy and daddy," the parents list the things they would have enjoyed buying for him, including "your first ball, your first bat, or when daddy buys your first Steeler's hat" (Martin and Martin 1995b).

Another example is found in a piece by Melanie Sheehan entitled "The Things I Grieve," describing her experience following the death of twin daughters due to prematurity. This piece was published in an issue of the SHARE newsletter devoted to "Surviving Grief without Any Surviving Children," and in it she compares her experience with those who already have children when they experience a pregnancy loss.

> I'd like to be able to walk down the Baby Aisle at Toys R Us and be sad with my losses and yet know at the same time that when I reach the Toddler Section, I have a smiling little face who sits in my cart and expects a toy. But, there's no one sitting in my cart; I have no

children who beg me to take them to Toys R Us. I'd like to take items off the shelf in the baby section of the store. I'd like to be piling them high in my cart instead of buying only one jar of baby food just to see how it feels (Sheehan 1996:1).

Linda Nucitelli, a part-time systems engineer who serves as the current editor of *UNITE Notes*, writes on the occasion of what would have been her son's second birthday of her fantasy that she could tempt him come back for just one day for a visit with the promise of presents, "[If you come back,] I will buy you the toys that I've dreamed should be yours. Footballs, Legos, and cars with real doors" (Nucitelli 1997).

The importance of consumerism to parenthood is also signaled by the fact that many baby-product companies buy mailing lists of names of pregnant women and send advertisements and coupons to expectant mothers (Larson 1992).[14] If a pregnancy loss occurs, these items are painful reminders of what could have been, and the SHARE and UNITE newsletters periodically provide instructions on how to get one's name removed from mailing and/or phone lists for baby products.

The pleasures of buying and giving are also denied the larger social network in the event of a pregnancy loss. Kathy Conners wrote a piece on what would otherwise have been her last day at work before beginning maternity leave, which tells of how her coworkers had planned on giving "a big shower,"—"Everyone was looking forward to buying little baby girl clothes for you" (Connors 1992).

As I described elsewhere (1994), the prospect of being reunited with one's baby in heaven provides an important source of solace for many. But in a poem, Marion Cohen, an avowed flea-market enthusiast (first published in the UNITE newsletter and then in one of her many volumes of poems and prose about her troubled reproductive history), points out that in heaven, at least as conventionally imagined, the sharing of consumer goods with one's child will not be one of the paradisiac pleasures:

When the Messiah comes
the little Carter's stretch-suits and pastel
    French undershirts will be
out of style,
She'll have soft fluffy clouds; she
won't need that pussy-cat pillow
She'll have angel harps; she won't
    need that clown musical mobile (Cohen 1981b).

Several women describe how their pregnancy loss prompted a reevaluation of their preoccupation with worldly goods in favor of things of more enduring value. (See next chapter for examples.)

"Baby Things"

Descriptions of baby things either acquired for the baby during pregnancy, or imagined as ones that might have been given to the child had it survived, are the most numerous and elaborated accounts of goods found in narratives of pregnancy loss. Clothing, bedding, toys, and food are the most frequently described categories of things. Not surprisingly, these goods do not seem to differ from those purchased for newborns. In both cases, baby things display characteristics similar to valued qualities of babies.

Clothing is one of the most frequently mentioned items in these accounts, which is understandable given how important clothing is as a marker of humanness, of personhood.[15] "Clothing is quite literally at the borderline between subject and object" (Buck-Morss 1989:97). As Cook notes, "Clothing, in particular, speaks daily, publicly, and bodily to the presentation of self" (1998:348). Schneider and Weiner have observed how common gifts of cloth are cross-culturally at life cycle celebrations and explain this by the way cloth can symbolically be seen to make "a continuous thread, a binding tie between . . . kinship groups, or . . . generations" (1989:3). They also note that in many small-scale societies the manufacture of cloth is analogized with gestation. For example, among the Kodi, "women's laments compare miscarriages to imperfectly dyed cloths" (Schneider and Weiner 1989:8).

Clothing also has a particular relationship to memories and loss. According to Stallybrass, the wrinkles in clothing "which recorded the body that had inhabited the garment . . . and memorized the . . . mutual constitution of person and thing" were called "memories" by nineteenth-century British clothes-makers and repairers (Stallybrass 1998:196, 1993).

Studies suggest that clothing is in fact the most popular gift item for Americans. Caplow's 1970s restudy of Middletown, the midwestern industrial city documented in the 1920s and '30s by sociologists Lynd and Lynd, showed that clothing was by far the most common type of gift (35 percent of all gifts). Caplow suggests that the American "preference for clothing over all other categories [of gift] is probably accounted for by the automatic individualization of items of clothing. In effect, they describe the receiver by age, sex, appearance, and style" (1982: 385).

This has not always been the case. According to Aries (1962), in Europe up until the thirteenth century children were not a distinct social category, and thus were not dressed differently from adults. It was not until the seventeenth century that noble and middle-class children started being dressed in special "children's clothing." Schneider and Weiner note that the present "consumption system of high-velocity turnover and endless ever-changing variation—[has] vastly inflated dress . . . as a domain for expression" (1989:4). The children's-wear industry has experienced exponential growth in the United States during the last five decades and "mass produced garments for children have become constitutive of childhood" (Cook 1998: 348).

An important part of this trend has been the development of gender-specific clothing. Although Willis asserts that "under capitalism . . . , gender like all our attributes and expressions, is bound up with the commodity form" (1991:33), the capitalist garment industry has only relatively recently produced gender-distinctive clothing for young children. According to Paoletti and Kregloh, "for most of our history, there has been little differentiation between the clothing of male and female children under the age of five. . . . pink and blue color coding was a novelty at the turn of the century and only became widely practiced after the Second World War" (1989:22). They attribute this phenomenon to changing understandings of infancy, specifically, our ideas about how and when children learn gender and to "the increasingly public lives of babies." Whereas in the nineteenth and early twentieth century infants mostly stayed at home, surrounded by people who knew their sex, today newborns are routinely exposed to strangers, and the color coding of clothing serves the important social function of enabling strangers to make appropriate social responses to the baby" (Paoletti and Kregloh 1989:29).

In narratives of pregnancy loss, clothing is almost always gender-typed, with clothing for girls being described more frequently and fully than for boys. This is to be expected. As Schneider and Weiner (1989:4) have observed, "in the fashion system of contemporary Western capitalism, women's dress is elaborated to a uniquely high degree."[16] Female gender is expressed via the now conventional color of pink, for example, "pink rosebuds," and by gendered patterns, fabrics, and trims, for example, "a red velvet dress with lace and Mary Janes."

The clothes that babies are buried in, oftentimes the same clothes the parents had planned to bring the baby home from the hospital in, are sometimes described in great detail. Susan Ashbaker, for example, whose daughter died two hours after birth due to an umbilical cord accident, wonders in a poem entitled "What Will You Look Like in Heaven?" (1994), "Will you still be wearing your long white gown with satin slippers and lace socks and panties?"[17] She (1993) describes this outfit in even greater detail in a poem entitled "Small White Box." "A small white box containing my baby, oh so precious, dressed in a beautiful white gown with ruffled socks and satin shoes carrying two gold hearts on a dainty chain around her little neck." (See Keener 1981/2 for another example.)

Of course, the size of infant clothing is by necessity small, yet it is telling how frequently this shared characteristic of babies and baby clothes is commented on in narrative accounts; for example, "precious little summer things," "little Carter's stretch-suits," "little diapers," "little baby girl clothes," "tiny pink rosebuds." This is sometimes accentuated by a double adjective, as in "tiny little clothes."

Beds and bedding are another frequently described category of baby things. Special infant furniture—cribs and bassinets—feature routinely in narratives of loss, the empty crib being one of the most pervasive images of loss. Baby blankets (and quilts) are also frequently mentioned, and bumper pads are sometimes described. Like clothing, these goods possess the physical qualities of cloth, qualities that Schneider and Weiner (1989) have noted underlie cloth's importance in ritual and social domains. "Malleable and soft, cloth can take many shapes . . . [and cloth] lends itself to an extraordinary range of decorative variation. [These properties] give cloth an almost limitless potential for communication" (Schneider and Weiner 1989:1). Cloth can readily "evoke ideas of connectedness or tying," and in many societies, even in large-scale industrial capitalist ones, people . . . acknowledge the birth . . . of children with gifts of . . . bedding" (1989:10).

At the same time, "the softness and ultimate fragility of these materials capture the vulnerability of humans, whose every relationship is transient, subject to the degenerative process of illness, death, and decay" (Schneider and Weiner 1989:2). In the case of pregnancy loss, the blanket in which infants are wrapped before burial may serve as a physical surrogate for the physical embrace of the parents. Another important quality of cloth in this context is that it is permeable with bodily fluids such as tears and body oil. Nanci Hyneman of the Boise, Idaho, SHARE tells of how after learning of a baby girl born with Trisomy 18 she made an "extra small" afghan for the child, who weighed only 4 pounds. When the baby died the mother told Hyneman that she wanted to bury her daughter in the blanket but was having trouble parting with it. Nanci made her another one just like it and the mom was able to keep the one that was "filled with her daughter's fragrance" to use "to sleep with or just hold" when she "needs comfort"

(Hyneman 1988). Barbara Knopf describes her need for "a very special place to keep all the things that had touched [her son's] skin and smelled like him." Hannah Campbell tells of a blanket that a friend had given her during her pregnancy in which she had hoped to wrap her child upon his birth.[18] After his death, instead of filling the blanket with her son, she "filled [it] with love" by hugging and kissing it and crying into it and then keeping it in the picnic basket with his other things (Campbell 1991a).

Here again one finds gender-typing a common feature. Hannah's baby blanket was white with "a pink and a blue ribbon . . . tied at either end" and she planned to "remove one . . . once our baby was born" (Campbell 1991a). Kristen Ingle, whose daughter died at thirty-three weeks gestation, tells in a poem entitled "Pink Blankets" of how much she cherished seeing her wrapped in these after her birth.

Another frequent category is toys. Like children's clothing, the market in mass-produced toys has grown dramatically since the 1950s (Seiter 1995). According to Sutton-Smith's (1986:2) report on the importance of the toy industry in the United States in the 1980s, "some 800 companies sell about 150,000 different kinds of toy products (with about 4,000 new items every year), involving about 250,000 tons of plastics, 200,000 tons of metal at 150,000 retail outlets, and employ about 60,000 people." Seiter criticizes those who have attributed this growth solely to the increasing sophistication of advertising directed at children. She explains that as more women worked outside the home, they had greater income and access to credit but less time. Increased geographic mobility away from traditional familial networks for child care also made toys especially attractive given busy mothers' need to keep children entertained. In addition, more families owned larger houses with space to keep the toys (Seiter 1995:13–16).

Here, as in the case of clothing, gender-typing is important, for example, "dolls and dishes and all the play-house toys," or "footballs, Legos, and cars" (cf. Miller 1997). According to Willis, "one of the strongest early influences on gender is the mass toy markets" (1991:24). In addition, toys have been found to "incite in parents strong feelings that are a tangle of nostalgia and generational and class values" (Seiter 1995:193).[19]

Special food items (like bottles and prepared baby foods) are also frequently described in these narratives (such as the woman who imagined buying a jar of baby food at Toys R Us). Hannah Campbell, the Irish-American woman with whose story I began this chapter, tells of a family tradition of presenting each new member of her extended family with a green lollipop at birth. Even though her son was stillborn, premature, and deformed, one of her siblings gave him the anticipated lollipop and he was buried with it

(Campbell 1990, 1991a). The association of children with lollipops and other candy marks not only children's fondness for such foods but also evokes the culturally valued "sweetness" of infants. These special newborn or children's foods highlight the way that the category of "baby" is so thoroughly constituted by special goods (for example, Blair 1990).

In addition to smallness, another remarkable feature of "baby things" is the prominence of certain representations of nature. Animals are one of the most common themes in baby goods (for example, "teddy bears," "bunnies," a "lamb chop toy," a "pussy-cat pillow"). These representations of animals are frequently personified and thus explicitly analogize animals and babies.[20] The presumed "naturalness" or "animality" of newborns can be understood, depending on one's view, either because they have yet to be civilized, that is, imparted with culture, or because they have yet to be corrupted by, and tainted with civilization (cf. Paoletti and Kregloh 1989, Miller 1997, cf. Slater 1977).

Stuffed animals, like many other baby things including blankets, bumper pads, and pillows, are soft, and this evokes the softness of the baby's body (both the proverbial soft skin of infants, but also the softness of their bodies due to undeveloped musculature). In addition to this tactile quality, softness is often expressed through the use of pastel colors for baby products.

Although as noted above, many baby goods are gendered, a striking characteristic of teddy bears and other toy animals is that they are asexual. According to Willis (1991:26), this complements children's understanding of multiple sexualities. (She gives the example of her three-year-old daughter, who insisted that her bear was both a boy and a girl.) But an alternative interpretation is that infants are considered to be gendered but asexual (or at least presexual), and these toy surrogates represent this characteristic.[21]

Another important decorative theme are those aspects of nature that change, particularly those that do so in a linear direction toward a more desirable end such as rainbows and butterflies (see also chapter 8).[22] Cyclical natural changes like the seasons, the related growth and decay of flowers and trees, and the melting of delicate snowflakes are used in narratives of pregnancy loss to symbolize the transformation of the child in death (from this world to the next) as a natural occurrence (Layne 1996b), but these motifs are not commonly found on infant consumer goods. Rainbows and butterflies, in contrast, are found frequently on memorial goods and are also very common motifs on toys, books, and clothing of young children and are considered appropriate decorative items for nurseries.

Another quality of "babies" and "baby things" of particular relevance in the context of pregnancy loss is that of "preciousness" in both its standard reference to great value and its colloquial sense of "cuteness." Since the early part of this century, children in the United States have been considered "priceless," valued for their sentimental rather than monetary value (Zelizer 1985). This expression of sentimental value appertains not only to the children themselves, but also to their things. Consumer goods designed for children are often described with this adjective, for example, "precious little summer things."[23]

After a Loss

After a loss, the goods that had been acquired for the baby are handled in one of two different ways, and these differences do not appear to be directly related to the duration of the pregnancy.[24] For instance, in a poem entitled "Baby Things," about the death of her baby girl two days after birth due to meconium aspiration and hyaline membrane disease, Cindy Foster names, one by one, the things that she accumulated and arranged for her baby during the pregnancy: "Your room was gaily decorated, a rainbow on the wall. I made bumper pads and a mobile. In gingham they were all. The playpen is blue. The crib is white. The quilt: blue, yellow and pink." She then tells of how these things were disposed of following the death. "Grandpa took the crib down. Grandma helped me pack, all the clothes and toys and things into a large sack." There is a parallelism being drawn here between the accumulation of baby things that both accompanied and instantiated the accumulation of personhood during the pregnancy. With the death, the parallel projects of both the new "person" and its things are brought to an abrupt end—put into sack and casket. With the baby go the things and all they stood for.

Others use the analogy between baby and baby things to different ends. Some use the things to symbolize the baby's ongoing presence in the family. Whereas Cindy Foster put away the baby things "until the time is right for me to have another to share in such delight" (that is, the ownership of these things are revoked with the death and reserved for the next baby), others grant an ongoing ownership to the dead. In these cases, their things are sometimes used as a stand-in or surrogate for the baby. One woman, for example, in a piece describing the death of her grandson seven weeks after his birth due to a heart anomaly, which was diagnosed via ultrasound during the seventh month of her daughter-in-law's pregnancy, writes, "Grief is . . . taking a family picture with Alexander's teddy bear instead of with Alexander" (Schneider 1995:7).

Goods Given to Others in the Name of the Baby or Baby-to-Be

Just as being given gifts is an important indicator of personhood, so too is the ability to give. Indeed, beginning with Mauss (1969) the anthropological literature on gift exchange has focused on the reciprocity that gift-giving entails (for example, Sahlins 1972a,b, Weiner 1976). Yet Zelizer (1985) describes how since the 1930s in the United States, the parent-child relationship has been defined as one in which goods and services flow unidirectionally from parent to child.[25] Nevertheless, children are still socialized to become givers (and shoppers) as well as receivers.[26] In fact, as Zelizer herself notes, since the turn of the century, allowances have been valued as an educational tool with which to teach one's children "to spend, to save, or to give away wisely" (from an 1893 article quoted in Zelizer 1985:105).[27] In middle-class families, children begin giving even before they are old enough to have an allowance.

Narratives of pregnancy loss indicate that during a pregnancy babies-to-be are sometimes constructed as both shoppers and givers. In our culture the ability to exercise consumer choice is a central aspect of our identity as persons, as individuals. As an ad for a special issue of *The New York Times Sunday Magazine* on American retailing put it (using Barbara Kruger's famous photo): "I shop therefore I am." In a poem by Pat Schwiebert (1985: 14) written in the voice of her baby, entitled "Please Don't Tell Them You Never Got to Know Me," the dead baby reminds her mother, "[It was] I who went shopping and helped you pick out the 'perfect' teddy bear for me." Carrier describes shopping as one of the most important methods of "appropriating" consumer goods, thereby transforming mass-produced, anonymous "commodities" into personal "possessions." It would seem that an analogous process may be occuring with the fetuses as well. Shopping is one of the strategies used by mothers and their social networks to transform an anonymous mass of cells into "our precious baby."

Sometimes gifts are given to others (usually extended family members) in the name of the baby-to-be. This is sometimes done by way of announcing the pregnancy. Thus, the first public act of the baby-to-be may be to enter into the gift-giving network of the family. I do not have much information on the nature of these goods, but they appear to be small, sentimental items.

For example, Pat MacCauley tells of how she and her husband planned to announce the news of her pregnancy on Christmas by giving their families "specially dated tree ornaments shaped as angels, signed from the

Christmas Card, Joe Kemp, 2000.

'baby.'"[28] She started to miscarry on December 12th and on Christmas, her "husband thoughtfully kept hidden those gifts from our baby-to-be which were intended for our families."

Another thing sometimes given in the name of the baby-to-be is greeting cards. One example of this is found in the personal Christmas card designed by the artist Joe Kemp in 2000 which showed a sonogram image of his baby-to-be wearing a Santa hat and read Fetus Navidad. Inside the card read "Happy Holidays from Steph & Joe & spawn (at T-months, pictured)." The September 2001 issue of *Self* magazine advertised a new line of "pregnancy announcement cards" from "Fetal Greetings" (www.fetalgreetings. com), which "lets parents-to-be send news of their pregnancy through the mouths of their growing babes."[29]

The giving of gifts or greetings in the name of a baby-to-be is an extension to fetuses of a class of distinctive North American practices by which

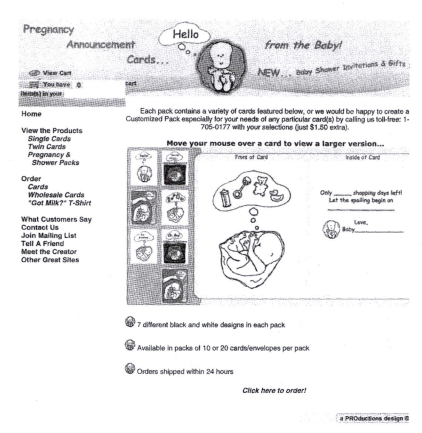

Web site, www.fetalgreetings.com

we treat infants as agents. One particularly clear example of this is found in Ochs and Scheifflin's study of language acquisition and socialization among Anglo-American white middle-class families, the Kaluli of New Guinea, and Samoans. Only in the United States did they find infants "treated as an *addressee* in social interaction" (Ochs and Schieffelin 1984:286). Other examples include writing thank-you notes or sending greeting cards in the name of preliterate children, or having one's answering machine list infants, along with other family members, as people who "are unable to answer the phone right now."[30]

In MacCauley's case, the item given symbolically and materially represents the child (that is, it is both evocatively and physically homologous). Angels are one of the most frequent symbols of babies (both dead and alive)

OUR ANGEL

Two   Souls in search of ONE
and You were the ONE.

TWO people so much in LOVE, for YOU were conceived in that LOVE.

TWO Arms that wanted to Hold You, for that's all I wanted to do.

Now You are gone, and I ache for You.

Grief has enveloped me like a cocoon waiting for THE LIGHT, when I will be with YOU.

For we Love You

Go my CHILD, where the Angels go

And may the Lord Bless Your Little Soul

For your Life has only STARTED and not as we believed that it just Ended.

Nino, Help those who Like me, had at one Time lost the will to Live

Embrace them with your Wings and show THEM the Light

For One Day we all shall find PEACE, and be within the Light.

We miss you and love you.

Mom, Dad, and Tiffany (Your little sister)

Our son Anthony died January 22, 1991 when he only took one breath and decided to leave us, for I believe only a few of us were chosen to feel the pain and grief in order to help others understand and show them how precious life is! "A Gift".

By Lucette Scalia

UNITE newsletter.

(Layne 1992). In this case the angel also represents the child through its material qualities—it is small, sentimental, and individualized by the mark of a "special" date. Thus the child is in effect giving the gift of itself (see next chapter).

After their demise, many parents continue to construct their children as givers. While this is usually done in terms of spiritual gifts (see chapter 7), Carol Winter reports buying "savings bonds each year for" her two surviving sons "from Jake on his birthday."

Goods Given to the Baby after Its Death

Just as gift-giving often begins before birth, it frequently continues after death. These gifts are often, but not always, presented to the dead child at the cemetery where s/he is buried, and they tend to be given on the major gift-giving holidays on which the child would have received gifts had it lived. For example, Marla Morgan's son was delivered at thirty-two weeks gestation because of low amniotic fluid and died due to a heart defect. In a piece written on the eve of what would have been his first birthday, she explains that she and her husband planned to commemorate the day by taking balloons and a gift to the cemetery (Morgan 1995). Corinna Mountain's (1996) son was born at 25.5 weeks gestation due to an incompetent cervix and died the next day. Corinna describes how "we put pretty things" like "bunnies" at Easter on his grave "to show we care." Michael Niehoff (1994) tells how their "surviving" son, Zachary, "usually makes a small gift or draws a picture which is . . . placed on the grave for Christopher."[31] Janet Jones (1992) also buys "flowers and balloons" to place on her son's grave on his birthday and holidays. Scarlett Hartzoge (1990) of Lincolnton, North Carolina, whose daughter died of prematurity after having lived a little over two months, anticipates that such practices may be met with social disapproval: "Why did we put an Easter basket with eggs, a bunny, pink grass and a card that read 'to our daughter' on her grave, even though she was dead?! . . . ' 'Are they crazy?' you ask when we plan to put birthday balloons on her grave."

In the next example, birthday balloons are sent up to the child in heaven. Traci McFaul wrote a piece entitled "Happy Birthday Sarah" on the occasion of what would have been the second birthday of her daughter, who died two days after birth during heart surgery. "There's no presents to buy. . . . So I'm sending to you in the heavens above, lots of balloons filled with my love. And each one I have personally kissed" (McFaul 1996).

Another woman tells of how she brings home a gift from each of her trips, just as many middle-class parents do for their living children. "Every new place I go, I bring something home in Matthew's memory. A shell sits on a shelf in the office. Matthew never went to the beach but this is Matthew's shell" (Boyette 1996).

Many of the goods given to the baby after its death are like those that the child would have received if it were living, e.g., birthday balloons or Easter baskets, but some gifts given on these occasions, such as holiday flower arrangements, are clearly gifts to the dead and inventions of the funeral and florist industries (Mitford 1963).[32] Gender is much less frequently mentioned in this context, but it is likely that the flowers, balloons, and even Easter baskets purchased are in fact gender-coded by color, for example, the "pink grass" in the Easter basket.[33] Balloons and flowers,[34] the two most frequently mentioned items given on such occasions, are both highly perishable, and thus mark the short, ephemeral worldly existence of these children via a material homology.

Not all of the goods given after the loss are commercial. Several of the gifts mentioned, such as a picture drawn by a sibling, or a shell brought home from a trip by the mother, are valued precisely because of their non-commercial nature. As in the baby things given to or from the baby during the pregnancy, smallness (either in terms of the physical size or the "tokenness" of the item) seems to be a common characteristic, like the "small gift" that the boy makes for his deceased sibling every year, and the purchases made by another family at the "dollar store."

In many respects these gifts are similar to those given in the "Romantic gift culture" of nineteenth-century America. Schmidt has documented the way that the domestic writers of this era extolled the virtues of "presents of 'small value' or of painstaking handicraft" (1997:83) and how often these goods were fragile, for example, "lace-work cards" or flowers, noting the "contradictory ways in which such tokens simultaneously bind together and ratify separation." As will be discussed in chapter 9, this valorization of the small also harkens to the nineteenth-century natural theologians' view that the miraculous, infinite, and sublime could best be found in the small.

There are also similarities between these practices and the practice of leaving gifts at the Vietnam War Memorial and its replicas documented by Hass (1998) and Kennedy (1990), and most recently at the sites of the 9–11 attacks (Sheehan 2001).[35] While Hass asserts that "mainstream funerary and memorial traditions in American culture do not involve the offering of things" (1998:8), narratives of pregnancy-loss support-group members suggest that such offerings are clearly part of a much broader set of contemporary memorial practices, and not a unique "new impulse . . . to speak publicly and privately, to the problematic memory of [the Vietnam] war" (Hass 1998:1).[36]

Goods Given in Memory of the Baby after Its Death

In addition to goods given to the baby after its death, goods and cash are frequently given by family members (and occasionally healthcare providers) to others in memory of the baby.[37] One important category of memorial gift is a monetary donation to a nonprofit organization. The organizations most frequently mentioned in the newsletters are the pregnancy-loss support groups themselves. The SHARE and UNITE newsletters regularly acknowledge contributions made to the organization, the vast majority of which are made in memory of a baby by family members and sometimes also by friends or medical-care providers.[38]

Memorial gifts are most commonly given on occasions at which the child would have been given presents had s/he survived, such as Christmas, Hanukkah, or birthdays. Each year, the editors of the SHARE and UNITE newsletters publish advice on how to deal with the holidays, and these pieces invariably mention the giving of memorial gifts. One example of such memorial gifts is found in a piece by Lauren Sariego, who describes how, since the stillbirth of their first child four years earlier, her family commemorates him at Christmas. Their family "participates in a Polyanna [a gift exchange system whereby each participant gives to another randomly selected participant]. Each year, my husband and I ask that whoever picks us in the Polyanna make a donation to UNITE in David's memory. . . . Other relatives always remember to make their loving donations commemorating David's small but everlasting mark on our family" (Sariego 1996).

The other important category of memorial gift is consumer goods for children. Sometimes these are given to particular needy children and other times to institutions that care for children. In a piece entitled "Holiday Help for the Bereaved," one of the coeditors of SHARE, Michael L. Niehoff (1994), discusses such gifts: "memorial gifts can . . . be comforting to bereaved families and a way to help others. Small gifts such as books, videos, games or toys can be given to school, church or temple libraries or nurseries. . . . clothing, toys, or other supplies [can be provided] to local children's centers such as a crisis nursery" (Niehoff 1994, see also Mellon 1992).

Sometimes these gifts may be generic baby gifts, while other times they are like those one might have been giving to one's own child had it lived.[39] For example, Maribeth Doerr (1992) tells how she "donated books in [her] son's name when and where he would have started kindergarten."[40] Bereaved parents often mention thinking about how old their child would be were s/he still alive and what kinds of things s/he would be doing. Shopping for age-appropriate gifts allows parents to experience in a material, though abbreviated way some of what might have been.

Memorial gifts serve at least two other very important roles. Since one of the most troubling problems encountered by members of pregnancy-loss support groups following a loss is the cultural denial of these events, the public acknowledgment that these memorial donations involve seems to serve as a welcome antidote. In addition, one of the challenges of such losses is to find meaning in what may at first be experienced as a brutally senseless event. The following example illustrates how memorial gifts may bring desired social recognition for a loss and also endow the loss with positive meanings. Janet Jones opened a memorial fund for her stillborn son and has $5 from each of her paychecks deposited into this account. She has used this money "to purchase a much needed organ lamp for our church, small Christmas gifts for needy children, monetary donations to charities, etc. All of these things were done in memory of Ronald, and we received acknowledgments to reflect that. It is a good feeling to know that he is, in a way, helping others, and at the same time others are learning of his short existence and remembering him" (Jones 1992).[41]

Memorial gifts are the least personal of all the gifts described in the narratives of loss. It is only in this category of gift that one finds money mentioned as an acceptable gift. Even though these gifts are typically given on occasions at which the child would have been given presents had he survived, and may be the type of gift one might have been giving to one's own child had it lived, the goods typically given on these occasions, such as toys, books, or videos, are less individual than items purchased for the baby during the pregnancy. These gifts are typically ones that could be used by a group of children.

Whereas clothing features so prominently in accounts of purchases made for the baby during the pregnancy, clothing is rarely mentioned as an appropriate memorial gift. Schneider and Weiner (1989) report that gifts of cloth are particularly common at rituals of death, but this does not seem to hold true in the United States. Although, as we saw, "grave-side" gifts like flowers or balloons tend to be perishable, memorial gifts tend to be "hard" goods, perhaps conveying the donor's wish that the memory of their loved one endure.[42]

Smallness remains a theme, as seen in the "small gifts" Niehoff (1994) recommends or in Janet Jones's purchase of "small Christmas gifts for needy children." Smallness not only indexically matches the physical size of the baby, it also corresponds with the norms regarding gift-giving to children. Caplow (1982:386) found that children in the United States were typically given many small gifts, while adults were given fewer, more "substantial" gifts.[43]

Goods Acquired by Family Members to Memorialize the Baby

Goods are also used to memorialize the child more privately within the family. Newsletters contain numerous advertisements for products designed to assist bereaved parents in commemorating their babies. Some are new products that have been developed, like "Recognition of Life Certificates," which are "suitable for framing" and "provide a record of birth and lasting keepsake" (*SHARE* 1991 January/February). Others are existing products now being marketed to a new consumer niche, such as "portrait plates" on which a photo of the child is laminated; advertised "as a means of preserving the memory of your child" (*SHARE* 1990 July/August).[44] For many of these products, a portion of the sales is donated to a support group.

For later losses, hospitals are an important source of memorabilia. Many hospitals now have a bereavement team and special protocols for stillbirths, which include providing parents with mementos. We saw already that Hannah Campbell was given her son's "I.D. bracelet, picture, and baptismal certificate" at the hospital. Elena Baker (1992) provides another example. Her baby was discovered dead during a twenty-one-week ultrasound (that is, it was thus technically a missed abortion, not a stillbirth). The following day labor was induced and after ten hours she gave birth to her son. The hospital gave her and her husband "pictures of him along with his crib card and his weight and length, the measuring tape used to measure him and a certificate with his footprints." Another woman who was seven months pregnant when she learned her daughter had died was given "pictures of her, her footprints, a small picture frame with her hand print, and a lock of her hair" by the nurses at the hospital (Connors 1992).[45]

These mementos from the hospital generally include two different types of goods—traces of the body, and artifacts of civil society. Mementos like locks of hair, or foot- or handprints are particularly important because they function indexically, that is, they are "signs whose relation to their objects [is of] a direct nature . . . by virtue of having been really connected with it" (Singer 1978:216).[46] Importantly, these elements denote humanness. Lovell, writing in the early 1980s before these practices had become common, describes one woman who regretted not having such a sign. "If only I'd kept a lock of hair to prove I'd had *someone*" (Lovell 1983:756). In addition to providing physical evidence of "someone," hair has since the eighteenth and nineteenth centuries been considered particularly appropriate for the commemoration of love and death because of its ability to endure, even after death.[47]

Handprints and footprints are one step removed from hair semiotically; the prints are formed by a direct, physical connection with the baby but then represent the baby from a distance. Like hair, hand- and, even more commonly, footprints have been common mementos of babyhood in Europe and America throughout the twentieth century.[48] Footprints and handprints are important symbols of humanness; bipedalism and an opposable thumb being distinctive characteristics of the species. Since the Victorian era and the discovery of the uniqueness of fingerprints, these prints have come to represent not only generic humanness but the idea of the unique individuality of each person. Infant footprints were also apparently used in this manner.[49] Until recently, New York state law required that the footprints of all newborns be recorded.[50]

In the rhetoric of pregnancy-loss support, as in the anti-abortion movement, footprints and handprints function as a synecdoche: Part A (fetal feet) equals A (a fetus), which in turn equals B (a human) (Condit 1990). Unlike the placenta and umbilical cord, and the tail of early embryo/fetuses that mark the difference between fetuses and children, fetal feet are "very close to baby feet in shape. . . . Our visual logic 'recognizes' such feet as 'small human feet' and we synecdochically expand the unseen picture to see a full 'small human'" (Condit 1990:68–69).[51]

In the case of pregnancy loss, footprints seem to have an additional meaning (one that privileges them over handprints) in that they can evoke the sense that someone was here and now is gone.[52] Like the marks left by someone walking in the sand, the footprint is a fragile trace that a person passed this way.[53] Unlike footprints in the sand, however, those imprinted on specially treated paper, or cast in plaster, are durable reminders of the baby's physical reality.[54]

As discussed in the previous chapter, photographic images of the child are another important commemorative item provided routinely by hospital staffs to parents. These artifacts straddle medical and social (see Taylor

CROSS-STITCH FOOTPRINT
Submitted by Ailene M. Lewis
Loves Park, IL

Use 14 count cloth. Can make a
magnet, picture or Christmas tree
ornament.

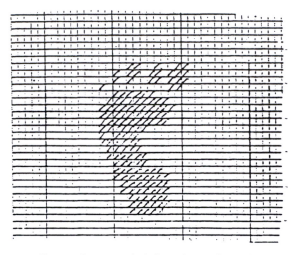

Pattern for cross-stitch footprint by C. Lewis.

1998). Sonogram images are generally provided while the pregnancy is still viable; I have no indication that these images are given to families if they reveal the fetal demise. Polaroids and snapshots, on the other hand, are routinely taken by the hospital staff and bereaved parents following a stillbirth or infant death.

As decribed in chapter 5, some women publicly display these images after a loss as an assertion of the motherhood role to which they lay claim. But even for women like me who do not consider themselves mothers based on a ten- to thirteen-week pregnancy, and do not consider that which was lost by the miscarriage to be a baby, but rather a might-have-been baby, sonogram images may have a powerful, if ambivalent charge. Somewhere in my bathroom closet, in among my cosmetics and cleaning supplies, is a sonogram image from one of my pregnancies. I do not know which pregnancy it is from, nor how it ended up in this closet. From time to time I am disconcerted to come upon it unexpectedly as I search for some item. Each time it happens, I think I ought to remove it, yet I can never come up with a

BABY NEWS

<u>Laura and Carl Brown</u> of Shiloh, Virginia joyfully announce the birth of Joshua David on September 15, 1986 by Cesarean weighing 9 lbs. 9 oz. He spent fifteen days in NICU recovering from pneumonia due to possible Beta Strep Toxemia. Joshua means "Jehovah Saves" and David means "Beloved" which fits him perfectly. Their first baby, Andrew Carl, was born February 28, 1985 and died March 4, 1985 due to meconium aspiration and Beta Strep Sepsis. (See **REACHING OUT** page 5.)

SHARE Newsletter.

more appropriate place to keep it—it certainly does not belong in the scrapbook with the sonogram images of Jasper, and for some reason I cannot bring myself to throw it out. What unexamined norms of decency prevent this? Also in that closet, on the uppermost shelf out of my children's reach, are my sons' baby teeth, surreptitiously collected in exchange for silver dollars. As with the sonogram image, I don't know what I'm keeping them for, what I'll ever do with them, but I have not been able to determine a suitable alternative. I fear if I throw out either the teeth or the sonogram image I would regret it, much as I did when I flushed the embryo down the toilet (chapter 1). It seems that the sonogram image substitutes for and/or is governed by the same norms that I apply to no-longer-needed bodies and body parts. I feel they should be "properly" disposed of, with "due respect" (Morgan 2002), but lacking culturally sanctioned models for this, I keep them, where they serve, like it or not, as occasional reminders of important biologically rooted life events.[55]

Artifacts of civil society are another important type of memorial good. This includes birth and death certificates, hospital identification bracelets, crib cards, baptismal certificates, and, in at least one case, a measuring tape.[56] Like visual representations, these items bestow authenticity but they do so via different means. Their authenticating power comes from the civil (or religious) authorities that grant them. This, in turn, rests on the power of positivism that forms the basis of these bureaucratic institutions. Such

goods traffic in weights and measures, dates and times, for these are the prerequisites of civil personhood—what it takes to be counted.[57]

Sometimes, as Hannah Campbell first did, these assorted mementos are
put away. Some use a box they have already, like the shoe box described in a
piece by that name by Lisa Davenport (1993), while others purchase "memory boxes" especially designed for this purpose like the ones SHARE markets and those given to patients by hospital bereavement teams or social
workers (see chapter 9).[58]

Other times, memorial items are displayed in a public area of the home,
as we saw in the example of Hannah Campbell's curio cabinet. Campbell
(1992) explains this choice for public display saying, "after all, he is more
priceless to us than all the crystal in the world."

Like other forms of public commemoration, these publicly displayed
memorial items serve several important functions. They make the claim that
the baby existed—in Campbell's words, "He was a real baby with baby
things" (Campbell 1992). They also make an assertion regarding the value
of that existence, that it was deserving of recognition. But unlike the other
forms of public commemoration, which tend to be periodic and directed at a
larger public, these household shrines to memory place the child within the
sphere of everyday family life. Campbell explains, "bringing them out helps
me and others be reminded of him on a daily basis" (Campbell 1992). She
obviously believes these daily reminders are a good thing and it appears that
her extended family shares her view. But this is a minority view and their
assertions are made in the context of a cultural denial of pregnancy loss.
Campbell discusses people's reactions to her display in this way, "now when
people visit our home, they sometimes peer into Marc's shelf. I see them
stand silently for a moment or two. I wonder what they're thinking." She
narratively counters any doubts she or her readers may have by projecting
empathy: "It feels good to see them care." But, given the dominant views on
these matters, one can safely assume that such displays will provoke discomfort and/or disapproval from at least some who view them.

One illustration of such reactions was recounted to me by an acquain-
tance who, when she learned of my research, told me this story in the hopes
I could help her and her colleagues better understand the behavior of one of
their coworkers. One of the secretaries where she worked had framed the
sonogram images of each of her several miscarriages and had them prominently displayed on her desk. The rest of the staff were horrified by what
seemed to them bizarre (and some felt, disgusting) behavior.

We also get a glimpse of the discomfort that such breaches of the cultural norm can create in a newsletter item discussing portraits as a way of

memorializing dead babies. "If you have pictures but . . . feel they may be frightening for others to look at, an artist may be able to do a sketch or painting from your photos that is more pleasing" (Doerr 1992).[59]

The dominant cultural attitude toward unhappy events like pregnancy loss is not uniformly distributed in society. A recurring theme at pregnancy-loss support-group meetings is the difference in the way women and men grieve; men tend to grieve in silence while women more often feel the need to talk. In our culture most men are socialized not to discuss their feelings and to avoid emotionally charged situations; women are more frequently taught to explore and express their feelings.

This difference is often a source of conflict in marriages. In her study of divorce in the United States, Riessman found that men constructed themselves "as the silent partners in marriage" and both men and women frequently identified this as a problem in the marriage (Riessman 1990:37). "Women want marriage to be eminently intimate through talking about feelings, problems, and daily experience . . . [and] they expect talk to be reciprocal." They want "their husbands [to] disclose to them" (Riessman 1990:69–70). The inability or unwillingness to do so is one of the problems frequently discussed at support-group meetings and in the pregnancy-loss support literature.[60]

Men's silence after a pregnancy loss is sometimes taken by women as a sign that their partner did not care. Take for example Michell Chiffens, who served for many years as a UNITE group facilitator. At age thirty-three she was employed as a systems manager for a law firm, was unhappily married, and had three children ages thirteen, five, and two, when she discovered she was pregnant again. She had been interviewing for a position at "a very prestigious" firm that would pay a lot more and included "a chance to travel," and this pregnancy meant she couldn't take the new job.[61] Nine months later her daughter was stillborn. In her piece "I'm Here, Daddy," Michell discusses the way that a consumer good helped her and her husband to overcome the breach in their marriage that had been exacerbated by the different ways they handled the stillbirth. "He couldn't talk about her; I thought he didn't care. He couldn't say her name; I thought he forgot" (Chiffens 1991a). Michell explains how she kept a duck that was placed on her daughter's grave at Easter on the sill between the kitchen and dining room. One day her husband was angry at the mess his three children had made, and, as was his custom on such occasions, he opened the door to the basement and threw all the toys down the steps. The duck got thrown along with the other toys. When he realized what he'd done and that his wife was angry, he said, "Well, she's just like the rest of them; leaves her toys all over the place" (Chiffens 1991a). The display of this item in a public area of the house was a daily assertion of the wife's view of the event, a tacit tool in the unspoken conflict over interpretations of the loss. Once her husband acknowledged the baby in this way, the duck was no longer needed. That day she retrieved the duck and "put it in the 'box' with all our memories."

In addition to asserting that a baby existed and deserves recognition, some use consumer goods to claim that the baby still exists and remains an important part of the family. For example, Janet Jones had two children when she experienced her loss. For two years following the loss, even though in the meantime she gave birth again, she found herself unable to have family portraits taken. She solved this problem by buying "a guardian angel pin with Ronald's birthstone on them" for herself, her husband, and three children one Mother's Day. "They are nothing fancy or expensive; I only spent a couple of dollars each. But the price wasn't important. They were bought to be worn on special occasions, at family gatherings, on holidays, and for family portraits. Now our family will be 'complete'" (Jones 1992).

A similar use is illustrated by Michael Niehoff (1994), who explains that when his family signs greeting cards they use "an angel teddy bear rubber stamp" as the "signature" of their stillborn son. These uses are similar to that mentioned earlier where a dead baby's teddy bear takes the baby's place in the family photo. In these cases, however, it is not one of the baby's things that is used as a surrogate for the child, but, rather, a consumer good purchased after the demise specifically for this purpose.

Another example of this can be seen in the common practice of bereaved parents buying a Christmas ornament to represent each of their children.[62] Cathy Hintz, an R.N. and UNITE member, tells how, on the basis of a suggestion she read in the UNITE newsletter, she bought four crystal snowflakes as Christmas ornaments one year, "one for each of our children which includes our six year old daughter, Carolyn, our survivor." After Christmas she hung the ornaments in her kitchen:

> Everyday as the sun kisses each snowflake, our home is filled with rainbows—unexpected gifts from our children in heaven. . . . The rainbows reaffirm symbolically how the children were and still are a good part of our lives (Hintz 1988).

Debbi Dickinson, a pastoral bereavement consultant and author of several collections of poetry about the four babies she lost "due to Antiphospholipid Syndrome and Lupus complications," also buys "special" Christmas ornaments every year "to represent each of our babies." She explains how these material representations help concretize her losses. "This year meant having to buy four ornaments instead of three. At first, I was thinking that I needed three ornaments and then I remembered. I felt guilty for having thought that momentarily I had forgotten Ashley Brooke. . . . But that was not the case. . . . I was trying to avoid the pain of truly acknowledging her death. Buying the fourth ornament would make her loss more real; make her absence more tangible" (Dickinson 1996).

Artistic renderings—sketches and paintings—are also sometimes used to memorialize dead babies. According to Aries (1962), this practice can be traced to the sixteenth century, when elite European families began to include their dead children in group portraits on or at the family tomb.[63] Not until the beginning of the seventeenth century were portraits of individual children common. By then, "it had become customary to preserve by means of the painter's art the ephemeral appearance of childhood. . . . henceforth every family wanted portraits of its children, and portraits painted while they were still children" (1962:43). According to Ruby (1995:38), posthumous mourning paintings, including those of children, were found "among the middle-class Protestants, primarily in the northeastern United States, in the middle of the nineteenth century" and in the western states as late as the 1890s.[64]

These paintings coexisted with postmortem photographs. In fact, according to Ruby, posthumous mourning paintings flourished in the Northeast during a period when the "general business of painted portraits was on the wane." He concludes that these two forms fulfilled different needs as they did not appear to be in direct competition with each other (1995:43). Both Ruby and Aries concur, however, that by the end of the century, "photography [had taken] over from painting" (Aries 1962:43, Ruby 1995:46).

While there is no denying the importance of photography in contemporary family life, photography has not completely replaced painting. Many middle-class North American families still have portraits done of their children, which they hang in public spaces in their homes. The greater cost of such representations and what Bourdieu (1984:39) has described as the "legitimacy-imposing effects of paintings" make these prestige items. Portraits are, like children, "one of a kind" and although painting is thought to be less "realistic" than photography, good art is thought to capture the essence of its subject.[65]

Another important set of memorial items are objects to be placed in a garden. Some commonly used items include trees, rosebushes, fountains, benches, birdbaths, and garden statues of children or angels. Miller (1997) has documented the preoccupation among a segment of British mothers (the same women who strive for "natural" childbirth) about preserving the "purity" and "naturalness" of their children through pure and natural foods (for example, avoiding sugar). (I know from personal experience that this same preoccupation is shared by many middle-class American mothers as well.) But one does not find reference to nature in this way in narratives of pregnancy loss, presumably because the baby's purity and naturalness is preserved through death.[66]

"Nature" holds a different place in narratives of pregnancy loss (Layne 1996b, 1994). As I describe in chapter 8, naturalistic settings feature prominently in narratives of loss. Many mention seeking out a beautiful, quiet space in which to contemplate their loss and attribute healing powers to nature. Others feel that their child is now immanent in nature and thus natural settings allow them to be closer to their child.

Whereas most memorial goods are the kinds of mementos that one might have had the child lived (such as hospital records, scrapbooks, portraits, toys, and balloons) and therefore work to normalize the baby's life, garden memorabilia normalize the child's death. The fact that plants are alive and capable of growth is particularly important in this regard. Cathi Lammert (1992) tells of "a very special gift" of "a little blue spruce" given to them by family members one December, on the first anniversary of their son's birth/death. (As with other memorial goods, the qualities of "smallness," "specialness," "loveliness" are stressed.)[67] The bush becomes a stand-in for a child who is not thought of as dead, but rather as an ongoing, living, miraculous, "angelic presence" manifested through this object of nature. According to Cathi, "Our little bush, . . . immediately named the little 'Christopher' bush, . . . nurtured and grew" even after having been transplanted when they moved to their new home. Each year they decorate "our little bush" with "bright white lights . . . the symbol of brightness and purity." Cathi remarks on the loving way her husband arranges the bush/child in "his radiant white garment of lights," thereby transforming Christopher's bush into Christopher who "stood glistening alone."[68] At other times the bush is construed not as the child himself but as a vehicle through which Christopher "do[es] his miracles" (Lammert 1992).[69]

Similar symbolism is found in a common pregnancy-loss support-group ritual—the planting of a tree as a living memorial, like that planted during the October 1989 Pregnancy and Infant Loss Awareness Weekend in Washington, D.C. (see chapter 8).

Jewelry is also a popular memorial good.[70] The most frequent type mentioned is a "mother's ring," which has the birthstone of each of the woman's children (whether living or dead).[71] When there are no surviving children, these goods serve not only to constitute what was lost as a "child" but, equally important, the woman who lost it as a "mother." Often memorial jewelry is more representational, as, for example, "precious feet pins" and guardian angel pins. These two most common pin motifs are sometimes combined. The July/August 1999 issue of *SHARING* advertises "Angel Feet Pins," which were created by Lisa Marie Pawelkiewicz in memory of her stillborn daughter. "She offers it to all parents (for $3.95) as an outward sign that stands for the loss of our precious children." The pin has gold wings and comes with "blue feet for boys, pink feet for girls or teal feet if the sex is unknown." This same issue suggests for others who feel "overwhelmed and need a 'team of angels,' . . . not just one, pins with three gold angels." At UNITE's twenty-fifth anniversary celebration one of the organizers wore a large wire-and-glass-bead angel pin that she got at a SHARE conference; one of the guests, a nurse, wore a gold pin representing six angels side by side, which a patient had given her; another wore a small angel pin decorated with a birthstone. These pins were the topic of casual conversation during registration as women complimented each other on them and, in exchange, volunteered stories about their provenance and meaning.

Sue Friedeck (1995a), a long-term *SHARE Newsletter* editor who had two miscarriages and then had a son who died thirteen days after birth, wears two pieces of jewelry representing her son: "an angel on a chain" and a ring with her son's birthstone, which was given to her as a Mother's Day gift. She writes that she would also like to get a butterfly and heart to wear on her necklace to represent "each child lost." For Sue, the angel, butterfly, and heart "each represent special qualities of my babies."

Sometimes more than one of the categories of memorial goods are combined in memorial jewelry. For example, the "keepsake pendant" advertised in an issue of *SHARE* as "a small decorative vessel that holds a portion of a cremated baby's remains or a lock of hair." The pendant can be worn as a necklace or displayed under a blown-glass dome (Madelyn 1996).[72]

Whereas balloons and grave flowers stress the fragility of life and the inevitability of change as time passes, jewelry is a "hard good" which emphasizes a lasting quality.[73] Memorial jewelry also makes tacit claims about the "preciousness" of these babies, a cultural notion that appears to have a particular prominence in narratives of loss. Like clothing, jewelry mediates between the body and others and as such is both public and private—memorial jewelry may be seen by others but not necessarily recognized as a symbol of a pregnancy loss.

Simulacra and the "Realness Problem" of Pregnancy Loss

In addition to the many consumer goods and memorabilia discussed in the preceding pages, familiar accoutrements of birth and death for middle-class

Americans, pregnancy-loss support newsletters reveal another category of goods unique to pregnancy loss—simulacra of the trappings of fetus- and infanthood. Certain goods act as substitutes for items that are desired but unattainable. In fact, since the goods that are desired but unattainable are often themselves used as stand-ins for the baby the parents so desperately desire but cannot have, these simulacra represent a particularly clear example of the way in which bereaved parents use the tangibility of goods to combat the "realness" problem that pregnancy loss poses for them.[74]

A number of these goods concern visual representations of the baby. As discussed in chapter 5, because embryos and fetuses cannot be readily seen, their "realness" is an issue for many pregnant women and their associates regardless of the eventual outcome. The importance of visual representations in establishing the "realness" of an embryo or fetus is even greater in the case of pregnancy loss.[75]

If a desired representation is unavailable, pregnancy-loss support newsletters provide suggestions on how to attain substitutes. For example, in an article on early losses a contributor to the *SHARE Newsletter* counsels, "If you didn't have an ultrasound, get a copy of Nile Newton's *A Child Is Born* from the library. Photocopy the picture closest to your baby's gestational age" (Lewis 1991). In this case, a photocopy of a reproduction of a sonogram image of some other embryo/fetus may stand in for the coveted image of one's own, which is in itself a substitute for the coveted child.

Another example is found in descriptions of artistic renderings. Sometimes, much like the case of surrogate sonogram photos, portraits are suggested as a way to fill a void. For example, Kelly Gonzalez, coordinator of the SHARE group in Colorado Springs, advises, "Even if you do not have any pictures of your baby or you were not able to see your baby, an artist can sometimes work with baby pictures of the parents and/or other children to create a likeness to what you may have envisioned your baby to look like" (Gonzalez 1995; cf. Doerr 1992).

Other times, portraits are suggested as a way of improving on the visual representation/s one may have, that is, a way of substituting a more desirable representation, one more like the type of representation one would have had if the birth had been "normal" and the baby survived. This is typically suggested for babies who survived for some time after birth. In these cases, portraits are specifically recommended because the image of the baby can be improved by the removal of unsightly/unpleasant reminders of the baby's traumatic birth, such as tubes and wires, bruises, and birth defects (Friedeck 1995b).

Like visual representations, when the artifacts of civil authority cannot be attained, simulacra are available. For example, the Association for Recognizing the Life of Stillborns (1992) sells "Recognition of Life Certificates" as does SHARE. These certificates are described as "suitable for framing" and "provide a record of birth and lasting keepsake" (Guenther 1991). In 1987 SHARE had two models: one for stillbirth and one for neonatal death. In 1991 they redesigned their certificates and now offer "three styles to best suit your experience." Space is provided for personalizing the certificate with "baby's name, parent's name, date and name of support person or hospital representative" (Voegele 1991).[76]

SHARE also provides copies of do-it-yourself baptismal certificates. The certificate was designed by Malinda Sawyer of Marion, Illinois, an active member of AMEND (Aiding a Mother Experiencing Neonatal Death), and shared at the 1983 SHARE conference Memorial Service and then printed in the newsletter (Sawyer 1983). According to Dorothy Van Sant in a piece in a subsequent *SHARE Newsletter*, "anyone can administer the rite of baptism, it is often carried out by a parent or by hospital personnel. For

Recognition of Life

This is to acknowledge the life of

_____

Who was born into the hearts of

_____

On _____

In an instant you and your
Little one touched hearts. . .
Love is for a lifetime . . .

Recognition of Life Certificate.

Ḥosanna Amen Ḥallelujah Shalom Praise Ḥosanna

Certificate of Baptism
for

_____

_____ *of* _____

LOVINGLY BAPTIZED
In the Name of The Father, Son, and Holy Spirit

Date _____ *Place* _____

Baptized by _____

"This is my beloved child,
in whom I am well pleased."
Matthew 3:17

Ḥosanna Amen Ḥallelujah Shalom Praise Ḥosanna

© 1982 Aiding a Mother Experiencing Neonatal Death

Baptismal certificate.

instance, a mother who miscarries at home may baptize her baby" (Van Sant 1986).

This class of goods raises authenticity and legitimacy questions that replicate similar questions regarding the status of the child itself. For example, does a photocopy of a sonogram image from a book count as much as a sonogram image attained from the obstetrician? Does a miscarried or still-born child count as much as one that lives? The equivalent materiality of both types of goods ("real" and "fake") provides a tacit answer to these questions. That is, while a do-it-yourself baptism certificate may not be considered by many to be authentic or legitimate, from the point of view of materiality, a homemade certificate is as tangible as any other. The same is true for sonogram images, whether they come from an obstetrician's office or out of a book.

Baudrillard defines simulation as "feign[ing] to have what one hasn't" (Baudrillard 1983:5).[77] "Feigning" has two valences. Its primary meaning has the derogatory sense of fabrication, making something up, or pretending, and it is with this more common sense that I first interpreted the use of these substitutes as "fake" goods. Its other, older meaning was to form or to shape, coming from the Latin *fingere*, meaning to touch, or handle. On reflection, it seems to me that this earlier meaning points to a deeper truth with regard to these goods and that is that pregnancy (and later mothering) are works of fabrication in the sense of being inventive, creative acts that rely heavily on physical touch. The bodily and social work of shaping a child that begins during a pregnancy, and is cut brutally short with a pregnancy loss, creates a painful physical void for bereaved parents. Things not only play an important role in the production of a child during pregnancy, they also help bereaved parents define and deal with the painful absence of their wished-for child once it is gone. One of the reasons that things are so effective in both instances is that they are tangible; they occupy a space, can be kept present and regarded, or touched, at will.[78]

"Baby Things" as Fetishes?

Gamman and Makinen (1994) begin their book on female fetishism with this quote: "a fetish is a story masquerading as an object" (Stoller quoted in Gamman and Makinen 1994:1). The baby things acquired and preserved after a pregnancy loss certainly fit this description. But it is not just any story such things tell. They are stories of thwarted desire and tragic loss.

Like narratives of pregnancy loss, contemporary theories of fetishization and the Baudrillardian notion of "simulation" are fundamentally about "lack" and "absence" (Baudrillard 1983:5). Both Freud and Lacan understood fetishism as an individual male solution to the fear caused by the sight of a woman's "lack" of a penis (Stratton 1996). Stratton has expanded this notion from the individual to the collective and argues that it is a "lack" which people who live under the power of the State feel "provides the overdetermining context for . . . the twentieth century expansion of consumption" (Stratton 1996:14). He cites Ewen, who has described how "twentieth-century advertising encouraged people—especially historically, women—to think of themselves as incomplete, as lacking" and in turn "encouraged a constant consumption of new products in order to . . . erase the discovered and naturalized lack" (Ewen quoted in Stratton 1996:14).

Psychoanalytically informed theories of fetishization begin with the fear of a fantasized potential loss. How can the use of things in response to the actual loss of a wished-for child be understood in terms of fetishization? Gamman and Makinen distinguish between three types of fetishism: anthropological, commodity, and sexual fetishism. Of the three, the anthropological model seems best suited for illuminating the ways in which goods are used to deal with pregnancy loss. Gamman and Makinen base their notion of anthropological fetishism on Tyler's *Primitive Culture* [1871], where he says, "to class an object as a fetish demands explicit statement that a spirit is considered as embodied in it or acting through it or communicating by it, or at least that the people it belongs to do habitually think this of such objects . . . " (Tyler quoted in Gamman and Makinen 1994:17). Clearly, the "angelic presence" of Christopher in the little blue spruce tree is one such example. Another example can be found in Hannah Campbell's story. She ends her description of "Marc's things" displayed in her curio cabinet by exclaiming, "His Irish ancestors must be proud *he's* in with their Waterford crystal from Ireland!" (Campbell 1992, emphasis added).

Much like the pop music fans studied by Fiske, who use things to "help them summon up the star's presence," by using spaces in their homes or their own bodies to construct "'temples' in honor of the star" (Gamman and Makinen 1994:19), we have seen how some bereaved parents place things in special places in their homes or on their bodies to similar ends. "What the cherishing of objects associated with those we love has in common with the behavior of fans is the desire to maintain a link to an absent person through a fetish object" (Gamman and Makinen 1994:27). One can also see how objects may be used during the course of a pregnancy, not so much to maintain a link, but to begin the process of constructing one with an "absent person," or at least, a not-yet-present one.

Gamman and Makinen note the special association of anthropological fetishism with loss and grief. "People mourning lovers, friends, parents, children or animals have been known to develop fetishistic behavior, in order to cope with the loss" (Gamman and Makinen 1994:27). A number of feminists have argued that loss is a defining quality of motherhood (not an experience restricted to those whose babies die). Simonds and Rothman, for example, argue that loss is a "universal" part of motherhood: "The dead baby, the well and truly gone baby, is a symbol for all the babies we lose: the babies of fantasy and the babies of reality, all of whom inevitably leave us" (1992:13).

A similar point was made by female "fetish artist" Mary Kelly in her exhibit *Post-Partum Document* (1976), in which "she displayed objects associated with her baby, charting his first move away from the breast, at weaning, to the move away from home to go to school" (Gamman and Makinen 1994:189). Kelly describes the objects exhibited (dirty diapers, a plaster cast of her son's hand, his drawings and gifts of bugs and plants to her, which she "carefully saved," her transcripts of his baby conversations) as "fetish objects that enabled her to disavow the separation" (Gamman and Makinen 1994:189).

According to Gamman and Makinen, Kelly "was really the first to put the issue of female fetishism on the feminist agenda by arguing that the mother was the prototype fetishist" (Gamman and Makinen 1994:187). Kelly's work, informed as it is by psychoanalytic traditions, seeks to address human universals: "For women, . . . the threat of castration does not focus on genitalia but instead takes the form of fear about losing children" (Gamman and Makinen 1994:189). But historians like Gillis (1994) illuminate the particular cultural and historical context for "the museological mania of the maternal collector/fetishist" (Kelly and Apter 1993:352). Gillis (1994) tells of how collective forms of memory have declined throughout Euro-America during the later part of this century. "Memory work" has become much more individualized and has dramatically increased in volume.

> As global markets work around the clock and the speed of communications shrinks our sense of distance, there is both more memory work to do and less time . . . to do it. . . . It is wives and mothers who pick up the slack. Every attic is an archive, every living room a museum. Never before has so much been recorded, collected; and never before has remembering been so compulsive, even as rote memorization ceases to be central to the educational process. What we can no longer keep in our heads is now kept in storage (Gillis 1994:14).

As Gillis (1994:10) points out, it is Euro-American women who have come "to serve in various (and usually unpaid) ways as the keepers and embodiments of memory."

Given the negative evaluation inherent in the concept of "fetishism," the application of this term to the collecting and preserving of baby things by mothers (whether or not their babies live) denigrates "women's work."[79] As Gamman and Makinen (1994:45) point out, all types of fetishism share "the process of disavowal." Whether it is the disavowal of human labor in commodity fetishism, or the disavowal of the fear inspired in the discovery that mothers lack a penis in sexual fetishism, or the substitution of an object for the original "suppressed" or "hidden" object of desire of anthropological fetishism, a fetishist is by definition someone who "believe[s] the false" (Gamman and Makinen 1994:45). Thus, fetish theory risks marginalizing and derogating the cultural work of memory assigned to women throughout contemporary North America. The maternal obligation to remember is particularly challenging for would-be mothers following a pregnancy loss.

Ultimately it is unclear whether the concept of fetish really adds anything to our understanding of the importance of things after a pregnancy loss. What is clear is that this concept emphasizes the notion of "disavowal" in the practices of individual bereaved mothers while ignoring the "disavowal" of pregnancy loss that our society engages in collectively. This is particularly problematic given that this collective disavowal serves as an important impetus for bereaved parents to use objects to make reality claims about their loss in the first place. In other words, if the "realness" of their "baby" and their loss were not disavowed in the first place, bereaved parents might not have such a need to use things in these ways.

Conclusions

Dead fetuses or newborns are liminal, and as such have the potential for great power and danger. This is even more the case if there is deformity. In our culture, the dangerous valence of these beings is predominant, and like other entities that do not fit into our cultural scheme, they are hidden and ignored.

Most members of our society deal with this challenge, and the threat that these liminal beings present, by pretending that such an event did not happen and that these betwixt-and-between beings never existed. This tendency contributes to additional and unnecessary suffering for those who have a pregnancy loss. In order to combat this tendency, many members of pregnancy-loss support groups often adopt the opposite strategy. They work to transform the dangerous ambiguity of that which they lost into power, and, as I have shown in this chapter, they marshal the efficacy of things for this task.

Throughout this chapter I have focused on the instrumental role material artifacts play in the construction of fetal and neonatal personhood and consequentially of parenthood. Scholars of material culture recognize that, as a medium of discourse, objects differ from language or behavior (Gorenstein 1996:3). The meanings that objects convey may reinforce or challenge meanings expressed through language and behavior. Baby things are used by members of pregnancy-loss support groups to do both. On the one hand, they reinforce the dominant cultural constructions of babies as precious, that is, sentimental objects of affection; on the other hand, they challenge existing definitions as to whether being alive is a prerequisite of this condition. Similarly, they reaffirm the rightness and powerful desirability of proper life trajectories but challenge prevailing notions as to what qualifies for inclusion in this narrative structure.

In a society so thoroughly imbued with the ideology of "possessive individualism" (that is, we are largely defined by what we possess, cf. MacPherson 1962; Handler 1988), to posses baby things is powerful proof that "a baby" existed. But not any "baby" will do. The insistence of bereaved parents on the notion of "real babies" points to the frightening alternative of "the unreal," that is, the liminal dangers of death and deformity. Through the use of both physical and evocative homologies, bereaved parents use objects to construct the "real babyhood" of their embryos/fetuses/neonates. They use the culturally prescribed, appealing qualities of baby things (smallness, softness, naturalness, sweetness, cuteness, preciousness) to normalize their child. These things assert not only that a baby existed but that this baby (even if born dead and/or malformed) possessed many of the shared qualities of babyhood that are so culturally valued. Unlike those middle-class parents in Britain (Miller 1997) and the United States who wage a constant and losing battle against the polluting effects of the artificiality of capitalist consumer goods on the purity and naturalness of their children, bereaved parents have different challenges. The naturalness and purity of their children is guaranteed. What is in short supply is evidence of the dead child's culturalness, and baby things are a valuable resource in this regard.

Baby things also help parents normalize and "make real" their experience as parents. Although for some bereaved parents the child continues to have an important spiritual presence in their lives, the physical, sensual aspects of mothering are sorely missed. Because things have sensual qualities, they play a critical role in helping bereaved parents to articulate and mourn this lack. As the advertisement for the keepsake pendants suggests, "holding a source of comfort in their hands" helps bereaved families "find peace in their hearts" (Madelyn 1996).

In addition, in buying, caring for, and preserving baby things, women are able to engage in some of the prescribed roles of motherhood. Many bereaved mothers describe feelings of frustration and helplessness. For example, Sue Friedeck (1995a) writes, "I felt so helpless, I could not protect my babies and it seemed that nothing I did could save them." Although unable to preserve their children, bereaved mothers, like other mothers, are able to use things to preserve their memory.

Scholars of material culture often remark on the subversive capacities of things and on their ability to proselytize (McCracken 1988:25). We have seen how members of pregnancy-loss support groups take the "cultural themes" inscribed in things (Gorenstein 1996), whether traces of a body or mass-produced consumer items, and use them to make their babies and their parenthood "real." In so doing they challenge the dominant cultural assessment of pregnancy loss.

CHAPTER 7

"True Gifts from God": Paradoxes of Motherhood, Sacrifice, and Enrichment

In addition to the "realness problem" discussed in the previous chapter, pregnancy loss poses a cluster of other historically and culturally defined problems for bereaved parents. In this chapter I describe the moral problems that pregnancy loss poses for individuals in a culture that often understands pregnancy in terms of capitalist production and deems moral stature and worldly success to be the result of purposeful, individual effort.

When a woman's "pregnancy fails,"[1] she is exposed to the judgment of others. Given that she, too, is a member of society, it is not surprising that she may have internalized societal norms and may judge herself according to these standards as well. Because of how closely motherhood and womanhood are tied in our culture, her virtue as both a woman and mother may be questioned. Put in their most brutal form these questions are: What kind of a woman kills her own child while in the womb? What kind of a woman mis/carries or "loses" this most precious cargo? What kind of a woman produces a baby that is so flawed that people tell her it was a blessing that it died, or nature's way of protecting itself from such aberrations? The answers to these questions are no less unkind. Women report feeling like "a human coffin," "a living tomb," "a baby killer," "a freak."[2]

In the face of these debilitating judgments, the rhetoric of the gift provides a powerful defense. Many bereaved mothers use idioms of the gift to construct (or reconstruct) themselves as exemplary women and mothers in and against a context of capitalist production and consumption. Just as it does for many other non-normative child getting and rearing experiences, the language of the gift "restores virtue to" (Modell 1999) the experience of pregnancy loss.[3]

One of the reasons that the rhetoric of the gift is so effective in this regard is the extent to which the meaning of "the gift" for Americans is still colored by Christian understandings of this notion.[4] And while I believe this is the case with regard to gift-giving in general, the sacred dimensions of gift-giving are particularly pronounced in cases like the one examined here, where the gifts in question are either children or transcendental gifts[5] like those that many members of pregnancy-loss support groups describe as being the result of their loss, such as greater faith in God, an improved set of priorities, or greater appreciation for what they have.[6]

Just as the Christian inflections of the gift may be most apparent in such exchanges, the paradoxical nature of gift exchange is also particularly clear in cases like these. In her book *Inalienable Possessions*, Weiner focuses on material things, yet her arguments about the paradox of keeping-while-giving can help illuminate exchanges that involve children and transcendental gifts. Indeed, as she notes, "the paradoxical tension created by keeping-while-giving exists at the root of all attempts to defeat loss . . . the motivation for keeping-while-giving is grounded in . . . the need to secure permanence in a serial world that is always subject to loss and decay" (Weiner 1992:10). In the United States, Christianity provides one of the main meaning systems by which people seek to "secure permanence" and "defeat loss." Thus, in narratives of pregnancy loss, the paradoxical nature of gift exchange is oftentimes reinforced and strengthened by the paradoxes of Christianity. As Baldick notes, "paradox . . . is pervasive in the literature of Christianity, a notoriously paradoxical religion" (1990a:160).

Pregnancy Loss as a Moral Problem

To an even greater extent than pregnancy, pregnancy loss is something that is largely beyond the control of individuals.[7] Yet a number of things in our culture serve to disguise this fact. The ethic of individual self-control and responsibility runs deep throughout North American culture. Newman (1988) has described how the "culture of meritocracy" functions to exacerbate the experience of unemployment and downward mobility in the United States. In this secular version of the Calvinist ethic, success in business is "viewed as a test of commitment, and the product of hard work and self-sacrifice" and therefore "a measure of one's moral worth" (1988:76). A lack of success is also evaluated in moral terms (especially by those who are accustomed to success). "If individuals are responsible for their own destinies, there is no one else to blame in case of failure" (Newman 1988:77).

This doctrine of individual responsibility is also evident in biomedical and popular understandings of health and illness. For example, in Martin's (1994) study of changing North American cultural models of the immune system she described an emerging form of social Darwinism. She observed that the immune system is coming to be used as "a scale measuring people and groups" and that this "allow[s] some people to feel especially potent" (1994:236) (and, one might extrapolate, others to feel especially impotent). Although Martin does not explicitly link her analysis to the Protestant ethic, there are clear connections. People are thought to vary in the "quality of their immune systems." The "elect," those with strong systems, will have lasting, if not everlasting life, while those with inferior systems will perish. The relative strength of immune systems is sometimes understood in terms of an individual's or group's genetics, but it is also frequently understood to be the result of an individual's conscious efforts at self-improvement (Martin 1994:237). Thus, if one is slothful, one will not achieve success/health; if one is well disciplined and gives one's system enough practice and training, one will be rewarded in the "currency of health" (Martin 1994:237).

Even in public health, there has been an increasing emphasis on individual "lifestyle" choices as the most important factor for improving (or diminishing) health. For example, Balshem describes how residents of a neighborhood with an elevated cancer rate in Philadelphia believed their illnesses were caused by toxic exposure from the chemical factories clustered in their neighborhood, and other sources of pollution. Representatives of the Fox Chase Cancer Center "sought to deflect this concern" and focused their efforts instead on getting individuals to "quit smoking, improve their diets, and schedule cancer screening tests at regular intervals" to reduce cancer risk (Balshem 1993:3).

The ethic of meritocracy is also conspicuous with regard to pregnancy and birth. In Ginsburg's (1989) study of abortion activists in the United States, she argues that with the advent of legal abortion, motherhood shifted from being a status that was ascribed to one that was achieved. Once women could safely choose not to become mothers, even after they were pregnant, the choice to keep a pregnancy and mother a child came to be seen as a moral achievement.

There are many other dimensions of contemporary North American culture that contribute to this understanding of pregnancy and childbirth as being the result of purposeful moral-laden activity.[8] Many feminist authors have observed the ways production metaphors inform our understandings of pregnancy and birth.[9] Martin notes that since the fifteenth century the same English word, "labor," has been used to describe "what women do in bearing children and what men and women do in producing things for use and exchange in the home and market" (1987:66). While in earlier times this notion of reproductive labor referred to preindustrial forms of production, it now has specific, if somewhat outdated, references to industrial production. For example, writing in 1971, Mitchell observed, "the child is seen as an object created by the mother, in the same way as a commodity is created by a worker" (Mitchell quoted in Martin 1987:67). The Calvinist ethic, and its more recent secular versions, see productive labor as both a sign of, and avenue for, achieving moral stature.[10]

To the extent that pregnancy and birth are understood in terms of production, pregnancy loss is, by extension, an instance of failed production.[11] Like success in business, reproductive success may be "viewed as a test of commitment, and the product of hard work and self-sacrifice" and thus, "a measure of one's moral worth" (Newman 1988:76). Like failure in business, reproductive failure may be read as the result of a lack "of willingness and ability to drive beyond the limitations of self indulgence and sloth" (Newman 1988:76).[12]

It is not surprising, since the "successful production" of a baby may be credited as a moral achievement, the result of self-discipline and labor, that the inability to bear children is oftentimes attributed to a moral failing on the part of the woman. As Sandelowski has observed, "In a cultural milieu characterized by the expectation that conception can be prevented, terminated, and initiated at will, and in which individual habits and life-styles have been persistently implicated in the onset of disease, not being able to have a child . . . is still often viewed as a kind of failure of will" (1993:22).[13] She delineates the (selfish and immoral) "life style choices" of women that are commonly blamed for infertility: the (selfish) postponement of childbearing, which brings with it in addition to age-associated risks, additional risks from prolonged exposure to contraceptive, occupational, and environmental hazards; sexually transmitted disease, associated with (immoral) early and frequent sexual contact and multiple sexual partners; and (selfish and immoral) personal habits such as overeating (the sin of gluttony) or undereating (the sin of vanity) and intensive exercise (1993:23).

Other reproductive experiences that do not measure up also tend to be blamed on women's moral failings. Schroedel and Peretz, for example, have noted that the current debate about fetal abuse focuses almost exclusively on maternal behaviors, particularly maternal substance abuse, rather than on the social and environmental hazards such as poverty, malnutrition, and inadequate medical care that have long been associated with poor birth outcomes, or on the adverse birth outcomes caused by male behaviors (1995:86).

When one looks specifically at obstetrical understandings of pregnancy loss, one finds contradictory messages. For instance, in their discussion of the causes of spontaneous abortion, Bourne and Danforth (1975) begin with a long paragraph designed to reassure the women that it was not their fault:

> It is certain that there is virtually nothing a woman could possibly do herself to produce a miscarriage, . . . in almost all miscarriages the fetus dies . . . for causes that are beyond anyone's voluntary control (Bourne and Danforth 1975:261).

This absolution is revoked, however, in a later chapter on perinatal death, where the authors argue that "the decline in the perinatal death rate over the years has been due directly or indirectly to improvement in prenatal care" (Bourne and Danforth 1975:522). They conclude by revealing that their reason for writing the book was to get "pregnant women . . . to . . . accept more stringent supervision during their pregnancy" (Bourne and Danforth 1975:522). According to the authors, in order for this to happen, women:

> must understand the reasons for any inconvenience which they may undergo and they must realize that everything they are asked to do is for their own and for their babies' benefits. Above all, the mother and all the members of her family must realize that they must accept the final responsibility for her welfare and that of the unborn child (Bourne and Danforth 1975:522).[14]

Regardless of patent reassurances that they were not responsible for a miscarriage, and in fact were incapable of producing a miscarriage if they wanted to, ultimately, "the final responsibility" for the health of mother and her fetus is placed squarely with the mother. Thus, while women are assured after the fact that there was nothing that they could have done to have caused the loss, this message contradicts all the messages they received from their doctors and popular culture throughout the pregnancy on the importance of their agency in "producing" a healthy baby through self-discipline and submitting to the authority of experts.[15]

Paradoxically, the women's-health movement has contributed to this ethic of individual achievement, and in so doing has made the experience of pregnancy loss (or any other less-than-ideal birth) more problematic for women (see chapter 10, Layne 2002). The fundamental premise of the movement that women must wrest back control of their bodies from physicians (especially during pregnancy and birth) reinforces the ethic of individual control and responsibility.[16] Childbirth educators who encourage pregnant couples to make a "birth plan" obscure the extent to which pregnancy and birth are unpredictable, largely uncontrollable processes. For example, throughout *The Bradley Method Student Workbook* (Hathaway 1989), the emphasis is on women's control over their pregnancies and births. Even in the chapter on "variations and unexpected situations," the message is not that these things sometimes happen, but rather that if one is only diligent and hardworking enough, such problems can be avoided (Hathaway 1989:64–65). It is clear that a "culture of meritocracy" applies as much here as it does in the business realm. Like those who suffer economic downward mobility, individual women may "fall from grace" and slip from "low risk" to "high risk" if they are not morally vigilant.[17] If the pregnancy does not end with a desired birth experience or birth outcome (for example, a healthy baby), it is hard to imagine a woman who could not go back over that daunting list and find at least some areas in which she should have done more, could have tried harder.

This ethic of individual achievement found in orthodox and alternative obstetrics and in popular culture exacerbates the experience of pregnancy loss. Among the middle classes, those who experience a loss may be cast (by themselves, at least) as failed achievers. One version of this focuses on the middle-class moral mandate to "finish what one starts." In the film *Some Babies Die*, a woman who had had three stillbirths in three years articulates these issues clearly. "You've failed, no matter how you look at it, you've failed, because if you set out to do something, I believe you've got to finish it, and here's something that you're trying to see through and you've got no control over, and that's one thing that is to me vitally important, control."[18]

Donna Brunner (1992) vividly illustrates how the rhetoric of natural childbirth exacerbates the experience of pregnancy loss in a piece entitled "Me? Guilty?" She describes how after her first pregnancy, which was a C-section, she attempted a "natural" vaginal delivery and lost her baby. She explains that she "held off those unnatural drugs for as long as possible" (19.5 hours) and now worries that if only she had taken some pitocin sooner she might have saved her baby.

> Guilty? Oh, I'm guilty all right. . . . How come the "childbirth education" didn't do any good?. . . . of course, the classes tell you (or strongly imply) the everyone can handle the birth process if you just get in tune with your body and breathe, breathe, and breathe some more. But what about us who don't have easy births and who don't

maintain the ability to "hout" during 26 hours of labor?. . . .

Guilty? Oh I'm guilty all right. I didn't do it right. I didn't hear her cry; I didn't see her move; I didn't hold her while she lived (guess I failed the "nursing on the table" criteria too).

Oh well, I'm guilty either way. I took it [pitocin] and Demeral and had an epidural and it was still a complicated birth, so I failed in the eyes of the natural childbirth/no drugs crowd *and* in the eyes of the world because I couldn't produce a baby that lived (Brunner 1992).

This creates a double bind for women who experience a loss. Either they accept responsibility for the pregnancy loss and therefore blame themselves for the death of their "baby," or they must admit that the loss was a bodily event over which they had no control. Despite the much-discussed dominance of the Cartesian split between mind and body, this is still experienced as "I am/was out of control." This alternative of acknowledging that one was not in control of oneself is hardly more palatable than self-blame. Lack of control is the first item Donna Brunner (1992) includes in her list of things she feels guilty for: "Guilty? Oh, I'm guilty all right. Guilty for not being 'in control.'" Sue Friedeck (1995a), whose son had survived fetal surgery for congenital diaphragmatic hernia but then was born prematurely and died thirteen days later, explains, "One of the hardest aspects of our loss of Michael was the feeling of helplessness and loss of control."

Nor is it easy to contemplate or accept the fact that the formidable forces of technoscience were not able to control nature when it really counted. Davis-Floyd has described "the need to create a sense of cultural control over birth, a natural process resistant to such control" (1992:63) and how the biomedical rituals of obstetrics "provide at least a sense of certainty and security to women that a natural process perceived as terrifying and uncontrollable can be controlled and rendered conceptually safe when its course is mechanistically channeled into predictable pathways" (1992:64).

Hence, it is not surprising that many North American women who experience pregnancy losses tell of feeling "out of control" and express an acute discomfort with this state of affairs.[19] At the same time, nearly all women worry that they were in some way responsible.[20] Indeed, one of the most disturbing findings of my research on the experience of pregnancy loss in toxically assaulted communities is how deeply ingrained and pervasive is this tendency to self-blame (Layne 2001). Even in communities where there is a ready-made, highly plausible external source of blame, many of the women I have interviewed persist in blaming themselves. The most notable example comes from Alsea, Oregon, where eight women signed a letter that eventually led to the EPA's ban on federal use of 2,4,5-T. In their community, the National Forest Service and timber companies had been routinely spraying the local roadways and watersheds with the ingredients of Agent Orange, and, each time they did, statistically significant numbers of the local women miscarried. Nevertheless, one of the women who signed still believes, twenty years later, that her loss was due to a hike she took.

Strategies for Dealing with Adversity

Newman identified two ways that downwardly mobile managers in the United States fend off the tendency to self-blame. Some use the concept of "categorical fate," that is, they see themselves as part of a group of victims whose plight is the result of large "social forces beyond their control" (1988:65).[21] Others focus on their individual personalities, but rather than finding fault with themselves, they attribute their difficulty to "manly flaws" such as exceptional "aggressiveness, rationality, and principled commitment, . . . praiseworthy attributes in American business" (1988:72). Neither of these strategies seem to work very well for women who have had a pregnancy loss. For most women in the United States, pregnancy loss is experienced as a highly private, individual, usually hidden event, and there is no equivalent for "manly flaws" for women who experience pregnancy loss. One cannot argue that it was because one was too much of a woman that this unfortunate event took place. On the contrary, since pregnancy loss is so directly tied to their sexuality, many women feel that these events threaten their womanliness.

And while a woman's role in reproduction (and pregnancy loss) is much more extensive and direct, men also suffer these losses, and their sexual identity may be significantly challenged as well. Men's sense of themselves as able reproducers may be threatened, and they may feel a sense of powerlessness at not having being able to avert disaster, to help their wives, and protect their children.

But members of pregnancy-loss support groups have found other resources for dealing with the threat to their identities as able, moral individuals that comes with pregnancy loss. The rhetoric of the gift appears to be one of the most widely used and versatile such devices. It enables bereaved parents to articulate and negotiate several of the tensions that result from pregnancy loss in our culture. It enables would-be parents to reassert some sense of control over a devastating personal event without condemning themselves. It also bridges the tension between the parents' sorrow and the moral mandate to be happy (Aries 1974:93–94). In other words, some of the most important redemptive resources for the "spoiled identity" (Goffman

1963) that pregnancy loss threatens are found, not within the sphere of secular production and commodity exchange, but in the spiritually infused discourse of the gift.[22]

One of the most important features of the rhetoric of the gift in this context is the way the notion of the gift functions paradoxically.[23] By situating their experience in the context of the paradoxical reversals of Christian dogma, many bereaved parents are able to reconcile the gap between their expectations and reality, and, in so doing, reassert a sense of themselves as virtuous and able.

Of Gifts and Agency

As we saw in the previous chapter, gifts play a prominent role in the personal narratives of miscarriage, stillbirth, and early infant death of members of pregnancy-loss support groups. Whereas in that chapter I described the way that gifts of consumer goods are used in the construction of fetal personhood during a pregnancy and after its demise, in this chapter I focus on the various types of spiritual gifts associated with pregnancy loss. I describe the trajectories of these gifts, paying special attention to the issue of agency in each case, and discuss the qualities most often described as inhering to these gifts.

Spiritual gifts routinely appear in the narratives of pregnancy loss in six ways. In three of these the parents are cast in the role of receiver: when the "baby" is interpreted as a gift from God; when the "baby's" life and death are experienced as a source of valuable spiritual and/or interpersonal gifts for the parents; and when other people's acknowledgment of the loss is defined as a gift to the parents. In the three other cases the parents take the role of givers: when parents (especially mothers) are seen as givers of life and/or birth; when the death of the child is interpreted, often in the language of sacrifice, as a gift from the parents to God; and when bereaved parents feel the need to "pay back" the help they received by helping others. These six trajectories are by no means exclusive. Indeed, contributors who embrace the language of the gift tend to use it in its many manifestations, thereby creating dense, intratextually woven accounts that are permeated with this imagery.

Parents as Receivers

Baby as a Gift from God.   The notion of the child as a gift from God is a common one in contemporary popular culture. An example is found in the soundtrack of the popular *The Rugrats Movie* released by Paramount Pictures and Nickelodeon Movies in 1999. The chorus of the duet sung at the shower for "Baby Dill" is "A baby is a gift, a gift from above. A baby is a gift from above."[24] As this example illustrates, all children may be understood in these terms. Nevertheless, the construct seems particularly apt in cases that highlight the un-inevitability of reproduction, as in cases of infertility, high-risk pregnancies, or pregnancy loss. For example, Christine Zemichielli, a contributor to the UNITE newsletter, describes how, when she learned she was pregnant in 1998, several years after having been diagnosed with poly-cystic ovarian syndrome, she "knew this was a gift from God."[25]

A number of contributors also cast their babies in this way after their loss. For example, Patricia Shute (1988) writes of her granddaughter, "God sent to us for six short days, Jennifer Maria to hold and love. And with his gift sent from above, came stronger faith and richer love," and Kathleen Bannon (1999) describes her son, who was stillborn five years earlier, as "God's special gift to me." The opening lines of a poem read by Denise Jones (1988) at the funeral of her son also use this image: "Your tiny body inside me—your tiny body to love. A gift from heaven—a gift from above." Marlene Castiaux of Hayward, California, describes how she learned that she was pregnant with "our second child three weeks before Christmas. What a Christmas present!" An ultrasound at nineteen weeks revealed that their baby had died. Six months after the loss, Marlene remarked that even though they had named their first-born "David Nathanael: beloved gift of God," she "had taken childbearing and children for granted!" She now understands that "children truly are a gift from God" (Castiaux 1988). Another example is found in the poem from which I take the title for this chapter. In a piece called "Two More Angels," Jennifer Habercorn (1996) describes her son and daughter as "true gifts from God."

The notion of these children as "true gifts" is remarkable in that in our culture, in order for a gift to be a "true gift" (or a "pure gift" to use Mauss's term), it is necessary for the gift to be alienable (cf. Parry 1986). According to Cheal (1988:10), "in modern western societies" the alienability of gifts "is a precondition for their being gifts rather than loans or shared possessions." The donor must have the exclusive right to freely dispose of the object (Cheal 1988:10).[26] Yet I would argue that the very idea of a child as a gift from God has within it the understanding that this individual will one day be returned to God. In other words, God never gives up his rights in the child.

This notion is present in Jewish tradition in the lore surrounding Beruryah (or Beruriah), a second-century Talmudic scholar from Tiberias.[27] Beruryah is said to have informed her husband that two of their sons had died while he was at Temple, by saying, "'Some time ago a certain man came and left something in my trust: now he has called for it. Shall I return it to him or not?' When told she must return it, she showed her husband their sons' bodies, and then in order to comfort him in his grief, reminded him of the verse from Job, "The Lord gave and the Lord hath taken away" (*Encyclopaedia Judaica* 1971, *The Jewish Encyclopedia* 1901).

A number of contributors make explicit a similar understanding of this arrangement with God, that is, they interpret the baby not as a "true gift" from God, but as only a loan. In a poem entitled "My Little Angel" a man identified as Uncle Rick states, "Children come to this world on borrowed time" (Alvarado 1995).[28] This notion is also found in a poem entitled "God's Promise" by the nineteenth-century American poet John Greenleaf Whittier, which is reproduced periodically in the UNITE and SHARE newsletters: "'I'll lend you for a little while a Child of mine,' He said. For you to love her while she lives and mourn for when she's dead. It may be six or seven years. Or twenty-two or three. But will you, til I call her back, Take care of her for me?" (Whittier 1995/6).[29]

In addition to the notion of true gifts, or loans, we also find examples of children being given to women in exchange for something, as part of a bargain struck with God. "If you only give me a child (or let my next baby live) I'll. . . . " For example, in a piece entitled "My Second Pregnancy," Kelly Gonzalez (1988) tells of how she "prayed and begged God to let me become pregnant" after the stillbirth of her daughter. When she became pregnant she felt she should not ask for more, for example, help with labor. "During 16 hours of labor I refused to ask God for any help. I needed to show Him that I could do this, no matter how bad it was. It all paid off."

Whether understood to be a gift, a loan, or part of a bargain, parents are required to give in return: to give the child love and care, and to give God thanks for this privilege. Whittier ends his poem with God overhearing the parents agree to be grateful: "for the happiness we've known, forever grateful stay" (Whittier 1995/6); and the piece by the grandmother ends, "For now we know the privilege given in caring for this gift from heaven" (Shute 1988).

Sometimes parents understand their baby, rather than God, to be the giver of this gift. In several cases the child is represented as giving the gift of her/himself to the parents. For example, a father from Canton, Massachusetts, in a piece written one year after his daughter was born and died at twenty-three weeks gestation, writes, "It's been a year since you gave us the gift of your oh so short life" (Atwood 1990). Another father thanks his son for this gift: "Thank you, Jonathan, for giving us the time you had. We will always love you for it" (Nagele 1986a). These are just two of a whole series of examples found in narratives of pregnancy loss where the dead fetus or newborn takes on roles traditionally attributed to God.

Baby Brings Transformative Gifts to Parents. Many members of pregnancy-loss support groups report feeling that the experience of loss resulted in valuable changes in their lives, changes often described as gifts. Of all the types of gifts discussed in pregnancy-loss support-group newsletters and literature, the idea that the life/death experience is a source of spiritual/personal enrichment is the most common and most thoroughly developed.[30] One remarkable feature of these types of gifts is that they are almost inevitably multiple, that is, if parents report any such gifts they almost always report several. Whereas in the case of the child as gift, it is typically God (and occasionally the child) who is the giver, in this case it is typically the child (and occasionally God) who has the active role of giver.[31]

The most fundamental gift the child is thought to give is that of making their mothers "mothers." For example, Bonita Martin (1995) dedicates her poem "I'm Still a Mother" to the memory of her son "who gave me the gift of being a mother."

In addition to this primary gift, the child is frequently construed to be the bearer of a whole host of other transformative gifts. For example, Diana Widell's daughter Kira died during labor two weeks before her due date. She had Down Syndrome and a serious heart defect. In a piece reprinted in the 1995 holiday issue of *SHARING* Diana writes:

> The Holidays are a time to count our blessing and to thank God for all we have been given. For those of us who have lost a child, giving thanks can sometimes be difficult. . . . Yet even in our grief we have found good. And there are things to be thankful for" (Widell 1995).

She itemizes the benefits:

> I became more certain of who I was and what I wanted as my faith and dependency on God became essential in just getting through each day. . . . We found much we thought important before, no longer was. We also found things we took for granted before were suddenly very important . . . Kira's death taught us . . . contentment. We try to live day to day and have learned there are no guarantees in life. We have learned just wishing for something does not make it true (Widell 1995).

She ends with, "While I am not happy about Kira's death, I am thankful for all she has given me" (Widell 1995).

Another example is found in a piece entitled "What I Learned from Baby Adam," written by Andrea D'Asaro, whose amniotic water started leaking at twenty-three weeks gestation, and after several days of hospitalization she developed a fever and the doctors induced labor. She gave birth to a "previable" son who stopped breathing once they cut the umbilical cord. As a result of "Adam's birth and death" she reports that she resolved "to give up complaining about my husband's faults, to throw out my lists of grievances I collect in a file by my bed waiting for a chance to read them to Ralph." She is still often annoyed by her husband's habits but she doesn't take them so seriously now, and instead turns her focus outward to others who are in distress: "my heart goes out to the homeless woman on the street, the stressed co-worker, the harried driver behind me" (D'Asaro 1996).

Most of the losses described in pregnancy-loss support newsletters take place well after the first trimester, but the notion that the child is a source of enrichment is not restricted to later losses. For example, Marie Allen and Shelly Marks end their book *Miscarriage* with a chapter entitled "Gifts," which focuses on how "our babies' lives and the process of grieving our babies' deaths brought us emotional, psychological, and spiritual gifts that changed our lives," gifts "that touched not only our lives but also the lives of countless others" (Allen and Marks 1993:211). Susan Erling (1984), who miscarried at ten weeks, writes, "It seems you only needed 10 weeks to make my life so much richer, and give me a small glimpse of eternity." Perry-Lynn Moffitt describes how the two miscarriages she had before the birth of her two healthy children helped her cope with her four subsequent miscarriages. She writes, "although their lives had been short, these miscarried babies had left an enduring legacy by augmenting my ability to order my priorities and cherish living loved ones more. . . . It is these babies' lasting gift to us as we struggle to integrate their absences into our lives" (1994:2).

This sense of gifts incurring from pregnancy loss is also a frequent topic at collective memorial services (which commemorate the full range of pregnancy losses from earliest to those that occur after birth). *SHARE*, for example, published a prayer written by its founder, Sister Jane Marie Lamb, for a memorial service held in Akron in 1986:

> Oh God, . . . we come to you with all that has been part of the special gift of our babies, the joyful anticipation, the mourning period, the memories and letting go—reaching out. We are grateful for all those times. . . . For the times of letting go, and for the times of reaching out, for each new day and each ray of hope, for the gifts our babies left us: in giving us new eyes with which to see, new ears to hear

more, a new heart to love with, and new values in many areas of our lives (Lamb 1986:4).[32]

The almost inevitable multiplicity of these gifts creates a sense of profusion and plenty. As we discussed in the previous chapter, narratives of pregnancy loss are fundamentally about "loss," "lack," and "absence," yet in these textually rich accounts one gets a sense of fruitful abundance.

For those who believe that their babies are still alive, now living in heaven, often in the form of angels (see Layne 1992), their children remain a source of ongoing gifts to their families on earth. Recall Cathy Hintz, the nurse/UNITE member mentioned in the previous chapter who hung crystal snowflakes in her kitchen window and described the rainbows they made as "unexpected gifts from our children in heaven" (Hintz 1988). Here it is the dead child who has replaced God as the giver of rainbows.

Another example is found in a letter written in the name of a dead baby, who explains, "I would like to share the full depth of love that one can only experience in heaven. I would like to share that love with you and ask that you use my gift well. I give you this gift . . . " (Kevin 1985/6).[33]

After a loss, a number of parents describe their subsequent children as a gift, not from God, but from their children now in heaven.[34] Laurie Holper (1991b) describes her subsequent daughter (who was born prematurely but survived) as "a gift from Josh," her son who had died two hours after birth.[35] In a piece called "One Mother's Feelings on Subsequent Pregnancy," Linda Rabinowitz (1983) writes, "In essence, she [her daughter who died after living two months] has given Joshua to us." Similarly, during an anxious pregnancy following the death of a son who died at forty-two weeks gestation, Debbie Hein describes how her husband reassured her by telling her that their daughter "would be a gift of love from Timmy" (Hein 1984). Another example is found in Linda McCann's (1985) "Love Letter to My Baby Girl," where she describes how when their subsequent child was born alive, "silently I thanked you over and over again. Joey is your gift to us."[36]

A few brave souls buck the mandate to find good in adversity. Pat McCann (1984) explains in her piece entitled "Growth Through Pain" that while she considers the fact that she has been forced to "grow farther than my years," "a very special gift from a very very special baby," she also acknowledges that "the knowledge almost never has been worth the pain." Marion Cohen, mathematician, author of numerous collections of poetry and essays on her many traumatic birth experiences, and UNITE member, writes in a poem titled "Bereavement and Growth": "It matures you they said. It matures you, they say. Wasn't I mature enough before? Was I really that bad? Was I one of the worst? How come God chose me?" (Cohen 1981a). Another example is found in the piece discussed above by Mary Doherty in which she compares her loss to that of mother Mary. She concludes by saying of Mary, "She knew friends would say His death would teach people to value life. She asked why her son's life needed to serve as a lesson" (Doherty 1988).

Acknowledgment of the Baby after Its Death—A Gift to the Bereaved Parents. The first two trajectories of giving concerned exchanges between the principal triad of God, child, parents. In this trajectory (and two others) the exchange takes place between bereaved parents and members of their wider social networks, including other members of support groups.

The acknowledgment of the loss is sometimes construed as a gift from others to the parents. Since our cultural norm is to ignore pregnancy loss—to avoid any reference to it, to act as if it never happened—the acknowledgement of the loss by family members, friends, the clergy, and so on may be experienced as a valuable gift for which the parents are grateful. For example, Janis Heil, during her editorship of the UNITE newsletter, wrote a piece entitled "Your Gift to Me" for the holiday issue in 1982. "What can you give me this holiday season? Your greatest gift to me is your listening" (1982/3). Cathy Holthaus, whose son was stillborn at full-term due to a knot in the umbilical cord, writes, "We know now that a friend who says, 'I've been thinking about you since you lost your baby' and waits for a response . . . is a gift" and goes on to say that an even "better gift is when someone" uses her son's name (Holthaus 1999). Another woman whose family gives a memorial gift in the name of their dead child every year at Christmas says, "We are grateful that they never forget" (Sariego 1996) (see chapter 9). Cathi Lammert describes her priest's recognition of her and her husband as parents as a precious and enduring gift: "I will treasure that compliment in my heart forever" (Lammert 1996). It is the fact that such acknowledgment is so rare and so much desired that qualifies it as a "gift."

Parents as Givers

Parents as Givers of Life and/or Birth for Which They May or May Not Receive Credit. Whereas in the first three examples parents are cast as receivers, some bereaved parents construe themselves as "givers" by virtue of the fact they created life and in some cases also "gave" birth. There are a number of possible recipients of this "gift of life," including the child, the world, and oneself. For example, Gia Strozzieri writes of the birth of her daughter who lived sixteen days: "Today I brought into this world. A gift of love, my little girl. My little girl so pure and sweet. A gift to make my life complete. . . . Consumed with love that all could see for this little girl, who came from me" (Strozzieri 1996).[37] In this piece the mother clearly takes credit for this gift and identifies two recipients: the world and herself. David Nagele (1986) casts his role as father as co–gift-giver. In a piece given to his wife after the death of their son he writes, "we have lost a part of ourselves, a gift to each other, to mankind, to time. For children are a gift."

Cathi Lammert (1996) tells of how at the funeral for her stillborn son, "the priest told Chuck and I that we needed to be congratulated for . . . for giving [Christopher] life, eternal life." It is unclear whether this gift of eternal life is understood to come from the act of conceiving and bearing him, or from the rituals of baptism and Christian burial that the parents arranged for him subsequently, but Cathi goes on to suggest that it is "the gift of love" that qualifies people as parents. She tells her readers that "you too need to be congratulated for being your child's parent; for loving and wanting them with all your heart and soul" (Lammert 1996).[38]

Not all women are acknowledged in this way and this lack of public recognition for their role as parent (that is, as giver of birth, life, and love) creates an imbalance in the reciprocity required at gift-giving events like Mother's Day.[39] Kelly Gonzalez, coordinator of the Pikes Peak SHARE group, writes, "You may not even have gotten 'credit' for giving birth at all . . . It can . . . be painful as you purchase a card for your mother or father and realize that you should be receiving one, not just sending a card" (Gonzalez 1996). Another woman complains that had she not lost her pregnancy in April, she would have received cards on Mother's Day as a "mother-to-be," but the following year, after her pregnancy loss she received no cards, even though she feels herself to be a mother. "As a mother of an angel, society does not make cards for me" (Morhardt 1999).

Although women are the ones normally cast in this way, fathers are also occasionally thought of in these terms. For instance, Karen Burton wrote a piece for the Mother's and Father's Day issue of *SHARING*, in which she contrasts the experience of parenting her three living sons with that of parenting her son Joey. Joey was born with a major heart defect. He underwent surgery but a few days later suffered a massive heart attack. The parents disconnected the life support and he died nine days after birth. "As most people celebrate Mother's/Father's Days, they will reflect on the gifts they have received from their own parents or on the gifts they have received in being a parent. I cannot help but reflect on the great cost many of us have paid to be a "Mom" or "Dad." . . . We are parents who have paid a great price and we deserve recognition on these special days whether we have surviving children or not" (Burton 1996).[40]

Sacrifice: The Baby as a Gift to God. Bereaved parents also sometimes construct themselves as givers by defining their child's death as a return gift to God.[41] For example, a poem by an uncle from Corpus Christi, Texas, written in the voice of a baby boy, Ray,[42] begins by granting God agency, "born out of love by God's design, a light for all to see" but ends by reversing the roles and stressing the agency of the parents as givers to God: "I'm now God's Ray of joyous light—a gift from Mom and Dad" (Dunham 1986). In another piece, John Fuchs of Indianapolis, the father of a baby girl who was born with lung and heart problems and lived for two days, depicts a similar two-way exchange—from God to them, then back to Him. In his piece entitled "Our Littlest Angel," addressed to God, he writes, "We didn't know why you'd required this baby we had conceived. Or why her time on earth was short, this daughter we'd received. We dedicated her to You before we gave her up" (Fuchs 1987). Even in cases like this, when the parents acknowledge that the logic of such gifts challenges their comprehension, constructing the loss as a gift to God edifies the loss and attributes agency to the parents at this moment of extreme helplessness.

One of the most common ways this is accomplished is by analogy with Christ's sacrifice.[43] With the crucifixion, God engages in what Kermode has called "the ultimate sacrificial excess" by allowing his only son to be killed for the salvation of sinners (Kermode 1987:393).[44] According to Miller (1998:115), in Christianity sacrifice serves as a "prevalent . . . model for appropriate religious behavior. The ideal of sacrifice and especially the abnegation of self-sacrifice remains close to the dominant ideals of Christian devotional love." But, as the reader may have noted, men write a disproportionately large portion of the pieces that cast the baby as a gift to God. It may be that given the Judeo-Christian examples of men who either sacrificed their sons or who were willing to do so, this notion may have special resonance for men.[45]

God's gift of his only son provides a model by which some bereaved parents understand their loss. The thought that because of his own son's death God can empathize with their grief makes the grief more bearable for some. One father writes, "We feel that if God so loved the world that He was willing to give up His Son, that we, too, could bear the pain" (Herr 1984). Judy Ward also compares her loss with God's: "for He too lost His precious Son before His earthly work was done. . . . so God understands our pain" (Ward 1987).

This analogy also helps bereaved parents transform/reverse the shame they may feel as a result of what, in another discourse, would be defined as a "reproductive failure," into pride. By analogizing their child to Christ, they reverse the valuation process that deems dead babies to be of no value. Not only are their babies of equal worth to other people's, in fact, they are of even greater worth, for they are, like Christ, not ordinary babies, but special, chosen ones (cf. Landsman 1999).[46] Ward, for example, makes explicit the analogy between Christ's death and that of her son by capitalizing "Son" in the final line of the poem: "Sweet little Tyler, God's chosen one. We are so proud you were our Son" (Ward 1987). Another mother (from Beaver, Pennsylvania) shares this view. Of her son who lived a few hours after his birth at twenty-four weeks gestation due to a uterine infection, she writes "Our infant son was born today, He came and died to show the way. As Jesus died, upon the cross" (Yoder 1985).

This analogy to the archetypical Christian sacrifice is also made by means of the symbol of the Lamb (see Hyde 1979:19). Jesus is often referred to as the Lamb because of his sacrificial death, and bereaved parents sometimes refer to their dead children as lambs. One poem, written in the voice of the child, reassures the parents, "I'm resting now beside the Lamb (Dunham 1986), and another poem written by a bereaved father (from Lexington, Nebraska) writes of his stillborn son, "Our little lamb has gone away" and later makes explicit this analogy with Christ, "My son I know you are not an angel, But a son of God I see" (Cantrell 1987).

In poems written at Christmas and Easter time, some bereaved mothers compare themselves to Mary. At Christmas the focus is on Mary's relationship with "baby Jesus" and the pangs that bereaved mothers may feel when they "view the manger scene" (Ingle 1982/83). Like "every baby in a stroller," each "Christ Child in a manger" may pull . . . at the core of [the] hearts and . . . souls" of bereaved mothers (Gana 1998). For example, a woman whose daughter was stillborn on December 15th and who left the hospital empty-handed the next day describes how hard it was for her, while waiting for her husband to bring the car, to see a woman with a new baby get into a car and to see the nativity scene set up in the lobby of the hospital (Amendolara 1997). In such cases, Mary may be a source of jealousy—just one more lucky woman who got the baby she desired.

At Easter time, the focus is on Jesus' death.[47] Whereas God actively chose to sacrifice his son, poor mother Mary didn't have much to say about it. Women empathize with Mary's powerlessness to prevent her son's death. For example, Mary Cushing Doherty, a lawyer and member of UNITE's board of directors, published a piece entitled "At the Foot of the Cross" in an April issue of UNITE's newsletter. She explains in a note preceding the poem that she "composed the following Easter remembrance . . . while thinking about the death of Jesus and about the death of my own son, Tommy [who died three days after his birth]. I began to understand the grief that Jesus's mother must have felt while watching the untimely death of her son." It begins:

> She stood at the foot of His cross.
> She asked God if she could pray hard
> Enough for a miracle to keep Him alive.
> She received Him into her arms
> Bruised, cold limp
> She wished to hold the warmth of His life.
> She cried because she could not protect Him from an untimely death.
> She asked if she had done something wrong (Doherty 1988).[48]

Whereas in the earlier examples parents were comforted by the thought that God could understand their pain, in this case a bereaved mother offers compassionate understanding to Mary qua bereaved mother.[49]

As this example makes clear, not everyone experiences their loss as a gift; for some it is quite the contrary. Other examples include Cindy Hunn (1995) who writes of the stillbirth of her twins, "I feel like I have been robbed of the two most precious things in my life."[50] Jody Kozak (1987) from Salt Lake City likened her stillbirth to having "Christmas treats . . . stolen in the night."[51] Kathy Rosso Gana (1985) likens grief to a number of socially mandated but onerous fiscal obligations—unwelcome solicitations for charity, the obligation to pay bills and dues. She writes, "Two autumns in a row a child died within me. When grief came knocking on my door the second time around, I tried to tell him 'I gave at the office' . . . whether I like it or not the dues must be paid—one year of pain and suffering per child. Well, my bill is almost paid up" (Gana 1985).

For still others, the emphasis is not on giving or sharing but on the pleasures of exclusive possession. Susan Erling (1984) of St. Paul, Minnesota, who miscarried at ten weeks, writes, "for just 10 weeks I had you to myself."

The Need to "Pay Back" Others for Their Support. The final example of ways in which bereaved parents construct themselves as givers is found in the common notion among members of pregnancy-loss support groups of their need to "pay back" the help and support they received when they were going through the "early stages" of grief. Hannah Campbell (1993) explains in a piece entitled "Going Back and Giving Back to Group

Meetings" that she still attends group meetings five years after the stillbirth of her son because "part of my remembering Marc is to give to others what I have gotten from others." In 1986 UNITE published a letter from Shelley Cocke thanking the organization for help in dealing with the stillbirth of her son. She describes how after a year she felt less grief and considered dropping out, but decided to continue attending. After the birth of her daughter, she "felt ready to try to give back some of the encouragement, the knowledge of the grief process, and the support [she] had received from other members" (Cocke 1986).[52] Her piece is followed by a note from the editors of the *UNITE Notes* thanking her for her return gifts: "Thank you Shelly, for your gift to UNITE—your time, your caring, yourself." Although this type of exchange is described in terms of "paying" or "giving back," in fact, it does not usually involve reciprocity within a dyad. More typically such gifts move from A to B to C, and so on. For example, Tami Leather credits a friend with enabling her to engage in this type of exchange. She thanks the friend for "loving support" and observes, "You have given me the courage to pass on to others the love and support that you have given to me" (Leather 1995). Sue Friedeck, while serving as editor of *SHARING*, tells how helping others can help restore the feeling of efficacy and control that is so challenged by a pregnancy loss. She refers to "A Hindu Proverb [that] says, 'Help thy brother's boat across, and lo! thine own has reached the shore'" (Friedeck 1995). While in this proverb the message is that one helps oneself by helping others, that is, that the two things can happen simultaneously, in her next sentence Sue stresses the more common temporal script of sequential role-shifting from helpee to helper. "At first, we may be the ones to be helped. In time, we can help others" (Friedeck 1995). Another female contributor worries about this time lag: "I know one can receive without giving for only so long, but I have not yet had enough energy to return the attention I've received" (Whipple 1995).

Hyde (1979) describes such exchanges as a common feature of transformative gifts and notes that spiritual conversions have the same structure.[53] "With gifts that are agents of change . . . passing the gift along is the act of gratitude that finishes the labor" (1979:46). This rhetoric may be a common feature of self-help groups in the United States. For example, the twelfth step in the Alcoholics Anonymous recovery program is the one in which "the gift is passed along" as "recovered alcoholics help other alcoholics" (Hyde 1979:46).

This form of gift-giving is especially important for bereaved parents in terms of reasserting their ability to act as able, moral agents.[54] The experience of pregnancy loss creates "children" of the would-be parents to the extent that the experience incapacitates them, and this type of gift-giving rein-states the normative structure of dependency wherein parents hold the primary role as helpers.[55]

The Qualities of the Gifts

We have examined six gift-giving trajectories involving God, dead babies, bereaved parents, and their social networks, including other members of pregnancy-loss support groups. Let us now focus on the gifts themselves. A number of qualities characterize the gifts involved in the gift-giving trajectories discussed above including preciousness and specialness, durability and inalienability.

By far the most common adjective used to describe such gifts is "precious." The most frequent use of this term is in the context of the child as gift. Take for example the summer 1995 issue of *UNITE Notes*. The first item is a thought from the director, Janis Heil, on the occasion of the twentieth anniversary of the organization, where she asserts, "grief is a natural response to the loss of a loved and cherished person. Our babies are precious beyond words." The next item is the poem mentioned above, which describes stillborn twins as "the two most precious things in my life" (Hunn 1995:1). On the following pages appear a piece that ends with the line "I thank you, my precious son"; another written "for my precious boy" (Warren 1995); and a birthday message "to our precious little girl" (Mommy and Daddy 1995:3).[56]

The term "precious" means "of great price or value; costly, of great desirability, held in high esteem, beloved; dear" (Guralnik 1970).[57] Like "precious," the adjectives "valuable," "priceless" and "cherished," which are also frequently assigned to these gifts, also highlight the great worth of these gifts/lives and in so doing reverse the social hierarchy of worth normally associated with such deaths.

Although the quality of preciousness is most frequently assigned to the baby, it is also sometimes used to describe subsequent children as well as other types of gifts associated with pregnancy loss. For example, Jean Schwabe (1984) of Kansas City, Missouri, writes of her son Nathan, who was born after a loss, "he is truly a 'gift given of God' which is the meaning of his name. We have found through this waiting time that the gift is more valuable, more priceless and cherished when one has waited for God's perfect timing." In 1987 *SHARE* reproduced the philosophy of a support group called Precious Parents (a not-for-profit group of parents offering support to parents who have experienced the death of a baby in Cuyahoga

Falls, Ohio), which delineates the many other ways the quality of "precious-ness" may be considered applicable to the gifts that result from a pregnancy loss. In addition to asserting the preciousness of their dead babies, they define both the relationship they had with the baby and the memories and keepsakes they have as "precious." The lessons learned as a result of the loss (i.e., to value life and relationships) are likewise defined as "precious," and of value not only to themselves, but to other bereaved parents and professionals as well. They also use the concept of "preciousness" to critique the way the experience of loss is handled in our culture—singling out the lack of "precious recognition" for them as parents, how "precious-little-time" they are given to mourn, and how "people make our baby. . . . less precious by believing babies can be replaced" (Precious Parents 1987).

"Specialness" is another related quality often attributed to the gifts associated with pregnancy loss.[58] It is sometimes intensified by the use of "very" or even "very, very" (McCann 1984). Like "precious," "special" means "highly regarded" or "valued" but it also stresses the exceptionality of that described. In this sense it is similar to "rare," another term sometimes used to describe dead babies, for example, Lisa Casimer describes her daughter's short life as "precious and rare" (1987). Pregnancy losses are not the statistical norm; most pregnancies do result in a live birth. Even miscarriages, which are relatively common, occur only in about 15–20 percent of all pregnancies (if one does not include those losses that take place during the first two weeks after conception), and the second- and third-trimester losses and early infant deaths that feature so prominently in pregnancy-loss support-group newsletters represent only a tiny minority of pregnancies. The infrequent occurrence of such events combined with the cultural taboo regarding discussion of these deaths leads some members of pregnancy-loss support groups to call themselves or their loss a "freak of nature" (chapter 8, Layne 1997b). According to Fiedler, in our not-too-distant history, all fetuses were considered freakish—"travesties of the human form even the normal among us are at two, three, or four months after conception" (1978:18). Throughout Europe during the sixteenth and seventeenth centuries the collections of "curiosities of nature" popular among the aristocracy, natural scientists, doctors, lawyers, and educators often included "bottled embryos" (Duden 1991:41) or illustrations of human malformations including those of miscarried or stillborn fetuses (Hood 1991). What in an earlier era might have been prized as an example of what Francis Bacon called "nature erring[s]" (Hood 1991:3) are now sometimes prized as "my precious baby" specially chosen by God.

Much like mothers of children with disabilities who respond to the cultural devaluation of their children by asserting their specialness (Landsman

1999), bereaved parents also use the rhetoric of "specialness" to counter the rhetoric of reproductive failure and to transform a statistical abnormality into something meaningful. The rhetoric of the gift transforms "a mistake" or "random error" into a "special child," "precious gift," "part of a special plan."

In a piece written for her grandson, who died during delivery and who is now pictured as "our precious angel up in the sky," Judy Ward of Willington, Colorado, writes, "you are gone from us, we don't know why," but then immediately provides an explanation—the baby was special and was chosen for this reason by God. "You were so perfect in form and face that He took you to His heavenly place. . . . He knew you were a special boy and He needed you to spread His joy" (Ward 1987). Another woman describes how, following the stillbirth of her son, she asked, "God, why my son? Then I remembered, the verse: I go to prepare a place for you. . . . Maybe my son has a special mission or job to attend to. Maybe he is helping in the preparations and getting everything ready for me" (Rodgers 1987).[59]

The notion of "special parent" is also found, though to a lesser extent than that of "special children." The reason that the quality of specialness is not as frequently used to describe bereaved parents may be that, unlike their babies, these parents are not in themselves considered gifts. In addition, unlike the foster mothers described by Wozniak (1999), they do not typically portray themselves as especially gifted parents. And whereas parents of foster children or children with disabilities face the day in/day out problems of caring and providing for the "special needs" of their children (Wozniak 1999; Landsman 1999), parents of children who die at birth or shortly thereafter do not face these special challenges and, in fact, are spared/denied even the normal demands of parenting. The extra needs of foster children and the extended dependency of children with disabilities on their parents contrast sharply with the experience of bereaved parents whose children no longer need them at all.[60] Nevertheless, as the givers and/or recipients of "special gifts" the parents are sometimes also construed as "special." For example, the "precious parent" group philosophy described above ends with the assertion "We are precious parents." This quality is derived from their role as both giver and receiver of "precious" gifts.[61] Kim Maycock (1999), a contributor to the Pikes Peak *SHARING*, writes, "I must be a special mother. Because I have been set apart. Some mothers carry their children in their arms—but I carry you in my heart." In addition, the typological thinking whereby the specialness of Christ is extended by analogy to the dead babies is sometimes, though much less frequently, found with regard to parents. For example, in a piece entitled "I was chosen. . . . ," Kathy Casey, leader of a support group, tells of the eleven weeks that she carried her baby, "Jesse."[62] She writes, "It still amazes me how I was chosen—It was as if I was favored, blessed among women to carry him on his brief journey" (Casey 1995).

The other set of qualities most frequently attributed to the gifts associated with pregnancy loss are durability and inalienability, and these qualities speak to an implicit and sometimes explicit contrast between material and spiritual gifts. A number of bereaved parents use the term "lasting" to describe the gifts they received from their babies. For example, Perry-Lynn Moffitt describes her "babies' lasting gift to us" (Moffitt 1994:2); and Andrea D'Asaro concludes her piece "What I Learned from Baby Adam" with the assertion that "This landscape, where the people in my life come first, is my lasting gift from Adam" (D'Asaro 1996:3). Cathi Lammert wrote in the 1995 holiday issue of the *SHARE Newsletter* about her experience during the first holiday season after the loss of their son on December 4th. "We didn't get caught up with the hoopla of the season that year because our priorities changed. Perhaps this is the gift we experienced from little Christopher that season. Hold on to the love; this gift no one can take from you" (Lammert 1995). Whereas the embodied baby as gift can and indeed was taken away, these spiritual lessons are lasting and inalienable.

Others describe how their pregnancy loss prompted a revaluation of their preoccupation with worldly goods in favor of things of more enduring value. For instance, Kristen Ingle ends a Christmas poem in which she mourns the fact that she cannot buy gifts for her daughter who died at thirty-three weeks gestation saying, "But I know in my heart you have the best Christmas gift, for you are with Him and no better gift could I give" (Ingle 1981/2b). Similarly, in a poem entitled "Chanukah Is Here," a mother describes buying Chanukah gifts for others, and although she mourns the fact that her son is not there to enjoy the pretty Chanukah candles, she casts the fact that she need not buy for him in a positive light: "This year, again, once more, I won't be in a quandary of what to buy. I give you my love . . . for that is eternal" (Kravet 1994). The notion of "true" gifts also points to the contrast between the glittery seduction of this-worldly consumer goods, which are soon outdated or broken, and the gifts of the world hereafter, which are eternal. In a piece called "A Gift of Meaning," in the winter issue of *UNITE Notes*, Janis Heil writes, "This is a season of gifts. Too easily it becomes plastic, artificial time of hurried irritation, looking for a gift that will fit, that will be the right color, or that will not break" (Heil 1985/6). She contrasts these superficial preoccupations of the Christmas season with four "realizations" that are "gifts"—"gifts from a child to its parents, and gifts we can, in turn, share with others." They are "(1) that people are important, no matter how small or how short they live, (2) that love exists in ways previously unknown, (3) life is delicate and precious and must be handled with loving care, and (4) as others were there to help us in our need, we want to be there to help others in their need" (Heil 1985/6).

Conclusions: The Paradox of the Gift

I began this chapter with a description of the moral problem that pregnancy loss often poses for individuals in our culture. We have seen how members of pregnancy-loss support groups use the rhetoric of the gift to negotiate the double bind of either blaming themselves for the loss or admitting that they were not in control of themselves. Like the classic elegists analyzed by literary critic W. David Shaw, these popular elegists turn "the wounds [death inflicts] on our consciousness. . . . into performances that are self-therapeutic and cathartic" (Shaw 1994:8),[63] and they do so by playing with and elaborating on the paradoxical nature of the gift.

The rhetoric of the gift is a morally laden one, and in the United States, especially when applied to life and death issues, it is colored by a Christian understanding of the gift. Through the use of paradox, the rhetoric of the gift effects a series of transformative reversals, reversals that are intertextually related to the classical paradoxes of New Testament Christianity. As Kermode explains in his literary analysis of the book of Matthew, "the new world is to be a world of paradox. . . . Under this new authority the world is turned upside down." Probably the best known of such paradoxes are those presented in the Beatitudes in the Sermon on the Mount: blessed are the poor, the mourners, the meek, the persecuted, the reviled (Kermode 1987:391), but the Gospels are teeming with them. Other examples include the parable of the laborers in the vineyard told by both Mark and Matthew, "so the last shall be first, and the first last." All of these paradoxes lead up to, and are transfigured, by the greatest New Testament paradox of all—that death is not what it seems.

As Shaw has observed, paradox has been a key trope in Anglo-American elegies historically. Paradox is defined as a "statement which seems false but is true" (Shaw 1994:2), and in the case of pregnancy loss, the principal example is that a "loss" is really a "gain." But as Shaw points out, paradox is a contradiction that "invites a solution" and the way it accomplishes this is by inviting "the thinker to remove the contradiction to [another] plane of consciousness," to cause "the mind to expand" (Shaw 1994:2,3). The paradoxical nature of the gift permits the "transcendence of the antinomies" by "allow[ing] one term to preserve its identity in a wider context" (Shaw

1994:3). This is what Shaw means by the "'both-and' of a genuine paradox" (Shaw 1994:3). Thus, pregnancy loss can be, and indeed is, frequently understood to be simultaneously a great loss and source of significant gain. "Paradox" is defined as "a statement contrary to common belief," a statement that seems contradictory but may actually be true (Guralnik 1970), and members of pregnancy-loss support groups, like "the righteous" described by Kermode, "must defy common sense" if they are to find some good in the death of a wished-for child.

From this principal paradox stem other paradoxes. As we have seen, the rhetoric of the gift addresses the problem of control by reasserting parents' agency as givers. When parents construe the death of their baby as a sacrifice to God, or when they describe their newfound wisdom as gifts they have to offer other bereaved parents and the professionals who care for them, they are reinscribing the conventional status hierarchy that privileges givers. But, at the same time, in narratives of loss that construe the baby as a gift from God, and the purveyor of valuable spiritual lessons for the parents,[64] they are, paradoxically, casting themselves as receivers and doing so in a manner which challenges the moral superiority of giving. In these cases, being the recipient of such gifts is understood as both an indicator of moral worth and a pathway for enhanced spiritual/personal growth.

This paradoxical aspect of gift-giving is also found in Christian teachings. Despite the biblical instruction that it is "better to give than to receive," Christianity hinges on the fact that believers must accept Christ's gift of salvation. Christians are fundamentally receivers. It is God the Father who gives His children blessings and peace, and grants eternal life.

This paradoxical status of gift-giving is also evident in secular arenas of contemporary capitalist culture. In tribal societies, social status is both marked and made via the exchange of gifts with status accruing to the giver.[65] But in Anglo-American culture, the status ramifications of gift-giving are not so clear. It is well understood that more is better and getting more by means of gifts (for example, inheritance) remains one of the more morally acceptable routes for acquisition. Furthermore, one is not morally required to give what one has to others. For instance, as Hayden has observed, the queen of England very rarely gives anything away.[66] Given the mandate for capital accumulation, the "collections" of rich people, especially if they are men, are often respected and admired (Goldstein 1987).

The rhetoric of the gift also addresses the problem of self-blame and it does so in a way that does not jeopardize the treasured notion of control. If one understands the baby's birth and death to be a part of a master plan, one is no longer accountable for the event. The loss is still not understood to be a random statistical event but one controlled by God rather than the self. Unlike the unemployed male managers and air-traffic controllers Newman studied who fended off the impulse to self-blame with the notion of categorical fate, these bereaved parents are achieving similar results by turning to a form of hyperindividuality via the notion of a special, precious, chosen child.

These narratives highlight the ways in which the spiritually infused rhetoric of the gift provides a valuable cultural resource that is mobilized by bereaved parents in their efforts to make sense of a culturally dissonant experience. The dissonance of their experience is reframed in a way that promotes the possibility of spiritual and social reintegration.

CHAPTER 8

"Never Such Innocence Again": Irony, Nature, and Technoscience

In addition to the primary loss of a wished-for child, the experience of miscarriage, stillbirth, or infant death often entails other significant losses. Many bereaved parents report, and rue, a loss of innocence as well. For example, Kristen Ingle, a facilitator for UNITE's subsequent pregnancy-support group, writes of her pregnancy following the stillbirth of her daughter, "Gone is one's innocence. Gone is the thought that pregnancy means you will have a baby"; and Mary Cushing Doherty observes, "Never again will I capture the innocent joy." Another UNITE contributor, Susan Erling (1988), writes following a stillbirth, "My spiritual, trusting innocence or naivete is gone now, never to be recaptured"[1] and Mary Davis writes after a miscarriage, "I'll never hear those words again ['You are pregnant'] with the same naive joy, the same innocence of spirit. I know that in future pregnancies, there will be a cloud over the news and I'll wonder if it is going to happen again" (Davis 1988:25).

The title of this chapter, "Never Such Innocence Again," comes from the concluding line of one of the poems on which Paul Fussell (1975:19) based his account of The Great War as a critical turning point in the way we think about the world and engage in the art of memory.[2] In this chapter I discuss how contributors to pregnancy-loss support-group newsletters use irony to confront and come to terms with their loss/es, noting a number of similarities with the ways that the British soldiers described by Fussell dealt with untimely death and the loss of innocence in the wake of the Great War.[3]

Irony, Innocence, and Loss

In the previous chapter, we saw how bereaved parents made use of paradox, particularly the paradoxical nature of gifts and the Christian paradoxes surrounding worldly death and eternal salvation to deal with the moral problems that pregnancy loss posed for them and to reestablish a sense of themselves as virtuous and able. In this chapter we focus on the related concept of irony. Like paradox, its "sister trope," irony, also uses "context to question straightforward meanings or interpretations" (Huber 2001:190).[4] But where irony shows apparent truths to be contradictory or false, paradox is a statement that seems contradictory but may actually be true.[5] And whereas paradox invites "transcendence of the antinomies" by "allow[ing] one term to preserve its identity in a wider context" (Shaw 1994:3) in what to recall Shaw's phrase is the "'both-and' of a genuine paradox" (Shaw 1994:3), irony focuses on the gap between antimonies.

Although many believe that we now live in "an age of irony" (see Fernandez and Huber 2001:5), certain situations lend themselves to ironic treatment. As Fernandez and Huber note in the introduction to their collection on the anthropology of irony, "when things seem misaligned, disproportionate, unexpected, or out of place, philosophers, poets, and everyday people (including anthropologists . . .), often use irony to capture and comment on the pattern of contrasts they discern" (2001:1).

The ironies of pregnancy loss hinge on the fact that things did not turn out as expected. In literary theory, it is understood that the depth of irony corresponds in large part to the extent of the gap between what one expects will happen and what actually happens (e.g., Muecke 1969). Thus, if as Fussell suggests, "every war is ironic because every war is worse than expected" (1975:7), a pregnancy that ends in a miscarriage, stillbirth, or infant death also lends itself to ironic treatment, for the outcome is certainly worse, far worse, than what the would-be parents anticipated.

As Jorgenson et al. note, "expectations of success are intrinsic to any action; culturally defined criteria of excellence and rules of behavior are invoked in most value judgments. Thus it is always possible to mention these expectations ironically when they are frustrated, or to mention these norms ironically when they are violated, and to trust that hearers will share them and so recognize them for what they are" (Jorgensen, Miller, and Sperber 1984:115 quoted in Fernandez and Huber 2001:3n3). Indeed, "irony's structure invites its use to criticize failure rather than to praise success" (Jorgensen et al., cited in Fernandez and Huber 2001:3).

The ironies that feature in narratives of pregnancy loss, like those explored by Fussell's memoirists,[6] are "ironies of circumstance." Such ironies are of the type Booth, one of the primary literary theorists writing on irony, describes as stable and overt. Unlike covert ironies, which require an act of ironic reconstruction (the reader must figure out what the author *really* meant), the ironies of pregnancy loss described in support-group newsletters "require no special act of reconstitution or translation. They simply assert an irony in things or events that the speaker has observed and wants to share" (Booth 1974:236).[7]

Of at least equal phenomenological importance to the gap between what is expected and what happens is the depth of conviction with which the expected is expected. This is where the issue of innocence comes in. According to Muecke, "innocence" is one of three essential elements for irony. He maintains that it is not enough that "there should be a confrontation or juxtaposition of contradictory, incongruous, or otherwise incompatible elements and that one should be seen as 'invalidating' the other" (his first two essential elements) (1969:29). In addition, there should be an "innocent." He argues that "simple ignorance is safe from irony, but ignorance compounded with the least degree of confidence" (1969:30) makes one vulnerable for ironizing and he illustrates this with the following example: "it is not in itself ironic if a man fails to get the promotion he expects, but it would be if he had expressed his confidence of being promoted and still more if he had anticipated his promotion by buying a new car" (1969:32). Pregnancy loss fulfills both of these criteria. Most women (and this is especially evident in the narratives that document later losses which feature so prominently in the newsletters) feel confident that they are having a baby, share this confidence with others, and act on their confidence by planning their life around the expected birth and buying gifts for the baby. Muecke goes on to say that the irony is even greater if what happens "is the *contrary* of what is expected," for example, "if the man expected a promotion and had been demoted instead" (1969:32). The death of a baby certainly fits this bill as well. Muecke concludes that ironies "may be made more striking either by stressing the ironic incongruity or by stressing the ironic innocence" (1969:32).[8] Members of pregnancy-loss support groups routinely use both of these strategies, often simultaneously, in their narrative accounts.

For most, a pregnancy loss is experienced as an abrupt, unthinkable deviation from the natural, normal biological and social progression that pregnancies are expected to entail. Both the social transformation of 'would-be parents' to 'parents' that wanted pregnancies normally accomplish and the 'natural' biological progression of a pregnancy over a period of nine months (now commonly understood in terms of a popularized medical model of fetal development) that such pregnancies ordinarily enact are suddenly and unexpectedly abrogated and annulled.

Such a challenge to deeply held beliefs about the order or nature of things is, as Fussell observes, often associated with an "ironic mode of understanding." For instance, continuing with our WWI example, according to Fussell, the world before the war was "a different world," a world in which "the certainties were intact" (1975:21); with these certainties gone, "the dominating form of understanding" has been "essentially ironic" (1975:35). Similarly, for many members of pregnancy-loss support groups the loss of a wished-for baby is a watershed event after which they will never experience the world or think about their lives in the same way. Their life narratives become punctuated by the loss, and other experiences come to be understood as having occurred either before or after this pivotal event.

According to Fussell the thing that made "the Great War . . . more ironic than any before or since" was the fact that "it was a hideous embarrassment to the prevailing Meliorist myth which had dominated the public consciousness for a century" (1975:8). But the Meliorist myth that Fussell believes was irreparably shattered by the Great War is, as we saw in chapter 5, still very much alive and well at least with regard to biomedicine; and it is at least partially because of the myth of biomedical progress that so many members of pregnancy-loss support groups find irony such an appropriate interpretive means.

Yet, despite their belief in a technologically improved and improvable nature, members of pregnancy-loss support groups also appear to hold views of nature very much like those of the nineteenth-century Romantics, that is, of a sacred nature that reflects God's glory. This alternative concept of nature, rather than counteracting the effects of the myth of biomedical progress, compounds the discrepancy between expectation and reality and thus, like the myth of biomedical progress, also contributes to the adoption of an ironic form of understanding. But ultimately (and perhaps ironically), many individuals find the means for negotiating the challenge that a pregnancy loss poses to a view of nature as the work of a just and providential God in the Christian conception of redemptive nature. By placing the ironies of their situation in the context of what, depending on one's view, are the ironic or paradoxical reversals of Christian dogma, many bereaved parents are able to reconcile the gap between their expectations and reality and in so doing make their loss a meaningful one.[9]

"She Was Born/She Died":
The Terrible Irony of Pregnancy Loss

Though the discrepancy between the expectation that "modern technology" can now "fix" all problem pregnancies and the actuality of pregnancy loss certainly creates the potential for ironic understanding (chapter 5),[10] the primary irony of pregnancy loss is the conflation of birth and death, of the beginning of life with the end of it. Contributors to pregnancy-loss support-group newsletters capture this irony in their poems with lines like "I gave birth to death once" (Heil 1982); "Two years since I never met you" (Hoch 1988c); "A little boy of no days old" (Aunt Debbie 1991).

This primary irony is compounded and reinforced in many narratives by the memory of other minor ironic details. The organization of their memory into "a series of little ironic vignettes" (Fussell 1975:32) provides these individuals (much as it did for WWI soldiers) a structure by which to remember and give shape to events that have challenged the certainties of their world.

Oftentimes these details are of mundane aspects of daily living that give us a sense of comfort and security. The narratives show how fragile is our existence; how quickly such well-being can be destroyed. For example, much like the WWI memoirist who remembers passing a "young and cheerful lance-corporal of ours . . . making tea" in a trench "one warm afternoon," a moment before a single shell is dropped in the trench, which blows this young man to bits (Fussell 1975:32),[11] I was struck in listening to a woman describe her loss at a support-group meeting by the emphasis she put on the fact that her mother had prepared her favorite dish the night that she went into premature labor.[12]

In Linda Iacono's account it is childbirth classes, a ritual of preparedness routinely engaged by middle-class American couples, that highlight how impossible it is to prepare for something as unpredictable and out of our control as birth. She writes:

> The baby wasn't due until August, but we enrolled in childbirth classes in May, as they didn't give the classes in the summer. The first class was a trip through the labor and delivery floors at the hospital. It was on a Sunday afternoon and while we leisurely strolled around, little did we know that the very next day I would be using all these facilities, 12 weeks too soon (Iacono 1982).

In "dramatic irony," including "tragic irony," "the audience knows more about a character's situation than the character does, foreseeing an outcome contrary to the character's expectations, and thus ascribing a sharply different sense to some of the character's own statements" [or actions] (Baldick 1990b). In narratives of pregnancy loss a bereaved mother can become the audience to her own actions. It is she, the main character, who now, with the benefit of hindsight, can revisit earlier scenes with the privileged knowledge of how things turn out in the end.

A number of contributors to pregnancy-loss support-group newsletters openly declare the irony of their situations. Margaret Donato describes the stillbirth of her daughter six and a half years earlier as "the lifelong sorrow of a catastrophe whose misery is only matched by its irony" (Donato 1988). The year after the birth/death of her first daughter, who unaccountably was born "twelve weeks too soon" and survived only two hours, Linda Iacono got pregnant again. When she reached twenty-eight weeks she thought she was "home free" but soon after discovered the baby had died in utero, again for no apparent reason. She carried the dead baby two weeks while waiting to go into labor and writes of that experience, "It really seemed ironic, although the baby was dead it wasn't ready to be born" (Iacono 1982). Others like Susan Ashbaker (1994), while not using the term "irony," comment on the ironies of their circumstance. In Susan's case, she notes that it was her daughter's umbilical cord, "the very cord that nurtured and sustained her life for 37 weeks" that "took [her daughter's life] in the end."

Like other ironies of circumstance, the ironies of pregnancy loss derive largely from the fact that things did not turn out as expected. Many pieces, like the poem "Dead, Instead" by Barbara Daniels of Lenexa, Kansas, use a contrasting structure to index and accentuate these discrepancies:

> I bought birth announcements,
> I used death announcements.
> I bought dresses and dolls,
> I used casket and plot.
> I wanted congratulations and baby gifts,
> I got sympathy cards and flowers.
> I wanted a beautiful new life,
> I got ugly death.
> I wanted a new beginning,
> I got an old ending.
> I wanted mornings filled with joy,
> I got mornings filled with mourning (Daniels 1988a).

Although the tone of another poem by the same author is not as brutal, because the positives are cast as dreams rather than legitimate expectations,

Daniels uses a similar structure in her poem "Dream":

> I am drawn quietly to her grave to check on her,
> Just as I'd have been drawn quietly to her crib.
> I trim the grass around her marker,
> and dream of trimming bangs from her forehead.
> I place the flowers in her vase,
> and dream of placing ribbons in her hair (Daniels 1988c).

Clearly, in these cases, it is not just that things did not turn out as expected but that things did not turn out as they *should* have. Even after the loss, many insist that their expectations were justified and reasonable. Writing on the first anniversary of her daughter's death, Michell Chiffens (1991b) asserts, "I am a woman who longs for what should have been but isn't." Joanne Murphy writes of her daughter who died six days after birth while undergoing surgery:

> Today I celebrate my baby's first birthday, without my baby. I'm sitting on the rocking chair in her room holding her stuffed musical lamb, lamb chop, who is wearing her pink hat from the hospital. I should be holding my baby. It is so quiet. This is not supposed to be. It should be loud and noisy with cries, laughter and baby babbling (Murphy 1991).

And in a piece entitled "Forever Baby," Lauri Dykstra writes of her stillborn daughter:

> My baby should have lambs on her cradle,
> not on her headstone.
> My baby should be covered by a warm, fuzzy afghan,
> not by a cold blanket of earth.
> My baby should be taking afternoon naps in the nursery
> Not sleeping for all eternity in the cemetery.
> My baby should be playing on the floor with a Cabbage Patch doll.
> Not romping in heaven with the angels.
> My baby should be growing into a beautiful little girl.
> Not remaining my FOREVER BABY (Dykstra 1991).

The sense of "how things are supposed to be" expressed in these texts reflects a conviction in a natural order of things in which pregnancies (unless voluntarily aborted) progress in a unidirectional, inalterable, and inevitable way over a nine-month period until the baby is ready to be born—

a benign nature takes its course. Despite the medicalization of pregnancy and childbirth and the associated mechanistic approach to women's bodies and the birth process that have been so well documented in recent years, the narratives of pregnancy-loss support-group members suggest that, for these individuals, the idea that a wanted pregnancy results in the birth of a baby had been, at least up until the time of their loss, a great incontrovertible fact of nature.

Mother Nature and the Cruel Irony of Spring

The nature portrayed in these narratives of loss is not the wild, chaotic, unruly nature needing to be subdued by science that Merchant describes, but rather a Romantic vision of nature more akin to that normally associated with Wordsworth, Turner, and Ruskin (Merchant 1980).[13] These same nineteenth-century figures informed the way that British soldiers experienced and portrayed the Great War. But whereas many of the British officers of Fussell's study were aware of the literary and artistic origins of this Romantic view of nature, contributors to pregnancy-loss support-group newsletters are most probably not. (I have found no equivalent to the British soldier who wrote, "Was it Ruskin who said . . . ?" (Fussell 1975:54). Yet contributors to these newsletters use the Romantically freighted significance of nature to many of the same effects.

Where sunrise and sunset were the primary images of nature used by the British officers recalling the Great War (Fussell 1975:52–63), in narratives of pregnancy loss it is the annual cycle of the changing seasons that is most typically employed.[14] Where the WWI authors achieved an ironic effect by "juxtaposing a sunrise or sunset with the unlovely physical details of the war" (Fussell 1975:55),[15] pregnancy-loss support-group members achieve a similar effect by juxtaposing the traditional meanings associated with the seasons, particularly spring, with the details of their loss.[16]

Mary Wallace develops this theme in a poem entitled "Spring":

Spring is a cruel irony:
So much life—
While one is missing.
A spring sun,
Drying the tears of winter,
Makes sport of sadness.
Birds ridicule the silence
Of a season of grief (Wallace 1991).

Another example is found in a piece by Hope Abel, who lost a son at five months gestation and then a year later lost another son after having carried him to term. Of this second loss she writes,

> Our son was born in April just as the trees budded and the birds began to sing with joy as Spring arrived . . . after having our bundle of joy home only one week, our son was hospitalized. . . . Our son never did come home (Abel 1984).[17]

Janis Heil explores similar tensions in two spring issues of *UNITE Notes,* "The sights and smells of Spring remind us of newness and life. Yet often in our grief we feel rotted and dead inside" (1986); and in another piece, entitled "A Prayer for Spring" Heil (1984) asks God to "Help me face the harsh reality of sunshine and renewed life."

Feelings of isolation are a frequent theme at pregnancy-loss support-group meetings. Participants repeatedly comment on their fear that they were going crazy because no one seemed to understand or find appropriate the feelings they were having. Another frequent topic is how they feel unable to take part in holidays (Christmas, Mother's Day, etc.). Many women also report having strong aversions to seeing or being around pregnant women, and this makes it difficult for them to enjoy the company of their pregnant friends, or attend baby showers, or even to go out in public (let alone the obstetrician's office for a follow-up visit), where they are likely to bump into pregnant women.

But in addition to feeling isolated and excluded from society (such isolation being the defining characteristic of tragedy according to Northrop Frye (1973 [1957]:41), accounts like those discussed above, which contrast the new life and hope of spring with death and feelings of despair, portray subjects who feel isolated and out of step with nature as well.

Like the survivors of natural disasters (for example, the Buffalo Creek Flood described in Erikson's *Every Thing in Its Path*), many pregnancy-loss support-group members no longer feel in harmony with their physical environment and describe feeling that their loss changed their experience of themselves vis-à-vis nature. For example, Barbara Daniels compared her experience to living through a natural disaster. "When my baby died, I felt as though I was suddenly caught up in a tornado whirlwind, spinning me around in circles and upside down, finally dropping at lightning speed back to earth, but in a totally different place from where I was first picked up, and unable to find my way back to the place I had been before. That place no longer exists" (Daniels 1988b).

This feeling is also expressed, though in a somewhat different way, by contributors who liken themselves and/or their loss to freaks of nature (Layne 1994). For instance, Janis Heil (1981b) "felt like a freak" following the stillbirth of her daughter, and another woman describes feeling "freakish" after experiencing a "double loss" (first losing a baby to Sudden Infant Death Syndrome, then having a stillbirth).

Narratives of loss point to two, in some ways contradictory, senses in which pregnancy losses are sometimes construed as freaks of nature.[18] The first refers simply to the fact that pregnancy loss is not the norm. As discussed earlier, the tendency to think that pregnancy losses are uncommon is paradoxically exacerbated by the confluence of what are normally thought to be two diametrically opposed approaches to pregnancy and childbirth: a mechanical, technocratic, biomedical model and organic models either from earlier times or current countercultures (Davis-Floyd 1992). Despite undeniably important differences in the approach and forms of understanding, the rhetoric of midwifery and the home birth movement, like the rhetoric of biomedical progress, reinforces and encourages the expectation that a pregnancy, unless voluntarily aborted, will result in a baby.

A variation on this view of pregnancy loss as freakish is illustrated in a piece by Perry-Lynn Moffitt. Following a miscarriage, Perry-Lynn entered into her next pregnancy reassured by her obstetrician that although one loss was common, "most women who suffer an isolated miscarriage go on to carry healthy, full term pregnancies." She likened her miscarriage to lightning, a rather common destructive act of nature, and felt "armed with the hope" offered by the aphorism "lightning never strikes twice in the same place." When the subsequent pregnancy also ended in a miscarriage, that is, "lightning had indeed struck twice," she "felt singled out, no longer a statistical norm" (Moffitt 1994).

The second sense in which pregnancy losses are construed as freaks of nature derives from the medical and popular belief that many such losses (approximately 50 percent of first-trimester miscarriages according to Pizer and Palinski 1980:83)[19] are the result of genetic abnormalities. Up until quite recently the medical explanations for miscarriage or stillbirth focused on human malformations, either of the woman's uterus, or more commonly of the fetus. *Coping with a Miscarriage*, a lay book published in 1980, which is distinctive in the level of detailed attention it gives to causes, devotes an entire chapter to "Genetic Causes of Miscarriage." All "Other Causes" are relegated to a single chapter (Pizer and Palinski 1980).

Whereas in the first sense it is the loss that is characterized as "freakish," in this case, it is the fetus/baby to which the term "freak" refers. Interestingly, once the fetus is defined as freakish, the loss can be defined as "natural." One hears regularly at pregnancy-loss support-group meetings reference to the idea that miscarriages are nature's way of taking care of itself (although many resist the framing of the event by others as "for the best").[20] As Pizer and Palinski explain,

> The theory states that a spontaneous abortion is nature's way of protecting humankind from the consequences of the mistakes that are sometimes made at conception. It maintains that since conception is very complicated, mistakes do occasionally happen. Since small mistakes can cause serious abnormalities, it is the job of the woman's body to keep mankind from perpetuating these mistakes (Pizer and Palinski 1980:56).

Although this view of things may offer comfort to some, it does so at a cost. The idea that one has produced and is carrying within a "freak," a "monster," a "mistake" so serious that humankind must be protected from it, is, needless to say, a chilling one.

In addition to the juxtaposition of their child's death with the thoughts conventionally associated with spring, members of pregnancy-loss support groups often use abnormal weather to convey the freakishness of their experience. For example, Dotti Brown writes of her daughter who survived one week on a respirator:

> The funeral was on Veteran's Day. . . . Rain had been forecast that day but instead, there was a freak snowstorm, totally uncharacteristic for early November. But then everything about Clare's birth and death seemed unreal, from her unexpected birth on Halloween night to her deformed face, caused by a condition called Trisomy 13 (Brown 1988).

Similarly, Lisa Casimer begins her account of her daughter's life/death by saying that "Nothing about Sarah was ordinary" and in describing her daughter's funeral mentions the abnormal weather that day: she "was buried on a bright, sunny day (uncharacteristic of winter in Chicago)" (Casimer 1987). Carl Jones of Bakersfield, California, remarks on the fact that his son was born on the same day as Halley's Comet and explains how Mark Twain, who apparently was also born on the same day as Halley's Comet, used to refer to himself and the comet as "two uncommon freaks of nature." He goes on to note the additional irony: whereas Twain had "planned to go out the same way," that is, seventy-six years later, their son "came and left with Halley's comet . . . the very same year" (Jones 1987).

Both of these literary devices (juxtaposing spring and death and the association of an abnormal birth experience with other abnormal natural occurrences) make ironic use of the standard techniques of pathetic fallacy, where nature is attributed sentiments that are in keeping with the dramatic action (as in Ruskin's famous example from a ballad by Kingsley of "the cruel, crawling foam" over which men retrieve the body of a young woman who had drowned). In the case of the juxtaposition of spring with death, the standard portrayal of nature in "solemn sympathy" with human endeavors is inverted. The association of abnormal weather and other unusual natural occurrences with the contributors' abnormal birth experience, on the other hand, constructs a parallelism between the actors and nature but does so by making freaks of both.[21]

Redemptive Nature

Despite the challenges that a pregnancy loss poses to these individuals' beliefs about mother nature, and God and the relationship between the two, nature continues to function as a spiritually healing force for many bereaved parents.

Accounts of pregnancy loss frequently portray the bereaved parents turning to nature as a source of comfort in their loss. It was just such an image that first drew my attention to the importance of nature in narratives of pregnancy loss. The first image that appears after the title of the film *Some Babies Die* is of a man walking alone among trees. As the camera moves back, the viewer sees that the man is on a golf course. This struck me as an incongruous image for the start of a film on infant death. As the man gazes off toward the horizon he describes the deaths of his two stillborn sons. Later we learn that he is also a physician, and that, as a result of his personal experience of loss, he helped to set up a perinatal-loss support team at the hospital where he works in Australia.

The image of the introspective mourner alone in nature is repeated later in the film with a view of a bereaved mother going for a solitary walk along a lake, a common theme in narratives published in pregnancy-loss newsletters. For example, one woman writes of how after the burial of their daughter (born at twenty-four weeks gestation) she asked her husband "if we could go to the beach to talk. . . . We sat on a large log, watched the waves roll upon the sand and cried our hearts out" (McGinness 1988:27). Another woman tells of how in response to the return of profound grief eleven months after the stillbirth of their daughter she "wanted to escape to a tree, a beautiful green meadow" (Gana 1984).

Such practices, though now common, are a relatively recent occurrence in the evolving, sometimes contradictory, Judeo-Christian attitudes toward nature.[22] According to Nash, early and medieval Christianity thought of wilderness as a place where "the powers of evil" dwelt (1982:17), but also maintained the idea that the wild country could be "a place of refuge and religious purity" (1982:18), at least for hermits and monks. By the eighteenth century a full-fledged appreciation of nature had emerged in Europe; but, as Williams describes, it was the British landed gentry who developed the neopastoral ideal along with their own "elevated sensibility" with which to appreciate the "pleasing prospects" of their estates and the sublimity of the "wild places" they toured (1973:121). The contemporary North American middle-class view that everyone, not just religious specialists or social elites, may find wisdom and solace in nature is clearly a relatively new one.[23] Halloran links this North American "idea of drawing 'inspiration' from direct communion with nature" with "the transformation of nineteenth-century rhetoric from an art based in the wisdom of communal consensus to one based on the individual's unique personal experience" (1993:231–232).[24]

While self-representations of bereaved parents communing with nature depict an important connection between these individuals and nature (a connection that may have been threatened by the loss), such depictions portray nature, as it was so often in eighteenth- and nineteenth-century British poetry, as "a retreat and solace from human society and ordinary human consciousness" (Williams 1973:129).[25] In other words, though these individuals may feel at one with nature, they still feel isolated from society.[26]

Eventually, though, most deal with their losses in a way that enables them to take up their everyday lives and to feel once more a part of their communities. The UNITE and SHARE newsletters suggest that the Christian narrative of redemption helps many to achieve this sense of reintegration.

In many of the accounts that are written some time after the loss, the feelings of isolation and despair expressed in earlier accounts become transformed into one moment in a spiritual journey—a journey from certainty to doubt and then ultimately to renewed and strengthened certainty. This journey of salvation and rebirth is frequently portrayed as one both paralleled in and learned from nature. As Frye noted, the pastoral images of sheep and pleasant pastures have been closely associated with the idyllic mode (a mode that normally portrays the incorporation of the central character into society), and such imagery is often used in literature "as it is in the Bible, for the theme of salvation" (1973:43). We find pastoral imagery employed in just such a way in the following account of the memorial services one couple held for their stillborn daughter four-and-a-half months after her birth/death:

> On a sunny September morning we drove out to the valley, passing the strawberry fields and cow pastures. We went to a state park that had an open field surrounded by a swiftly flowing river and towering cliffs. We walked to the center of the field and stood there in the wet grass with the sun warming our bodies. In a circle we celebrated the life we had (Cruickshank-Chase 1988).

The redemptive capacity of nature is even clearer in poems that relate the transformation of the seasons:

> We must live through the weary winter,
> If we would value the spring
> And the woods must be cold and silent,
> Before the robins sing.
>
> The flowers must be buried in darkness,
> Before they can bud and bloom.
> And the sweetest and warmest sunshine,
> Comes after the storm and gloom.
>
> So the heart, from the hardest trial,
> Gains the purest joy of all.
> And from the lips that have tasted sadness,
> The sweetest songs will fall.
>
> For as peace comes after suffering
> And love is reward of pain
> So, after earth, comes heaven
> And out of our loss, the gain (Unknown 1988).

Another contributor writes:

> You have to believe the buds will grow,
> Believe in the grass in the days of snow.
> Ah, that's the reason a bird can sing
> On his darkest day he believes in Spring (Mallock 1985).

Margaret Donato writes in an open letter six-and-a-half years after the still-birth of her daughter:

> Lessons to be learned when birth turns into death, just as death turns to birth, as these trees here shedding the last of their spring

and summer life will bloom again. Mothers who suffer those losses stand in the shade of an actuality where hurt and anguish can turn itself into love (Donato 1988:33).

In other words, in these later narratives, the ironic distance between how things ought to be and how they are that had been expressed through the jarring juxtaposition of spring and death is bridged by the paradoxical portrayal of death (even such an untimely one) as an essential part of nature. By situating death in nature in this way, and by defining nature as essentially a reflection of God's triumph over death, the loss becomes both intelligible and tolerable. In this Christian concept of redemption, Christ redeems humankind from the senseless cycles of death and rebirth that belong to the realm of a fallen nature. Indeed, in the narratives of loss examined here, the seasonal cycle is in fact routinely transformed into a linear narrative always culminating in spring (and implicitly the resurrection).

The symbolism of redemptive nature is also used in a common pregnancy-loss support-group ritual—the planting of a tree as a living memor-

Tree-planting ceremony during 1989 Pregnancy and Infant Loss Awareness Weekend in Washington, DC.

ial.[27] One of the activities of the October 1989 Pregnancy and Infant Loss Awareness Weekend in Washington, D.C., was a tree-planting ceremony. In addition to such collective rituals of tree plantings, many contributors tell of planting some sort of living memorial in their yards (see chapter 6). In a handbook on organizing pregnancy-loss rituals compiled by the founder of SHARE, Sister Jane Marie Lamb offers suggested scripts for tree-planting ceremonies that make explicit use of this symbolism:

> We are aware of the symbolism of the tree's life and death cycle according to the seasons. In spring new life follows the death evident in winter, summer bears fruit and autumn again brings colorful beauty. Each season has its own gift. We accept the gift of each season, just as we appreciate the gift of each child however short his or her life may have been (Lamb 1988b).

This imagery does more than suggest an acceptance of life as it comes ("to every thing there is a season"); it offers the hope of death defeated and transformed:

> May we come to know more fully in visiting this place and our tree, that nothing dies, rather life is transformed into new life. . . .

> We have placed their names within the soil around our tree. As the paper degrades and becomes one with the soil, our tree will be nourished to grow and bring forth new life (Lamb 1988b).

In addition to the analogy between the survivor's journey and evolving understanding of her/his loss, analogies are made between the particular tree (or type of tree) and the particularities of dead children, or if a familial rather than collective memorial, of a particular child (cf. chapter 6). Lamb explains why she sees the Bradford Pear as a particularly appropriate tree for pregnancy-loss memorial services. "Each tree, [like each child], has its own gift. The Bradford Pear tree was chosen for its special qualities and gifts: The Bradford pear remains small, does not produce fruit, has blossoms which are pure and sweet and remind us of innocence, requires little care just as 'the children who had died cannot receive the care you longed to give them'" (1988a:7).

In addition to the seasons (and trees portrayed therein), the images of flowers and snowflakes, rainbows and butterflies,[28] frequently appear in narratives of loss (see below and also chapters 6, 7, and 9). These images, which stress the transience of nature, often serve to naturalize the loss.

Artist: Wendi Hunt, Middletown, CT, October 1992. "For all the babies who have fallen from the tree." Yale New Haven Hospital and Yale University School of Medicine.

Flowers were a common symbol for dead children in the nineteenth-century consolation literature examined by Simonds and Katz Rothman (1992:54), and they remain symbols today.[29] During the memorial service at the end of one of UNITE's conferences, bereaved parents were invited to pin felt flowers with the names of their dead babies to a banner. In a poem entitled "A Little Flower," baby David's great grandma writes, "One day God walked in His earthly garden. . . . he saw a bud, not yet opened but beautiful inner strength and vigor. This, he thought was too beautiful to leave wither on the vine, and stopping, He gently plucked our baby, to live eternally in His heavenly bouquet" (Taylor 1993; cf. also Golden 1994).

This flower/child analogy was also elaborately developed in a letter written by Kathy Kuhn of New Tripoli, Pennsylvania, to her stillborn son one year after his death:

The daffodils in our woods bloomed this week. The same week that you died. I took a walk today, down to our stream, and on my way I

Felt banner representing dead babies displayed at a UNITE Memorial Service.

picked one of those "wild" daffodils. It was cool and damp, just like you were when I held you. It felt small and fragile in my hands, just as you did. It smelled sweet and felt soft on my cheek, just like you did. It was beautiful and perfectly formed, you were too, Brian. I held it for a short time, then I had to let go. I dropped the daffodil in the stream and watched it drift away . . . just as you did (Kuhn 1984).

And Lisa Casimer (1987) tells of how she buried Sarah with "a small bunch of pink Sarina 'roses.' We chose to have those rare and tiny blossoms buried with Sarah because like her, and unlike all of the other flowers, those little roses were too precious and fragile to make it on the outside."

The fragility of flowers is also sometimes used to naturalize the parents' experience. Peggy Kociscin writes:

A blossom looks so delicate,
So fragile to the touch;
As if the least disturbance
Could crucify . . . and crush.
Tossed about and battered . . .
with petals bruised and torn (Kociscin 1993).

She concludes with, "How well I understand its plight. My life, it seems, is but a blossom, Blowing in the Wind" (Kociscin 1993).

Snowflakes are another natural symbol of transience sometimes employed by bereaved parents. As a fund-raiser in 1995, SHARE sold holiday greeting cards that depicted a little girl outdoors trying to catch a snowflake. Inside is a poem about the pleasures of the holiday season and how those pleasures end. The final line is "there's a place in our hearts where the memories live on" and on the inside flap is a space to write the name of a dead baby: "In Peaceful Remembrance of _____ (picture of snowflake)." The child is thus analogized to the fleeting, culturally valued pleasures of the holiday season and to the lovely transience of snowflakes.

Rainbows and butterflies also make good symbols of a fleeting life—they can be here one minute and gone the next. These two symbols are also particularly apt because of their location in the air/sky (that is, close to heaven). In addition, the transformative character of rainbows and butterflies, changing as they do from something with a negative valence, that is, dark, violent storm and creepy, crawly bug to something with a positive valence, makes them particularly appropriate symbols of redemptive nature (cf. chapters 6 and 7).

Cathy Hintz (1988), you will recall, combined the symbolism of snowflakes and rainbows in her memorial practice of hanging crystal snowflakes, which produced rainbows in her kitchen.[30] Teresa Page of Rockford, Illinois, wrote a poem entitled "Robins and Rainbows" for the "child" she miscarried at nine weeks gestation, to whom they gave the gender-neutral name of Robin:

Robins and rainbows
Always turn our thought to the hope of spring
May the rainbow of hope and joy that our Robin gave to us always
turn our hearts to God in thanksgiving (Page 1987).

In addition to the above-mentioned qualities, rainbows are particularly appropriate symbols in the context of pregnancy loss because of their reference to God's covenant following the flood. This reference seems to be most frequent with regard to subsequent children. For instance, Linda Rabinowitz (1983) says of children born following a loss, "They're a rainbow after a storm," and from 1984 to 1987 a drawing of a rainbow and dove with olive branch illustrated the "Baby News" section of *SHARE Newsletters* that reports subsequent live births of members.

Butterflies have also been common illustrations for both newsletters and in fact sometimes appear in conjunction with images of rainbows, as in the drawing used as the illustration for Rabinowitz's poem. From 1984 (and perhaps before) through 1987, the front page of the *SHARE Newsletter* and frequently the two pages of poetry that followed were illustrated with hand-drawn butterflies. *UNITE Notes* used a series of hand-drawn butterflies as a runner separating the poems in their first issue. Butterflies have continued to be a frequent choice of the editors of both newsletters[31] (see examples in chapter 6).

Butterflies are sometimes explicitly used as a symbol of redemption in narratives of loss. An advertisement for "Mizpah butterfly pins . . . beautiful pewter pins symbolizing hope after death" appears in a 1988 issue of the *SHARE Newsletter*. They are used in a similar fashion in the iconography of organ-transplant procurement (Sharp 2001:120). This association between butterflies and triumph over death has apparently been a part of popular American culture for some time. A 1836 issue of the American women's magazine *The Lady's Book* included a short notice entitled "A Striking and Beautiful Emblem of Immortality," which reported that "The Greeks sculptured the butterfly upon their tombstones." The author suggests that "the Creator appointed insect transformations to excite the sentiment in the human heart, of death being only one step in the path of life" (Unknown 1836).[32]

Healing Grief cover image.

In several instances bereaved mothers liken themselves to butterflies. Janis Heil utilizes the metaphor of the butterfly's transformation in describing her experience of personal transformation as a result of her loss:

> let me unfold and grow, fresh and anew, from this cocoon of grief that has been spun around me. . . . Give me strength to break out of the cocoon of my grief. But may I never forget it as the place where I grew my wings, becoming a new person because of my loss (Heil 1984).

More recently (2001), Janis has used the metaphor of a butterfly to depict how, now twenty-one years after her stillbirth, she remembers her loss. "The quality of my remembering on this anniversary . . . was different than ever before—my mind 'lit' on the memories. The clear and striking image of a butterfly came before me, lighting on a remembrance most gently, then flittering on" (Keyser 2001).

Another woman writes, "a trip to the cemetery helped me feel alive again. What more fitting a place to leave one's cocoon and to fly freely away" (Gana 1984).

Butterflies are also sometimes used to represent deceased children. Nanette Wagner of Cincinnati, Ohio, ends a poem addressed to God by saying, "She was a little cocoon to us. She'll be a butterfly for You" (Wagner 1984), and a seven-year-old boy writes in a piece addressed to his deceased little sister, "You were like a caterpillar who turned into a beautiful butterfly then went to heaven to be with God" (Jordan 1988). As you may recall from chapter 1, at UNITE's annual conference in 1991 participants were invited to write the name/s of their "baby/ies" on tissue-paper butterflies, which were hung on a tree during the ritual of remembrance that culminated the conference.[33]

Several of these elements of nature are understood to be "signs" from the dead babies to their parents. In a special issue of *SHARING* on "love signs," Raye Diaz (2001) describes how after her daughter died from a metabolic disorder following five months in the NICU, she has sent her and her husband many signs of her love through butterflies. "Whenever we are having a difficult moment in our grief, a butterfly seems to go by." In that same issue Jami VanDer Meer's (2001) poem called "Signs" begins "My angel sends a butterfly." Following stanzas report on rainbows and snowflakes sent as a sign from this same angel. Other examples of such signs include "a little pink cloud" (Pines 2001), "a tiny perfect white feather" (Lykens 2001), both of which clearly are metaphors for the child, in their color (either gender-coded, or representing innocence), size, location in the sky/heavens, and transience.

The Politics of Irony

Irony has its victims and the perfect victim for ironies are "innocents" like the women and men who turn for help to pregnancy-loss support groups.[34] As Jorgensen et al. (1984:115) observe, "In ridiculing a proposition, the ironist ridicules whoever holds or held that proposition to be true." In the case of pregnancy-loss narratives, the ironist is also the victim. Through her use of irony, the narrator may ridicule herself for her "naive" acceptance of propositions like "a pregnancy means you will have a baby," or that because "of our prenatal care, . . . we would experience a normal pregnancy" (Casimer 1987), or that good amniocentesis results means you are assured a healthy baby, or that after reaching a certain point in a pregnancy you can relax in confidence, or that after birth, a premature infant who has been given a good medical prognosis will live, or that babies only die if there is clearly something wrong, or if they are from another country, or born to bad mothers who don't take care of themselves and abuse drugs.

According to Baldick (1990b:114), the additional knowledge that the audience possesses in ironic dramas gives those in-the-know a "sense of detached superiority." It is true that in ironic accounts of pregnancy loss bereaved parents do look back with the benefit of hindsight (and a loss of innocence) and see how "little did we know" (Iacono 1982). And in the future, women who experienced a pregnancy loss may be horrified to see others blithely enter into a pregnancy without this "privileged" knowledge, or may feel appalled by the hubris of women who plan a pregnancy so that their child's birthday will not conflict with holidays or other family member's birthdays, or so that the birth will not interfere with vacation plans. Yet, any sense of "detachment" or "superiority" that this privileged knowledge brings is tempered by the fact that the poor dupe in these narratives, who does not know what the narrator and audience know, is the narrator herself.[35] Furthermore, given the sentimentally freighted maternal discourse of pregnancy loss, which valorizes the special qualities of children, including innocence, knowledge of "how things really are" is not necessarily deemed "superior." Indeed, as we have seen, rather than simply welcoming this new knowledge as superior to their old, flawed knowledge, this change is frequently cast as "a loss of innocence," another loss to be mourned. Narratives of loss express and reflect a cultural tension between the value of hard-nosed realism, seeing things as they *really* are whether the picture is a pretty one or not, and the American moral mandate for optimism and our penchant for happy endings. As discussed in chapters 2 and 7, the knowledge that, even if one is a good, morally upright, hardworking, well-disciplined, middle-class American, things do not always work out as one plans runs counter to a profound, broad-based ideological commitment to success and narratives of linear progress.

This tension helps to explain why it is that although there is an "edge" (Hutcheon 1994) to the ironies deployed in narratives of pregnancy loss, one rarely finds what Fernandez and Huber (2001) call the "militant forms of irony," sarcasm, satire, and parody. The ironic accounts of pregnancy loss have more in common with what they call, in an extension of Burke's concept, "true anthropological irony," which shares the generic "sense of the discrepant," but does not lend itself to "malice and parody" (Fernandez and Huber 2001:22).

This brings us to another dimension of ironic expression. As a number of authors have noted, irony runs the risk of contributing to a "politics of complicity" (Fernandez and Huber 2001:7). Given irony's association with postmodernity, the political critiques of one, to a certain extent, can be applied to the other. For example, Fernandez and Huber (2001:16) question the efficacy of irony deployed by the impoverished Mexican tomato workers documented in the ethnography *The Force of Irony* (Torres 1997) and point out that irony may contribute to a "politics of accommodation" rather than helping the workers to improve their lot. But unlike these tomato harvesters, for whom much could be done to ameliorate their living conditions and health, "accommodation" is perhaps the most "pragmatic" outcome possible for members of pregnancy-loss groups. As Bakhtin observes, "under conditions of . . . futility, irony can serve as a special substitute for silence" (Bakhtin 1986 quoted in Fernandez and Huber 2001:5). Think again of Barbara Daniel's poem (quoted above). For her, as for many other members of pregnancy-loss support groups, the alternative to ironic acknowledgment of the irreparable gap between what she longed for, and no doubt expected, and what she got may have been silence. Given our cultural taboo prohibiting the acknowledgment of things that don't work out, voicing these gaps and using the powerful, cutting trope of irony to do so can perhaps be understood as a political act in and of itself.

In addition, as Fernandez and Huber (2001:4) point out, "while it may be most common to use irony to criticize someone or something for not meeting expectations or cultural norms, . . . irony is also sometimes used to question those expectations or cultural norms." Irony is "bound up in categorizing-conceptualization processes" and can be used by "those who have in one way or another been left out of or disfavored by a privileging set of conceptualizations and distinctions" to "contest . . . the adequacy of such categories" (Fernandez and Huber 2001:9). This can be seen in the way some bereaved mothers use ironic contrasts between normative expectations about pregnancy and birth and the reality of pregnancy loss to challenge the norms about what it takes to be included in the category "mother." Take, for example, the following two poems, which use a structure of ironic contrasts similar to that used by Daniels in her poem "Dead Instead." The first is a poem by Bonita Martin (1995) entitled significantly, "I'm Still a Mother." Martin begins and ends with a paradoxical assertion that even though it may not appear to others that she is a mother, she is in fact just that. In contrast to Daniels, who is unrelenting in her focus on the brutal distance between what she hoped for and what she got, Martin intersperses stanzas stressing the ironic gap between expectations and reality with paradoxical stanzas that challenge the meaning of that gap (Martin 1995):

> I would have had you today
>> I have you
> I would have cried for joy
>> I cried for help
> They would have announced "it's a boy"
>> I had a boy
> All the excitement and happiness
>> All depressed and alone
> Everyone congratulating us
>> No one was there
> Balloons, cards and flowers
>> just lights, doctors, and needles
> Your little scream lighting up the whole room
>> quiet and silent
> 7 pounds, brown eyes, black hair
>> 7 oz., no hair, eyes closed.
> Would you like to hold him?
>> I held him
> I would have said "I love you"
>> I said "I'm sorry"
> You would have went home with us today
>> Now I stand over your grave with loneliness, hurt, pain, anticipation, suffering, tears, with all of my body and soul, with all my love.
>> I still have a baby boy today.

Despite her paradoxical insertions/assertions, the weight of the poem is with the ironies, both in terms of sheer numbers (eight ironic stanzas to four paradoxical ones), and in the structure of the penultimate verse, which is written in the present tense. Compared to all the other verses, this one is much longer, weighted down metaphorically with all the things she has, "loneliness," "hurt," "pain," "suffering," "tears" (and even her body and soul); visually/aurally overwhelming the final paradoxical assertion that what she has is "a baby boy."

Judy Smith extends this technique further in a piece called "We Wanted a Baby," describing her stillborn son. She lists a series of discrepancies between what they wanted and expected and what they got, but, in this case, Smith consistently structures the contrasts to show that what they got, though unexpected, is at least as good as, and in some cases better than, what they had hoped for, even if on the surface this does not seem to be the case:

> We wanted a baby,
> but had an angel. . . .
> We wanted to watch our baby grow,
> instead our child helped us grow. . . .
> We wanted to hold our baby in our arms,
> instead we hold him in our hearts.
> We wanted to be a normal family;
> We have an angel. . . .
> We wanted to be parents
> and we are (Smith 1997).

This is a political act, a protest, a heterodox insistence. Here the unfairness is shifted from the fact of the death, about which there is nothing now to be done, to the unfairness of social categories that exclude women whose babies died from the motherhood club, from enjoying the social recognition that motherhood brings.

Smith's poem provides a vivid example of the way paradox can "take the very disparities that irony disparage[s], and give them a positive—even transcendent—twist" (Huber 2001:190). According to Booth, "irony is usually seen as something that undermines clarities, opens up vistas of chaos, and either liberates by destroying all dogma or destroys by revealing the inescapable canker of negation at the heart of every affirmation" (1974:ix). As we have seen, for many pregnancy-loss support-group members, the irony of pregnancy loss does appear to have "undermined clarities, opened vistas of chaos" in challenging deeply held beliefs about the power of biomedicine and the order of a benign nature, the virtues of innocence, one's confidence in the adequacy of one's own understanding of the world. But the narratives of loss published in support-group newsletters indicate that many have found alternatives to the two subsequent scenarios sketched by Booth. Many draw on the rich rhetorical resources that Christianity provides. Christian dogma presents ready-made a framework for dealing with discrepancies between our cultural models of nature, of science, of a normal life course and the harsh reality of pregnancy loss. As Sontag has observed, there is no Christian tragedy. "In a world envisaged by . . . Christianity, there are no free-standing arbitrary events . . . , every crucifixion must be topped by a resurrection. Every disaster or calamity must be seen . . . as leading to a greater good" (Sontag 1966:137).

Fussell, following Frye, was correct, then, in positing a close connection between ironic and mythic modes of understanding, even though Frye's rationale for doing so (a theory of cyclical history) is ill conceived. The relationship, at least when it comes to ironic tragedy like that explored here, lies in the very preconditions to ironic understanding. It is precisely because of deeply held beliefs, beliefs that are not confirmed in life, that irony comes about in the first place.

Sontag has taken issue with Abel's assertion that one cannot create tragedy without accepting some implacable values as true. Narratives of pregnancy loss support Sontag's view that "It is not the implacability of values which is demonstrated by tragedy, but the implacability of the world" (1966:136).

CHAPTER 9

"I Will Never Forget You": Trauma, Memory, and Moral Identity

A Traumatic Experience

Many members of pregnancy-loss support groups experience their loss as traumatic. Brison (1997) begins her piece "Outliving Oneself: Trauma, Memory, and Personal Identity," from which I adapt my subtitle, with the observation that "survivors of trauma frequently remark that they are not the same people they were before being traumatized." Though originally used to refer to "a physical wound (a . . . break in the body produced by an outside force or agent)," trauma has come to be used to describe "invisible injuries inflicted on the mind, self, or soul" (Young 1996:89). Along the same lines, Hacking describes trauma as "painful experiences that corrupt . . . one's sense of oneself" (Hacking 1996:75).

Pregnancy loss clearly poses challenges for would-be parents' sense of themselves. As Kristen Ingle put it, "Once you have had a child die, you are never the same" (Ingle 1986/7a). Not surprisingly, this appears to be especially true for women. Lois Dubin (1995/6:68), a professor of religion at Smith College, recalls that when at age thirty-four, after eight years of marriage, she lost her first two pregnancies at eleven and seven weeks gestation, "my husband and I were saddened . . . but my despair was overwhelming and the sense of death afflicted me uniquely. . . . Swirling fears threatened to engulf me." Marion Cohen vividly conveys a number of the "invisible injuries" she suffered as the result of repeated reproductive traumas in three poems published in the first volume of *UNITE Notes*. In her "Kerin-self-image poem," she confides, "I don't exactly blame myself./I don't exactly feel less of a woman/and I'm not exactly ashamed of my body . . . ," while in her piece "Intensive Care Nursery" she worries, "I forgot to explain to her that it was my body that betrayed her, not me," and, in "Poem to an Impossible Fetus," she wonders, "did I smell bad?" A similar sentiment was shared with me by UNITE facilitator Michell Chiffens. Michell remembers, "after the birth of our baby and subsequent burial I felt my baby didn't want me as a mommy and she asked God to let her stay with Him" (personal communication, 2000).[1]

In addition to feelings like these of fear and guilt, of having been rejected as unsuitable or unworthy by one's baby or by God, and/or of having proven oneself untrustworthy, incompetent, and unwomanly, many members of pregnancy-loss support groups express a "corrupted" sense of themselves in terms of a sense of fragmentation.[2] Frequently, bereaved parents say that they feel they have lost a part themselves.[3] For example, Laura Brown (1985), whose son died four days after birth due to meconium aspiration, wrote, "Part of me is missing. The part that was you. I'll never be whole again."[4] Gail Fasolo (2000) says of her daughter's stillbirth, "It made me less than whole," and Barb Knopf (1999:2) explains, "There is a hole inside of me where my son should be and it can not be filled." While such feelings may be especially acute for women, they are not confined to them. Four months after the loss of his son, David Nagele (1986a) gave his wife a poem in which he wrote, "we have lost a part of ourselves." Many others describe broken hearts. For example, Erica Frank (1999), whose twins died at twenty-two weeks due to a placental abruption, feels that her "heart will be forever torn," and Peter Cornell-Drury (2000), founder of a support group for fathers of stillborn children called "StillFathers" in Washington (www.stillfathers.org), describes the birth and unsuccessful attempt at resuscitating his daughter as a "trauma," which created an "immense hole in [his] heart" that he cannot "repair."

Another common experience of those who undergo trauma, including members of pregnancy-loss support groups, is an altered sense of time. For example, Barb Knopf (1999) says of the three weeks her son survived, "It was a little capsule of time that now seems so awesome and monumental and yet, so hard to believe it was real." Ann Bachman (1999:2) describes how, during the lengthy period that she carried her twins after one had been diagnosed with a condition incompatible with life outside the womb, she "felt like I was living in a different time zone."[5] Numerous contributions to the newsletters are simply titled "Time" (e.g., Hoch 1987b). In a poem by that name, Karen Gardner (1986), of Scottdale, Pennsylvania, describes her experience of time passing at dramatically different speeds during the distinct phases of her pregnancy and loss. Time passed quickly while her pregnancy was going well ("Time-passes quickly-swiftly speeds along./ Waiting a new, sweet life to call our own"); but crept during the month that transpired between when they learned that the baby had died in utero and her delivery. "Time-so slow, so agonizing-painful, each second takes forever. You forgot to move—to turn, to play, day after endless, endless day." Time slowed to a standstill with the stillbirth and then gradually, with the slow passage of time from day to day, began to move again. The poem ends with the reassurance that despite the resumption of the normal movement of time, "we'll love you forevermore."

An altered sense of time is also evident in the way many bereaved parents rewrite their life story with the pregnancy loss as a turning point. Much as events like Pearl Harbor and September 11 provide a "watershed," "pivotal moment," "great divide" for collective, national narratives, pregnancy loss is experienced by many as a "moment that divides time" into preloss and postloss eras (White 1992:4). For example, Mickey Hoch writing "one year and nine months" after a loss at seventeen weeks gestation right after Christmas describes viewing "a videotape of Christmas 1985. What a happy time! Everything was going well in our lives. We looked so happy; who would have thought . . . ? Well our lives have changed dramatically. . . . My heart has been broken. I've also had a subsequent pregnancy and what joy my new son brings into my life. Joy yes, but fear also. . . . I look back and I can't believe what my loss . . . has done to me. I am not the same person I was on December 25, 1985."

Many people also express their sense of trauma in terms of an altered relation to space. Some describe feeling "lost" (Craig 1999). Recall Barbara Daniels, quoted in chapter 8, who said it felt like being picked up by a tornado and dropped down "in a totally different place . . . unable to find [her] way back to the place [she] had been before. That place no longer exists" (Daniels 1988b). Similarly Emma Mellon (1999) writes, "you have redrawn my internal country, uprooted trees and changed the course of lanes."

Narratives of loss often employ the simultaneously temporal and spatial metaphor of journey to describe their experience. For example, in her piece "My Journey . . . My Memories" Barb Knopf (1999) said after the death of her son, "I feel changed, like I am on a different road than I was before,"[6] and in a piece called "My Journey," Janis Heil describes her realization, in looking back at the journal she had started during the period when she had "felt so scattered" after her daughter's stillbirth, that it "represented a journey I was taking, winding through the rough road of my grief." In a letter to UNITE thanking the organization for support after the loss of a daughter at seventeen weeks gestation due to an undiagnosed incompetent cervix, one couple observes, "We have come a long way in the past year" (Ferrante 1999.

Trauma, Identity, and Problems of Memory

Memory is "an intrinsic part of selfhood" and given the havoc that trauma can wreak on the self, the "identity-building act" (Lambek 1996:243, 249) of remembering is critical. Yet pregnancy loss poses a number of challenges in terms of memory. Some of these problems, such as the deleterious effects of time on memory, are general problems of memory, at least as memory is understood in our culture. Others, such as difficulty in finding empathetic listeners and social pressure to forget, appear to be widely shared by those who suffer trauma. Still others, like the scant number of memories, the fact that the person being remembered was known to so few, and indirectly, appear to be, if not unique, at least a distinctive consequence of this particular type of trauma.

Members of pregnancy-loss support groups, like the general population, are troubled by the effect of time on memory. Memories are commonly understood to be like photographs (Lambek 1996, Kirmayer 1996, Forty 1999); an analogy that highlights the perceived objectivity and accessibility of memories. Kirmayer explicates this analogy: memories are believed to resemble "snapshots, laid down at the time of experience through a process of registration" (Kirmayer 1996:176). One recent example of this can be found in a Father's Day card marketed in Macy's department store in May 2001. Featured on the front, amid sparsely fallen leaves, blooms, and old stamps, is an old black-and-white snapshot of a man squatting with arms outstretched to receive a beaming toddler. The text reads, "Special memories are the snapshots we carry forever in our heart."

At the same time, the analogy with photographs focuses attention on the deleterious effects of time on memory. "Like photographs, memories may fade and this can limit the vividness and detail of recall" (Kirmayer 1996:176). As Forty (1999:4) put it, "the faded Daguerreotype, the result of inadequate fixing process, is the perfect metaphor for forgetting." It is this aspect of memory that most concerns members of pregnancy-loss support groups. Just as snapshots fade and classic feature-film footage is reduced to dust, members of pregnancy-loss support groups fear the corroding effects of time on memory.

Iris Rubinstein (2001), a UNITE support counselor, tells of meeting a woman at a craft class who had lost her third child at full-term twenty-five years earlier. Although people had told her that "time heals all wounds and

Father's Day card. Credit: © Ferrel Rao.

she would forget this pain, . . . she had not. In fact, the pain seemed to be
getting worse as the years went on." Iris asked her to come share her story at
a UNITE meeting, explaining that "Many of us fear that we'll forget our
lost babies as we move through the years . . . [You] would provide great reassurance that these precious souls are never forgotten."[7]

This fear explains why bereaved parents are so determined to "fix" their
memories securely. Janis Heil (1989) recalls how during the first week after
her daughter's stillbirth she felt she "had to record every detail of her life
and death for fear that I might ever forget her."[8]

We all rely on others to help us construct and maintain a sense of ourselves, and this is particularly important for people who have experienced
trauma. As Brison (1997) has observed, it is essential for survivors of trauma
to have empathic listeners. "In order to construct self-narratives . . . we
need not only the words with which to tell our stories but also an audience
able and willing to hear us" (1997:21). Antze and Lambek (1996:xvii) concur: "stories require interlocutors, and the right to establish authoritative
versions never rests with the individual telling the story alone." Dubin's

(1994) analysis of the Old Testament story of Naomi provides an apt example. Naomi "went out full" but was returned by God empty, having lost her husband, two sons, and her fertility while in Moab. Dubin stresses how important it was for Naomi to return to Bethlehem where women knew her (1994:135). "The women's listening and acknowledgement is a first step in Naomi's gradual recovery, and eventual return to satisfaction and wholeness. Public acknowledgement of private grief is essential" (Dubin 1994: 136).

But as survivors of trauma often learn the hard way, many people do not wish to hear their sad, disturbing stories. Brison describes the "intense psychological pressures" that make it so difficult "for others to listen to trauma narratives," noting that this reluctance stems from "an active fear of empathizing with those whose terrifying fate forces us to acknowledge that we are not in control of our own [fates]" (Brison 1997:26). Similarly, in his discussion of how "gentility and optimism" hindered WWI soldiers from being able to adequately express their memories, Fussell observed, "What listener wants to be torn and shaken when he doesn't have to be?" (Fussell quoted in Brison 1997:21).

The difficulty of finding empathetic interlocutors is one of the most common themes in narratives of pregnancy loss. For example, Karen Craig, whose nephew died for unexplained reasons after one week in an intensive care unit, describes how hard people's unwillingness to hear was for her sister. What hurt her sister most was not the insensitive things people said, like "At least you didn't have a chance to get to know him" or "At least you have your daughter," but "those people who didn't know what to say so just avoided the issue, or my sister, or both, altogether." She felt she "needed to talk about what happened to accept it, and having people avoid the issue" made it worse. Another example is found in a piece by Cathy Conners describing how "traumatic" it was for her, nine years after the stillbirth of her only child at seven months gestation, when her entire family gathered to celebrate her parents' fiftieth wedding anniversary. This was the first time that the entire family had been reunited since her loss and each time the grandchildren were "rounded up for a picture" or when five grandchildren instead of six were toasted, she fell apart. She explains, "Much of the hurt was the result of my family not acknowledging our daughter during this time. It was as though she never existed. My family is very loving but unfortunately take the old fashioned 'better not talk about it' approach."

Several authors have adopted a didactic voice in pieces addressed to potential interlocutors. For example, in a poem entitled "Remembering," Elizabeth Dent instructs the reader to "Go ahead and mention my child. . . .

Don't worry about making me cry. . . . Help me to heal by releasing the tears that I try to hide. I'm hurt when you just keep silent." Linda McCann (1984) pleads, "Ask me what her name was. Ask me what she weighed. Ask me what color her eyes were. . . . Tell me you don't know what to say. But please don't turn your back. Don't not say anything." Recall, too, Janis Heil's (1982/3) characterization of people "listening" to the story of her daughter's stillbirth as the "greatest gift" they could give to her.

A related, though different problem that affects those whose memories are of traumatic events is social pressure to forget. Like other trauma victims, members of pregnancy-loss support groups keenly feel such pressure.[9] Carolynn Zorn (2001) describes how she keeps finding her silver-framed photograph of her daughter holding her stillborn grandson face down on the credenza in her office. She wonders, "Who is doing this? What is their problem? Do they wonder what kind of person would love a picture like this?" and ends by asserting, "we should be allowed to remember him . . . " Frank Pavlak (1984), who along with his wife formed the Association of Recognizing the Life of Stillborns writes of his stillborn daughter, "Sadly, our society does not recognize the fact that she was ever alive. I will remember Sarah for eternity even though some others think we should forget her" (Pavlak 1984). Lisa Jeffries (1998), the UNITE group facilitator quoted in chapter 2, ends with the defiant declaration "What they think has never mattered as much as how much I will always remember you."

One way to understand this pressure is in terms of culturally specific schedules for forgetting. LaFleur describes how in Japanese ancestor worship as time passes the tablet representing the dead is raised gradually on the family altar at home as "the spirit of the dead is elevated out of human place and time as the dead person fades from memory" (LaFleur 1992:33). He notes that "in the long run to forget the dead . . . is not only necessary but desirable: one could not possibly keep alive forever the memory of all one's deceased ancestors. But forgetting has a schedule and is part of a process" (LaFleur 1992:33). Brison has commented on the socially approved schedule for forgetting in our own culture. "As individuals and as cultures, we impose arbitrary term limits on memory and on recovery from trauma: a century, say for slavery, fifty years, perhaps, for the Holocaust, a decade or two for Vietnam, several months for mass rape or serial murder" (Brison 1997). It should be no surprise then that the length of time considered appropriate for grieving and remembering a pregnancy loss is so brief.[10]

Barb Knopf speaks to this. She acknowledges the excellent support she received from her family and "everyone around her" at the time of her loss "and even a long time afterward," but then observes that "four whole years" later she feels as though she "shouldn't be crying about Danny anymore, . . . everyone assumes that four years should surely be enough time to 'get over it'" (Knopf 1999).

These pressures often lead bereaved parents to silence. Iris Rubinstein (2001) concludes her piece "Storytelling with Our Hearts" by noting, "frequently we censor ourselves before we speak and as a result, the story often doesn't get told. But the tales of our babies—loved and lost—need to be told."

While difficulty in finding empathetic listeners and social pressure to forget are problems that appear to be widely shared regardless of the type of trauma, other problems of memory seem to be particularly associated with certain types of trauma. For instance, for those who suffer childhood sexual abuse, the problem tends to be retrieving buried memories so that painful experience can be consciously dealt with (cathected) and integrated into one's life (Antze 1996, Hacking 1996, and Young 1996). For rape or Holocaust survivors or those who undergo "combat trauma," however, the problem is more likely to be one of disruptive, overwhelming memories that come unbidden (Kirmayer 1996, Brison 1997).[11] For pregnancy loss, the challenge is neither to uncover buried memories nor to keep them at bay, but rather to create adequate memories and then to retain them. As Kirmayer notes, "the validation of suffering depends on . . . enough memory to make it real for others" (Kirmayer 1996:190).

"Babies" that die during a pregnancy or shortly after birth pose special problems because of how little there is to remember.[12] Recall Lisa Jeffries (1998), who wrote of the "baby" she miscarried at eleven weeks, "I will remember you in so few ways it hurts," or take the example of Mary Zeches (1989), who writes of a boy who died at birth due to prematurity, "I hunger for images—there was so little time and so little to remember," or David Nagele (1986a), who observes, "The reminders will always be with us, but not in the things we remember; his life was too short." Instead he anticipates that they will remember their son through reminders of "the things that will never be—No first steps, no words, no baseball gloves or scraped knees" (Nagele 1986a). Similarly, Stacy Bricker (2000) describes sitting each Mother's Day in the garden she has planted in honor of her stillborn son Geoffrey and "dream[ing] of our missing memories."

The problem is not only that the "life was too short" but also that this "life" was experienced by so few, and oftentimes indirectly at that. Frank Pavlak (1984) describes his daughter "Sarah's Secret Life" in a piece by that name. He begins by noting the fact that she was "made in secret" and describes how "very few people knew Sarah. My wife knew her very well. I knew Sarah indirectly through my wife but only saw her for part of one day." His son, two friends, and his parents saw her for a short time at her baptism. "No one else really knew Sarah" (Pavlak 1984). Sue Palmer of Winterville, Ohio, also addresses this issue in her poem "Knowing You": "You are so real to me. But this is understandable because I am the only one who ever knew you."[13]

The risks of forgetting are greatly increased by the fact that there are so few social reinforcements for these memories. Time and time again, contributors comment on the fact that others have forgotten. For example, Colene Rose (1984) of Grand Marais, Minnesota, in a piece written one year after the stillbirth of her daughter, writes of this anniversary, "it's nothing special to others, even those who were there. They won't remember that one year ago today, our beautiful little girl was born. But, my darling Erin, I will never forget." Similarly, Sue Chaidez writes, "Everyone's forgotten you, Lacy. Everyone but me . . . " (1985:16), and Audrey Hess (1991) of Springdale, Arizona, writes of what would have been her stillborn son's first birthday, "Not even your father remembered." Cathi Lammert recalls how after the death of her son in December, "she did not want to turn over the calendar page . . . I wanted to remember my pregnancy with him and all our moments together. I was also afraid that everyone would forget him."

In dealing with these problems of memory, leaders and members of pregnancy-loss support groups do not work in a vacuum, but draw liberally and creatively from the cultural resources available to them. In this chapter I will focus on two of the major sources from which pregnancy-loss support group leaders and members routinely borrow in crafting pregnancy-loss rituals of remembrance and memorial practices: consumer culture and postwar commemorative culture (including the Judeo-Christian traditions that inform it). Although I draw out points of similarity and difference between the experience of pregnancy loss and other traumas, I want to be clear that I am not equating, or even attempting to compare, the seriousness of these different types of trauma. Rather, I want to illustrate how the public, collective ways these historic incidents have been memorialized provide powerful, culturally validated models for dealing with private, individual loss. Furthermore, given the lack of social recognition for pregnancy losses, the adaptation of memorializing practices that are associated with losses that are collectively acknowledged and socially valued is particularly important.

Consumer Culture and Technologies of Memory

Consumer goods are routinely employed as technologies of memory by pregnancy-loss support group leaders and members as they make, maintain, and share memories.[14]

Preserving Memory. In an era in which children have great sentimental value (Zelizer 1985, Spigel 2001),[15] childhood, especially babyhood, is felt to be a precious time that is over all too soon. Part of the ideology of contemporary middle-class motherhood is that one should raise healthy, happy, competent, self-confident children, *and* also be sure not to get so caught up in all that is required to accomplish this that one forgets to, or is too tired to, enjoy them. Mothers must constantly self-monitor to be sure not only that their children have all they need, but that they are enjoying each moment of their childhood. That is not all. One must also record these "precious moments" so that they can continue to be enjoyed as memories for years to come. This two-part enterprise—providing children with "memorable" experiences and then assisting them to remember them—is an exercise in the contemporary management of childhood and hence an enactment of love.

Bereaved parents engage in these prescribed, value-laden practices as much as they are able. As outlined in chapter 6, for early losses, there may be sonogram photos or nothing at all; for late losses, there are often baby blankets, caps, hospital ID bracelets, locks of hair, photos, foot- and handprints, and perhaps a toy. But even for late losses, compared with the attic-full of such trappings that one can accumulate over the course of one's children's childhood, there are so few mementos that special care is often taken to preserve them.

Support-group newsletters give advice on how to care for "precious photos"[16] and periodically provide contact information for a company that "produces a line of archival quality photo albums and storage boxes which preserve photos" (*SHARE* 1988 11(5):8).[17] As Michael Niehoff explains, such photos "deserve special care. Many commercial photo albums and mounting devices damage rather than preserve these precious pictures utilizing harmful adhesives which can tear, stain or fade photos and actually erode the images over time" (Niehoff 1994). He had photographs taken of the five ultrasound images of his stillborn son because "ultrasound pictures given parents are not a permanent record and will fade over time" (1994:4). Others have photos transferred onto commercial products like plastic plates or mugs, or commission paintings or drawings based on them. Jane Dirks (1988) from Pittsburgh explains that she and her husband "thought of a safe deposit box because there is only one [picture of their daughter]. What if the house burns down?"

And, like other parents, some members of pregnancy-loss support groups have their infant's shoes bronzed. Cheryl L. Miller of Perry, New York, explains that even though her baby never got to wear the shoes she had purchased for her, she had them "forever bronzed" to "withstand the test of time. A frozen memory of your quiet departure. The shoes you left behind."[18]

As these examples suggest, rather than thinking of memory as a cognitive phenomenon, pregnancy-loss support members oftentimes treat memory as things.[19] This model of memory has a number of consequences. Once memories are understood as things, they then share with things a number of important characteristics. They can decay and decompose, be lost, or ruined; they can be also be kept, stored, lovingly cared for, and preserved for posterity.

Another instantiation of memories as things can be found in the use of "memory boxes." Many hospital bereavement teams present memory boxes to bereaved parents, and UNITE presented attendees at their twenty-fifth anniversary celebration with a small, white, heart-shaped "memory box." SHARE markets "padded, fabric covered" boxes produced by Memories Unlimited and advertised as "the perfect place to hold the cherished mementos that connect with the tiny child. With the ribbons tied, the box is closed and the memories are kept safely inside. When the bow is untied, the open box reveals the things that touched the tiny life and left footprints on the heart" (*SHARE* 1994 3(5):13). A number of contributors to the newsletters mention using "memory boxes." For instance, Mary Zeches (1989) laments, "that all our dreams should come to this—a box of memories and my mother's sketch." (For other examples see chapter 6.) Pieces like these reveal the common elision between mementos and the memories they evoke.

Memories are not just any sort of thing, however, but special, precious things and, like the babies, sometimes likened in size and value to jewels or other treasures. Schwiebert and Kirk (1985:38) reproduce a quote from Dietrich Bonhoeffer, which likens memories to "a treasure" or "valuable present." [20]

Memory boxes, bronzing, acid-free paper, and various techniques used to reproduce and preserve photographic images each constitute technologies for dealing with the corrosive effects of time on memory.

Prompting and Sharing Memories. Consumer goods are also employed to address the problem of inadequate social prompts for these memories and outright social pressure to forget. These may be the same items used to preserve memory (things purchased for the baby in anticipation of its birth, or traces of the baby's body) or they may be goods acquired after a loss specifically for the purpose of acting as aide-mémoire. For instance, as seen in chapter 6, memorial jewelry, figurines, Christmas ornaments, and items for the garden are often used to stimulate or prompt memories.[21]

The choice of aide-mémoire and where they are stationed signal differ-ent goals in terms of whose memory is meant to be aided. They may be aimed at prompting memory from one or more of the following: oneself, members of one's family, guests to one's home, coworkers, or strangers (who might perhaps comment on an unusual piece of jewelry).

There are clear differences in understanding, both between bereaved parents, and between parents and members of their social networks about the appropriate place for such mementos and of such memories in one's life. As described in chapter 6, memorial objects are sometimes placed in a box in a closet, in a curio cabinet or on the mantel in one's living room, on a win-dowsill in the kitchen, on one's desk at work, in one's pocket, or on one's person. In other words, they are sometimes kept in private spaces or segre-gated to the more formal, ritual spaces of one's home. In other cases, people attempt to integrate memorial goods and the memories they prompt into the ebb and flow of daily life. Some explicitly use goods to assure that the dead baby is included in the annual holiday cycle, with, for example, Christmas stockings and birthday gifts. Some also endeavor to make sure that the child is not just recognized as part of the family on special ritual occasions but part of everyday family life. For example, Michael Niehoff (1994) explains that "a week before Christopher was stillborn, we bought him a soft, cuddly raccoon puppet named Ragamuffin," which is "now one of Zachary's [the surviving older brother's] favorite buddies to sleep with, and is one of our most constant reminders of Christopher." Recall also Cathy Hintz (1988), who hung the crystal snowflakes in her kitchen window and felt the rain-bows they produced "reaffirm symbolically how the children were and still are a good part of our lives." Memorial jewelry is another way some be-reaved mothers endeavor to integrate these children into their daily lives. Although most jewelry is intended to be seen by others, at UNITE's Twenty-Fifth Anniversary I was introduced to a type of memorial jewelry that is not visible. Pewter "pocket angels" and hearts, sold for $.50 a piece, are trinkets meant to be kept hidden in one's pocket where one will come upon them periodically throughout the day and be prompted by the touch to recall the absent loved one.

Thus, for some the goal is to continue to remember an important event in their lives—that they had a baby who died. For others, the goal seems to be more. By keeping "the memory alive," they may feel that, in a sense, they are keeping their baby alive. As Martin (1995) explains in a piece addressed to her child, "Only in our memory do you live." This sentiment is also ex-pressed in a prayer from the Reform Judaism prayer book reproduced in the *SHARE Newsletter* entitled "We Remember Them." The prayer consists of a list describing various moments in which "we" remember [the dead] and ends with the verses "For long as we live, they too shall live, For they are now a part of us, As we remember them" (*SHARE Newsletter* 8(6):1).

Making Memories. We have addressed strategies for combating the effects of time on memory, compensating for the lack of social support for remembrance, and challenging social pressure to forget. Let us now turn to the problem of quantity. Bereaved parents handle this problem in two rather contradictory ways. One strategy is purposively to increase the number by "making memories." For at least twenty years, anthropologists and historians have embraced a model of memory (and history) as constructed, as an account of the past that is made and remade in the present. The concept of memory-making prevalent in narratives of pregnancy loss likewise shares an understanding of memory as something that can be constructed. But whereas the anthropological/historical understanding of constructed memory focuses on present reconstructions of the past, in the case of pregnancy loss memory-making is proactive.[22] This model of memory draws heavily on the rhetoric of advertising, particularly for leisure activities which encourages us to make certain consumer choices in the anticipation of making "priceless," enduring memories. For example, the header on a summer 2001 advertising flyer for CVS pharmacy devoted to Kodak products reads, "Memories in the Making" and the introductory section, touting the virtues of disposable cameras, explains, "ball games, picnic, boating, weddings, fishing, the beach—these are the places where summertime memories happen." In other words, one should be sure to provide oneself and one's family with pleasurable memory-making opportunities like these and also be sure to capture these moments on film. Other similar advertisements are found in the 2001 AAA tour book for Colorado and Utah. Mountain Waters, a riverboat company operating out of Durango, has a colored photo of a family in a white-water raft, with a header reading, "Share an adventure. Make a memory." The Lake Powell Resort and Marina has a large colored photo of a houseboat, and the header reads, "This year, enjoy the best of Utah and make the memories of a lifetime."[23]

The rhetoric of memory-making is not confined to activities, however, but also applies to some consumer goods. This seems to be especially true for certain categories of gifts. For example, precious, enduring, romantically freighted gifts like diamonds are often marketed this way.[24] I also found this rhetoric on the brochure of a high-end infant and youth furniture manufacturer, Moosehead Manufacturing Company, for their "Memory Lane" collection, "furniture from which memories are made . . . " Another place one finds this trope is with handmade gifts. This seems to be particularly true for individuals at the beginning or end of their lives, that is, with a lifetime of memories ahead or behind them, such as children or grandparents. An example can be found in The Vermont Country Store's mail-order catalog for Christmas 2000, which begins with a letter from the proprietor explaining why he has filled the pages of his catalog "with items that will create lasting memories for your family to cherish" (2000:2).[25] The header on this and the facing page reads, "Making Memories."

Children, especially girls, are socialized into such memory-making practices at a young age. For example, the popular children's "Dear America" series of historical novels structured around the diaries of children (mostly girls), marketed in elementary schools by Scholastic, has a "My Memories Club." In addition to books, members receive a "memory-making kit" and instructions to guide them on how to "create your own memories through hand-made keepsakes."[26]

Leaders of pregnancy-loss support organizations and pregnancy-loss bereavement counselors tend to agree that memories are something that not only can but *should* be created. For instance, in his article on the "psychological consequences and strategies of management" for stillbirth, bereavement counselor Emanuel Lewis recommends that in order "to facilitate mourning" for a stillbirth one should "aim . . . to make history, to make memories that can be thought about and talked about, which will then fill the emptiness" (Lewis 1983:218 quoted in Ruby 1995:181). Bernadette Foley, a social worker who became a UNITE support-group coordinator after the loss of her daughter, contributed a piece in 1985 speculating on what pregnancy loss had been like in "our Grandparents' day." She explains that she had not known that each of her parents had "lost a sibling in infancy until her own daughter died" and mourns the fact that "today, as in my family, many of us don't even know these children existed because no one has memories of them to share." She goes on to suggest that even though "making memories of a child who never lived outside the womb or whose lifetime after birth was brief, seems very difficult," bereaved parents should "make memories of your child, for yourself, your family, and your future" (Foley 1985:2). In a piece entitled "Healing Memories," Michael Niehoff describes how during the two-and-one-half days after learning that their son had died in utero and would be stillborn, the SHARE director "worked with us to create and collect as many memories of our little boy as possible." He explains, "this was especially important to us because we wanted 'material memories' that our then 4-year-old son, Zachary, could cherish with us for years to come." He goes on to instruct his readers, presumably the caregiving segment of the membership, that "someone must help [parents] create memories. They may not want to save anything at the time, or think taking pictures is repugnant" (Niehoff 1994).

The suggestions Niehoff gives for "creating memories" are ways to document the baby's life by "collecting" and "saving" things that were the child's and also by purposively creating documentation of the baby's life, for example, by taking photos. Some parents go further and continue to "make memories" after the loss. Recall for example, the woman described in chapter 6 who brings home a small gift from each of her trips, just as many middle-class parents do for children who stayed behind at home as evidence that they were thought of, "remembered," while physically absent from their parents. Yet the example she gives of a shell she brought back and now keeps on a shelf in her office, with the explanation, "Matthew never went to the beach but this is Matthew's shell" (Boyette 1996), conjures the image of mother and child collecting shells together and bringing them home as a souvenir of a vacation spent together. In either case, this mother continues to enact motherhood as she creates/provides memories of/for her child.

More Is Not Necessarily Better: A Critique of Consumer Culture. The other, not necessarily mutually exclusive, strategy for dealing with the scant quantity of memories available in cases of pregnancy loss is to challenge quantity as a measure of importance. In doing so, members of pregnancy-loss support groups articulate a critique of a number of related core values of capitalist consumer culture. For example, a foundational premise of contemporary North American consumer culture is that "more is better." One version of this is found in the words of Morrie Schwartz as conveyed in the best-seller *Tuesdays with Morrie*, "We've got a form of brainwashing going on in our country," which works by repeating "something over and over," for example, "Owning things is good. More money is good. More property is good. More commercialism is good. *More is good. More is good.* We repeat it—and have it repeated to us—over and over until nobody bothers to even think otherwise" (Albom 1997:124 emphasis in original).

Members of pregnancy-loss support groups frequently challenge these standards of value. They argue that size and amount, whether it be of the body, length of a lifetime, or number of memories, are irrelevant as markers of value. Sometimes they claim an equivalency, as, for instance, when Schwiebert and Kirk (1985:17) assert, "A single picture of this child will be something you can value as much as dozens of pictures of this child's brothers and sisters who survive."

Other times they go further and stress the superior merits of the small and the few instead. This ironic reversal—that a little is not what it seems, but is actually quite grand, grander in fact than things that are of more apparent size and worth—is a common theme in narratives of pregnancy loss. Rhetorically, this move is in the style of the late-eighteenth-, early-nineteenth-century natural theologians like Paley, Bucke, and Carlyle who refocused "the sublime from the vast and infinite to the small and immediate" (Cooksey 1992:6). "This perception of the miraculous in the ordinary, the infinite in the small becomes the basis of a sort of finite sublime (what Bucke termed 'the infinite little')" (Cooksey 1992:7). This sensibility is well captured in the familiar lines of the still popular poem "Auguries of Innocence," by William Blake [1863] (1970): "To see a world in a grain of Sand/And a Heaven in a Wild Flower/Hold Infinity in the palm of your hand/And Eternity in an hour . . . "

Images of nature are often used in narratives of loss to similar ends. For example, in a piece reprinted in the *SHARE Newsletter* from an anthology on pregnancy loss, Kim Steffgan elaborates an analogy between miscarried babies who never get a chance to develop and "brown dwarfs" or "prestars," which "have all the same elements to become a star, [but] for some reason" do not. The author describes the "full lives" that most "stars" go through, from the hot, bright, white dwarf stage to their aged, cooler and dimmer red giant stage, but explains,

> "brown stars" only go so far. Instead of being born to live a normal star's life, they remain cool and dim. . . . But like our babies, their roles in the universe are very important. In fact scientists believe they serve as a link between the small things and the big things, holding the universe together, a mid point between the beginning and ending of our universal story . . . our babies who died before reaching the stardom of their earthly lives [may also have been] designated for this very special, universal role (Steffgan 1999).

In another piece, it is memories rather than the babies that act as a link or bridge between this world and the next. As Connie Harmon puts it, "memories are the bridge between heaven and earth, cherish your memories, even if they are few, They are like a rainbow, from you to heaven, from heaven to you" (Harmon 1988).

Flowers are probably the most commonly employed analogy from nature for dead babies. In an interesting variation on the "little equals a lot/more is not better" theme, Susan D. Schwaegler of Moline, Illinois, uses a "full-blown flower" to symbolize her stillborn daughter, Mary Rose. She explains why instead of choosing an unopened bud to represent her child, she chose "full-blown" pink roses with which to remember her on her birthday. "A life full-lived. For a thimble of water is as full as a pail . . . her life as complete in all its brevity" (Schwaegler 1989).

With or without analogies to nature, bereaved parents routinely contrast worldly time and value, which we obsessively measure, with transcendental time and things whose value is beyond measure. For example, David Nagele (1986a) deploys this trope, both in terms of describing the enormity of that which was lost, "We lost something . . . that cannot be measured—a lifetime," and in describing his memories of his son. "Jonathan's memories are in hours and not in years as we had hoped. Just an instant, an instant an eternity of emotions grasped in a handful of time" (Nagele 1986a).[27] Elsewhere (1986b) he offers the aphorism—"Time should be measured in intensity, not duration." Similarly, Anthony Smith (1986) writes in his piece "The Last Hour," "I will never know an hour/ So precious as this./ An eternity/ Gone by too fast/ Every moment/ A lifetime/ Must last."[28]

The remarkably undertheorized notion of "love" plays a critical role in these narratives.[29] Love appears to be simultaneously measurable and uniquely elastic. Several poems suggest that love can be measured. For example, mothers like Anne Ciany assert that their love is equal to that of other mothers. "If motherhood is measured in minutes and hours, then maybe I don't qualify, but if motherhood is measured in terms of love, then I'm a mother too" (Ciany 1999). Schwiebert and Kirk (1985:17) assure mothers that their baby was "equal to your other children in the love you gave, if only while inside you."

Love is also felt to be capable of transcending time and space and therefore beyond measure. Love's ability to endure "forever" is a common theme in these narratives. In a piece signed "Mom," a woman writes, "Your body will soon be gone, but the love goes on forever" (Mom 1985:22), and Cindy Lee Foster (1985a) ends her piece with a quote attributed to M.D. Hughes.

Another variation on this theme is made in terms of the conventional contrast between quality and quantity. This distinction is found with regard to the value of a life. Bereaved parents frequently make assertions like "you taught your parents more in an instant Than they had learned in thirty years" (Laux 1985), or "you accomplished more in your short life than many do in their lifetimes." The quality/quantity distinction is also employed in terms of memories. For example, Jennifer Ryan asserts of her son who lived eight days, "Although our time was very brief, I remember each minute clear" (Ryan 1999), the implication being that if one had a lifetime of memories, some would inevitably fade, but in this case, these few memories are indelibly imprinted on her mind/heart.

"The Replacement Child."   Another way that members of pregnancy-loss support groups critique consumer culture is in rejecting the oft-suggested notion of the replacement child. One of the most common ways that others encourage bereaved parents to "get over" a loss is by having another baby.[30] The support-group newsletters periodically discuss the insensitive, hurtful things that well-meaning but misguided bystanders often say. Always high on this list is "well, you can always have another." Bernadette McCauley's (1986) poem " . . . Only a Miscarriage" illustrates this. "'It was only a miscarriage.'/ That's what they all said./ 'Why are you so depressed and upset?'/ 'There will be others.' . . . 'You can try again.'/'It was only a miscarriage'—/'Pull yourself together.'"[31] David Nagele (1986b) instructs, "Don't say you're young, you can have more children. Because we don't take things for granted anymore. Besides babies cannot be replaced."

Parents who have subsequently borne children frequently assert, rather defensively, that their new child is NOT a "replacement child" and will not erase the memory of the one/s who died. For example, Terry Weeden's (1985) first daughter was stillborn due to Turner's Syndrome. After the successful birth of another daughter, she asserts, "She won't replace our first daughter—for one person can never replace another. We will always remember our first baby . . . " Similarly, in a piece addressed to her stillborn daughter after a subsequent birth, Kelly Gonzalez ends with the avowal "No one can replace you!" Writing during a subsequent pregnancy on what would have been the first birthday of a daughter who died shortly after birth while undergoing surgery, Joanne Murphy assures the reader and/or herself, "My new baby is not going to replace Amanda and he never will," then switches voices and assures her daughter, "Amanda, my Forever Baby, you will always be special and never forgotten by your Mommy" (Murphy 1991).[32]

These concerns are shared by those who anticipate having another child as well. For example, Denise Lohr (1986), a facilitator of the Pittsburgh SHARE group, wrote of the stillbirth of her first child, "someday we may have another baby, but there will never be another Daniel; he will always be our firstborn, our son." This sentiment is even more dramatically expressed by Colene Rose (1984), who ends her piece, "How could I forget you? My firstborn, my precious baby? I could have ten more children and still you would be special because you will always be my first." In other words, she not only rejects the one-to-one equivalency implicit in the idea of a "replacement child," but asserts that ten to one would still be an inadequate rate of exchange.

These pressures and resistances resemble those experienced by parents who give birth to children with disabilities. In her article "Too Bad You Got a Lemon," Landsman (in prep) comments on philosopher Peter Singer's controversial position that it is not only morally acceptable but often desirable to kill disabled infants so that their parents can replace these defective children with more fulfilling ones. According to this position, "infants not only can but should be understood to be replaceable" (Landsman in prep:2). Singer's argument is a utilitarian one. His concern is that such children require such an extraordinary commitment of time, money, and energy that the parents are much less likely to have another child. In the case of pregnancy loss, there are no such demands on familial resources. Nevertheless, the commodified logic of replacement and the damning evaluation of the worth of their child are staunchly rejected.[33]

Postwar Commemorative Culture and Technologies of Memory

In the context of the many forces that encourage forgetting, such as a scant number of memories, the effects of time, pressure to "move on" and have other children, remembering is understood to be a matter of individual, deliberate choice. Kathy White Casey (1999), mother of four living children ages four to twenty-two, and founder and leader of HUGSS (Help in Understanding Grief and Successfully Surviving) of Louisiana, describes in a piece entitled "I Choose to Remember" her experience of two miscarriages one year apart. "There were many choices to be made following the loss of my sweet babies, Jesse and Shelby. The one choice I made, with great determination and resolution to fulfill, was in remembering them."

Choosing to remember is not a neutral choice. The commitment to remember, especially in the face of subtle and not-so-subtle pressures to forget, is clearly understood by bereaved parents to be an honorable, moral choice.[34] This is not our ordinary understanding of memory. As Lambek observes, memories are more readily thought of in terms of "passive absorption and playback" than in terms of "ongoing engagement." We tend to think of memories more as objects "which may be more or less accurate, more or less complete" than as acts or claims that may be more or less "justified" (Lambek 1996:238, 239).

Although an understanding of memory as a moral act is not the dominant one, there are clear cultural models for it. This brings us to our second set of cultural resources from which bereaved parents draw in crafting tech-

Photo by author, September 2001.

nologies of memory—postwar commemorative culture[35] and the Judeo-
Christian traditions that inform it.

Memory as a Moral Choice—The Old Testament.   The Old Testament is an important source for the view of remembrance as a moral act and
no doubt informed postwar commemoration.[36] In the introduction to his
book on Holocaust memorials, Young (1993:2) describes the "traditional
Jewish injunctions to remember," noting that Genesis mentions both the
"tombstone Jacob erected on Rachel's grave," and "a small pillar and witness heap of stones," signifying an important historical event; two examples
of "everlasting remnant-witnesses by which subsequent generations would
remember past events and people" (1993:3). These traditions certainly inform Holocaust remembrance, including special ceremonies designed for
"remembering the children," like the observance of Yom Hashoah, with a
Holocaust Remembrance Service, May 1, 2000, at Rensselaer Polytechnic
Institute, which included the reading of a poem, "I Cannot Forget," by
Alexander Kimel, a Holocaust survivor, which begins with the question

"Do I want to remember?" and ends with the reply "No. I Have to Remember and Never Let You Forget" (2001).[37]

Among pregnancy-loss support groups, it is the Old Testament verse Isaiah 49 that is most frequently drawn upon.[38] In this verse God's unique powers and commitment to remembering his children are stressed by means of comparing him with those one can most count on to remember, that is, mothers.

> Can a woman forget her sucking child, that she should have no compassion on the son of her womb? Even they may forget, yet I will not forget you. Behold, I have graven you upon the palms of my hands; your walls are continually before me (Isaiah 49:15–16 quoted in *UNITE Notes* 8(4):3).[39]

Several contributors express a similar equation between motherhood and remembering.[40] In her piece entitled "Am I a Mother?" Julie Boyer Smith (1986) writes, "I remember every moment of those nine long months./ I remember every kick inside me./ I remember the hopes and plans and dreams./ I remember the love./ Yes, I must be a mother!" Gail Fasolo (2000) echoes this truism in a poem called "A Mother Always Remembers": "Others think that I've forgotten,/ Can they really be so naive?/ A mother always remembers/ the child she conceived."

Isaiah 49 provides a cultural and literary template for pieces like those quoted above, which are addressed to the deceased and report that others have forgotten her/him, but conclude with the author's promise "I will never forget you." In adapting this scriptural model, authors, whether consciously or not, place themselves, like God, as superordinate rememberers. Those who remember babies who die during a pregnancy or shortly thereafter cast themselves as even more exemplary than normal mothers who provide the benchmark in this arena.

In narratives of pregnancy loss the decision to remember is represented, as it is in Scripture, in the morally charged language of vows, promises, and pledges.[41] For example, in a piece entitled "Winter Vow," Chuck Clark of Springfield, Illinois, describes visiting the "lonely hill" where his son was buried two years earlier, and how there alone atop the hill he made a vow to his son: "I haven't forgotten, and standing here. I swear I never will" (Clark 1984). This is in fact the most common way contributors end their pieces.[42] To give just a few other examples, in a piece read at the funeral of her nephew, Lori Jordan Wood (1988) closes with the following pledge: "But there is one promise we want to make./ We'll never forget you/ 'till we meet our fate." A sister ends a piece addressed to her baby brother, "You shall never be forgotten—not for an instant!" (Stover 1989), and Jacki Bergels concludes, "You are not forgotten little one/ Nor will you ever be./ For as long as life and memory last/ We will remember thee" (Bergels 1989).

These vows recall the verbal injunctions to "Remember the Alamo," "Remember the Maine," "Remember Pearl Harbor"[43] (White 1992:3) and to "Never Forget" the Holocaust, or more localized imperatives like "Ne les Oubliez Jamais" referring to the fallen of the 551st Parachute Infantry Battalion who fought in World War II.[44] The vows of pregnancy-loss support-group members differ in several respects, however. Remember the Alamo, the Maine, and Pearl Harbor were American "war cries," meant to rally popular support for military action (White 1992:3). Exhortations to "never forget the Holocaust" are, as Young (1993:xiii) explains, intended as "history lessons," so that it will never be repeated. Furthermore, these war-related injunctions are aimed primarily at people who did not directly experience the events. In other words, they are designed not so much to preserve memories as to construct what Liss refers to as "postmemories" of the events. The vows made by bereaved parents, on the other hand, are directed to the dead. As speech acts, their vows resemble more the POW/MIA movement slogan, "You Are Not Forgotten," in that both are addressed to the subject of remembrance.

The pledges of members of pregnancy-loss support groups are replete with words like "thee," and "shall," and phrases like "meeting one's fate," examples of what Fussell (1975:21, 22) refers to as the "high diction" of the essentially "feudal language" (1975:21) found in "Arthurian poems and pseudo-medieval romances," which conjure white knights battling evil foes, and reflect a "confidence in Divine assistance" (1975:29). According to Fussell, before World War I this language was associated with "personal control and Christian self-abnegation ('sacrifice')," themes which, as we saw in chapters 7 and 8, are important in narratives of pregnancy loss. He (1975:22) argues that this language was one of the "ultimate causalities" of WWI, but, evidently, archaic language like this is still compelling as a means for communicating the out-of-place/out-of-timeness of these traumatic experiences.[45] Just as the use of language like this helped transform "compulsory service . . . into voluntary sacrifice" during World War I (Sherman 1999:86), it helps transform a biological mishap into a transcendent moment in narratives of pregnancy loss.

Memory as a Moral Choice—War Memorials. The public commemorative practices and rhetoric of remembrance that emerged following the

Great War provide a well-developed model of remembering, not as an automatic physiological phenomenon, but as a self-willed, moral choice. War memorials manifest the view that remembrance, at least of certain collective traumas, is something to which one can, and should, make a commitment.[46] Those involved in designing, funding, and building twentieth-century war memorials have, according to Young (1993:27), been "ethically certain of their duty to remember," even when they have not been certain what form this remembrance should take (Liss 1998, Young 1993, Kirmayer 1996, Sherman 1999:66).

The period following the First World War saw an unprecedented level of monument-building. According to King, "The commemoration of the dead of the First World War was probably the largest and most popular movement for the erection of public monuments ever known in Western society" (1999:147). The erection of war memorials continued throughout the twentieth century. In fact, during the same decades when pregnancy-loss support groups were being established there was "a tremendous growth in . . . the building of war memorials" (Rowlands 1999:129). Given the sheer number of war memorials built during the twentieth century, and their remarkable popularity, it is not surprising that they are so "closely connected in modern consciousness with memory" (Forty 1999:9).

One subset of these that witnessed a "veritable explosion" in numbers in the last decades of the twentieth century is Holocaust memorials (Young 1993:x). According to Young, "the number of [these] monuments and memorial spaces in Europe, Israel, and America . . . now reaches into the thousands, with dozens more being proposed and erected every year" (1993:ix). Many of these, particularly the more recent ones, are located in the United States, which, according to Rabinbach (1997:226), became after 1985 "the preeminent nation of official Holocaust remembrance."[47]

In recent years, often in conjunction with fiftieth anniversaries, there has been a flurry of remembrance activities commemorating the turning points in WWII, for example, organized tours for veterans to revisit Iwo Jima and participate in commemorative rituals honoring the dead (Howard Layne, personal communication), the release of the high-budget film *Pearl Harbor*, and the dedication on June 4, 2001, by President Bush of a National D-Day memorial in Bedford, Virginia, a tiny town which had the highest per capita loss on D-Day (twenty-two of its thirty-five soldiers died the first day of the invasion) (Lewis 2001). Plans are now under way to construct a World War II memorial on the mall in Washington, D.C.

What is even more important for the argument I am developing is the growing popular appeal of these memorials. Rowlands (1999:129) reports that the memorial sites of the First World War "now receive more visitors

than ever before" and Young estimates that "as many people now visit
Holocaust memorials every year as died during the Holocaust itself"
(1993:x). The Vietnam War Memorial in Washington, D.C. "has become
perhaps the most famous and one of the most visited monuments of the late
twentieth century" (Rowlands 1999:129). By 1998, "more than 20 million
visitors, about one in ten Americans, [had] visited the wall" (Hass 1998:8),
and thousands of others visited a replica of the wall which toured American
cities (Kennedy 1990).[48] In the wake of September 11, ground zero has now
perhaps surpassed the Vietnam War memorial as pilgrimage site.

Bodies and Names.   In addition to providing a compelling model of remembrance as a moral choice, postwar commemorative culture informs
pregnancy-loss support in several other ways. Laqueur has argued that the
innovative ways of burying and commemorating war dead that developed in
the aftermath of the Great War created "a distinctively modern way of
creating meaning" (1994:158). Laqueur (1994) and Sherman (1999) have
explored the special importance of bodies, names, and the relationship between the two in this regard. Unlike previous wars where only "men of
name" were memorialized, World War I ushered in a new ideal. No longer
would the dead be "buried where they fell," but each and every casualty de-
served an individual, personally identified grave in consecrated ground
(Laqueur 1994).[49] According to Laqueur, "this represented a radical departure not only from earlier military practice . . . but also from nineteenth-
century British domestic custom" of burial in "collective . . . shaft graves."
Efforts to achieve this ideal were prodigious. Laqueur (1994:155) remarks
on the "sheer magnitude of the commitment to remembrance" evident in
the number of servicemen and Red Cross volunteers assigned to the task of
attempting to identify corpses, and of marking graves at the front, often
while under fire, and recording their exact location so that they could later
be retrieved and moved to more appropriate locations.

Despite these great efforts it is estimated that "no more than a quarter of
the four hundred thousand Frenchmen killed [in the Verdun theater] would
ever be buried in individual graves" (Sherman 1994:189), and, by the end,
the remains of approximately 517,000 were "unknowns" (Laqueur 1994:
156). Sherman (1994) and Laqueur (1994) concur that the rapid spread of
monuments following WWI was in large part spurred by the "plight of families who lacked the demarcated site of mourning that a tombstone offered,
as well as the consolation of proximity to physical remains" (Sherman 1994:
189).

Although this problem was not as acute for soldiers during the Second World War, the Holocaust produced "a murdered people without graves, without even corpses to inter" (Young 1993:7). Much as WWI memorials stood in for missing bodies, following the Holocaust things like memorial books ("Yizkor Bikher") "came to serve as symbolic tombstones . . . substitute graves," which functioned as "sites for memory" (Young 1993:7). In the weeks following the World Trade Center attack, as rescue workers continued to sift through the rubble, it became apparent that this was another tragic instance of brutality so extreme that most of the bodies are no more.

Pregnancy loss, too, often poses a "crisis of substantiation" (Scarry quoted in Sherman 1999:102, cf. Ruby 1995:181). Especially for first-trimester miscarriages, by far the most common form of pregnancy loss, those who grieve do so without the body and without traditional funeral services, both of which are generally understood to aid in the mourning process (cf. Sherman 1999, Young 1993:7). Even for later losses, before the advent of the pregnancy-loss support movement, the body would be discreetly slipped away and disposed of by the hospital.[50] Dr. Berman (2001:xvii) reports that during his obstetrical training in the 1970s he was taught "that if a baby was stillborn or born with a serious, 'unsightly' birth defect, the physician should attempt to protect the parents from the 'shock' of seeing their dead child by covering it with a blanket, quickly removing it from the delivery area, and sending the body to the morgue to be buried in an unmarked grave."

In the absence of bodies, names play a particularly important role. Like anthropologists (Bodenhorn and vom Bruck in prep), members of pregnancy-loss support groups are cognizant of the sociocultural constructivist power of naming.[51] As Di'Saro (1988) observed following her decision to name a baby in the final month of her pregnancy after having learned that it had died in utero, "having a name feels so close to having a baby."

In some narratives, both the presence of and relationship between a name and body is assumed. For example, in her piece "Angel Children" Laura Phillips (1995) writes, "Angels in Heaven, that's what they became, after leaving this Earth with a body and name." Yet, as other narratives make clear, pregnancy loss potentially uncouples the assumed axiomatic relationship between bodies and names.

For example, whereas in the earlier cited military examples, it is absent bodies that present an obstacle for adequate mourning, in the case of pregnancy loss names, too, are often absent. They are not available, either for having never been given, or sometimes for having been provisionally given and then revoked for use with a subsequent child. According to family historian Lawrence Stone, during the Middle Ages and up through the first half of the eighteenth century, "it was common practice to give a new-born son the same first name as an elder sibling" who had recently died, "especially if it was the traditional name for the head of the family" (1979:257). Sometimes the patronym was given to more than one living child in case the eldest son died (1979:257).[52] Stone writes, "so far as I am aware, this practice died out by the late eighteenth century, indicating a recognition that names were highly personal and could not be readily transferred from child to child" (1979:258). Yet in their "guide for parents whose child dies before birth, at birth or shortly after birth," Schwiebert and Kirk (1985:19) "strongly encourage you to give your baby a name, preferably the name you had been planning for the child all along. Don't 'save' the name for your next child. It rightly belongs to this one." Thus we may be witnessing a historical process similar to that documented by Stone. Just as at the close of the early modern era the "right to a name" was extended to infants, a similar process may now be under way with regard to embryos and fetuses.[53]

Other times there is a name but no body; not only in the cases where the hospital disposed of it, but also sometimes because a body never developed. For example, in a piece called "How Early Is Too Early? Mourning a Baby Lost Through Miscarriage," Kathy White Casey (1997) tells of how she named her two first-trimester pregnancy losses. The first she miscarried at eleven weeks gestation; the second was part of a double conception from which one embryo developed into a living child but "its twin," whom she named, was a "blighted ovum," lost at six weeks gestation.

Names and Memory. Pregnancy-loss support leaders recognize the important link between names and memory. *SHARING* editor Sue Friedeck (1999:5) places "Name your baby" first on her list of ways to "remember your child" and she instructs, "If he/she was lost early, use a name that is gender neutral or use "Baby" with your surname" (Friedeck 1999:5). Schwiebert and Kirk (1985:19) advise, "You will find it easier to connect your memories to this child if you can refer to him or her by name." Their pamphlet devotes an entire section to naming, which begins with the heading "human beings should not die without their names being remembered or else human beings don't count" (Schwiebert and Kirk 1985:19).

Not only are members of pregnancy-loss support groups naming their dead babies, some are doing so many years after the loss. In 1986 the *SHARE Newsletter* reported on a bill that passed in 1984 in New York State "concerning naming our babies—even after a death certificate has been filed." This bill overturned a law that had stated "if a child dies without a given name, there shall be entered in the space provided for the name the words 'died unnamed.' This law made it impossible to name a baby once a death certificate had been filed. The new law changes this unfair, insensitive law so that it is now possible through a designated form to finally name our unnamed babies if we so desire" (*SHARE* 1986 9(1):6) reprinted with permission from REACHOUT). In that same issue, cross-referenced to the notice about the new law, appears a letter by Mary Lou Eddy (1986) of Schenectady, New York, who reported that she had recently named her baby who had died ten years earlier, presumably by grace of this new law.[54]

Once a name has been given, pregnancy-loss support organizations encourage its use.[55] Of particular note are inscription practices in this regard. For example, UNITE's 1985/6 list of suggested ways of "remembering your child at the holidays" includes a number of suggestions that involve inscribing the baby's name on a memorial object: "Buy an ornament to hang on the tree or by a window. You can have your baby's name and birth date inscribed on it. Give yourself a gift of a charm upon which your baby's name is engraved" (*UNITE Notes* 1985/6 5(2):2).[56] As in the case of war memorials, the engraving of the names on objects like these may be felt to help engrave them on memory (Sherman 1999:76).[57]

These inscription practices illustrate an extension of practices associated with 'the invention of childhood' (Aries 1962; Stone 1979). According to Stone (1979:257), the inclusion of "very short-lived infants" in official genealogies of aristocrats reflected "a greater concern to register the existence on earth, however brief, of all infants born." He cites naming as "evidence that, for the first time, parents were beginning to recognize that each child, even if it lived only for a few hours or days, had its own unique individuality" (1979:257). The pregnancy-loss support movement is extending this logic to a new category, to include even those who did not even live "a few hours or days," or perhaps more accurately, by redefining the definition of "living."

In both cases, the early modern practices of inscribing the dead baby's name along with those of other family members on a tomb or genealogy, and the contemporary practices of pregnancy-loss support members of inscribing the baby's name along with those of other children on a set of Christmas stockings or a charm bracelet, the baby is being constructed as part of the collective identity of the family.

Lists of Names and Collective Identity. Pregnancy-loss support groups also frequently orchestrate the listing of unrelated dead baby's names together. In so doing they are drawing on a distinctive commemorative practice introduced following the First World War. Lists of names of the dead became "the keystone" of the new commemorative practices following the war (Sherman 1999:66). Sherman and Laqueur agree that these lists are evidence of the "fruits of mass democracy" and represent a "distinctively modern form of commemoration" (Sherman 1999:66). According to Laqueur (1994:154), the "central problem of . . . design [of the major monuments of the western front] was to find room for the plethora of names." He describes two of the largest: the 54,896 names inscribed on Monin Gate and "the seemingly endless walls of Tyne Cot . . . inscribed with 34,888 names" and then describes the "string of names" that continues down the front in smaller clumps. "The names of 11,447 . . . line the colonnades of the Ploegstreet Memorial. Fifteen kilometers south, . . . 4,843 names of missing Indian soldiers fill the walls. . . . Another fifteen or so kilometers away . . . the Duds Corner Memorial . . . [with] a courtyard formed by panels with 20,589 names," and so on.

This World War I innovation was the inspiration for Lin's design for the Vietnam War Memorial (Sherman 1999:67) in Washington, D.C., and her wall, in turn, has inspired other "walls of remembrance." For example, a wall of remembrance inscribed with the names of the thirty-five students who died aboard Pan Am flight 103, which was blown up by terrorists in December 1988 over Lockerbie, Scotland, was constructed by Syracuse University in front of the oldest building on campus. A wall inscribed with the names of children killed by gunfire in this country was constructed on Mother's Day, 2000, in Washington, D.C., by the Million Mom March Foundation.

Related practices involving the listing of the names of the dead are now also found at memorials for victims of September 11, AIDS, DWI, school violence, and terrorist attacks, and for organ donors. The AIDS Memorial Quilt was displayed for the first time on the Mall in Washington, D.C., on October 11, 1987, as part of a Lesbian and Gay Rights March on Washington.[58] It consisted of 1,920 panels and was viewed by an estimated half a million people that weekend. It then went on a four-month, twenty-city tour, growing in size to "more that 6,000 panels by the end of the tour." The Quilt was displayed in October of 1988 in Washington again, where the names of the 8,288 people represented on the panels were read aloud, and then again in October of 1989, 1992, 1996. The Quilt now has approximately 44,000 panels, and it is estimated that over thirteen million people have seen it (www.aidsquilt.org).

Quilts on display at 1989 Pregnancy and Infant Loss Awareness Weekend in Washington, DC.

A Rensselaer County DWI Victim's Memorial was erected in Troy, New York, in the 1990s near the site where a Troy teen was killed by a drunk driver. The shiny black granite stone is surrounded by a "circle of evergreen shrubs." As deaths occur, names are added. At a recent memorial service, New York State Senator Bruno remarked, "unfortunately the list is growing," as he called for "a renewed commitment to fighting drunk driving so no more names need be added to the memorial stone" (Bolton 2001).

The Oklahoma City National Memorial has the name of each individual who died inscribed on an empty chair (large ones for adults, small ones for children), organized in rows representing the floors of the building where the victims were at the time of their death (www.oklahomacitynational memorial.org).[59]

In recent years, such lists are also appearing in the form of webpages. The names of the Oklahoma City dead are also listed on the Memorial's webpage (along with hyperlinks that provide a short biography of each) (www.oklahomacitynationalmemorial.org).[60] "Virtual cemetaries" for organ donors have also been constructed by surviving kin, listing the names and a short biography of each donor (Sharp 2001). A similar website with biographies of fourteen victims of the August 1, 1966, University of Texas Tower shootings now exists (Eberly 2001).[61] Following the September 11 attacks, newspapers and a host of websites published regularly updated lists of the names of the dead, the missing, and confirmed survivors.

In each of these cases, the shared circumstances of untimely death serves to create a collective identity. Likewise, collective rituals of pregnancy-loss support place the names of dead individuals together, thereby forging a common identity based on the circumstances of their deaths rather than biological relatedness. For example, in 1985 a Memorial Plaque was placed on the wall near the entrance to St. John's Hospital, home of the National SHARE office. The announcement in the *SHARE Newsletter* listed each of the eighteen babies' names "embossed in bronze" and invited others to send a donation and "their baby's name if they wish[ed] to have it added to the plaque" (*SHARE* 1986 9(5):7).[62] In 1987 a "Cherished Children's Park" was dedicated on the grounds of the hospital "in honor of the little ones everywhere." Kathyrn E. Simonds, *SHARE* editor from Jacksonville, Illinois, published an account of the remembrance service in the *SHARE Newsletter*. "Dozens of families gathered to publicly 'remember' their children—the precious children who have died. . . . Inside the hall, the children's names were called out one by one and their families came forward to accept a white rosebud in remembrance of each."[63]

In October 1989 a commemorative quilt which appears to be a direct borrowing and adaptation of the AIDS quilt was displayed on the mall during the Pregnancy and Infant Loss Awareness Weekend March to Remember in Washington.[64] Members from around the country created like-sized quilts commemorating the lives of individual "babies."

Each of UNITE's conferences ends with a memorial service at which the names of participants' dead babies are inscribed and collectively displayed. As mentioned in chapter 8, at one of these events participants were invited to write their baby/ies name/s on felt flowers, which were then displayed on a felt banner; on another occasion, the names were inscribed on tissue-paper butterflies, which were then displayed together on a tree. At UNITE's twenty-fifth-anniversary event, people were invited to write the name/s of their dead babies on lavender index cards when they registered. At the end of the ceremony one of the UNITE facilitators read the names out loud to a musical accompaniment. Parents were asked to stand when their baby's name was read so that they and their baby could be "acknowledged." Because of the Web, babies' names honored at pregnancy-loss support events, which in the past would have not retained a group identity after the event, are now being preserved as a group on the organization's website, and can be viewed on the "virtual tour" of their twenty-fifth-anniversary celebration (http://region/philly.com/community/UNITEINC).

Lists of names like these clearly derive from the lists of names that became the hallmark of World War I commemoration. Other elements of collective pregnancy-loss commemoration harken to more recent developments. According to Hass, following World War II the United States embraced a "powerfully forward-looking" approach to memorialization, bent on improving the country for which the dead had sacrificed their lives.[65] "In most cities and small towns, the names of the World War II dead were simply added to the World War I memorials or a second modest plaque was added to the memorial gazebo or obelisk in the town square. But when a new local or state memorial was erected," it almost always embodied a new vision of "practical war memorials" (Hass 1998:60). "The whole country became in a sense, a living memorial to World War II." Recreational spaces for children, such as parks, memorial football or baseball fields, and playgrounds, were particularly popular (Hass 1998:61).

The collective pregnancy-loss memorial practice of tree planting and dedication participates in this post–WWII memorial impulse for "civic beautification" and the enhancement of recreational spaces.[66] Sister Jane Marie Lamb (1985) published a report of one such event held in October 1985 in a park in Illinois; Kathy Kuhn did the same for one held in Allentown, Pennsylvania, in 1987, and I attended a similar event during the 1989 Pregnancy and Infant Loss Awareness Weekend in Washington, D.C. On each occasion, "families were offered the opportunity to write their babies' names on paper and place it near the roots of the tree. At the conclusion of the ceremony, many families took the shovel and covered the paper with soil so their precious babies' names could integrate into the soil and nurture the tree" (Lamb 1986).

Together these commemorative practices signal important extensions in the historical processes of the "democratization of memory" (Laqueur 1994:159). Such lists of names of the dead, whether recited, displayed, or buried among the roots of a tree at collective pregnancy-loss support rituals, appear to be the next step in the process documented by Laqueur (1994). During World War I the honor of being remembered was extended from noble men to ordinary soldiers, and is now being extended to embryos, fetuses, and neonates. What is more these new, memory-worthy "individuals" are sometimes being constructed as belonging to a social group made up of others with similar identities.[67]

Keepers of the Flame. Another apparent borrowing from postwar commemorative culture is found in the appropriation of the symbol of the eternal flame. Like flowers (chapter 6), candles are symbols of the fragility of

life, and flames are sometimes used in narratives of loss to stress how
quickly a life can be snuffed out. For example, this is the thrust of a piece
written by a grandmother, called "Keith, Our Brief Incandescent Flame"
(Sheppard 1990).[68] In contrast, the notion of an eternal flame focuses on the
difference between eternal God and mortal human beings, between our
bodies and everlasting souls.[69] The earliest "eternal flames," like the one
that burns in front of the Torah, represent God's eternal presence and in
this distinguishes God from mortals.[70]

Following WWI, "eternal flames" emerged as part of national memorializing efforts. They were constructed as part of the Tomb of the Unknown
Soldier, itself a WWI innovation,[71] in France and Belgium.[72] There is not an
"eternal flame" at the U.S. Tomb of the Unknown Soldier in Arlington National Cemetery, but there is one at the lesser-known Tomb of the Unknown Soldier erected in 1957 in Washington Square, Philadelphia, which
commemorates the "thousands of unknown soldiers of Washington's Army
who died of wounds and sickness during the Revolutionary War" (www.
ushistory.org/tour/). With the death of President Kennedy in 1963, the
symbol of "an eternal flame"[73] was adapted to represent, not those who died
in battle, but one who gave his life to national service. At Jackie Kennedy's
request, "an eternal flame similar to that of the French Unknown Soldier in
Paris" (www.arlingtoncemetery.org) was placed in front of President John
F. Kennedy's grave in Arlington (library.thinkquest.org/2901/jfk.htm). In
this case, the flame is made to represent not his enduring soul, but Kennedy's enduring legacy, which will live on through others. This "eternal
flame" is intended to "forever burn brightly in honor of [his] legacy. . . .
The legacy of President Kennedy's ideals lives on as the eternal flame continues to light his final resting place" (library.thinkquest.org/2901/ jfk.htm).
(Kennedy's grave, which also contains the bodies of son Patrick and an unnamed infant daughter, was one of the sites visited by those attending the
1989 Pregnancy and Infant Loss Awareness Weekend in Washington, D.C.)

Following the untimely death of Princess Diana in 1997, this symbol
was once again adapted through a process of popularization and generaliza-
tion. No longer confined to official state monuments of those who died in
the line of service, candles were a common element of the memorial displays
constructed in shop windows in England during the week following
Princess Diana's death.[74] One of the display designers interviewed by Bowman explained that "she deliberately bought a huge candle, because she
wanted it to be untouched once lit and wanted the flame to burn for the
whole time the display was in the window" (1999:223). In 1998, on the one-
year anniversary of their deaths, Harrods erected an "eight-foot-high shrine

to Diana and Dodi which included "photographs, white flowers, and ever-lasting candles" (Bowman 1999:225). In this case, the candles apparently represent not only their everlasting souls, but also their everlasting love.[75]

Candles feature in a number of individual and collective pregnancy-loss rituals (Lamb 1988a section 3:12–14) and the metaphor of an enduring flame is used by several contributors to the newsletters. In Lisa Walsh Combes's (1999) piece "The Daniel Flame," she portrays her stillborn son as having become an "eternal flame," which wells up inside of her: "Silently the light shines forth. It burns within my heart." Through this image she reclaims the experience of having another living inside of her. Any birth entails separation, but the superordinate separation entailed with a stillbirth is metaphorically overturned and rejected. "In this way, you and I will never be apart." This relationship is transformative: she "shall never be the same." One of the ways it changes her is by transforming her into a vehicle for carrying out her son's legacy: "This flame is not a burden. Oh the opposite is true. It is my strength to carry out, the legacy of you." She ends by asserting that if she looks carefully enough she can see "Daniel Flames" shining forth from the others who loved him (his father, grandparents, aunts and uncles, and brothers).

In "The Keepers of the Flame," written by Mary Cushing Doherty (1991a) eight years after her son's death, she pays tribute to those who "personally experienced his brief life" and help keep his memory alive like an "eternal flame." In this piece the emphasis is less on the child as flame and more on the responsibility of tending his memory so that it will not be extinguished through neglect.

Many bereaved parents mention the use of candles as part of their rituals of remembrance. For example, "Buy a special candle. Keep it lit through the holiday season" (*UNITE Notes* 1985/6 5(2):2) is on UNITE's list of recommended ways of "remembering your child at the holidays." In their familial ceremony which they enact each Christmas for their son who was "stillborn" at five months gestation, Bonita and David Martin "light the middle candle," "once a year in remembrance of your little life here." The candle "represent[s] your life with us becoming one forever." Although in this case the flame is not eternal, the Martins associate their candle-lighting ceremony with eternity—"through the death of our lord Jesus Christ . . . you have everlasting life" (Martin and Martin 1995b).

Candles have also been a part of collective pregnancy-loss support memorials. For example, Sandy Smith, cofacilitator of the Chester County UNITE Group, describes how, at the group's memorial service held in August 1999 in the garden of one of the members, "we lit floating candles, and placed them in a small pool in remembrance of all our babies." The group walked a short distance from the pool, "yet they still burned. It's not as if we forgot about the candles, but when we turned our faces back towards the garden, we saw the glow, and wondered what it was. We remembered it was the light of the candles still burning, even though we had walked away. It was comforting to see them still glowing" (Smith 2000).

Conclusions

Remembering is one of the few maternal acts that bereaved mothers can engage in. This is powerfully expressed in a poem by Jana Laux (1985) of Belleville, Illinois, about her son who was stillborn nine days after his due date. Laux contrasts all the things she longs to do for her son with what she is able to do. Three stanzas begin "all I want is," followed by things like, "[to see] you asleep in your crib," "to hold you," "to feed you," "to give you the world." These multiple wishes/stanzas, which give a sense of some of the mundane fullness of a normal parenting relationship, are contrasted with the meagerness of what remains. The poem ends with one brief line: "All I can do is love you and remember."

And yet as we have seen, remembering, in these cases, is not an easy matter. As Kirmayer notes, "memories are most fully and vividly accessed and developed when they fit cultural templates and have a receptive audience" (1996:193). Leaders of the pregnancy-loss support movement are acutely aware of the problems of memory that face those whose babies die before or shortly after birth, and an explicit part of their agenda is "helping parents know what rituals, procedures and mementos will be helpful in remembering their babies" (Laux 1988).

In making sense of their loss and developing ways to remember their babies, members and leaders of pregnancy-loss support groups draw on, adapt, and sometimes critique the powerful and readily available cultural resources of consumer culture. Since there is so little to remember in these cases, what memories and/or physical traces or reminders there are are conscientiously preserved and stationed strategically to serve as aide-mémoire for oneself and others. In addition, the notion found in contemporary consumer culture that memories can be made is sometimes embraced as a strategy for dealing with the small number of available memories. Consumer goods help make both the "baby" and the memory of its existence and loss more tangible and enduring. In the absence of a baby, Dickinson (1995) explains, we have "only memories to hold."

Since the advent of the birth control pill and the legalization of abortion, having a baby in the United States has come to be understood as a matter of choice (Ginsburg 1989). Middle-class women in the United States choose when and with whom to start a family, and sometimes plan the timing of their pregnancies with the idea of choosing an optimum birth date for the child. Once a pregnancy is under way, a woman is intensively involved in a host of consumption choices: what to eat, what to refrain from ingesting (Markens, Browner and Press 1997), which health caregivers to use, which purchases to make (Taylor 2000a, Layne in prep b).[76] As described in chapter 6, it is clear that mothers and members of their social networks use a great deal of care in making these choices. As Peggy Swanton (1985:21) explains to her stillborn daughter, "every decision was made with such great care, What color to paint . . . " In making choices like these, women are not only engaging in the act of "making love" (Miller 1998), but also in the act of making "mothers" and "babies."

When a pregnancy ends in death, the fallacy of control that a consumer-oriented model of pregnancy and birth engenders and perpetuates is brutally exposed. Although many bereaved parents count among the moral lessons they learned from this life-changing experience the fact that we are not as in control of our lives as we assume, bereaved parents do not abandon "choice." The use of consumer goods for "singularizing" and "appropriating" the baby that begins during a pregnancy often continues after the demise. As one woman explained in answer to a questionnaire on post-mortem photographs, "I wanted a picture in a dress of my choice. I want to make her a part of my life, not just a remembrance, but something I can see and show other people" (Laux 1988b).

At the same time, bereaved parents often redirect choice away from the mundane, transitory realm of consumer culture. Memory comes to be understood as a matter of individual, deliberate choice. This choice, made in the face of social pressure to forget, to have a replacement child, to move on, is a moral one, which focuses on the transcendental, oftentimes religiously infused, value of loyalty and love.

In this way narratives of loss reflect a "widespread ambivalence about consumerism and children." On the one hand, "the ability to provide children with wondrous products . . . is a hallmark" of good parenting. On the other hand, parents worry about "overindulgence, in the 'synthetic pleasures' of consumer culture" (Spigel 2001:248).

We also saw how members of pregnancy-loss support groups are borrowing from and contributing to the extensive, often state-sponsored, efforts to develop new ways of memorializing Americans who die untimely deaths. Twentieth-century war memorials as well as more recent memorials collectively commemorating untimely deaths provide a powerful model for how one might or even should properly remember the dead, particularly those whose lives have been cut short. In each of these cases survivors mourn their loved ones and seek ways to ensure that "the remembered death had a purpose" (Sherman 1999:64). This shared symbolic vocabulary communicates both "the prevalence" and "transcendence of suffering." Drawing from this sanctioned "public repertoire" helps members of pregnancy-loss support groups move from social isolation to "greater connection to others" (Lambeck 1996:236).

The memory work of members of pregnancy-loss support groups demonstrates the currency of a contemporary American view of memory as a moral act. When bereaved parents vow to remember in the face of social pressure to forget, they are engaging in "memoro-politics" (Hacking 1996) and defining themselves as people of substance who honor social commitments even in the face of adversity. They are also championing democratic ideals regarding the unique worth of each and every individual, regardless of her/his physical attributes and capacities.

The burden of finding appropriate ways of acknowledging these largely unrecognized losses should not be placed solely on those individuals most directly affected. As Kirmayer puts it, "The moral function of memory is to compel us to confront what we . . . wish to leave behind. . . . Societies . . . must provide cultural forms and occasions for remembering" (1996:193). Feminists have an important role to play in this cultural work.

CHAPTER **10**

Breaking the Silence:
A Feminist Agenda
for Pregnancy Loss

Like pregnancies, books inevitably end. But whereas my pregnancies all ended after uncommonly short gestations, this book, perhaps in compensation, was atypically long in the making. And whereas in all but one of the pregnancies my creative desires were thwarted, I have a profound sense of satisfaction with this book that resulted in their stead. I was never able to enjoy the full extent of any of my pregnancies. Even my one successful pregnancy was cut short at seven months gestation. Although Jasper is now a strapping, well-built eight-year-old boy, I was never filled with his body, was never so large "with child" that I had trouble getting up from a couch or getting in and out of a car. With this book, on the other hand, I have had the luxury of working on it until I was sated. There is still much more to be said and learned about pregnancy loss, such as what the experience of loss is for those from other class and racial backgrounds, or those from other cultures, and the history of pregnancy loss's medicalization, but these are topics for other books. This book now feels pleasingly replete and complete and so I find myself, at last, ready to let it go, to launch it into the world.

This book begins with recollections of my own pregnancy losses, and, given the profound meaning they had for me, I was surprised at how difficult it was to remember the details of those losses. By the time I completed the ninth chapter, which explored problems of memory associated with pregnancy loss, I had a better understanding of why my memory was so sketchy. Of equal importance, no doubt, must be the fact that during those years I spent my creative energy documenting the losses and memorial practices of others rather than my own. This book clearly represents my own chosen form of commemoration.

In the decade and a half during which I have studied pregnancy loss, the conceptual apparati of anthropology changed and a number of exciting new fields of interdisciplinary scholarship emerged. As Csordas (1997:xiii) observed, "long-term research becomes transposed across a variety of theoretical developments." In earlier paradigms, long-term research was understood to "deepen and intensify anthropological knowledge." While this is no longer in fashion, I still believe it to be true. In addition, we [anthropologists] are now expected to "account reflexively for temporality and history in our analytic construction of the ethnographic object and to explicitly recognize the autobiographical element in ethnographic writing" (Csordas 1997:xiii).

Motherhood Lost reflects my personal coming to terms with multiple miscarriages, documents the evolution of the pregnancy-loss support movement in the United States, and engages current theoretical issues in anthropology and a number of interdisciplinary areas of scholarship that emerged during those same years.

Since my first miscarriage in 1986, the pregnancy-loss movement grew and transformed. By the end of the century the movement had entered into a new phase, with less emphasis on peer-support groups (see chapter 2 for figures). There are two possible, not mutually exclusive, explanations that may account for this. First, I believe that the last quarter of the century was a unique moment in the experience of pregnancy loss. This book documents the historically and culturally specific forces that shaped the experience of pregnancy loss during those years. Enduring taboos regarding unhappy endings, "dirty" and "unruly" female biology, "wasted production," corpses, and malformations collided with changing childbearing patterns and an increasingly developed sense of fetal personhood.

Kleinman and Kleinman (1997:23n39) conclude their essay on "suffering in our times" with a quote from Hobsbawm's *The Age of Extremes: A History of the World 1914–1991* to describe how the current "transformation of epochs" is changing "social experience": "The old maps and charts which guided human beings, singly and collectively, through life no longer represent the landscape through which we move." This aptly describes what befell middle-class Americans who suffered pregnancy losses during the '80s and '90s, and was a primary factor in the emergence of the pregnancy-loss support movement. Those who experienced pregnancy loss during these years found themselves on an unanticipated journey with outdated maps that no longer accurately represented the sociocultural geography. As they made their way through this altered terrain, they created new maps, piecing together in novel ways bits and pieces of what they found at hand. *Motherhood Lost* documents the creative ways members of pregnancy-loss support groups drew on cultural resources to deal with their losses and, in so doing, actively contributed to the development of emerging sociocultural practices. Now, thanks to the pregnancy-loss support movement, pregnancy losses are somewhat more visible, and the plight of those whose pregnancies end without a baby to take home somewhat better recognized.

Another important factor leading to a diminution of face-to-face peer-based pregnancy loss support is the advent of Web-based support. SHARE and UNITE each now have a Web presence. In addition, there are numerous other electronic sites devoted to pregnancy-loss support. Some of these include "Heartbreaking Choice," "a nonjudgmental place to find support . . . for people who have chosen to terminate pregnancies due to severe fetal health problems," "Christian Pregnancy Loss Support," which offers "spiritual comfort, solace, prayer and emotional support" to "women who have suffered from miscarriage, stillbirth or neonatal death or infertility," as well as list serves for "Miscarriage after Infertility," "Multiple Miscarriages," "Pregnancy after Miscarriage." One site of particular interest is that of a nonprofit organization founded by Dr. Michael Berman, a Yale ob/gyn. Hygeia seeks to create "a global community using 'new technologies' to assuage the hurt, grieving, and sorrow experienced by families who have endured the loss of a pregnancy, newborn, or infant child" (www.hygeia.org 1–14–02).[1] Visitors to the site are invited to "exchange stories and thoughts" on message boards and to participate "in a private international email community." Hygeia also provides "moderated chat rooms" for siblings. Dr. Berman explains to new users that they will "find original poetry of loss and hope, medical information about maternal and child health, and the ability to share [their] stories with thousands of registered families world wide" in a "safe and secure on-line environment." The Hygeia Foundation is, as far as I know, unique in its efforts to make computer-mediated support for pregnancy loss "universally" accessible by placing Internet access in "medically under served and economically disadvantaged neighborhood communities."

Scholars of "computer-mediated social support" have identified a number of features or "affordances" that may make this form of peer support particularly attractive. Walther and Boyd's (in press) online survey of 340 users from 57 usenet newsgroups designed to offer support for a wide range of issues, including one devoted to pregnancy loss (soc.support.pregnancy loss), indicates that users appreciate the greater ease of access. Computer-

mediated support is available every day, around the clock, and allows access
to people who are geographically distant. Computer-mediated support is
also perceived as providing access to a greater range of expertise.[2] Walther
and Boyd (in press:12) also found computer-mediated communication allowed participants to "optimize their expressiveness," noting that "participants may craft their messages and their self-presentations with greater care
than may be possible in spontaneous FtF settings. They may stop and think,
edit, rewrite, even abort and re-start a message." Because people do not
need to monitor "their gestures, facial expressions, voice or physical appearance," they may pay more attention to their desired message and may have
heightened "self-awareness" (Walther and Boyd in press:12). In addition, it
offers a higher level of anonymity and social distance, which are considered
beneficial because they enable participants to be more candid and to "manage stigma" with greater ease. These features also reduce the obligation to
reciprocate. Unlike face-to-face support groups, where members may feel
"social pressure to participate actively and disclose their thoughts and feelings" (Gallagher et al. quoted in Walther and Boyd in press:5), with computer-mediated support people may participate as "lurkers," reading others' contributions without revealing their own presence.

One of the major goals of the pregnancy-loss support movement has
been to bring pregnancy loss out into the open. According to Schwarcz, "to
suffer is to be shut in, to be locked up by grief in a world without light. A
pane opens when sorrow is somehow voiced, shared, spewn out of the
closed world of the individual in pain" (1997:128). Similarly, Shay concludes from his research with Vietnam veterans, "one cannot recover in isolation since narrative heals . . . only if the survivor finds or creates a trust-
worthy community of listeners" (Shay quoted in Brison 1997:25). This is
exactly what bereaved parents have done through their creation of and participation in pregnancy-loss support groups, and more recently with computer-mediated support.

But meeting together in support groups or participating in electronic
chatrooms or bulletin boards is a partial and imperfect solution. In both
cases discussion of these events is post facto. If people only learn about
pregnancy loss after they have one, and if the only people who know about
such losses are people who have had them or been directly affected, then
women and people who undertake a pregnancy will continue to be unin-
formed and unprepared for this not uncommon eventuality. These types of
support keep the topic hidden in protected real or virtual spaces. In either
venue, bereaved parents seek support from strangers, and although the
anonymity of computer-mediated support and of face-to-face support-

group meetings (where participants normally use only first names and are reminded each week about the importance of confidentiality) is clearly of a certain value to those seeking support, it also flags a problem. As Kirmayer has observed, "there is a crucial distinction between . . . a public space of solidarity and a private space of shame" (1996:189).

Throughout the '80s and '90s, in addition to providing peer support to bereaved parents, leaders of the pregnancy-loss support movement also worked to bring the topic out into the open.[3] As described in chapter 4, they achieved some success in this regard. Perhaps the clearest measure of their success is in the creation of an official, publicly recognized awareness month and day. By 2001, forty-seven governors had signed a proclamation "honoring October 15 as Pregnancy and Infant Loss Remembrance Day" (*SHARING* 2001 10(6):10). The topic is also now more frequently covered in the popular media. Some laws have been passed at the behest of the movement concerning the "disposal of fetal remains" (see also Morgan 2002), civil records, and insurance coverage. Many, perhaps most, hospitals now have designated staff and explicit protocols for caring for the special needs of women who have pregnancy losses.

There has also been some modest success in terms of getting pregnancy loss onto the scholarly map. Chapter 2 described a number of volumes devoted to, or touching on, this subject written by historians, sociologists, and anthropologists. Another small indicator is the fact that the proposal for an Encyclopedia for Science and Literature included pregnancy loss as a heading.

But by and large, in the realm of feminist scholarship the topic of pregnancy loss remains an orphan. It is time for feminists to move pregnancy loss from "a private space of shame" to a "public space of solidarity." The first thing that must be done is to lift the taboo surrounding pregnancy loss. In retaining a studied silence on pregnancy loss, feminists have not only abandoned their sisters in hours of need, they have contributed to the shame and isolation that attends these events, and have, de facto, surrendered the discourse of pregnancy loss to antichoice activists. Feminists must frankly acknowledge the frequency and import of such events in women's lives and create a women-centered discourse of pregnancy loss. We are, in fact, well placed to do this cultural work. As de Certeau (1984:74) has noted, in order to authorize "new language," one must first critique the established discourses. Feminists have already critiqued the patriarchal dimensions of biomedicine and Judeo-Christian traditions, two of the primary resources currently shaping the meaning of pregnancy loss. Why is it, then, that feminist agendas still do not include the issue of pregnancy loss?

One of the most important factors is, of course, the way the subject of pregnancy loss (particularly early losses) overlaps with issues central to the abortion debate. Because anti-abortion activists base their argument on the presence of fetal, and even more important, embryonic personhood, feminists have studiously avoided anything that might imply or concede such a presence. The fear, in the context of pregnancy loss, is that if one were to acknowledge that there was something of value lost, something worth grieving in a miscarriage, one would thereby automatically accede the inherent personhood of embryos and fetuses.[4] This is not the case, however, unless one accepts the anti-abortion view of personhood in the first place. If, on the other hand, one accepts an anthropologically informed view of personhood, that is, that personhood is culturally constructed (and that the ways it is constructed differ between cultures and within a given culture over time), one can see that the process of constructing personhood may be undertaken with some embryos and not others.[5] The cultural construction of personhood is a gradual process, one that continues through the course of a lifetime (and often beyond, for example, with "ancestors"[6]). During the course of a pregnancy (and even before conception occurs) one may begin to establish a social relationship with a wished-for child. True, these relationships are "relatively one-sided," but as Rothman (1989:104) has pointed out, "all relationships with babies, for quite some weeks or months after birth, are relatively one-sided."

To illustrate the distinction between these two models of personhood, let us take the examples of two types of miscarriage that do not involve an embryo. Not infrequently a sonogram exam will reveal an empty embryonic sac. Although the woman would test positive on a pregnancy test because of the changes in her hormones, no embryo would have formed. Similarly, in some molar pregnancies (Chelouche 2001), fertilization of an empty egg results in the abnormal growth of placental tissue and no fetal tissue. In other words, fertilization may result in a cancerous or precancerous growth instead of an embryo. According to the logic of "inherent personhood," there was no "person" in either of these cases since there was no embryo, but according to the cultural model of personhood, if that pregnancy was known and desired, the would-be mother (and others) may have already begun the process of constructing a new person. If she has, that protoperson is part of what is lost and mourned. Speaking of American middle-class married women, Reinharz (1987:232) remarks, "For many women . . . the child begins when the decision is made to bear it. When a woman decides to become pregnant, her child, which hitherto had been only a potentially wanted thing, is transformed into an actually wanted thing. The child begins to exist." Of course this is not always the case even for desired pregnancies. As Reinharz (1987:243) also noted, after one or more losses a woman may "dehumanize, minimize, and medicalize" her experience of a subsequent pregnancy, or in my terms, she may postpone and/or attenuate the sociocultural work of constructing a person. To deny that such practices take place is simply foolish; to fear these practices is to give credence to the anti-abortion stance. If we can dispel this fear and overcome our paralysis, there are numerous ways feminists can help alleviate some of the unnecessary suffering and alienation that now accompanies pregnancy loss. A cross-culturally informed, progressive, "social constructionist" (Layne 1999b) model of personhood would help feminists deal with the thorny issue of how to reconcile "the increasing and undeniable moral and social importance given to fetuses in European and North American society" (Morgan 1996:2) with a pro-choice position.

Another factor hindering the inclusion of pregnancy loss (including perhaps especially stillbirths and early infant deaths) in feminist agendas is the fact that pregnancy loss contradicts two fundamental premises of the women's-health discourse of pregnancy and birth—that women can control their reproduction and that birth is a natural, joyful experience. The liberal emphasis on self-determination that has been used effectively to secure for women the right to contraception and abortion (Rothman 1989:68–74) is often understood to mean that we have the right, ability, and, in fact, responsibility "to control our fertility" (Rothman 1989:72). An unintended and unexamined consequence of this is that women may be assumed to be responsible for their pregnancy losses. Despite the women's-health movement's sustained critique of biomedical models of reproduction, it in fact shares with biomedicine a belief in the ability to control reproduction.

In addition, both share an emphasis on happy endings. So focused has the women's health movement been in challenging biomedicine's pathologization of pregnancy and birth, it has systematically minimized and marginalized negative reproductive outcomes.

In *Our Bodies, Ourselves*, negative reproductive outcomes are segregated to a chapter of their own instead of being integrated into the four chronologically ordered chapters on pregnancy and birth. In the second edition (Boston Women's Health Book Collective/1976), the subsections on miscarriage and ectopic pregnancy were not in the chapter on pregnancy; the subsection on stillbirth was not in the chapter on childbirth. Instead these topics were lumped together in a chapter entitled "some exceptions to the normal childbearing experience" found after the chapter on postpartum. In addition, in stark contrast to the other chapters on childbearing, which were

Mother with newborn. Photo by Harriette Hartigan.

peppered with appealing photographs of pregnant, laboring, and mothering women, not a single photograph is included in the "exceptions" chapter. There women and their longed-for babies are visually erased. It is worth noting that the chapter on elective abortion *is* illustrated: there is a photograph of women at a pro-choice demonstration, one of a lone woman "deciding what to do," one of a female physician operating a vacuum suction machine, and one of a woman supported by a female companion during an abortion (Boston Women's Health Book Collective 1976:217–231). One might deduce from this that elective abortions are events worthy of feminist support and that spontaneous abortions are not.

The 1998 version, *Our Bodies, Ourselves for the New Century*, is identical to the second edition in terms of organization and the lack of illustrations. Part four of the book is devoted to childbearing and includes an introduction followed by chapters on pregnancy, childbirth, postpartum, and "child-bearing loss, infertility, and adoption." Every chapter save the one on loss has photographic illustrations. The chapter on childbirth ends with an afterword directed to women who had healthy babies but are dissatisfied with their birth experiences, and may "feel ashamed of not having had that 'natural' birth we'd prepared for" (1998:493). This section has a footnote acknowledging that babies can die "before, during, or just after delivery" and pointing those "women who face this rare and heartbreaking occurrence" to the appropriate chapter. Others, that is, the lucky ones, need not trouble themselves by reading about such unpleasant topics. The unrelenting focus on happy outcomes also colors the coverage of postpartum depression. The postpartum chapter is illustrated with six photographs of happy new mothers snuggling or breast feeding their healthy infants. One of these photos is placed directly above the subsection on the "baby blues" (1998: 504).[7]

Another example is found with the Bradley Method of Natural Childbirth, an approach that "has been closely linked to the homebirth movement and particularly to the National Association of Parents and Professionals for Safe Alternatives in Childbirth" (Rothman 1982:99).[8] Their literature portrays birth as "the most joyful event" in one's life (1989:1). Even in the section "Variations and Unexpected Situations" of *The Bradley Method Student Workbook* (Hathaway 1989), where one might expect to find examples of difficulties, reproductive mishaps are starkly absent. The page is dominated with a large photograph of an attractive smiling white woman nursing twins. Thus, even "variations and unexpected situations" are cast as ones with idyllic endings. The authors take pains to assure the reader how unlikely it is that the variations listed—breach presentation, Cesarean section, meconium staining, postmature baby, premature baby, vBac—would occur to them. The very real risk that these "variations" may result in the death of the baby/ies or the birth of a child with birth defects is left unsaid, and the horror of birth disasters[9] minimized as "unpleasant possibilities."

In addition to the erasure of negative reproductive outcomes, the rhetoric of the women's-health movement, and of the natural childbirth movement in particular, champions the ethic of individual responsibility. The fundamental premise of the women's-health movement, that women must wrest back control of their bodies from physicians, *especially* during pregnancy and birth, reinforces the notion that positive birth outcomes are something women can control.[10] In *Our Bodies, Ourselves* the subtitle of the chapter on pregnancy is "what you can do to prepare yourself" and is followed by the key words "choice, commitment, preparation" (1987:251). The chapter on childbirth is called "*preparation* for childbirth" (BWHC 1987, emphasis added).

As discussed in chapter 7, the ethic of individual control is embedded in a culture of meritocracy. The Bradley Method workbook contains a forty-four-item checklist of things women should do on a daily basis (for example, six different types of exercise, drinking eight to ten glasses of water, and avoiding pesticides and stress) to be sure they "Stay Healthy and Low Risk." Women are not only expected to control their own bodies, but those of their partners ("Make sure your coach is adequately rested"), and their work and home environments ("Avoid stress and overdoing at home and at work") (Hathaway 1989:65). This list, which appears immediately after the pages explaining Cesarean section (Hathaway 1989:64–65), includes space for pregnant women to engage in self-criticism and write in plans for how to do better in each area. The message is clear: if they are not morally vigilant, women may "fall from grace" and slip from "low risk" to "high risk." If a pregnancy ends with a less-than-desired birth experience or birth outcome, it is hard to imagine a woman who could not go back over that daunting list and find at least some areas in which she should have done more, could have tried harder.

This liberal emphasis on individualism also deflects attention from social causes of pregnancy loss. Although most pregnancy losses are thought to be the result of random genetic errors, some losses can be reasonably considered to be the result of "social problems," such as domestic violence, inadequate prenatal care, and exposure to environmental toxins (see Layne 2001).

In the United States, the women's-health movement has had many positive effects on women's reproductive experiences. Fewer anesthetics are used; some of the "prep" practices, such as shaving the genitals and enemas, have been eliminated; women are not as physically constrained during labor; many middle-class women now give birth in relatively cozy, lower-lit "birthing suites" in hospitals; babies are not swept away from their mothers right after birth, and breast-feeding is encouraged. These positive effects should not be minimized. Nevertheless, it is time to own up to the fact that there have been a number of unintended negative consequences of the women's-health movement's position on pregnancy and birth. Radical feminists have resources ready at hand to illuminate the limits of an ideology of control and the pitfalls of individualism in this context. It is time to do so.

Much of the feminist scholarship on reproduction has clustered around the beginnings and ends of pregnancy, that is, on the assistive conception technologies and on the medical management of birth. Rothman (1989) and Stabile (1998) have convincingly argued that pregnancy itself, the process of gestating, has not received the recognition it deserves. Rothman explains why gestation (along with all the other nurturing aspects of motherhood) are systematically undervalued in terms of our patriarchal ideology, which privileges "the seed." Kinship is reckoned based on genetic ties. Rothman (1989:36) explains, "unlike what happens in a mother-based system, . . . the relationship between women and their children is not based on . . . the long months of pregnancy, the intimate connections with the baby as it grows and moves inside her body, passes through her genitals, and sucks at her breasts." Instead, women are understood to be related to their children the same way men are—through their "seed." Another indicator of this patriarchal bias is found in the language of birth. "In acting as if the baby 'arrived' from the outside, 'entered' the world, we are making it sound like children start as separate people, arriving in our lives as babies" (Rothman 1989:98). We treat "the baby as if 'delivered' from outside;" the baby is "'brought home' (as if for the first time)," as if it hadn't been there all along as part of the woman (Rothman 1989:100).

Stabile (1998:183) makes a similar point in her discussion of the fact that fetal images are now considered acceptable for public display (for example, the Volvo advertisement using a sonogram image, and anti-abortion protest films and posters), but the image of Demi Moore's nude, pregnant body which appeared on the cover of *Vanity Fair* provoked public outrage. "With the advent of visual technologies, the contents of the uterus have become demystified and entirely representable, but the pregnant body itself remains concealed."

Stabile (1998:183–4) argues that this blind spot is not restricted to mass culture but notes that the pregnant body also remains "invisible and undertheorized in feminist theory," which she links to the "overarching goal" of feminism to "extricate 'woman' from a purely reproductive status." She notes how much of the scholarship on reproduction has focused on "labor and childbirth" and argues that "despite critiques of the product-oriented, capitalist management of labor and childbirth," feminists who have focused "on the climax of reproduction—the aspect of the process that literally introduces the product into the marketplace—the concept of labor exists only in relation to activity expended during childbirth" (1998:185–6), not to the nine months of activity preceding birth.

Surrogacy clearly raises questions about the value and meaning of gestation.[11] While an issue in both traditional (Artificial Insemination) surrogacy and gestational (GIFT) surrogacy, the issue is particularly clear with gestational surrogacy, where the surrogate is not genetically related to the child.

The issue is also an important one in the context of pregnancy loss. At first glance, pregnancy loss is another subject that seems to focus on the "climax" of birth, but since there is no baby to bring home, little or nothing beyond the pregnancy itself, the process of gestation in fact looms large. Over and over again bereaved mothers proclaim the value of those months.[12] A better-developed feminist theory of gestation will be beneficial for those who suffer and/or study pregnancy loss.

Another stumbling block to the development of a feminist response to pregnancy loss may come from the degree to which women who join pregnancy-loss support groups reveal their deep desire to become mothers. Their efforts to "join the motherhood club" even if their baby died may strike outsiders as desperate and pathetic. In at least some feminist circles, members of pregnancy-loss support groups risk being condemned for their "maternal desire," and the anthropologists who study them may be castigated for "condoning" this desire. For example, one reviewer of *Transformative Motherhood* (Layne 1998, 1999a) criticized the foster, adoptive, and bereaved mothers we studied for aspiring to be "mothers within patriarchal culture" (McLeod 2001:70). As Stabile (1998:185) points out, one camp of feminists views "pregnancy as the ultimate act of female complicity, as the exemplar of feminine false consciousness." Although this stance is perhaps less common in feminism today than it was in earlier years, cases like pregnancy loss, which expose thwarted maternal desire, still tend to provoke strong judgements. As Sandelowski (1993) noted in regard to infertility, the motivations of women who choose to bear children and do so without difficulty are not subject to the same feminist critique of those who try but fail. Sandelowski (1993:40) quotes feminist scholars Birke, Himmelwieit, and Vines on this issue: "Understanding where a need comes from does not remove it. Nor indeed is there any difference in the desire for children from any other in that respect. All needs and desires are socially produced."

These are substantial but not insurmountable obstacles. In addition to developing ways to acknowledge pregnancy losses without undermining women's right to terminate unwanted pregnancies, or overpathologizing pregnancy, or suggesting that women's only source of value is their reproductive capacity, there is much to be done.

Feminists active in the women's-health movement need to put pregnancy loss on their agenda and to critically evaluate the sociomedical management of pregnancy loss. Pregnancy loss needs to be chronologically integrated into manuals on pregnancy and birth rather than ghettoized and secluded in chapters on abnormal pregnancies. Pregnancy loss also needs to become a regular part of prenatal education and childbirth classes. Models for "natural" and/or "prepared" pregnancy loss should be developed, just as they have been for birth.[13] At a minimum, pregnant women should be informed well in advance of the standard medical procedures in the case of miscarriage or stillbirth and informed of their options and alternatives. Whereas midwives and childbirth educators have questioned the medical necessity of episiotomies, painkillers, anesthesia, and C-sections, to my knowledge no comparable questioning has been done of the standard practice of performing a D&C for miscarriage, sometimes with general anesthesia. Furthermore, now that many miscarriages and most stillbirths are discovered earlier via prenatal diagnostic technologies, there exists the possibility of developing new, more supportive ways of helping women under these circumstances, such as developing appropriate office protocols for what to do when a loss is detected during a routine prenatal visit.[14] In recent years some hospitals have started to assign women who are delivering stillborn babies to rooms off the maternity floor. There may be other aspects of the medical management of these events that could be tailored to meet the special needs of these women and the nursing staff who cares for them.

Science reporting on reproductive issues, like science reporting in general, tends to highlight the promise of new technologies while giving short shrift to failures and costs. Feminist science reporters could offer more measured perspectives, which might help reduce unrealistic expectations that are fueled by sensational portrayals of "revolutionary breakthroughs" in reproductive medicine.

Another way in which feminists could contribute is with the development of feminist rituals of pregnancy loss. There are at present no culturally sanctioned rituals by which to mark a pregnancy loss in our society. Over the past twenty years, pregnancy-loss support organizations have been active in creating rituals of remembrance for pregnancy loss, but these rituals have focused on concretizing and sacralizing the personhood of the baby. We saw how such groups encourage bereaved parents to concretize their loss by retaining keepsakes, and, even with very early losses, to name the "baby." Likewise, communal memorial services focus on the special qualities and value of "the babies."

Feminist rituals might focus on the woman and provide scripted ways for friends, relatives, and colleagues to offer support, acknowledge her loss, reaffirm her connection to others, and her sense of belonging and identity. One possible model comes from a ritual I participated in during the course of my dissertation research in rural Jordan in the early 1980s. A schoolteacher I knew had a miscarriage and at the end of a short period of seclusion/recuperation her colleagues and I were invited to her home for a ritual meal. We offered our condolences and presented her with a gift of a blanket, an important form of women's wealth (Layne 1994). The following day she returned to work.

In Jordan, the serving of a ritual meal to guests is a central element of all rites of passage (for example, marriage, high school graduation, death), except childbirth. My friend prepared and served the meal herself and this occasioned some disquiet in me, since my own cultural background dictated that we ought to have been taking care of her and not vice versa. Upon reflection, I realized that, given the cultural logic of gift exchange in Jordan (and the honor associated with giving), it was essential that she give as well as receive. And since this ritual took place a few days after the miscarriage and immediately prior to her return to work, it was not only possible, but ritually critical, for her to demonstrate her competence in this way.

In contrast with the new rituals of loss being created in the United States by pregnancy-loss support groups, this Jordanian ritual focused on the woman. Given the differences between Jordan and the United States, there are aspects of this ritual that may not be appropriate in our culture, but it provides a wonderful model, I believe, for a feminist ritual of pregnancy loss. As Turner has noted, "a primary function of ritual is to connect the individual with the group—dramatically, indissolubly. . . . The specific rites which comprise many feminist rituals reaffirm relationship, belonging, and identity" (1982:226). Through this Jordanian ritual, my friend's loss was shared as we collectively acknowledged the event, offered our support, bore witness to her competence, and through that rite provided a bridge back to her everyday life, no doubt making it easier for her to return to work, no longer a pregnant woman and yet, not a mother.

Another even more ambitious intervention would be to alter the occupational structure to ensure that women who choose both families and careers need not delay childbearing, but may have their children during the years when the risk of pregnancy loss is less without jeopardizing their careers (cf. Maranto 1995). The women's movement that helped liberate a whole generation of career women has inadvertently contributed to the problem of pregnancy loss by encouraging women to delay childbearing. The rate of pregnancy loss is lowest for women twenty to twenty-four (10.6 percent) and increases steadily thereafter to a high of 20.5 percent for women thirty-five to thirty-nine (Ventura et al. 1995:20). The cover story of the August 13, 2001, issue of *Newsweek* reported on a new move among fertility specialists to encourage women to have their children earlier. The American Infertility Association, a patient advocacy group, had recently undertaken a campaign to educate women about the effects of age on fertility and "the American Society for Reproductive Medicine, the nation's largest professional organization of fertility specialists" was planning a "bold ad campaign" to "debut on buses in New York, suburban Chicago and Seattle encouraging women to have their children in their twenties and early thirties" (Kalb 2001). Clearly we must work to ensure that women who choose to begin their families during the biologically optimum childbearing years are not penalized at work.

It would also be desirable to facilitate alternative modes of forming families, such as, for instance, with fostering systems like those in Africa or among native Hawaiians (Goody 1970, 1971; Bledsoe 1990a, 1990b, 1999, Modell 1996), whereby one does not have to produce a child of "one's own" in order to enjoy the experience of nurturing. This is a task that radical feminists have long acknowledged (Rothman 1989:256). And there is still clearly plenty of work to be done to make sure that womanhood and motherhood are not equated, that women have many, varied opportunities for leading fulfilling and productive lives, whether or not they choose to be mothers.

In the meantime, we can no longer afford to put our heads in the sand. According to Melucci (1996:1), social movements in complex societies are like "prophets, 'they speak before': they announce what is taking shape even before its direction and content has become clear. The inertia of old categories may prevent us from hearing the message and from deciding, consciously and responsibly what action to take in light of it." During the last quarter of the twentieth century, the pregnancy-loss support movement announced changes in the experience and meaning of pregnancy and pregnancy loss which we cannot afford to ignore.

In a recent issue of *UNITE Notes*, Marty Heilberg describes her experience of having an ectopic pregnancy in a piece called "Out of Place," which she explains is the meaning of "ectopic." She concludes by describing how out of place she feels in "a society that loves pregnant women, but only if the pregnancies work." We have blindly been a party to this. In that same issue Julie Gimmi, a mother of two living children, published a series of vignettes about the loss of her daughter Zoe. The first reports the reaction of an associate to the news of her loss. "'I don't like death' she says. 'I try to surround myself with good things, positive energy.' For a fleeting moment I see the ghost of recognition in her eyes. But only for a fleeting moment, then it's gone. She doesn't realize or she's more wicked than I ever imagined. She doesn't apologize" (Gimmi 2001).

Pregnancy loss is not a nice topic. None of us "like death," and all of us would prefer to be surrounded by "good things and positive energy." But pregnancy loss is a fact of life and the pain that members of pregnancy-loss support groups express is real. Grief for a dead loved one may be both inevitable and necessary, but the additional hurt that bereaved parents feel when their losses are dismissed and diminished by others is needless and cruel. It is high time we recognize pregnancy loss and offer our support.

Notes

Chapter 1

1. Apparently we are not the only ones to display such hubris. Fillion (1994:35), writing from Canada, describes "proud we've-decided-to-start-a-family announcements."
2. The admission forms in Emergency were not transferable to another ward.
3. The nineteenth edition of *Williams Obstetrics* (Cunningham 1993:662) gives a rate of 10 percent for first-trimester spontaneous abortions for "healthy, fertile women" but adds that "spontaneous abortion rates of nearly 25 percent are frequently reported." The rate may also increase with parity and if a woman conceives within three months of a live birth (Cunningham 1993:666), but there is no evidence that the rate is greater if conception occurs in the next cycle following a miscarriage (Wilcox et al. 1988).
4. A 1988 study (Wilcox et al.) found that 31 percent of all pregnancies end in miscarriage. Macfarlane and Mugford cite studies that report even higher rates: one estimates that married women aged twenty to twenty-nine in England and Wales spontaneously abort 78 percent of their conceptions and two other studies suggest that 40 percent of the conceptions that survive to the time of implantation are spontaneously aborted (1984:84). Standard demography excludes such embryonic deaths from their measures of spontaneous intrauterine mortality (Bongaarts and Potter 1983:38).
5. I also remember the impact of all those losses on the pregnancy I did manage to carry to viability; how I shifted my conviction that things could and would go wrong from one source of anxiety to the next, throughout the course of the pregnancy. First I was certain that I would lose it between the eighth and tenth week, as was my pattern. Once I made it past that critical point I transferred all my anxiety to the amnio. I was so worried that the amnio would cause a miscarriage that I made myself physically ill. What at first appeared to be an impacted tooth turned out to be the result of clenching my jaw. Then I worried about the amnio results, and, once that was behind me, about whether I would make it to twenty-four weeks gestation, after which fetuses sometimes survive outside the womb.
6. This is not a pseudonym. I gave the participants in my study of pregnancy loss in toxically assaulted communities the choice of pseudonym, first name only, or full name.

7. When we put together our résumé to introduce ourselves to potential birth mothers, we included a photo of us with our dog. Later we learned that, like us, nearly all of the other infertile couples using our adoption agency had gotten a dog as interim child.

8. According to Valian (1998:21), luck plays a much greater role in explanations for women's successes (by both men and women) than it does for men's successes.

9. I first presented the story of Jasper's birth at the American Anthropological Association's annual meeting in November 1991, just months after he had come home. I also presented the paper to the Albany Medical Center's Early Intervention Staff, and, on another occasion, to their Obstetrical medical residents.

10. See Martin (1998) for a critique of this view of fetuses.

11. See Layne (nd) and chapter 10 for a feminist critique of the impact of the natural childbirth movement for women whose pregnancies end badly.

12. I have been moved by those whose stories share commonalities with my own, but in writing the book, have been drawn even more frequently to those who have made sense of their loss in ways quite differently than I have.

13. See Layne in prep a on the role of naming.

Chapter 2

1. See (Morgan 2002) for a discussion of the ambiguity of the term stillbirth in the early years of the twentieth century, years during which embryology was emerging as a specialty and states were passing laws regulating the treatment of stillborn infants.

2. The rate of loss also increases at a similar rate with paternal age (Cunningham et al. 2001:856).

3. The causes for a large proportion of late losses remain unexplained (Cunningham et al. 2001: 1074).

4. See Boddy (1998) for a comparison of rates in Canada and Sudan.

5. "Low birth weight" (less than 2,500 grams or about 5.5 pounds) is the leading cause of neonatal mortality for blacks and the second leading cause overall. In 1997, 291,154 low-birth-weight births were recorded (U.S. Dept. of Health and Human Services 1999).

6. Cutbacks in mental-health care during the 1980s led to a decrease in relatively costly one-on-one psychotherapy and greater use of medication (Irvine 1999:37) and group therapy. Many support medical self-help/self-care as a way of reducing healthcare costs (Gartner 1982:64).

7. I follow Makela et al. (1996:13) in my preference for the term "mutual-help" (over that of "self-help") to describe pregnancy-loss support groups given the ideological importance in pregnancy-loss support of mutually helping others who have had similar experiences.

8. Katz (1993:1) provides similar figures for both time periods. A recent study by the surgeon general (1999) suggests that 2–3 percent of all Americans have participated in a self-help group at one time or another.

9. Irvine (1999:101) has suggested that peer support groups, like the codependency groups she studied, help provide "a sense of self attuned to [the] new realities of an era in which "institutional anchors are dissolving," and we are leading more "complex, fluid, rootless lives." In contrast, pregnancy-loss support groups are designed to resist rather than adapt to the centrifugal forces and to aid individuals in creating and maintaining enduring familial relationships.

10. This explains why "feelings" are not the focus of AA but are so clearly at the center of pregnancy-loss support (cf. Irvine 1999 on feelings and Codependents Anonymous).

11. Canada ranks second to the United States in terms of numbers of pregnancy-loss support organizations (Lammert, personal communication, July 2000).

12. Examples include forced medical treatment of pregnant women (Daniels 1993, Hartouni 1997), social opprobrium of women who smoke (Oaks 2001) or drink during a pregnancy, prosecution of pregnant substance abusers (Boling 1995), ex utero (Casper 1998) and in utero fetal surgery (Blizzard 2000, in press).

13. In the 1980s and '90s, large numbers of women underwent fertility treatments. More than one million new patients were reported to have sought treatment for infertility in the United States in 1990 (Sandelowski 1993:7). For these women and their partners, the increased level of financial, emotional, and time commitment entailed in their quest for a biologically related child led to a huge investment in the pregnancy (Sandelowski 1993:126–127).

14. Lovell described a case of a late pregnancy loss involving a physical malformation, in which the attitudes and practices of the medical staff and the woman's network "may have led to the deconstruction of the baby's identity altogether."

15. An interesting comparison can be made with adoptive mothers, who have the requisite experience of raising a child but lack the required biological link.

16. Irvine makes a similar point with regard to codependency. Members of CoDA consider codependency to be a "condition" rather than an "injury" and therefore do not attempt to "recover" (1999:151, 61).

17. Like Csordas (1997:xii), I hope to show "that people who might be regarded by many [academics] as '. . . wierdos' are quite like ourselves, and at the same time that people who might be our neighbors in fact inhabit a substantially different phenomenological world."

18. Several nonanthropologist critics of my edited anthropological collection *Transformative Motherhood: On Giving and Getting in a Consumer Culture* have mistaken presentation of ethnographic data as an endorsement of those views. One reviewer, a professor of human ecology and women's studies, admitted to feeling "extremely uncomfortable" when reading the essays but had trouble identifying the source of her discomfort (Apple 2001:11). Ultimately she attributed her reactions to the "emotional uniformity" of the essays. I think she was both right and wrong in this assessment. The methodological uniformity of these anthropological essays does result in something that might be understood as "emotional uniformity," in that each author takes seriously and conveys in re-

spectful ways the points of view of the women we studied. This critic, however, mistakes these disciplinary conventions. She believes that we "expected that the women we based our studies on (women who gave up children for adoption or surrogacy, raised foster children and/or children with disabilities, or suffered pregnancy loss) would "have a similar outlook." Leaving aside the fact that each of the authors had independently noticed the prominence of gift rhetoric in their unique areas of research, the attribution of "expectation" runs counter to the anthropological mandate to suspend one's own "ethnocentric" expectations and be open to alternative approaches, practices, and understandings of those we study.

19. The association of certain forms of Christianity and anti-abortion politics (Ginsburg 1989, Press and Cole 1999) may make this even more of a lightning rod than it would be otherwise.

20. One type of action research described by Reinharz (1992:191) concerns "demystification": where there is a "paucity of research" about certain problems, "the very act of obtaining knowledge creates the potential for change."

21. For example, I have been welcomed by UNITE as semi-official chronicler of their organization; my photographs and transcriptions of the twenty-fifth-anniversary celebration are posted on their website.

22. For a small sample of these studies see Best 1981; Cote-Arsenault 2000; Cote-Arsenault, Bidlack and Humm 2001; Cote-Arsenault and Dombeck 2001; Cote-Arsenault and Mahlangu 1999; Forsyth 1983; Johansson and Bickman 1982; Neugebauer 1987; Neugebauer et al. 1992a, 1992b, 1997; Swanson 1999a, b, 2000; Swanson-Kauffman 1983, 1986. Swanson (2000) provides an excellent review of the extensive literature on depressive symptoms after miscarriage.

23. An exception to this is found in Scholten's 1985 book *Childbearing in American Society: 1650–1850*, which unaccountably does not deal with the issue of infant mortality.

24. Although the book illustrates broad differences, the author's afterword takes a universalist position. Sha hopes that women and men who experience a loss will be consoled by the fact that they "belong to an enormously large and ancient fellowship" and "are anything but alone" (1990:113).

25. On the other hand, Reinharz (1988a:6) notes that knowledge about how to prevent miscarriages could also be used to produce them, and that the possibility of miscarriage can be used to shield women who need to hide their abortions.

26. In her introduction to the volume, Cecil (1996) provides a description of the way miscarriage has been depicted in fiction and poetry by a number of British authors as well as a survey of the way in which the topic has been treated (typically mentioned only in passing) by other anthropologists.

27. Then as now, infant mortality "varied enormously" by class. Of the women who delivered at the General Lying In Hospital between 1870 and 1890 "a horrendous 62 percent had had two or more children die" (Ross 1993:182).

28. Ross (1993:185) tells of one early-twentieth-century London mother who prepared herself and her family for the likely death of a weak little boy by telling

them "He's only lent to us for a little while." Members of pregnancy-loss support groups use this same trope retrospectively (see chapter 7). It is much
harder to imagine them doing so in advance.

29. This belief underlies their questionable assertion that the current body of consolation literature "is being supported not only by those who have themselves
lost babies but also by a larger book- and magazine-reading public" (1992:9).

30. In Morris's (1997:26) essay on literature and suffering he observes that Marxist
critics are likely to "show how suffering is bound up with social class . . . ; psychoanalytic critics will show how it taps into mechanisms of desire; feminist
critics will show how it follows the fault lines of gender." *Motherhood Lost* illustrates how the suffering of pregnancy-loss support-group members does all
three.

31. In addition to those discussed below, *Motherhood Lost* contributes to studies of
popular culture, in particular those that have taken seriously women's "sentimental," "low brow" cultural productions (Douglas 1977, Radway 1984, Wright
1997, see also Kovacik 2001) as well the social scientific and humanistic studies
of medicine that focus on narrative (e.g., Kleinman 1988, Becker 1994, 1997,
Sandelowski 1993, Jackson 1994).

32. According to Stearns (1999:175), in the 1920s psychologists and other experts
argued that "mother's love, that quintessential Victorian emotion" was a danger to children. "Mothers risked suffocating their children with excessive
displays of emotion. Scientific child rearing, not 'superheated' passion, was required."

33. Barad (1998) discusses a parallel discussion in the feminist literature regarding
the "agency" of fetuses. Barad argues against the view that sees the "attribution
of agency to the fetus" as a "universal culprit" and suggests instead that we
frame agency as "a localizable attribution" (1998:114). Barad distinguishes
agency and subjectivity and argues that it "is the latter . . . that has played such a
crucial role in abortion debates in the country since the 1980s." Although in this
particular passage she focuses rather narrowly on "the pregnant woman" as the
primary apparatus/phenomena out of which the fetus is constituted, in her earlier discussion of apparatuses, where she uses the example of a computer
(1998:98), it is clear that this Bohrian-informed understanding of the term can
be quite broad. I would argue that it is not subjectivity per se that is problematic
but a particular ontological understanding of subjectivity. Barad's understanding of the fetus "as a phenomenon" which "'includes' those apparatuses/
phenomena out of which it is constituted" (1998:115) appears to be complementary to the model of relational fetal personhood that I endorse.

34. Certainly some women are having babies who would not otherwise be able to,
and some babies are surviving who would otherwise die, and many genetically
flawed fetuses are being aborted before birth. But IVF still has notoriously low
success rates and feminist critics have thoroughly documented the physical,
emotional, and financial costs of these treatments to the women who undergo
them (Becker 2000, Franklin 1997). In saving infants who would otherwise die,

neonatal intensive care enables the survival of babies with disabilities, while pre-natal diagnosis is contributing to a culture even less tolerant of differently abled people and places blame on women who bear children with disabilities (Lands-man 1998, 1999, in prep).

35. As Tenner (1996:9) notes, "Technology alone usually doesn't produce a re-venge effect. Only when we anchor it in laws, regulations, customs, and habits does an irony reach its full potential. . . . Revenge effects happen because new structures, devices, and organisms react with real people in real situations in ways we could not foresee."

36. I recognize the irony that my goal of finding ways of doing better is couched within the same narrative framework of linear progress that I critique.

37. Fernandez defines "edification" as "the cognitive construction by suggestion of a larger integration of things, a larger whole," as, for example, between animate and inanimate objects or between nature and culture (1986a:178).

38. See also Markens, Browner, and Press (1997).

39. Schrift considers the gift "one of the primary focal points at which contempo-rary disciplinary and interdisciplinary discourses intersect" (1997:3).

40. According to Radstone (2000b:1), memory has become a "central" and "orga-nizing concept within research in the humanities and in certain branches of the social sciences." The late-twentieth century "memory boom" is not restricted to academe, however. As Antze and Lambek (1996:vii) observe, "We live in a time when memory has entered public discourse to an unprecedented degree."

41. See Kleinman (1995) for a critique of post-traumatic stress syndrome.

42. Brison's (1997:13) definition of a traumatic event as "one in which a person feels utterly helpless in the face of a force that is perceived to be life-threatening" is apt for pregnancy loss.

43. Janet, the psychologist whose work has inspired the "recovered memory move-ment, contrasted this desirable type of memory which "narrates the past as past" and demonstrates "the capacity to distance oneself from oneself by representing one's experiences to oneself and others in the form of a narrated history" with what he called "'traumatic memory,' which merely and unconsciously repeats the past" (Leys 1996:122). See Radstone (2000a, 2000b) for a discussion of the change in Freud's understanding of the role trauma played in neuroses and the influence of Freud's theories on contemporary memory scholarship.

44. Critics also note that the "cultural and personal, and to a lesser extent, political and economic" resources needed "to pursue self-fulfillment" are "unevenly dis-tributed" (Irvine 1999:130).

Chapter 3

1. Janis and Kris remained the editors of and major contributors to the newsletter for six years.

2. Janis also holds dual certification as a Death Educator and Grief Counselor from the Association for Death Education and Counseling (ADEC) and is chairper-son of ADEC's Special Interest Group on Children's Grief Programs.

3. They recently issued an updated version of their pamphlet, which is prepared and published jointly with the Mount Sinai Medical Center, called "Understanding Your Pregnancy Loss: Coping with Miscarriage, Stillbirth or Newborn Death" (Pregnancy Loss Support Program of the NCJWNYS et al. 1999).

4. After an introductory meeting the topics were "Response of Family, Friends and Medical Community," "The Grieving Process and Coping with Grief," "Impact of Pregnancy Loss on Primary Relationships," "Individual Responses to Pregnancy Loss," "Where Do We Go from Here?"

5. For example, UNITE receives donations via the United Way and the SHARE newsletter has been partially funded by McDonnell Douglas Employees' Community Fund.

6. Limbo has been described as a "La Crosse, Wisconsin, nurse who has conducted programs in over 500 hospitals training more than 2,000 bereavement counselors" (Ruby 1995:185).

7. This guideline seemed most important when people had complaints about physicians and, although criticizing particular healthcare providers was discouraged in group meetings, people had the chance to compare notes and offer advice regarding who to go to for future care informally after the meeting.

8. Resolve, the largest United States infertility mutual-aid organization, is also a "predominantly white, middle class organization" (Becker 2000:105).

9. The relationship between economic status and pregnancy loss is disputed, however. According to Bongaarts and Potter, comparative studies show little difference in intrauterine morality between developing and developed countries. They agree that "further research is required before one can accept the hypothesis that intrauterine mortality is relatively invariant among populations" but they reason that intrauterine death is "relatively independent from social, economic, and health factors (except a few specific diseases)" (Bongaarts and Potter 1983:40) because of the fact that the majority of fetal deaths are attributed to genetic defects. Genetic explanations have dominated biomedical etiologies of miscarriage throughout the twentieth century. In the last ten years, however, there has been increasing attention paid to possible immunological explanations as well as the relationship to toxic exposure. It seems reasonable in both of these cases that socioeconomic status might be a significant factor.

10. The other reason Landsman puts forward is that "discrimination against persons with disabilities extends broadly across class lines in American culture" (2000:26). In chapter 4 I show that stigma is a problem for middle-class American women who do not "successfully" complete a pregnancy; it is an open question whether pregnancy loss is also stigmatizing for women from lower socioeconomic backgrounds.

11. It is difficult to know whether participants in these groups are typical of the American middle classes in terms of religious beliefs. A 1988 report by the Office of Technology Assessment estimated that 60 percent of Americans belong to some established religious community.

12. See Edelman (1995) for narratives of loss following an elective abortion.

13. I have consulted SHARE's newsletters from 1984 to 2002 and *UNITE Notes* from 1981 to 2002.

14. Just as at support group meetings, the pieces printed in the newsletter are each unique and reflect the particularities of an individual's experience yet still have some degree of overlap, drawing as they do on shared cultural resources. The women who participated in Simonds's study noted that the repetition of self-help books can be comforting (1992:27–29); it seems likely that this would be the case for newsletter readers as well.

15. Research on computer-mediated support suggests that a higher proportion of females than males participate but that this difference may be significantly less than in face-to-face support groups (Walther and Boyd in press:6).

16. Of 387 personal items in the SHARE newsletters published from 1984 to 1994, women authored 294, girls 1; men 45, boys 2, and in 23 cases the gender of the author is unknown. Twenty-two items were signed by both a man and a woman, and it is impossible to know the extent to which such items were in fact coauthored or simply written by one person and attributed to both. In addition, these issues contained 31 professional-advice articles.

    Of 372 personal items published in the UNITE newsletter between 1981 and 1993, 330 were written by women, 7 by girls, 11 by men, 3 by boys, 12 were coauthored, and 9 unknown. Forty-nine professional articles also appeared.

17. At UNITE's twenty-fifth-anniversary ceremony two men spoke during the open mike time for "parents"—an uncle who had flown in from California for the event and a man who had married a woman he had known for thirty years after she experienced a stillbirth.

18. An interesting contrast could be made with Alcoholics Anonymous. For a discussion of the male dominance of AA see Makela et al. 1996.

19. In Simonds's view, although "self-help reading may be seen as a feminist activity in that readers come away feeling they have been addressed as women" and readers of self-help books gain "a sense of commonality with other women through their reading," this activity "falls short" as "feminist practice" because it encourages "individually oriented and adaptive endeavors" and "represses a definitive challenge to the ways in which the social construction of gender works against women" (1992:48).

Chapter 4

1. Miller (1997:69) describes how members of Britain's National Childbirth Trust, an organization that encourages "natural" childbirth, dwell upon "the specific experience of childbirth both before and after the event." The fact that these women are more likely to experience extreme pain because they do not use pain killers increases the efficacy of this rite, "whose subject is not merely the birth of a new infant, but in equal measure the birth of a new form of adult—the mother."

2. Death and rebirth symbolism is common to all rites of passage: the old self dies, the new one is born. It is not surprising, then, that this imagery is common in contemporary accounts of childbirth (for example, Chesler in Bergum 1989:37).

3. Egyptian women who have recently given birth are thought to be capable of producing infertility in other ritually vulnerable women (Inhorn 1994:115).

4. In a sense, a pregnancy that ends in miscarriage or stillbirth might more accurately be described as what Crapanzano (1981) has called a "rite of return" in that, despite having gone through many of the rituals of pregnancy such as doctor's visits, maternity clothing, abstention from coffee, alcohol, and cigarettes, the woman returns to her prior, prepregnancy, status rather than advancing to the new (or renewed status) of "mother."

5. In many cultures gender influences the way that grief is expressed. The folk knowledge of pregnancy-loss support is that men and women react differently to a reproductive loss, and grieve differently, and that these differences often place a strain on marital relations. To fully understand the impact and meaning of a miscarriage or stillbirth for women, one must also understand what it means to their partners.

6. Cook (1988) adopted a men's-studies perspective for her study of father's bereavement for children who died of cancer. She describes a number of strategies used by fathers for dealing with their grief and describes the double bind men are in because of the societal expectation that men should comfort their wives, and the assumption that "healthy grieving cannot be accomplished without the [verbal] sharing of emotions" (Cook 1988:305). She concluded that much of our understanding of bereavement, especially parental mourning, is shaped by concepts formulated through the study of grieving mothers: "male behavior typically is seen as inferior or deficient to the 'female standard'" (Cook 1988:287).

7. For example, for poor urban Egyptians death is so powerful a source of pollution that one need not have physical contact with the dead to be affected; seeing a corpse is enough to ensure pollution. Even individuals who have passed a funeral procession in the street, or crossed a cemetery on a journey, or given condolences to a dead person's family are considered capable of binding the fertility of a ritually vulnerable woman (Inhorn 1994:126). Among the Konjo of Indonesia, the ghost of a woman who has died in childbirth, one of the most feared evil spirits, is believed capable of causing pregnancy loss (Gibson, personal communication), and magicians go to "meditate on top of graves" when they seek "birth magic" (Gibson 1995:135).

8. Similarly, among the Marquesans, if "an accident should occur" during the final stages of pregnancy or birth, the sleeping house and the special birth hut that had been constructed adjacent to it must be burned (Paige and Paige 1981:196).

9. The fetal or newborn corpse, or a part thereof, can be stepped over a ritual number of times, or soaked or boiled in water and the water used for bathing, or the sponge used to wash the corpse can be used for bathing or ritually stepped over

(Inhorn 1994:table 2). Thirty-three percent of Inhorn's sample of ninety-six in-fertile women had engaged in these types of rituals, or other similar rituals in-volving feline placental tissue or blood.

10. Some stillbirths or early infant deaths involve babies who appear perfectly nor-mal. In these cases they may have a hidden defect such as a heart problem, may have died because of a cord accident, or the cause of death may remain unex-plained (see Layne 1995 for a historical discussion of medical understandings of the causes of pregnancy loss).

11. Stacey (1997:88–90) presents a number of accounts that portray the pregnant body as monstrous.

12. The able-bodied commonly deal with physical malformations "by setting up so-cial distance by avoidance, . . . physical isolation and noncommunication" (Murphy et al. 1988:238). (See also Landsman 1999.)

13. See Stacey (1997:252 n10,11) for a discussion of recent critiques of the use of the concept "taboo." We both use the concept in a way that highlights the "gen-erative dynamics of such cultural processes" (Stacey 1997:252 n10).

14. The horrifying terrorist attack of 9-11 was a watershed event that may alter in fundamental ways American optimism, our belief that bad things happen to bad people, and our unwillingness to acknowledge the ever present possibility of un-timely, unanticipated death. The fact that America's twentieth-century wars were fought almost entirely on foreign soil, and because news coverage of those wars minimized American casualties (Ruby 1995), we have as a nation been buffered until now from such large-scale suffering. Langer (1997:50) has re-marked on how "the system of values cherished by the American mind, with its stress on individual success and an infinitely improving future, nurtures a psy-chology of mental comfort that discourages encounters with tragedy." Writing in 1997, Langer called for Americans to embrace what he calls an "alarmed vision," which entails a set of reduced expectations regarding guaranteed, auto-matic happiness. Though it was necessary, he anticipated that no such shift could occur "until we find a way of toppling the barrier that sequesters mass suffering in other regions of the world from the comfort and safety we enjoy far from its ravages" (1997:47). The events of 9-11 may have done just that and, as a nation, we may now become better able to come to terms with "unprovoked suffering" (Langer 1997:47), regardless of the scale.

15. See Lasch (1991) and Nisbet (1980) on the history of Western ideas of progress.

16. See chapter 7 for more on greeting cards.

17. Of course, pregnancy losses do not always involve hospitalization. Early losses usually involve a D&C or D&E, the same procedures used for elective abor-tions, and can therefore be done on an outpatient basis. I have not been able to determine the percentage of pregnancy losses that take place in emergency rooms. Anecdotal evidence supports my experience that having a miscarriage in an ER is not ideal. In her description of her miscarriage, Ilse mentions, "The cool reception we received in the Emergency Room did not make it easier to ac-

cept" (Ilse and HammerBurns 1985:1). MacFarlane and Mugford report that in 1978 in England and Wales approximately 46,030 women were admitted to the hospital after a spontaneous abortion (1984:84). They do not specify whether these admissions were to emergency or not. They believe that this figure is much lower than the total number of miscarriages, representing only "the tip of the iceberg." The history of the medicalization of miscarriage will be explored in a subsequent book.

18. Panuthos (1984:157) asserts that "very few childbirth-preparation courses discuss abortion, miscarriage, stillbirth or infant death" but gives no indication as to how she ascertained this.

19. The same holds true for statistics in the U.K. According to MacFarlane and Mugford (1984:82), "There is no comprehensive source of routinely collected data about spontaneous abortion (miscarriage). . . . Spontaneous abortions are only included in official statistics if they result in a claim being made by a GP for attending a miscarriage, or if they lead to admission to hospital or death." See also Reinharz (1988b:87) on the problems with epidemiological data on miscarriages.

20. The situation is no better internationally. One of the ways that the World Health Organization tries to coordinate the compilation of health statistics is via the International Classification of Diseases (ICD). In its ninth revision the ICD defined fetal death as "death prior to the complete expulsion or extraction from its mother of a product of conception, irrespective of the duration of pregnancy; the death is indicated by the fact that after such separation the fetus does not breathe or show any other evidence of life . . . " (in MacFarlane and Mugford 1984:5). In the United Kingdom as of 1984, fetal deaths were registered from the twenty-eighth week of gestation onward (and then only in the case of legitimate children), in which case they are know as stillbirths (MacFarlane and Mugford 1984:5, 8). For statistics on perinatal mortality (as opposed to fetal death), the ICD recommends a gestational age of at least twenty-two weeks for national statistics and twenty-eight weeks for international statistics (MacFarlane and Mugford 1984:6). Since gestational age is so difficult to determine with accuracy, it also provides suggested minimum birth weight and body length for inclusion in perinatal statistics.

21. According to Bongaarts and Potter (1983:39), studies that attempt to estimate the risk of intrauterine mortality often suffer from "(a) incomplete reporting of fetal deaths, especially of early spontaneous abortions in retrospective studies; (b) unrepresentative nature of the study population; (c) overestimation of spontaneous fetal mortality due to inclusion of induced abortions or misreporting of delayed menses; (d) errors in statistical estimation procedures; and (e) sampling errors if only a small number of fetal death are observed."

22. Bledsoe found it difficult to investigate "reproductive mishaps" in the Gambia because these events tend to be underreported since they "connote infertility and cast dispersions on a woman's conjugal worth" (1999:62). She also believes

that her own lack of understanding about the importance of these data contributed to the low reports. She notes that the questions in her survey about last
pregnancy assumed a live birth and would have discouraged respondents from
reporting on a miscarriage or stillbirth (1999:80); "careful probing" would have
"undoubtedly elicited" more such events (1999:63).

23. Reinharz (1987, 1988a,b), Simonds and Rothman (1992), and March (2001) are
notable exceptions.

24. The following publications focus on pregnancy loss: Pizer and Palinski (1980);
Peppers and Knapp (1980); Borg and Lasker (1981); Church et al. (1981);
Friedman and Gradstein (1982); Berezin (1982); Ilse (1985, 1989); McDonald-
Grandin (1983); Johnson and Johnson (1983); Panuthos and Romero (1984);
Schwiebert and Kirk (1985); Ilse and HammerBurns (1985); Hagley (1985);
Cohen (1983a, 1983d, 1988); Gryte (1988); Lamb (1988a); Davis (1991), Rich
(1991); Gilbert and Smart (1992); Allen and Marks (1993); Faldet and Fitton
(1996); Lammert and Friedeck (1997); Cardin (1999); Kohn and Moffitt (2000).

Chapter 5

1. Developments in biomedicine are affecting the experience of pregnancy loss in
other ways too. For example, new research foci and treatments regarding the
etiologies of pregnancy loss are shifting the landscape of blame and providing
bereaved couples with new narrative resources (see Layne 1995).

2. In the last few decades there has been some decentralization in both birthing
and dying with a small but significant resurgence in home birth and hospice
care. According to Davis-Floyd 2002, about 1 percent of births in the United
States take place at home. But even when these events take place in nonclinical
settings, one should not assume that they are free from a technoscientific mode
of understanding.

3. See Lock (1997) for a comparative discussion of these issues in Japan.

4. This has not meant a diminution in the power and control of ob/gyns, however.
The results of home pregnancy tests are often confirmed by a test in the doctor's
office and the early detection of pregnancies in this way generally results in earlier and, therefore, more prenatal visits.

5. These tests feature prominently in the story that Chrissy Coggins shared in a
UNITE newsletter. She begins, "For the last eleven years, I'd been trying to
conceive. Month after month, prayer after prayer, and one home pregnancy test
after another, it was all I could think about. While my peers were raising children and getting pregnant, I was crying. . . . At one point, I believe I psychologically made myself pregnant. I had all the typical symptoms, but I still got a
minus sign." She then tells of how in December she finally decided to "accept
the fact that I would never be a mother, but then "on January 27, 1999, my
dream came true . . . I saw a plus sign! Hallelujah! My first thought was 'Thank
God I don't have to buy anymore of those pregnancy tests' (I should have been
buying stock in them instead). My second thought was 'Is it really a plus sign or

are my eyes playing a trick on me?'" She woke her "significant other" up "so that he could confirm the test result. I had blood tests done to verify everything." Then they "began putting a plan together for [their] future. "Two ultrasounds, three blood tests and eight weeks later I was told 'there is no heartbeat and your hormone levels are dropping'. . . . My fetus was dying" (Coggins 2000).

6. See Jordan (1993), and Davis-Floyd and Sargent (1996) on authoritative knowledge in the context of pregnancy and birth.

7. New obstetrical practices are also contributing to the emergence of what one might call a "prepregnant" or "incipiently pregnant" status. For example, many obstetricians recommend that women start taking prenatal vitamins before they try to conceive.

8. He went on to explain that he did not share his wife's feelings of grief: "It was as though a close friend of hers, who I'd never met, had died. My feelings were primarily a reaction to hers" (quoted in Fillion 1994:50).

9. See Mitchell (1994) for mention of the controversy in Canada over the use of ultrasound for fetal-sex identification.

10. The long wait for the doctor, one assumes, took place at a subsequent ultrasound when the technician saw something wrong and went to get the doctor. These other losses may have taken place earlier in gestation since this pregnancy was experienced as "our dream come true," and she and her husband appear to have fully invested in the pregnancy ("Our whole world revolved around waiting for you") (Simons 1995), perhaps because they had made it through the period of greatest risk for miscarriage. Another woman, Tara Niles, describes a similar scenario. She writes, "I looked at your motionless heart on the screen. This can't be happening, is it just a dream????" describing the death of her daughter, Alli Renée, who died in utero in January 1995 and was delivered June 6, 1995, along with her surviving twin (Niles 1996).

11. Rev. Terry Morgan (1985) tells of a similar experience from the husband's point of view.

12. See Lamb (1982) for a critique of the methodology of their studies on bonding.
   Trevathan's (1988) study of childbirth among Hispanic and Anglo women in a maternity center in El Paso indicates that the "species specific" behaviors described by Klaus and Kennell were not universal but varied systematically according to sociocultural background.

13. See Yoxen (1989) on the development of this technology and Rapp (1997) on it in relation to prenatal testing.

14. This is also true for women in Canada, where universal and comprehensive health insurance includes at least one prenatal scan (Mitchell and Georges 1998:114) and women attended at teaching hospitals usually have "two 'routine' scans" (Mitchell 1994:148). Ultrasound has also become common in Australia and Greece (Mitchell and Georges 1998, Georges 1995), and in many parts of Europe (Saetnan 1996, 2000). In the public hospital in a small city in Eastern Greece where Georges undertook research in 1990, she found that "no preg-

nancy went unscanned, and women typically had three to five scans over the course of a normal pregnancy" (1995:161). She also found that medical students in Athens are taught to do one scan each trimester of a normal pregnancy and cites a recent survey that found that in practice the rate was even higher, with about one-quarter of the 500 women surveyed having "two or more scans in the third trimester alone" (Georges 1995:161).

15. There are other important differences in addition to timing: whereas women feel life inside their bodies, with sonograms they see it on a screen, across the room, outside and disconnected from their bodies. And whereas in the past fathers-to-be could feel movement in/of their wife's body, they now have direct access to "their baby." Several men have told me how much they liked sonograms because it made them feel more a part of the pregnancy.

16. Fletcher and Evans went on to discuss the uses to which ultrasound might be put in the struggle surrounding fetal rights, such as requiring that women considering abortion or refusing fetal therapy be forced by court order to view an ultrasound (1983:393). Such suggestions have received the outraged condemnation they deserve (Petchesky 1987:277).

17. I found it quite easy to tell when there was a heartbeat, when there wasn't, and when there was an empty sack.

18. Mitchell identifies a quarter of the women in her study as having "miscarried or are particularly anxious about miscarriage" and asserts that for these women "ultrasound echoes are especially and poignantly meaningful as reassuring 'proof' that they will have a baby" (Mitchell and Georges 1998:115).

19. According to Klaus and Kennell, the loss of previous children "may delay preparation for the infant and retard bond formation" (1976:46).

20. A related and normally unexamined belief is that "technological progress" improves our lives. Rarely do we stop and seriously consider whether "our impressive scientific and technical powers produce a world genuinely superior to that which came before" (Winner 1986:172).

21. Similarly, in their book *Born Early*, Avery and Litwack discuss the "greatly improved (and *ever-improving*) outlook for normal development" of preemies and their expectation that "ever more effective drugs" will be found through clinical trials (1983:31, emphasis mine).

22. For Donna the clash of expectations and reality does not concern medical technologies per se, but the unrealistic expectation that "knowledge" in the form of prepared childbirth classes from "experts" on birth will assure a successful pregnancy. This will be discussed further in chapter 7.

23. As an anonymous reviewer pointed out, one can equally imagine that technology might work to absolve doctors of responsibility.

24. According to Mitchell, the second routine scan had much less impact. "Aside from those who were told whether they were having a boy or girl, only a few women used the second fetal image to further construct the social identity of the fetus," fetal movement having supplanted these images as the primary indica-

tion of the fetus's "health, sentience, character, emotion and behavior" (Mitchell 1994:155).

25. See Sherman (1999:50, 64) on the relationship between the visual, the aural, and memory.

26. In an essay on the meaning of personal possessions for the elderly, Sherman and Newman (1977:186) found that photographs were the most frequently identified "cherished possession." This was particularly true for women, and their photos were most commonly of their children.

27. Newman argues that new image-producing technologies, including ultrasound, "are quite different from and noncontinuous with the modes of historical anatomical inscription" that have traditionally been used to represent fetuses (1996: 107), but I cannot agree that unlike earlier techniques, "ultrasound, color Doppler sonography, and fetal laser imaging are not visual techniques that depend on an observing subject" (Newman 1996:107).

28. Sonogram images of fetuses, particularly those of one's own, do not require the kind of photographic juxtaposition Newman describes as used in a National Geographic article to humanize highly abstract MRI images. As I have shown in my article "Of Fetuses and Angels," such "realist" images are supplied in the imaginations of the would-be parents (see Layne 1992).

29. The Centering Corporation publishes a manual on how to take photographs of stillborns and infants who die (Johnson et al. 1985).

30. The Johnson collection at the Strong Museum in Rochester, New York, has an extensive collection of nineteenth- and early-twentieth-century postmortem photographs. See Bowser's (1983) MA thesis for a discussion of this collection. The George Eastman House in Rochester also has several daguerreotypes of dead children. Bowser observed that in early photographs the dead body was the primary subject, but that, over time, the body was gradually replaced with images of the funeral, especially the floral arrangements (1983:51). (See Schmidt 1995 on the history of "floricultural" industry in the United States.)

   The early photographs were often framed in elaborately decorated union cases, which were held and gazed on privately (personal communication, Joe Strubel). Once photographs began to be printed much more inexpensively on paper, they came to be used more for public commemorations. For instance, it became common to put a photograph of a person, taken while alive, on her/his funeral floral arrangement. Such photos are now sometimes mounted on tombstones. See Meinwald (1990), Ruby (1995), for more on postmortem photography. Thanks to Joe Strubel, archivist at the Eastman house; and to Nick Fricket, Leah Maxwell, and the librarian at the Strong Museum.

31. According to Aries (1985:245), photographs of dead children had become "extraordinarily popular" by the second half of nineteenth century. During this period, children, unlike adults, were pictured with their eyes open, that is, as if alive, and he concludes that "the deaths of children were the first deaths that could not be tolerated" (1985:247). Ruby believes that photos of dead loved ones

are still quite common, especially by middle- and lower-class immigrant groups. However, he notes that they are now taken and used "in spite of and not because of society's expectations about the propriety of these images" (1995:1).

See Williamson (1994) and Hirsch (1981) on women and "family photographs" and Wozniak (1999) on the importance of photographs in rituals of remembrance among foster mothers in the United States.

In Benjamin's comparison of painting and photography, he argues that with photography (and even more so with film) "exhibition value" displaces "cult value" but notes that in photography "cult value" remains with photos of people. "It is no accident that the portrait was the focal point of early photography. The cult of remembrance of loved ones, absent or dead, offers a last refuge for the cult value of the picture" (Benjamin 1989:577).

32. Ninety-five percent of the respondents to the SHARE survey "felt that it is important to have pictures of the baby" (Laux 1988a). If the parents do not want the photos, the hospital often keeps them for some time in case the parents change their mind.

33. I have no evidence of bereaved parents using sonogram images for this purpose after a death, but Taylor (2000a) and Mitchell (1994) report North-American women engaging in the practice during real-time sonogram exams.

Chapter 6

1. From the late 1980s on, after the popularization of desktop publishing, there are pictorial representations of many of these items, or the motifs which decorate them included in the "clip art" illustrations of the newsletters (such as teddy bears, butterflies, balloons, balls, cribs, angels, bunnies). As a member of the same consumer culture, I also have firsthand knowledge of many of these consumer goods.

2. Sue Friedeck (1995a) describes how important the senses are in linking parents to their children: "Our senses of sight, touch, hearing and smell link us to . . . our children" and how much bereaved parents long for these connections: "When our babies have physically departed, we want to . . . hug that sweet precious child. We want to feel baby kisses and to smell sweet baby smells."

3. Sue Friedeck (1995a) hung wind chimes at home and in a tree near her son's grave as a way of remembering him: "When I hear one, I think of the other."

4. Strathern (1988) discusses a number of feminist critiques of this understanding of women as gifts/consumables but ultimately finds the model useful in the Papua New Guinean context.

5. For example, in my own case, while traveling in my twenties I bought a number of consumer goods (bibs decorated with the days of the week in Russian and silk-screened blocks in Moscow, and inflatable camels in Jordan) for my future children.

6. Much of the consumption during a pregnancy is focused around "the nursery," an individualized, specialized space in the home furnished with the "baby's

things" in anticipation of its "arrival." The making ready of the nursery (painting, wallpapering, etc.), like the making of baby things, is another example of the importance of personal, manual labor in social construction of fetal personhood by the woman, her partner, and their social network.

The nursery serves as a common place of mourning after the loss. For instance, Susan Ashbaker's (1993) daughter died two hours after her birth due to an umbilical-cord accident. Even though her daughter was never in the nursery they prepared for her, Susan describes how she would "rock in your room and stare at your little white bassinet crib and changing table, touching all the reminders, trying to comfort my sorrow with surroundings of you."

Lynne Blair, in a poem entitled "An Empty Room," ironically details how, in fact, the nursery is actually full of "baby things." "Little diapers that will never be changed . . . cute stuffed animals never to be hugged . . . plenty of bottles that I don't need. Many story books that I won't read. Bright shiny rattles that won't make any noise. A big wood box filled with untouched toys. A fluffy pillow—it will feel no head. A brightly colored quilt covers an untouched bed" (Blair 1990).

7. I also bought yarn and a pattern book for my mother, which I sent as a surprise announcement of my happy news. My parents, in turn, used the gift of a consumer good to announce the anticipated arrival of what would have been their first grandchild. They gave each couple in their bridge group a Christmas bell with a typewritten note which read "Let all bells ring with 'Joy in July' when Beth and Howard become grandparents." My subsequent pregnancies, including the one that resulted in the birth of my son Jasper, were not publicly acknowledged in this way.

8. This is, I am sure, what made knitting such an eminently satisfying experience for me. In my case, baby- and sweater-making were even longer processes than they usually are. With each of my miscarriages I would stop work on the sweater and resume again with my subsequent pregnancy. I eventually finished that sweater and several others while waiting for my adopted son to be born as I closely followed the progression of his birth mother's pregnancy, which she so generously shared with me.

9. Shopping is one of the activities that give child-waiting couples "something to do while waiting" (Sandelowski 1993:171). I used shopping in this way while waiting for our adopted son to be born. His birth mother experienced false labor two weeks before his birth. By the time we got to Wyoming, her labor had stopped. During the two long weeks until his birth, we bought a gift for our son-to-be each day. Several of these were linked to the place of his birth—for example, infant cowboy boots, a tiny pair of polar fleece mittens, and coloring books about Wyoming's history; in this way we began constructing one element of his personal identity and history.

10. The circumstances of the baby's death are not clear. One gathers that she died after three hospitalizations and a surgery. On this shopping excursion, which

takes place after the baby's death, they saw a dress "identical to the one she wore home from the hospital and on her Christening day, and home from the hospital twice again. It had been a present from the other three children. He took them shopping the day after the baby was born. They bought it here in this store and he had it gift-wrapped. This was an extravagance for his practical nature . . . . She was buried in that dress. It caresses her body" (Keener 1981/2).

11. This public, collective celebration of the pregnancy and child-to-be/parents-to-be is one of the things that birth mothers and adopting couples miss out on. Sometimes, however, showers or welcome parties are given for the child and adoptive parents after the baby/child arrives.

12. In their book *The World of Goods*, Douglas and Isherwood analyze things as part of an "information system," functioning as "markers" of cultural categories (1979:5). They describe how, by attending other people's rituals and bringing appropriate gifts to these functions, "people render marking services" to others (1979:74–5).

13. See Hyde (1979:41) on "threshold gifts," or "gifts of passage." According to Hyde, "threshold gifts may be the most common form of gift we have." Willis, in contrast, believes that under capitalism ritual ceremonies have become "marginalized, dismissed or assimilated to the commodity form" (1991:28).

14. To gather material on "synchographic" or "life-event" marketing for his book, Larson (1992) registered a fictitious wife with *American Baby*, a magazine for expectant mothers offered free of charge for six months and available in obstetricians' offices and baby-supply stores. Shortly thereafter this fictional new mother began receiving letters, catalogs, and phone calls trying to sell her baby products with an average of 4.6 offers per week (1992:84).

15. Guillemin and Holmstrom (1986:135–7) describe the various ways that physicians and nurses in neonatal intensive care units "personify" critically ill newborns, some of whom in the past would have been classified as miscarriages or stillbirths. Possessions are a central aspect of this activity. The staff of the NICU they studied "encouraged parents to . . . bring in toys and clothes. If the parents were reluctant, . . . the nurses would make or buy toys, clothes, and decorations for the isolette" (1986:136–7). Other personification practices engaged in by the medical staff included giving nicknames and the attribution of will, for example, the will to live. In my experience as a NICU parent (Layne 1997), we were not allowed to dress Jasper in clothing until he was deemed stable enough to place in an isolette. Before that point he was kept naked in a warmer to allow ease of access to his body in case he "crashed." In other words, although this clinical practice is explained in practical terms, nakedness symbolically expresses the tenuous personhood of the most critically ill neonates. During Jasper's first weeks in the NICU this tenuous personhood created quandaries for me about whether to continue to socially construct his persona by sending out birth announcements and asking people to be his godparents.

16. See Buck-Morss's (1989:99) description of Benjamin's understanding of the special relationship between women and fashion.

17. See Morley (1971) on the similarities between Victorian burial gowns and those for infants.

18. Instead, he was brought to her by a nurse wrapped in one of the hospital's "duck-patterned blanket[s]" (Campbell 1991a).

19. Brand names are rarely mentioned in the textual descriptions of "baby things." One may assume, however, that the actual purchases embody the style, taste, and class aspirations of the parents and their social network (Bourdieu 1984, Fussell 1983).

20. McVeigh (1996) describes the attribution of "cuteness" to animals, infants, and women in Japanese culture. He remarks that animals are considered cute because they "require loving attention from people, . . . they need to be 'protected, cuddled, and held.'" As living, breathing, active things, they exist somewhere in between being human but not quite human" (McVeigh 1996:295). Thorsen's study of dogs in Euro-America reveals striking similarities between the attributes of infants and dogs. According to Thorsen (1996:6), "infantilized, feminized and de-sexualized dog[s]" are the ideal both as reflected in nineteenth-century European dog-care books and "in the range of goods in present-day American pet stores."

21. Oaks recounts how for some North American women "imagining the baby's identity was complicated because they chose not to know the sex of the fetus. Calling the baby-to-be 'it' was mentioned by several women as unacceptable, perhaps because that label is less human then 'he' or 'she' or a specific name" (1998:246).
    See Cook (1998) on the trend toward sexualizing children.

22. It is interesting to note that a dramatic linear transformation is not sufficient, for example, frogs are not often used on infant goods though they are sometimes used on consumer goods for school-age boys.

23. See Layne (1999) and the next chapter for more on the "preciousness" of babies and their gifts.

24. See Wozniak (in prep) on the strategies used by foster mothers for dealing with the belongings of their foster children after the child has been returned to its natal family or placed permanently; and Clarke (1998) on how some British women manage their children's outgrown clothing.

25. This is the type of exchange that Sahlins would label "generalized reciprocity." In these types of exchanges, "reckoning of debts outstanding cannot be overt and is typically left out of account. This is not to say that handing over things in such form, even to 'loved ones,' generates no counter obligation. But the counter is not stipulated by time, quantity, or quality: the expectation of reciprocity is indefinite" (1972b:194).

26. See Foster and Foster's account of trading-card exchanges among children in the United States. Schoolchildren "appropriated objects they themselves had not created as resources for creating social relations and identities" (1994:2).

27. In McCracken's (1988:20) account of the consumer revolution in the eighteenth century, one of the fundamental reforms was the "inculcation of a willingness to

consume. . . . The consumer is not born, but produced by processes that teach him or her to want." This is not only true for that first generation of modern consumers described by McCracken but true for each subsequent generation and an important part of childhood socialization. Likewise, Willis notes that in the past children were incorporated into capitalist society as laborers but "now capitalism seeks to incorporate children as the reproducers of society. Children learn and want to be consumers at an ever earlier age" (1991:26–27).

28. Caplow (1982:386) found that ornaments were a common Christmas gift and that women were much more likely than men to give them.

29. They also make holiday cards including Father's Day cards and baby shower invitations and will customize with due date and "baby's name," gender, and for single or twin pregnancies. One satisfied customer commented, "The baby is the one arriving, so why shouldn't he be the one to announce it? These cards make great keepsakes" (Fetal Greetings 2001).

30. One woman who miscarried at eleven weeks due to a uterine septum describes how her "baby became a member of the family from the day the test came back positive." They nicknamed her "peanut" and her husband "left messages for her on [the wife's] voice mail and asked her to call her father." The woman recognizes that this "was crazy" but justifies it, saying, "we were so excited about her" (DiFabio 1997). [It is unusual to know the sex of a fetus this early. I assume this was learned via a chromosomal study done after the D&C.]

These practices are part of a historical movement over this century toward "enfranchising children as full persons in Western culture" (Cook 1998:349).

31. Like many other support-group members, the Niehoffs also hang a stocking with their dead son's name on it at Christmastime along with those of the other family members. It is unclear whether this stocking is filled on Christmas morning or hangs empty. Their surviving son is given "a special stocking-stuffer gift . . . to remember Christopher" (Niehoff 1994).

32. See Schmidt (1995) on the proliferation of Easter goods in the 1880s–90s. According to Schmidt (1995:200), it was during this period that Easter became "the festival of sacred remembrance," with Easter lilies becoming hopeful symbols of "the restored wholeness of familial circles" in heaven.

33. Recall also the pink roses that Sarah Casimer's mother buried her with (Casimer 1987) and the pink balloon which features in Diaz's (2001) description of the funeral for her second daughter, who died after five weeks in a NICU due to a metabolic disorder.

34. See chapter 8 for more on the analogies with flowers. Balloons are also frequently the centerpiece of collective memorial services. Lamb's 1988 book on planning farewell rituals provides a number of possible scripts for balloon releases. Some groups no longer do such releases because of environmental concerns.

35. Hass begins her book on the gifts left at the Vietnam War Memorial with an account of a mother who travels to the Memorial "a couple of times a year, usually once around Christmastime and then close to her son's birthday" and leaves

gifts, "a birthday card, a loved childhood toy, or a small Christmas tree decorated with strands of silver tinsel and bright red globes" (1998:1). Since the average age of the soldiers who died there was nineteen, the similarities are perhaps not so surprising.

36. A recent example of this is seen in the mementos left by relatives and friends on a cluster of hay bales near the site of the September 11 crash of Flight 93 in rural Pennsylvania a week after the crash. Items included "candy, baseball caps, photographs, teddy bears, and a flight attendant's jacket." Also present were flags representing the backgrounds of the 44 victims (Sheehan 2001).

37. It would be interesting to trace the history of such memorial donations. Were they practiced as part of the middle-class Victorian cult of the dead? Or did they come about as part of the democratization and changing attitudes and practices following World War I by which the dead were remembered? And who counted as worthy of such public memorialization—were infants always included in this category? Stillborn, or miscarried embryos/fetuses?

38. In the 1995 SHARE newsletters, these announcements are accompanied by the following explanation: "A love gift is a donation given in honor of someone or as a memorial to a baby, relative or a friend or simply a gift from someone wanting to help. We gratefully acknowledge these love gifts which help us to reach out to the daily needs of bereaved parents."

39. This raises the interesting question of whether babies in heaven mature. There appears to be no cultural consensus on this matter and some mothers imagine these babies as their "forever baby" while others picture their child opening birthday presents in heaven each year, and still others openly speculate on this issue. (See Layne 1992 for more on the imagery of babies as angels in heaven.)

40. In a piece entitled "My Special Christmas Gift," Kathleen Bannon tells how her son who was stillborn near Christmas five years earlier had been "God's special gift to me." She then reports another gift from God she received while delivering toys to a needy family. As she handed out the toys to the five-year-old girl and saw her happiness, Kathleen saw her son in her. "His gift to me this Christmas was to see [him] somehow through this five-year-old child."

41. Collective commemorations are frequently announced in the newsletters. For instance, in 1992 the SHARE newsletter published a notice asking for contributions to defray the cost of a group memorial at the Central United Methodist Church in Honesdale, Pennsylvania. A SHARE member there had bought a brick for the church's "memorial wall" in their new church annex and had it inscribed, "In Loving Memory, Our Precious Babies of SHARE." The brick was to be "placed in the foyer (hallway) wall, for all to see when walking past" (*SHARE* 1992 1(5):7). In 1994 a "Remembrance of the Innocents Memorial" was announced in the SHARE newsletter. It was described as a "personalized memorial dedicated to the ministry of mourning and healing the loss of a preborn child through miscarriage, stillbirth, and abortion. This memorial, to be located in Southeastern Wisconsin, will be the only memorial in our Nation, to date, dedicated this way. Estimated cost of each personalized stone is $50.00."

42. Schneider and Weiner note that the "spectacular cloth presentations" that had been a part of aristocratic funerals became less common during the seventeenth century as funerals became "more expressive of private rather than collective loss" (1989:11).

43. Women gave many more "token" gifts than did men (most of which went to children) and men were the most likely to give "substantial" (that is, expensive) gifts (Caplow 1982).

44. A recent issue of *SHARING* announced a "new line of affirming and uplifting bereavement products" and provided the address for requesting a catalog.

45. The Twin to Twin Transfusion Syndrome Foundation (1994) suggests providing parents with footprints, handprints, locks of hair, baby bracelets, the measuring tape, the paper the baby lay on, blankets, hats, and photos of each baby whether born alive or not.

46. Another bodily trace sometimes mentioned is the fragrance left on cloth. Although people often comment on the special smells of babies, because they do not last they are not normally kept as mementos of babyhood. But the smelling of clothing of an absent loved one is an act frequently portrayed in film.

47. Hair has been associated with mourning since antiquity and was used in the United States as a memento of loved ones, either absent or dead, since the eighteenth century. According to Sheumaker (1997:423), from the 1780s to 1820s hair was often woven as the backing for miniature portraits and mourning scenes, which were either worn or displayed in the home. Between the 1830s and 1880s the hair of beloved relatives, and sometimes even pets, was woven, braided, and twisted by middle-class American women, or the professionals they hired, into jewelry, wreaths, or pictures for display behind glass in the parlor (Sheumaker 1997, Morley 1971). Hair was believed to embody "the . . . essence of individuals and their relationships, symbolize . . . ties . . . in its tenuous strands" and, because of its durability, "it could transcend time, reaching past absence to presence" (Sheumaker 1997:422).

48. *Journal de Bébé* by Franc-Nohain, published in Paris in 1914, from which The Metropolitan Museum of Art's *Baby's Journal* (1978) was adapted, included a page for the *"empriente du pied et de la main de bebe"* and a page for *"boucles de cheveaux"* (personal communication, Valerie von Volz, Dept. Drawing and Prints, Metropolitan Museum of Art). The importance of such prints as symbols of early childhood is also evidenced in the frequency with which they are used as motifs in preschool art projects and consumer goods.

49. AC Controls Ltd., a British firm that advertises itself as a team of "integrated security specialists" markets a "baby footprinting identicator" kit. According to their promotional material, "obtaining fingerprints and footprints of young children has been undertaken since the early eighties."

50. This was discontinued recently as they proved to be nearly useless for forensic purposes, able to identify less than 1 percent of babies (Dr. Pinheiro, Albany Medical Center, personal communication). According to Dr. Joaquim Pinheiro, neonatologist at Albany Medical Center, they still do them "because parents

like them—they're cute." A nurse educator and social worker at St. Joseph's Hospital in Tampa explains the practice of giving parents footprints as "a token or remembrance of how small the baby was" (personal communication, Deborah Blizzard).

51. Still, the choice of footprints rather than handprints in anti-abortion campaigns is intriguing and can also perhaps be explained in part by the special place that feet hold as a symbol in Christian traditions regarding social worth. Feet, which touch the ground, are associated with a low position in the status hierarchy and sitting at another's feet was (and still is) a way of acknowledging that person's social superiority. See for example Lazarus's daughter who sat at Jesus's feet (Luke 10). But Jesus turned this tradition on its head in one of his final acts on earth by washing the feet of his disciples in order to teach them that "the master is not greater than the servant." He also requested that they wash each other's feet in order to learn that they were all equal. Feet thus provide a powerful rhetorical tool for those who would assert the social value of traditionally little-valued persons/entities.

52. Since 1996 the SHARE newsletter has illustrated the back page of the newsletter (the one that is visible during mailing) with the image of fetal footprints. A piece that was published in the September/October issue that year is entitled "Footprints on Our Hearts" and the title is framed with even smaller footprints, perhaps via the technique of Xerox reduction. The flyer put out by SHARE advertising the annual National Pregnancy and Infant Loss Awareness month activities for 1996 also uses this image: a picture of fetal footprints superimposed on hearts with the words "you have left your footprints on our hearts forever." The Centering Corporation, which describes itself as "a friendly non-profit organization in Omaha, Nebraska, providing a wide variety of grief resources," sells a baby book for stillborn infants entitled *Little Footprints: A Special Baby's Memory Book.* The advertisement includes some of the "meaningful poetry" in the book, some of which we are told "have been carved on headstones," namely, "How very softly you tiptoed into my world. Almost silently, only a moment you stayed. But what an imprint your footsteps have left upon my heart."

53. See Jasper Johns's sculpture *Memory Piece (Frank O'Hara)*, which is a box that has a positive cast of a human foot on the underside of the lid and three drawers filled with sand. "Close the lid, and the top tray of sand receives the imprint of the foot which survives [only] as long as the box remains undisturbed" (Forty 1999:1).

54. Another way of preserving this physical trace is through plaster casts. In the section, "ideas for remembrance," SHARE mentions "a kit for casting baby's hand or foot . . . available from American Baby Products. The copy-tot kit duplicates in lifelike detail" (Smith 1988). Footprints are also a common symbolic motif in memorial goods. The SHARE newsletter periodically includes the pattern for making a cross-stitched footprint. For example, in 1991 a pattern is presented along with an article on "keepsakes following a miscarriage." The author suggests that the footprint "could include baby's name and date and be framed

as a tree ornament." Replicas of tiny feet are also apparently sometimes purchased as memorial objects. According to a piece in the SHARE newsletter, "pewter feet the size of a 10 week gestation baby are available from religious stores" (Lewis 1991).

55. This reluctance is not restricted to bodies and their visual representation, however, but seems to inform my feelings about other traces of people (or protopeople) that I was emotionally attached to/invested in. For example, I cannot bring myself to erase the many old e-mail messages from a recently deceased friend and colleague, which inhabit my mailbox, preferring instead to let "nature take its course" and wait until the university mail system erases them gradually as time passes.

56. The measuring tape may also be valued for reasons of contiguity, that is, because it touched the child.

57. According to Hacking, "positivism . . . took for granted that positive facts were measured by numbers." He traces the "avalanche of numbers" to the period between 1820 and 1840 and maintains that by the end of the nineteenth century, no one would disagree with the statement of physicist Lord Kelvin "that when you can measure what you are speaking about, you know something about it: when you cannot measure it . . . your knowledge is of a meager and unsatisfactory kind" (1996:186).

58. St. Joseph's Hospital in Tampa, Florida, also presents such boxes to women who suffer a perinatal death while under their care. Doherty (1991a) describes her memory box as "an altar in my home with relics of our son. . . . It's really just a box of papers—Hospital records, Mass cards, ID bracelets."

59. It is the breaching of this cultural norm that lends dead baby jokes whatever humor they may have.

60. Allen and Marks (1993:87–92), Gilbert and Smart (1992), Davis (1991:112–117), Borg and Lasker (1981:80–81), cf. Lasker and Borg (1987:140–143) report a similar pattern in the way women and men deal with the crisis of infertility.

61. Michell quit her job six weeks after Lorraine's birth and became a "full-time mommy." She reports that she "is still married to her daddy (happily)" and believes their renewed love is something her baby gave her (Chiffens, personal communication June 2000, on the occasion of Lorraine's twelfth birthday).

62. In 1995 SHARE sold "hand cast pewter finish ornaments which depict three angels standing on a cloud. Their lighted candles and the holly-entwined bow are symbolic of hope, as etched on the ornament itself. The back of the ornament displays the SHARE Logo and has a blank nameplate suitable for engraving." In 1998 their "keepsake" ornament was "a clear acrylic teardrop featuring a child-like cherub whose wings are edged in gold. The attached heart is gold and the multi-faceted teardrop is tipped in gold."

63. This novelty "marked a very important moment in the history of feelings" (Aries 1962:40).

64. Although these paintings were normally commissioned, Ruby describes how the wife of the nineteenth-century American cleric Lyman Beecher did a pencil drawing of their daughter "after she was laid out" (Beecher quoted in Ruby 1995:34).

65. According to Sheumaker (1997:423), in eighteenth- and nineteenth-century America, "portraits were meant not only to be accurate depictions of the physical appearance of the sitter, but also to be character studies revelatory of the individual's inner self."

66. Similarly, where British women resist the gendering of their infants (Miller 1997), members of pregnancy-loss support groups welcome and seek out this reassuring evidence of identity.

67. For instance, Cathi writes, "It was a lovely small bush!" In the one-page account she refers to the bush as "little" or "small" ten times (Lammert 1992).

68. A similar example is found in a piece written by a father in memory of a baby whose sex is not known but who is imagined as now living in heaven: "I wish you could be here with me. Instead, we planted you a tree. We'll feed and water, and watch it grow to be beautiful just like you, I know" (Capps 1999).

69. Memorial goods for the garden traffic in an iconography of the dead that has been present in our culture since the rural cemetery movement of the nineteenth century (French 1975; Aries 1985:237–238). Since the establishment of Mount Auburn in 1831, the first "garden cemetery" to be built in the United States, cemeteries have been designed to combine "the plentitude and beauties of nature" with art and as a result to be "enchanting places of succor and instruction" (French 1975:78–79). These narrative accounts indicate that in the late twentieth and early twenty-first century some American families are using the same design principles to create similar places in their own backyards.

    See Schorsch (1976) on the importance of garden iconography in American Federal mourning art. As she notes, "the verdant garden is a setting for the Resurrection, the great Christian symbol of everlasting hope" and "upward pointing, candle-like" evergreen trees, which frequently appeared in the background of mourning art, reinforce the theme of life-in-death (1976:3–4).

70. Most of the jewelry described in pregnancy-loss newsletters is memorial jewelry worn by bereaved mothers (and occasionally other family members), but Susan Ashbaker describes on two occasions the necklace she buried her daughter in— "two gold hearts on a dainty chain" (1993); "our hearts around your neck on the dainty gold chain" (1994). Whereas in memorial jewelry, the jewelry represents the child, here the hearts represent the two parents. Campbell reports that she buried her son with the cross she wore on her wedding day (1990).

    Sherman and Newman (1977) found symbolic jewelry was the second most common cherished personal possession of elderly women in their sample, but the jewelry usually was associated with their spouse rather than children.

71. Other examples include the "beaded bracelet keepsake with your baby's name" advertised in the "resources" section of a SHARE newsletter (Herda 1989), and "Baby's Breath Lapel Pin and Pendants" offered by a SIDS group in Canada

(Mills 1988) as "meaningful symbols to help preserve the memory of a loved child."

72. According to Aries (1975), there were mourning lockets in the beginning of the eighteenth century. During that century, the goal of such lockets and other memento mori "had been to prepare the wearer for death." During the nineteenth century, the primary goal was "to perpetuate the memory of the deceased." Victorian mourning lockets often held a lock of hair or a reproduction of the loved one's tomb. Aries (1985:195, 243) and Morley (1971) provide illustrations of mourning pendants from the Elizabethan and Victorian eras.

73. Simmel (1950:341) places various kinds of adornment on a scale in terms of their closeness to the physical body. He deems tattooing the closest, then dress, which can be exchangeable and takes on the shape of the body; metal and stone adornments are at the other extreme because they are "entirely unindividual and can be put on by everybody." Yet, as we have seen, memorial jewelry is personalized.

74. As discussed earlier, gender is an important quality of both babies and baby things. In a piece called "Remembering Your Baby," Hely suggests that "even if you miscarried too early for the sex to be determined" you might want to "assign . . . a sex to your baby," noting that "many times a parent feels s/he knows what the baby's sex is going to be right from conception. Even when parents don't feel they know the sex, they can choose the sex they would have liked for their baby. This makes the baby more real, a person in his/her own right" (Hely 1994a).

75. Benjamin (1989:575) describes "the desire of contemporary masses . . . to get hold of an object at very close range by way of its likeness." Bereaved parents try to get close to their baby by way of its likeness and sometimes, as in the case of "fake goods," they do so by way of a likeness of a likeness of the child or by a representation of something that would have been a representation of a child, such as a baptismal certificate that is a substitute for an authentic birth certificate, which would have represented an authentic child.

76. The earlier versions were offered to "parents" at no charge by SHARE and sold to organizations in bulk for 50 cents apiece. They were printed "on white parchment-like paper in soft brown with a pair of green stemmed red roses" (Guenther 1991). The new designs are "elegantly outlined with bronze metallic trim on hard linen stock ivory paper. The sea shells add to the delicate beauty of this special remembrance of your baby" (Voegele 1991).

77. Baudrillard (1983:5) contrasts this with dissimulation, which is "to feign not to have what one has."

78. Barbara Knopf, who delivered at term a boy who had been prenatally diagnosed with a brain condition that was incompatible with life, but who nonetheless survived at home for three weeks, describes how she "spent months creating a photo album with all my mementos from Danny's life . . . .Working with my hands to make something tangible for Danny was very therapeutic for me."

79. Browne (1981:1) defines fetishes as "misshapen, bastard icons" and asserts that "the fetish carries the taint of the off-color, an abnormal attachment, a 'closet'

devotion, something that the person attached to [it] should be . . . ashamed of."
Even Gamman and Makinen, who choose not to use Freud's label of "patholog-
ical" when discussing sexual fetishism (1994:38), use the pejorative phrase "ob-
sessive hoarding" (1994:27) to describe the activities of widows or widowers in
preserving some of their partner's effects or of mothers in collecting their
child's memorabilia.

Chapter 7

1. See Borg and Lasker's (1981) book by that title, and Reinharz (1987:233). Many
   women explicitly use the language of "failure" to describe their experience of
   loss; for example, after her second consecutive miscarriage Perry-Lynn Moffitt
   (1994) "felt like a failure."
2. Their infants may be regarded as freaks by others.
3. See Layne (1999a) for a discussion of the way that the opposition in North
   American culture between the ideologies of gifts and commodities provides a
   powerful resource for valorizing non-normative family-making practices and
   experiences like foster, adoptive, and surrogate mothering, and mothering infants with disabilities, as well as pregnancy loss.
4. In comparison with the Old Testament, where "gift" refers primarily to material gifts or services, that is, the topics historically covered in anthropological
   analysis of giving, the New Testament scriptures refer to gifts like "eternal life,"
   "God's grace," "the gift of the Holy Spirit," and "Christ Jesus," notions more
   akin to "the child as gift" and "unconditional love." See the introduction to the
   volume *Transformative Motherhood: On Giving and Getting in a Consumer Culture* (Layne 1999c).
5. Another example of this type of gift in popular culture can be found in the 1999
   American Cancer Society fund-raising sale of daffodils, which used the slogan
   "The Gift of Hope."
6. Landsman (1999) discusses how mothers of children with disabilities emplot
   themselves as the recipients of gifts from their children, such as "enlightenment" and "knowledge of unconditional love."
7. See also Reinharz (1987) on this topic.
8. Feminist critics of obstetrics have sometimes overstated the extent to which obstetrical knowledge and practice cast pregnant women as passive, and pregnancy
   as an involuntary process over which the woman has little to actively contribute.
   For example, according to Davis-Floyd, the fetus is understood to be "a being
   separate from its mother and [that] can grow and develop without the mother's
   will or involvement" (1992:58) and Martin depicted the obstetrical understanding of women's role during the first stage of labor as "a passive host for the
   contracting uterus" (1987:61). This is only half the story for women are also
   chronically cast as responsible for the outcomes of their pregnancies.
9. Feminist scholars have frequently decried the "commodification of children
   and the proletarianization of mothers" (Rothman 1989:66). For example, both

Martin and Rothman have been concerned not only by the application of the values and images of capitalist production to pregnancy and birth, but also by women's relatively low status "as laborers" in this system. But when the alternative is not to produce, to be outside the realm of production, one can see that the role of producer, even such a lowly one, is a culturally more desirable one; for in our system, production is understood to be active, willful, and moral.

10. This language of production is found not only in obstetrical discourse (and its feminist critiques), but is also used by women to describe their experience. For example, Peggy Morton, whose dissertation in social welfare is on subsequent children following pregnancy loss, explains that she chose this topic after suffering from post-traumatic stress syndrome following a successful but difficult pregnancy after five years of pregnancy losses. Others could not understand why she wasn't finally happy, after having "attain[ed] the goal, producing a child" (1996:xi). She also uses this terminology in her acknowledgments section where she thanks her therapist who made it possible for her "to produce both: a child and a dissertation" (1996:ix).

11. Martin (1987) uses the term "failed production" in relation to menstruation and menopause, but not pregnancy loss. According to Fillion (1994:35), for many of the women she observed who were undergoing fertility treatments in Canada, this was "the first time they'[d] failed at anything. They did the difficult things—climbing the career ladder, buying a home . . . "

12. Martin (1987) described the way that gynecological textbooks portray menstruation in these terms and noted the horror that the "lack of production" evokes in our culture. She cites Winner's (1977) depiction of "the stopping and breakdown of technological systems in modern society" as "the ultimate horror" (quoted in Martin 1987:45). She also quotes a nineteenth-century inventor who understood the world to be a factory that God designed (1987:45). "In this great workshop, human's role is to produce: 'God employs no idlers'" (Ewbank quoted in Martin 1987:46).

13. Sandelowski (1993:32–37) also discusses the Freudian understanding that infertility is caused by "a true lack of desire for children."

14. Similarly, in *Williams Obstetrics* (1956), a "there is nothing to be done" explanation is quickly countered with the prescription of numerous things for would-be-mothers to do "for their own good and their babies' benefit," such as "a good schedule of diet, exercise, and rest with limitations of alcohol, tobacco and drugs and [avoidance of] excessive fatigue, insufficient sleep, nervousness, and tension due to overwork or social activities" (Eastman 1956:533). The primary responsibility incumbent on would-be-mothers, however, is clearly to trust their doctor and follow their orders.

15. The extent to which physicians and popular books on pregnancy loss feel the need to reassure women that there is nothing they did that could have caused their loss attests to the strength of this problematic tendency to self-blame (cf. Simonds and Katz Rothman 1992). In nearly every interview I have done with

women who have had a pregnancy loss, they have spontaneously produced a litany of the culturally defined prescribed and prohibited activities that they scrupulously abided by during their pregnancies. See also Landsman (1999) on this phenomenon among mothers of infants and toddlers with disabilities.

16. Another example can be found in a brochure put out by the birthing center that I went to during my first pregnancy. It begins, "You've nourished a credo of 'yes, I can!'" (Familyborn 1985). Just like the little engine that could, the implication is that if one believes in oneself and tries hard enough, one can achieve one's goal, in this case having a healthy baby and a drug-free labor.

17. The worst birth outcome mentioned is Cesarean birth (as opposed to say, a stillbirth or the birth of a child with disabilities). The authors assure those who must settle for this dreaded outcome that they "should be just as proud of themselves as other couples, since they *worked* just as hard (perhaps harder)" than other couples (1989:61 emphasis added).

18. Women who are unable to conceive, even with all the latest "technological wizardry," express similar feelings—"'I feel out of control,' they say again and again" (Fillion 1994:35).

19. The first in a list of valuable things that Kathy Wucherpfennig (1999) mentions as having been brought to her life by her daughter Kristine, who was stillborn at "38 weeks, with no medical explanation" is the lesson of "how little control I have over major events in my life."

20. Even Mother Mary is imagined by one contributor to the UNITE newsletter to be vulnerable to self-blame for the untimely death of her son: "She asked if she had done something wrong" (Doherty 1988).

21. I am currently investigating the extent to which pregnancy loss is experienced as a matter of "categorical fate" in toxically assaulted communities in the United States (Layne 2001).

22. Another important resource for both physicians and bereaved parents is an equally spiritually infused idea of "nature" (Layne 1997b). See chapter 8.

23. See Huber (2001) for a discussion of the differences between irony and paradox in the context of missionary experience.

24. The younger children make one of their typical mistakes and confuse this Godly gift with the profane gifts brought to the shower and thus surmise that the baby must be in one of the gift-wrapped packages. They also mishear the lyrics and substitute "a baby is a gift from our Mom."

25. She later developed a uterine infection in her twenty-first week and had to "evacuate the uterus to stop the infection."

26. Furthermore, one of the characteristics of modern Western economies is the rigid ideological distinction between people and things. As Kopytoff (1986:84) documents, "conceptually separating people from things" is intellectually rooted in classical antiquity and Christianity but does not become culturally salient until the onset of European modernity. And although he makes clear that things can be commodities and people cannot, it is unclear why people can be given (that is, alienated) in the form of gifts. In Parry's

(1986) discussion of Marx's and Mauss's evolutionary schemes, what distinguishes gift exchange in modern societies is that "persons and things, interest and disinterest" have been fractured, "leaving gifts opposed to exchange, persons opposed to things, and interest to disinterest. The ideology of a disinterested gift emerges in parallel with an ideology of a purely interested exchange" (Parry 1986:458).

27. According to the *Encyclopaedia Judaica* (1971), Beruryah was "the only woman in the Talmudic literature whose views on halakhic matters" were taken seriously by the scholars of her time. Thanks to Walter Zenner for sharing this with me.

28. His nephew was born at thirty-three weeks gestation and died one day later. The cause of death was oxygen deficiency from placenta abruption.

29. This poem also appears in the September/October 1985 issue of the *SHARE Newsletter* as "Understanding," "author unknown" and in the December 1989 *UNITE Notes* as "God's Lent Child," "author unknown" and in *Bittersweet . . . Hellogoodbye* (1988:4–57) as "God's Promise," "author unknown." See Ross (1993:185) for another example of this usage from pre–World War I England.

30. In early-twentieth-century American gift economy, there was an association between suffering and spiritual gifts. These associations are well developed in the devotional book *Streams in the Desert*, by Mrs. Cowman, which has been continuously in print ever since its publication in 1925. Forbes explains Cowman's remarkable success by the fact that "she assures women that their suffering *counts* and that their lives have meaning; they are significant to the one who counts the most, to God" (1997:130). In one entry Cowman writes, "comfort does not come to the lighthearted and merry. We must go down into the 'depths' if we would experience this most precious of God's gifts" (Cowman quoted in Forbes 1997:130).

31. In one case, a mother imagines her child as giver within a heavenly family instead. In poem entitled "Miscarried Joy," Teresa Page (1986) of Rockford, Illinois, whose baby "Sammy D. Page" was miscarried at ten and a half weeks gestation, wonders, "What gifts and talents do you share in heaven, with God's family there?"

32. Another example is found in a 1995 *SHARE* issue where the editors printed a piece they planned to use at their upcoming "day of remembrance." One of the refrains is "Let us treasure the gifts you left us as you have etched your mark on our hearts."

33. Much like what one finds in pregnancy-loss support-group newsletters, Sharp (2001:126) reports that the parents of young organ donors (approximately 40 percent are under twenty years of age) often memorialize their dead children on websites in the form of poems written in the voice of their child.

34. Rabinowitz (1983) likens her children born after a loss to a "sweepstakes prize"—unlikely, unexpected, unearned, based solely on chance.

35. She also lists a number of less tangible gifts: "Why am I so grateful to you? For making me appreciate more than ever the good in people—the giving, caring, comforting, and sharing. For forcing me to *really* feel—sorrow, hurt, anger, and

love. For teaching me the immeasurable value of life, the importance of health, the beauty of true friendship, and the priceless gift of love" (Holper 1991a).

36. The substitution of the child for God as giver of children is part of the move towards the sacralization of children (Zelizer 1985). I have described elsewhere how dead babies sometimes replace God as an immanence in nature (Layne 1997b, Layne 1999d). This fits with Miller's observation that God was replaced first by husbands and more recently by children as the object of devotion (1998, 1997).

37. In some cases, it is unclear who is responsible for the gift of a child. For example, Cindy Lee Foster of Venice, Florida, whose baby girl was born on Christmas Eve and died the day after Christmas due to meconium pneumonia and hyaline membrane disease, wrote, "You were with me for the holiday. A gift I'll always love" (Foster 1985b).

38. An interesting comparison can be made with Ragoné (1994), who describes how both the surrogate and the adoptive mothers she studied framed love as constitutive of kinship.

39. See Schmidt (1995) on the history of Mother's Day.

40. It is unclear from these pieces about Mother's Day and Father's Day the extent to which this notion is meant to apply to and/or is embraced by women who have first-trimester losses.

41. See Slater (1977:38) for examples from Puritan New England of dead children being construed as a sacrifice or offering to God.

42. This child died due to a rare genetic disease after living for twenty-one months, much longer than most losses mourned at pregnancy-loss support groups.

43. Sometimes Christ's sacrifice appears without the analogy between Christ and their child; for example, an anonymous woman explains that because God "gave his son's life," she and her deceased son are assured salvation (Anonymous 1995). Self-blame prevents the author from considering her loss as a gift to God. In the first stanza of her poem she construes herself as the agent in the conception, in the second, as agent of the wrongful death of her child, "because I didn't take care of myself." In the third and final stanza she (and her son) are cast as receivers of salvation (thanks to God's sacrifice) despite their status as sinners.

44. I am indebted to Mary Huber for this reference.

45. I have not found similar use of the Old Testament story of Abraham, who proves his devotion to God by his willingness to sacrifice his son. Hyde discusses the Old Testament scriptures regarding the sacrifice of first fruits, including the first-born son. "In the pentateuch the first fruits always belong to the Lord. The Lord gives the tribe its wealth, and the germ of that wealth is then given back to the Lord" (Hyde 1979:19). Miller offers a possible explanation for this in that Judaism turned away from human sacrifice and used a symbolic substitution in place of Isaac, whereas Christianity distinguished itself from Judaism by the actual sacrifice of the son (1998:115–116).

Also see Miller's (1998) discussion of theories of sacrifice and how they relate to shopping as transcendent giving and Gibson (1994:192) on the way

Ibrahim's sacrifice figures in the Islamic rituals that take place seven days after birth in Bahasa, Indonesia.

See Harding's (1987, 1992) account of the way an evangelical preacher used New Testament resources to tell the story of how he accidentally killed his own son.

46. The notion of the baby as specially chosen sometimes appears without a direct analogy between Christ and the baby. For example, in a piece written the day his daughter was stillborn, Michael Stagoski writes, God "said to her, 'I have chosen you little one to share My kingdom and be part of My Special Flock" (1995). He goes on to explain, "I have chosen you for a reason. You will be your family's guardian angel" (Stagoski 1995). Another author writes "Souls so perfect that God up above called them back home" (Phillips 1995).

47. Although I have come across no reference to this in pregnancy-loss narratives, Langer (1997:48) remarks of the story of Abel told in the book of Genesis, that the "loss of a single son was the start of the Jewish narrative."

48. She also attributes to Mary doubt as to whether she will be reunited with her son in heaven and acknowledges that, even if she were certain, that would not negate the fact that she was deprived of his company in the present. "She wanted to believe in heaven, another existence with her son. But she knew that time would come later. And she wanted Him to be with her now" (Doherty 1988).

49. Linda Nuccitelli (1999) is author of a poem, "One Tiny Baby" in which she expresses envy because "Holy Mary" got to have "Him for so long," imagines the pleasure that Mary took in her son's "good works and deeds," and conveys her admiration for Mary's courage and grief at Christ's death.

50. Another woman who lost twins reassures herself that she can bear the pain: "God never gives out an impossible sacrifice" (Clancy 1995). This is a variation on the saying that "God never gives burdens greater than one can bear," but in this case what God is giving is the obligation to give (cf. Landsman 1999).

51. She develops the theme that it does not matter if the items taken "are imperfect to some eyes . . . or incomplete" (Kozak 1987). Because they were theirs, they are loved and cannot be replaced.

52. Shelly ends by saying, "I treasure the lessons of love and caring, listening and sharing, that I received from the members of the group" (Cocke 1986).

53. According to Hyde, "the Word is received, the soul suffers a change (or is released or born again), and the convert feels moved to testify, to give the Word away again. . . . The transformation is not accomplished until we have the power to give the gift on our own terms" (Hyde 1979:46–47).

54. This is also accomplished in the Jordanian ritual I observed (see chapter 10).

55. See Cheal (1988) on the unequal flow of material gifts between generations.

56. This little girl died seven days after her birth.

57. I use *Webster's* in lieu of the *Oxford English Dictionary* as it is likely to reflect popular American understandings of the term more accurately.

58. The theme of *UNITE*'s fourth annual regional conference, held in 1988, was "Grieving a Very Special Baby: Miscarriage, Stillbirth, and Infant Death."

59. This woman uses a Christian paradox to reverse the view that it is better to live than to die. In this poem heaven is portrayed as the more desirable place to be. Therefore her son is lucky and those remaining in this world are to be pitied. "Through my soul searching I have come to believe: we live in a fallen world, and pain and suffering from this fallen world touches our lives. It doesn't seem fair, but nothing will until we reach Heaven" (Rodgers 1987).

60. Many narratives of loss include a list of missed opportunities to care for their babies, and such lists often include the less-desirable child-rearing tasks, such as caring for a sick child, or the night feedings. In an unusual piece by Sarai Rodgers of Lake Charles, Louisiana, written a year after the stillbirth of her son, she construes these missed moments as a gift. "I was never hurt by my child's rebellion, was never embarrassed by my child's actions, and I never had to discipline him. This was a gift only God could give" (Rodgers 1987). She gave this as her personal testimony in her church on the one-year anniversary of her son's stillbirth due to renal vein thrombosis (Rodgers 1987).

61. In the Whittier poem we learn that the parents were chosen because they were gifted teachers. "I cannot promise you she will stay since all from Earth return; But there are lessons taught down there I want this child to learn. I've looked the wide world over. In search of teachers true, And from the throngs that crowd life's land I have selected you" (Whittier 1995/6). This is more in keeping with the "special parents" notion described by Landsman (1999).

62. This piece was read at the dedication of the Littlest Angels Memorial in Baton Rouge, Louisiana.

63. I am indebted to Mary Huber for this reference.

64. This also applies, though to a lesser extent, when bereaved parents define acknowledgment of their loss by others as a valuable gift.

65. See Layne (1994) for a discussion of gift-giving as a hierarchical identity-making practice in the Hashemite Kingdom of Jordan.

66. See also Carrier (1993:65) on year-end giving in England where historically gifts flowed from subordinates to their superiors.

Chapter 8

1. See Sandelowski (1993:130–138) for a description of similar feelings by couples who achieved a pregnancy after struggling with infertility.

2. The poem is "MCMXIV" by Philip Larkin, written in the early 1960s in contemplation of "a photograph of the patient and sincere, lined up in early August outside a recruiting station" (Fussell 1975:19).

3. Other similarities between the "discourses of remembrance" (White 1992) found in these narratives of loss and those relating to twentieth-century Euro-American war dead will be discussed in the next chapter.

4. As Muecke explains, "To ironize something is to place it in whatever context will invalidate or correct it; to see something as ironic is to see it in such a context" (Muecke 1969:23).

5. See Shaw (1994:2), Guralnik (1970), Huber (2001), Fernandez and Huber (2001), Baldick (1990a, b), Muecke (1969), for definitions.
6. Likewise, the ironies found in the poems of Thomas Hardy described by both Booth (1974:238) and Fussell (1975:3–7) are of this type.
7. Booth notes that "overt assertions about irony can range from the most minute local observations to claims about the infinite" and that "most . . . particular ironies can be easily turned into ironic generalizations" (1974:236).
8. Another dimension of supreme importance in the case of pregnancy loss, and one not considered by Muecke, is the extent to which that which was expected mattered.
9. Literary theorists have used many of the same New Testament scriptures as examples for both irony and paradox. For example, Kermode (1987:391) uses the Beatitudes as an example of Christian paradox, while Booth (1974) uses them as illustrations of irony.
10. Carol Winter's daughter was only one year old when her little brother Jake died after having survived in the NICU for three weeks. Later, when this daughter needed to go to the hospital for tests, Carol had trouble reassuring her "that the doctors and nurses are there to help fix her." Her daughter wanted to know "Why couldn't they fix Jake?" (1996). The doctors had had no explanation for his premature birth and had given the parents a positive prognosis for his survival after his birth.
11. He continues, "Irony engenders worse irony: At this moment, while we looked with dreadful fixity at so isolated a horror, the lance-corporal's brother came round" (Fussell 1975:32).
12. WWI poets often commented on the "ironic proximity of violence and disaster to safety, to meaning, and to love"; the trenches being a mere seventy miles from home (Fussell 1975:69).
13. Of course, these Romantic figures were not in complete agreement about the meaning of nature. See, for example, Helsinger (1982:41–66), on how Ruskin's views departed from those of Wordsworth.
14. It would be interesting to know how frequently the seasons are used in thinking about successful pregnancies. One bereaved mother makes use of this imagery in describing her pregnancy: "July was such a long long time away . . . . Finally the seasons began to change and the anticipation grew" (Fitzgerald 1988:23).
15. Ruskin devoted an entire chapter of the first volume of *Modern Painters* to "the Open Sky," which he believed was "'intended' by 'our maker' for our pleasure as well as our moral instruction" and by the time the war had begun, "over a century of Romantic poetry and painting" had established sunrises and sunsets "as tokens of hope and peace, . . . [and] emblems of infinity" (Fussell 1975:53,52).

The sunrise/sunset contrast is sometimes used, though not nearly as frequently as seasons in narratives of pregnancy loss. For instance, the theme for the tenth national perinatal bereavement conference held in 1996 in Scottsdale, Arizona, was "Beautiful Sunrises, Bittersweet Sunsets."

16. This rhetorical strategy has been used by bereaved mothers in the United States since the nineteenth century. Simonds and Rothman found "pleasant weather" used "as a foil to a mother's distress" (1992:59).

17. He was diagnosed with sepsis and died during the hospitalization for that from a reaction to the dye used to test his kidney function.

18. The double meaning of "freak of nature" is paralleled in the notion of "natural," which can mean both that which is normal and that which is of nature, that is, free from human influence.

19. Genetic abnormalities are also implicated in many neonatal deaths. Second- and third-trimester spontaneous abortions, on the other hand, generally involve "normal fetuses" (Pizer and Palinski 1980:30).

20. See for example the piece by Rowe (1993) entitled "For the Best" that begins "Who are you to tell me that the loss of my child is FOR THE BEST? Is it for the best that I will never experience the joy of his birth? Is it for the best that this child will never hear my voice or know my love?" (See also Wiley 1987.)

21. Of course, one does also find more standard instances of pathetic fallacy, including those involving weather. Some authors do report feeling that the weather expressed sentiments similar to their own. For example, Dotti Brown describes the burial of her child "on the bleak hillside in November. I feel the cold, bone-chilling and penetrating, like death, so appropriate for the day" (Brown 1988). Similarly, Darlene Boggs (1988) of Visalia, California, writes, "The weather's cold and the rain seems right, as you go in the grave, out of sight" and Jacqueline Savageau writes, "the ground is covered with a fresh blanket of white just as you were several days ago. Just as the ground, you were still and silent, not a cry" (1991). Simonds and Rothman (1992:59) also found examples of this. They note that "Winter and stormy weather [were often used to] emphasize women's depression and passion."

22. According to Nash (1982), following the exodus from bondage in Egypt, the Jews wandered in the wilderness for forty years; there Moses received the Ten commandments, thereby creating the covenant between God and Israel. This experience gave wilderness several new meanings: "a sanctuary from a sinful and persecuting society; . . . the environment in which to find and draw close to God; and . . . a testing ground where a chosen people were purged, humbled, and made ready for the land of promise" (Nash 1982:16). (See also Albanese 1990.)

23. A classic nineteenth-century North American example of this attitude can be found in Emerson's influential *Nature*, published in 1835: "To go into nature, a man needs to retire as much from his chamber as from society. I am not solitary whilst I read and write, though nobody is with me . . . .In the woods we return to reason and faith" (Emerson in Finch and Elder 1990:147).

24. It is important to note that the "nature" in which bereaved parents find comfort is not by any means necessarily "wild, untouched nature" but, in fact, is quite

often domesticated nature, including golf courses, cemeteries, and their own backyard gardens or even kitchen windows. Since the advent of the "rural cemetery movement" in the nineteenth century, beginning with the opening of Mount Auburn in 1831, there has been a North American tradition of cemeteries providing by virtue of "the plenitude and beauties of nature combined with art . . . a place of succor and instruction" (French 1975:78–79). Nehemiah Adams, commenting on Mount Auburn in 1834, wrote that the beauty of nature in the rural cemetery would help people to realize that "in the mighty system of the universe, not a single step of the destroyer, Time, but is made subservient to some ulterior purpose of reproduction, and the circle of creation and destruction is eternal" (in French 1975:79).

25. See my review of the film *Some Babies Die* (1986) for other examples.

26. Given the lack of social support for such losses, one may ask, as Williams (1973:130) does of Wordsworth's poem "Michael," whether the narratives of these mourners can be interpreted as a form of social criticism—of evidence of the lack of community and of social life as a life of pain.

27. Sharp (2001:125) reports a variety of practices involving "memorial gardening" in the organ transplant industry, including tree planting ceremonies, which he describes as "the most popular form of professional commemoration." The sapling is meant to "embody all local donors who died that year" and to represent "transplantation's miraculous ability to regenerate life." He says that "for some, the tree transforms donors into another life form that will continue to grow; for others, however," it reminds them of a "'mass grave' of forgotten dead."

28. Another small, transient object in the sky reported as a sign from the baby is "a lone pink balloon," which floated by miles away from the cemetery after a balloon release at the funeral (Diaz 2001).

29. Lilies were the favored flower in this regard. Simonds and Rothman (1992) do not mention references to butterflies or rainbows, however. The other metaphor they did find, the bird, is no longer as common.

    Ruskin also utilized the flower/child analogy: "the simplest forms of nature are strangely animated by the sense of Divine Presence, the Trees and Flowers seem all, in a word, children of God" (quoted in Fuller 1988:17).

    Sometimes, however, the flower metaphor is used to highlight the unnaturalness of perinatal death. For example, in a letter to God, another woman describes her daughter as a "bud that never opened" (Wagner 1984) (cf. Taylor 1993, Golden 1994).

30. These crystals were originally hung up as Christmas ornaments, but she decided to leave them up year-round. She notes this anomaly of nature: "Snowflakes in July? Yes!" (Hintz 1988).

31. During 1988, the first year the *SHARE Newsletter* was illustrated with clip art, an image of a butterfly on a flower was used to illustrate the first page of each issue.

32. Thanks to my research assistant, Jennifer Snediker, for this find.

33. Sharp (2001:125) reports a similar practice at a conference of the Transplant Recipients International Organization, where organ recipients are invited to "decorate 'donor trees' with highly personalized ornaments reflective of the love and gratitude they feel for their anonymous donors."

34. Muecke (1969:34) defines a "victim of irony" as a "person whose 'confident unawareness' has directly involved him [sic] in an ironic situation."

35. Muecke uses an example like this to illustrate his concept of "simple irony." "In the light of greater awareness, or of . . . subsequent knowledge (sometimes supplied by the ironist himself [sic], an assumed or asserted fact is shown not to be true, an idea or a belief to be untenable, an expectation to be unwarranted, or a confidence to be misplaced" (Muecke 1969:23).

Chapter 9

1. Similarly, Leonard Clark's (1985) piece "Stillborn" is written in the voice of a mother who wonders if "you rejected us?"

2. In a letter addressed to bereaved parents, Cathi Lammert (2000) uses the metaphor of a jigsaw puzzle to capture this sense of fragmentation: "Your life is comparable to a 500-piece jigsaw puzzle that has been scattered."

3. Becker (2000) describes how infertile couples often express feeling "incomplete."

4. There are other potential losses to be feared as well. Pregnancy loss often puts a strain on a marriage. In a piece on fathers, couples, and grief, Janis Heil (1983) counsels, "When a couple has lost a baby, they don't need to lose each other."

5. Another example is given by Kathleen Depres, who had become pregnant later in life and then lost a baby girl at thirty-one weeks gestation. She describes the four days between when the baby was found dead by ultrasound and she delivered after an induced labor as "the longest four days of our lives." Of course, pregnancy and having a newborn themselves produce an altered experience of time. As one author wrote, in the voice of her dead baby recalling the experience of the pregnancy, "I, who couldn't seem to tell time and got your days and nights mixed up" (Schwiebert 1985).

6. Knopf uses this journey metaphor several other times in her account—she describes her "small steps of progress" and assured others at her support group that "it will eventually get easier as you get further down the road."

7. Similarly Foley (1985:2–3) writes, "So many of us wonder, fear almost, 'Will I forget my baby?'" and then tells a reassuring story of how, in helping a lawyer go through the things of her recently deceased neighbor, she found "what we'd call a 'memory box.' It held an assortment of toys and clothing and cards ("To Aunt Bert and her baby"). All the material hopes and dreams representative of that little child who never came home . . . all these memories of a child who had lived only one day, sixty-seven years ago!" She concludes, "the importance of

this child in their lives is shown by the memories of her which they kept in their room . . . all those years. Even if they couldn't share their child with family, friends, or neighbors, these items kept her memory alive to them."

8. Heimer (1999) found that "parents of NICU patients" seemed to be "especially likely to produce extensive documentation" of their child, "perhaps because their child's life hangs in the balance."

9. Given how common it is for others to forget, the act of remembering is particularly appreciated. A piece by Lauren Seriego (1996) called "They Never Forget" acknowledges how much it means to her that now, four years after the stillbirth of her son, her extended family still remembers him.

10. Kirmayer (1996) has a somewhat different view. He compares survivors of sexual abuse and the Holocaust, and concludes that because of "the transhuman scale of what" Holocaust survivors suffered, we "do not see their failure to surpass their traumas and move on as a consequence of personal weakness." The "landscape of 'ordinary' family life," where memories of childhood sexual abuse [or pregnancy loss] are situated, however, "does not allow the same tacit validation" (Kirmayer 1996:190).

11. Although members of pregnancy-loss support groups do discuss sometimes "being caught off guard" by their memories (e.g., Keyser 2001), this is not a primary problem of memory for them.

    In an article describing her rape and attempted murder, Brison conveys the horror of traumatic flashbacks and quotes Shay's study of flashbacks among Vietnam veterans: "[o]nce experiencing is under way, the survivor lacks authority to stop it or put it away. The helplessness associated with the original experience is replayed in the apparent helplessness to end or modify the reexperience once it has begun" (Shay quoted in Brison 1997:17). According to Kirmayer, "Survivors of the Holocaust are usually depicted as overwhelmed by memories and unwilling to recount their tale for fear of the pain it will re-evoke" (Kirmayer 1996:174–175). This is also conveyed by Kimel's poem, "I Cannot Forget."

12. Several bereaved mothers assert that they will remember the moments shared while the baby was inside of them: "I'll always remember the kicking I felt, and him growing inside" (Palekar 1988); "But, baby, just remember this:/I never will forget/how you moved inside me full of life/and brought me happiness" (Wojtowicz 1987).

13. While, for most, the fact that so few people knew their child is seen as a problem, others cast this singularity as a privilege, akin to private, exclusive ownership of an unique object. Sue suggests that when her baby died in utero it was "as if to say, 'You're the only one who will know me.'" This not only attributes the ability to the fetus to decide whether to live or die but also suggests a kind of privilege in this exclusive relationship. See also Miller (1984), who seems pleased that "You'll be a memory no one shares but me."

14. According to *Webster*'s, technology is defined as things "by which society provides its members with those things needed or desired," "tools used to enhance

human's capacity." Because of the multivalence of material culture, the same goods are often used to address more than one problem of memory simultaneously.

15. The twentieth century has been referred to as the "century of the child," an era in which children became discrete individuals (Spigel 2001:189). In 1993 President Clinton instituted National Children's Day, which was meant to complement Mother's and Father's Day (Spigel 2001:219).

16. In Ruby's (1995:1) seminal work *Secure in the Shadow: Death and Photography in America*, he attributes "photography's amazing popularity over the last century and a half [to] its capacity to help us remember people, places, and events." Ruby explores the "apparently obvious connection between photography and memory on the one hand, and memory and grief on the other" (1995:9). Photos also played a prominent role in the wake of September 11. First, on posters as people sought missing loved-ones, and since that time in informal and formal memorials.

17. See Hendon (2000) for a discussion of storage and memory based on archeological evidence.

18. See chapter 6 on the importance of feet in the imagery of pregnancy loss. Some narratives of loss mention shoe-bronzing among the list of things that "should have been"; for example, Mary Zeches writes, "there should have been small white orthopedic shoes I would have saved and later bronzed."

19. A recent example of this model of memory was a winter 2001 billboard for a Massachusetts ski area, which advertised, "Memories—come and get 'em."

    Memories are also sometimes construed in pregnancy-loss support rhetoric as something more like spirit, something that cannot be seen but whose presence is still felt. For example, the memory box given out at UNITE's twenty-fifth-anniversary celebration was so small as to suggest that the memories meant to be stored in it would have to be of this immaterial kind. These memories suggest something akin to a magical genie, a powerful spiritual force that does not actually occupy worldly space but that nonetheless can be stored in a physical location and accessed at will.

20. A number of parents note the likeness between their babies in size and value to jewels or other treasures. Joann Meredith of Beebe, Alaska (1988), wrote a piece in the form of a question/answer session with God in which God explains "your little jewel was mine to have"; another woman describes the tiny casket her daughter was buried in as a "treasure box"; and another woman who identifies herself simply as "Mommy" writing three years after the burial of her stillborn daughter recalls the funeral: the priest brought the coffin in his car, and is described as having delivered "my precious gift to me . . . you lay in your beautiful white box . . . Today, . . . we realize that was the most important Little White Box I will ever receive."

21. With children who survive there is little need for this: they are supremely present in one's life. Yet even in such cases, they are not always in our presence (e.g., they may be at school, day care, camp, friends' houses, with the other parent or other relatives).

22. Another difference is that an appreciation of the social-situatedness of the author/rememberer found in anthropology and history is not present in the case of pregnancy loss.

23. In this, and a related advertisement by this same group in the Arizona and New Mexico tour book, the issue of the relative durability/fragility of memory is simultaneously addressed. In this second ad, the colored photo image is of a tour boat and the header reads "Tours of Lake Powell Depart Daily. The Memories Never Leave" (2001b:51).

24. "Things Remembered: Personalized Gifts," an eight-hundred-strong, nationwide chain of shopping-mall kiosks, uses a series of imperatives like "Make the moment last with gifts they'll never forget," "Keep the memories alive with something they'll always treasure," "You must remember this . . . ", as headers in their brochure for wedding gifts (Things Remembered: Personalized Gifts 2001).

25. His letter is titled "Remembering the Greatest Gifts of all" and begins by recalling the year his parents gave him a much desired toboggan for Christmas. "Today I no longer have the toboggan, but the memory of that special time remains dear to me and becomes more treasured as time goes on" (Lyman Orton 2000), hence the header on the facing page, "Today's Gifts Are Tomorrow's Memories." The items include five kits for handmade gifts: a gingerbread house that requires no baking, a rag doll, a loop loom, a make-a-plate kit like those sometimes advertised in pregnancy-loss newsletters, and a "Grandmother Remembers" book promoted as "a Gift of a Lifetime."

26. The "premiere issue" is packaged in a decorative box labeled "my memory maker" and includes, along with the fictional diary of a girl who survived the Titanic, materials for creating and personalizing a "journal album," and instructions on how to make a Memory Quilt.

27. Another father writes, "The shortest moments we had together were the longest memories we shared," describing the moments after the doctors had given up hope and had asked if he wanted to hold his son during his last moments of life (Kocan 1984).

28. See also a piece written in the voice of the baby, "It is I who was able to put a lifetime of joy into an instant" (Schwiebert 1985:14).

29. See Landsman (1999, forthcoming) on the transformative power of "unconditional" love.

30. Stone (1979:408) describes the early modern "concept of the family as a group of replaceable surrogates, both spouses and more particularly children."

31. The related difficulty of finding empathetic listeners and the cultural mandate to buck up and quit whining was vividly brought home to me when the woman I had hired to transcribe my interviews one day included with the transcripts a copy of a poem by Brooke Astor called "Discipline." The poem begins with the author looking back on a life that has had "my share of good and bad," including "sudden death," and midway through tells of the discovery of "discipline." "I

learned to take the good and bad and smile whenever I felt sad." Not only is dissimulation seen as a virtue, grief is selfish and narcissistic. "[I] began to forget both 'me' and 'I' and joined in life as it rolled by. This may not mean sheer ecstasy but it's better by far than 'I' and 'me.'"

32. Unlike normal mortals who age, these special ones will remain forever young. This theme of being a "forever baby" is a common one in narratives of pregnancy loss and echoes memorials for WWII war dead, like the plaque placed by the National WWII Glider Pilots Association in Arlington National Cemetery in 1991, "In Memory of our Heroic Dead of WWII—Who Shall be Forever Young." Soldiers, especially the ones who die in combat, tend to be young men (Hass 1998:9).

33. The irreplaceability and uniqueness of children is sometimes addressed through analogizing children to elements from nature. For example, Linda Visconti (2001), who types *UNITE Notes*, likens her baby and all of the other "UNITE babies" to "snowflakes on a winter morning. Each unique, special, and different."

34. Like the women who earned "gold stars" for their role "as heroic mothers who bravely gave up their sons to the nation" (Piehler 1994:170), some pregnancy-loss support-group members use the language of sacrifice and cast themselves in equivalent roles as exemplary mothers. According to Piehler, the American War Mothers, a predominantly white Anglo-Saxon Protestant organization founded in 1919, "combined with the momentum of the women's suffrage movement to define. . . . the role of the good citizen as mother" (1994:175).

35. The pregnancy-loss support movement draws extensively from postwar commemorative culture, yet there are obvious social impediments to making an explicit comparison between these types of loss. It is one thing to liken oneself to Mother Mary—she is not likely to take offense—but quite another to liken oneself to a contemporary whose full-grown child died in the line of duty.

   One woman who lost her son on Veterans Day (Evans-Smith 1999) compares herself with wounded soldiers in a piece written on the anniversary of her baby's death. She begins with a discussion of the "wounds" inflicted on her by this death, remarking that in the intervening five years "time has healed most wounds" but yet every year on Veterans Day she discovers that "the wound is [still] fresh—like it all happened yesterday." She concludes, "Veterans Day is celebrated for the soldiers of battle and I celebrate for the remembrance of the day you left my womb but never my life."

36. As Sherman notes in his study of war memorials, the "church has been in the memory business for generations." More recently, Dubin and Cardin have searched Jewish texts for resources in building new women-centered rituals for pregnancy loss, and Lamb has compiled materials for religious services of various kinds.

37. With the exception of this last stanza, each of the five stanzas ends with, "No, I don't want to remember, but how can I forget?" In this last stanza the piece sud-

denly addresses the reader. This survivor changes his focus from his obligation to remember to his obligation to "Never Let You Forget." A Kaddish for the children by Miriam Diskind, "in memory of the one-and-a half-million children" killed in the Holocaust, was also read.

38. This is reproduced from time to time in the newsletters and on products marketed through pregnancy-loss support organizations, such as a sympathy card sold by a pregnancy-loss organization on which a picture of a statue of God's hand cradling a child appears with the biblical verse on the front of the card. The interior is blank but the back cover is printed with "the song text of 'Isaiah 49' from the recording 'I Will Not Forget You,' by Rev. Cary Landry": "I will never forget you, my people; I have carved you on the palm of my hand. I will never forget you; I will not leave you orphaned. I will never forget my own. Does a mother forget her baby? Or a woman the child within her womb? Yet even if these forget, Yes, even if these forget, I will never forget my own" (North American Liturgy Resources 1974).

39. Another version appears in *UNITE Notes* 3(2):2.

40. Dubin describes another connection between motherhood and remembering in the Jewish tradition. In Pesikta Rabbati 43:5 the infertile matriarchs Sarah, Rebekeh, and Hannah are each first tried and then "remembered" by God. In these passages, being "remembered by God" means to be given a child (Dubin 1995/6:73).

41. Some reverse this and cast the fact that they have not forgotten, even though they feared they would, as proof of the importance of this life/event. For example, in a letter to a son who had been stillborn the year before at 38.5 weeks due to uterine rupture, Meghan Boyd (1999) writes, "I am not forgetting you; . . . I have no choice." Although at first Janis Heil (1989) was concerned that she would forget her stillborn daughter, she came to realize that this was impossible. "Now I know I could never forget her."

42. For example, Ingle (1981/2a) ends "Pink Blankets" with the vow "I will never forget you" and Nagele (1986a) ends, "You will not be forgotten. Just missed."

43. According to White, this refrain became a "rallying cry" within days of the attack. A popular Sammy Kaye song "Remember Pearl Harbor" was released eight days after the bombing and a *Life* magazine issue designed to help Americans "Remember Pearl Harbor always" appeared three weeks after the event (Linenthal quoted in White 1992:3).

44. A plaque with these words is found in Arlington National Cemetery at the foot of a tree so dedicated.

45. As Preminger notes, elegies are "usually formal in tone and diction" (1974:214). Bereaved parents most frequently write poems in what is known as "elegiac stanzas," or "elegiac quatrains," an iambic pentameter quatrain, rhymed abab. According to the *Princeton Encyclopedia of Poetry and Poetics*, these quatrains are not restricted in their use to elegies but since Thomas Gray chose this form for his *Elegy Written in a Country Church Yard* in 1751, the pentameter quatrain

was "almost invariably employed for the writing of elegiac verse" (Preminger 1974:216).

46. History museums are another example of the new public commitment to memory. According to Leon and Rosenzwieg (1989:xv), "there are more history museums than all other kinds of museums combined" in the United States, approximately 47 percent of which were founded after 1960. In these cases, what is being remembered is at least as likely to be triumphant as traumatic.

47. Some of these, like that created by Israeli sculptor Edward T. Gordan for the Moraiah School in Englewood, New Jersey, focus specifically on memorializing the children who died in the Holocaust.

48. The notes and letters addressed to the dead left at the Vietnam Memorial and at spontaneous memorials for Princess Diana are similar in genre to many pieces published in pregnancy-loss support group newsletters.

49. See Aries (1974:72) on historical developments that led up to this "concern for marking the site" of burial. "Now people wanted to go to the very spot where the body had been placed and they wanted this place to belong totally to the deceased and to his family" (1974:72).

50. Pregnancy-loss support activists are trying to get a Massachusetts state law amended to assure that "hospitals . . . respectfully care for the remains of unborn babies" (*SHARING* 2000:14).

51. Heimer (1999) has remarked on the person-making powers of naming in the context of neonatal intensive care units. She reports how important it was to one mother of a critically ill newborn to have the "hospital staff members use the baby's name because I just wanted to make sure that he was a person" (1999:23). The NICU staff she studied encouraged parents to name their children and "bed spaces [were] labeled with babies' names inscribed on pink or blue cards" as a reminder to the staff that "in discussions with parents the child should be referred to as 'Linsday,' not 'baby Jones,' even though when the parents are not present there is little effort to "cloak patienthood with a veneer of personhood" (Heimer 1999:10).

    The revocation of names is well known to be a dehumanizing/depersonifying practice. See for example the fictional account of how American census-takers at the end of the nineteenth century "neglected to list [the Japanese living on San Peidro Island, Washington] by name, referring instead to them as Jap Number 1, Jap Number 2, Jap Number 3, Japan Charlie, Old Jap Sam, Laughing Jap, Dwarf Jap, Chippy, Boots and Stumpy—names of this sort instead of real names" (Guterson 1995:75). See Bodenhorn and vom Bruck (in prep) for a collection of recent anthropological studies on naming.

52. According to Scholten (1985:61), during the colonial years New England "parents delayed recognizing their children as individuals, frequently referring to their infants as "it," the little stranger," or "the baby." In choosing a name, she reports practices in the United States through the middle of the eighteenth century similar to those described by Stone for England.

53. As personhood is increasingly attributed to them, and they come to be considered "children," they are then entitled to the same rights and privileges as other children, as Schwiebert and Kirk assert in the title to this subsection of their pamphlet "Your Child Deserves a Name." Becker (2000:99) describes one woman who had undergone IVF and become pregnant with what her hormone levels suggested was a multiple gestation. "We are talking to the little embryos, you know, making up all these silly little nicknames for them."

54. She mentions that she "couldn't remember if we had decided on a name before she was born." Given the cross-reference, one assumes that she made use of the new law, and perhaps was even prompted to name the baby by learning of the law.

55. Janis Heil assured parents attending UNITE's twenty-fifth-anniversary event that "facilitators will remember your baby's name, even if they don't remember yours. And they will say their name."

56. Another of the suggestions, to "hang a Christmas stocking, as you would for your other children," may or may not involve personalizing with the name.

57. Sherman quotes a speech in a town in rural France at the dedication of their memorial, "Though we cannot visit them, let their names remain engraved in our memories" (1999:76).

58. According to their website, the quilt was conceived in 1985 by San Francisco gay-rights activist Cleve Jones, while planning the 1985 annual candlelight march honoring Harvey Milk and George Moscone, who had been assassinated in 1978. "He learned that over 1,000 San Franciscans had been lost to AIDS. He asked each of his fellow marchers to write on placards the names of friends and loved ones who had died of AIDS. At the end of the march, Jones and others stood on ladders taping these placards to the walls of the San Francisco Federal Building" (www.aidsquilt.org/Newsite/history/htm 9–30–01).

59. The guidelines composed by the "Families and Survivors Subcommittees" instructed that the memorial must "incorporate the names of those who died (noting in some way, if the family desires, each victim who was carrying an unborn child)." It is unclear whether any of the nineteen dead "children" represented were "unborn."

60. The "survivors' names" are also listed, but "in a manner separate, distinct and apart from the . . . names of those who died" (www.oklahomacitynational memorial.org).

61. In both of these cases, the individuals being commemorated are for the most part young people who died sudden, unexpected deaths.

62. A notice advertising the 1986 October memorial service held by SHARE explained that "as parents arrive, they will be asked to write the name of their child in a book so their child can be remembered during the service. We want to remember your child with you." It also encouraged people "unable to attend for any reason," including if people were from "other parts of the country," to "have their child remembered by sending the names" (1986 9(5):9).

63. Later "each person tied a greeting for their baby to a helium balloon and again gathered in the courtyard" where they were, "at a signal," released simultaneously.

   Sometimes, as at the Central United Methodist Church in Honesdale, Pennsylvania, rather than inscribing individual names, a collective inscription such as "In Loving Memory, Our Precious Babies of SHARE" is used (*SHARE* 1992 1(5):7).

64. Because of the stigma attached to death by AIDS, pregnancy-loss support organizers appeared to try to distance themselves from the source from which they clearly borrowed. Apparently, although it was first conceived of as a "quilt," in 1989, in a message from Sister Jane Marie reporting on preparations for the Awareness Month Activities, she explains "because blankets are more common than quilts . . . with babies we have begun speaking of the *baby blanket*" (1989:13).

   Sharp (2001:125) reports that a similar adaptation of the AIDS quilt was created by the relatives of organ donors and called the "Donor Quilt" or "Patches of Love" Project. Sharp contrasts this donor-kin-initiated memorial practice, which stresses the individuality of each donor, with the memorial practices of the Organ Procurement Organizations like collective tree-planting ceremonies. "Each panel potentially defies professional expectations" regarding the importance of anonymity (Sharp 2001:125).

65. According to Hass (1998:58), the World War I memorials built in the United States differed from the European ones in that they were "relatively practical," but this forward-looking ethos was not fully developed until after World War II.

66. Throughout Arlington National Cemetery one finds plaques documenting the dedication of a tree to a particular group of war dead. This practice has also become popular on college campuses in recent years to commemorate faculty or staff who dedicated their lives to the institution. Tree planting ceremonies were one of the common forms of commemoration used to mark the one year anniversary of September 11.

67. A related phenomenon might be seen in the various WWI memorial practices described by Laqueur (1994). He contrasts the lists of names and markers that gird the battlefield, which stress "specificity" and individuality, with the tomb of the unknown warrior and the cenotaph, the empty tomb, which stress universality.

   Another interesting comparison might be made with the shared kinship described by Rapp (1999:273–278) that some see between children with Down syndrome although in the case Rapp describes, this shared kinship is often used to diminish kin ties with the natal family. In the case of pregnancy loss, the shared social identity with others who died during or shortly after a pregnancy does not diminish, but in fact augments claims of natal familial kinship.

68. It is this valence of the candle symbol which was forefronted in the Elton John song "Candle in the Wind," sung at Princess Diana's funeral.

69. As discussed in chapter 8, members of pregnancy-loss support groups some-times seem to deify their dead babies, attributing to them qualities and powers in the past reserved for God. One of these qualities is the way God and Jesus are portrayed as a source of light/wisdom. Of her anencephalic grandson who lived three hours after his birth at thirty-seven weeks, Sheppard wrote, "How brightly your tender flame lit our hearts." Similarly, Chuck Morgan (1995) de-scribed his son who died shortly after birth due to severe microcephaly and complex heart defect as "a small light that shined brightly." They put these words on the baby's headstone and on a framed keepsake they made with his hand- and footprints.

70. The lighting of candles is part of Jewish, Catholic, and Greek Orthodox tradi-tions for remembering the dead. In these cases, candles are not snuffed out, but allowed to burn out "naturally."

71. Tombs of the Unknown Soldier were also built in London (1920), Rome, the United States (1932), and more recently in Australia (1993), Canada (2000).

72. There are also apparently "Eternal Flames" at the Tomb of the Unknown Sol-dier commemorating those who died in the Stalingrad Battle (ITAR-TASS News Agency, 2–22–2000) and an eternal flame was lit as part of the one year anniversary memorial activities for the victims of September 11.

    The "Olympic Flame" was also instituted during the first half of the twenti-eth century. This flame, described by the Olympic Information Center's official website as "the most revered and visible symbol of the Olympic Games," was first used at the 1928 Amsterdam Games. The idea is credited to Theodore Lewald, a chief organizer of the 1936 Berlin Games, and it was at the 1936 games that the first Torch Relay was held. The relay is meant to "symbolize the link between" the modern games and those held in ancient Olympia, at which "a sacred flame burned continually on the altar of the goddess, Hera" (http://www.aafla.com/OlympicInformationCenter/OlympicPrimer/).

73. Another website that includes a photo of this grave refers to the "eternal flame" which "burns bright" (http://nimbus.ocis.temple.edu/~jsiegel/texts/pericles/jfk.htm 2000). Earlier sources used a wider variety of terms. The 1935 *World Book Encyclopedia* uses "continuous fire" and "perpetual fire" in reference to the "eternal flames" at the Tombs of the Unknown Soldier in Paris and Brussels (1935:7418).

74. They were also common features of "the spontaneous memorials" erected to her in the United States (Haney and Davis 1999:231).

75. Everlasting flames have also come to represent earthly love. According to one popular music database, there are at least six popular songs with "eternal flame" in the title. One of the better-known ones is the 1980s Bangles song in which the lover/singer wonders whether the burning s/he is feeling is a dream or an "eternal flame."

76. Birth itself has become a plethora of consumer choices. Where will one give birth—at a hospital, in a birthing center, at home? Who will attend—physician,

certified nurse midwife, lay midwife? Will pain medications be used? What music will one listen to during the birth? (See Davis-Floyd in prep, Klassen in prep, and Layne 2001 and in prep b).

Chapter 10

1. Hygeia also uses new technologies to "alleviate angst which accompanies the parenting and caring for of a critically ill newborn or older child" by placing video cameras in NICUs which allow parents to check on their child remotely at any time.

2. In the case of pregnancy loss, such sites allow bereaved parents to locate not only other bereaved parents, but also those whose child died under similar circumstances or due to similar causes. This function is also accomplished through the newsletters. The SHARE newsletter includes a "parent connection" section where parents ask to be contacted by others who had similar experiences, for example, "anyone who has experienced a loss due to incompetent cervix" or "anyone whose baby died of a rare heart condition, subendocardial fibrosis" or "anyone who experienced a stillbirth, and then went on to have another baby" (*SHAR-ING* 1999 8(1):7). The SHARE office serves as an intermediary in these cases; someone wanting to respond to such a solicitation contacts the SHARE office for the person's contact information.

3. In my own way, through presentations at professional conferences, in my courses, and with the publication of this book, I have joined the leaders of the movement in this endeavor.

4. Curiously, Reinharz (1988b:90) does not mention the way miscarriage articulates with the abortion debate in her discussion of the "possible reasons that feminists have not contributed much to understanding women's experience of miscarriage."

5. Rothman has made a similar point about women's experience of elective abortions (1989:123). Several studies have found that the depth of grief following a pregnancy loss corresponds "with the intensity of the desire for the child, not with the length of its life" (Reinharz 1988a:27–28). Peppers and Knapp found no significant statistical difference in the emotional reaction of mothers but Lovell found that the reactions of health workers varied sharply depending on length of gestation: miscarriages were viewed as less sad than stillbirth and stillbirth as less sad than losing a baby who had lived.

6. As Fortes (1976:5) remarks, "death does not extinguish a person's participation in the life and activities of his family and community." The iterative process of constructing personhood after death is particularly clear in the Japanese case: "full ancestorhood is conferred by worshipers in stages over a stretch of years and by cumulative rituals that simulate the ideal life cycle of the living" (1976:8). LaFleur describes the similarities in Japanese Buddhist beliefs about the way that people are understood to come into and leave the social world of

human beings "bit by bit." He describes a process of "thickening or densifica-
tion of being" (1992:33) during the first years of life and the "structural opposite" at the end. Like birth, dying is "a prolonged, protracted, and many staged
passing" with "more and more time [being] permitted to elapse between temple
rites as the "deceased becomes more and more reified, progressively integrated
into the world of gods and buddhas."

7. The only illustration of a reproductive disaster is the heart-rending photograph
of Geraldine Santoro, lying naked, face-down on the floor, having bled to death
following an illegal abortion.

8. Rothman has criticized the Bradley Method for the primary role given male figures, for example, husbands and doctors as coaches who are directive, supervis-
ing the woman in labor.

9. See Layne (2002) for some disaster stories.

10. Martin (1990) has noted that this emphasis on control found in the rhetoric of
"the largely middle-class women's health movement" appeared with much
greater frequency among the middle-class women in her sample. Working-class
women, in contrast, more readily articulated the aspects of birth that were less
controllable (1990:309). See also Reinharz (1988a:12) on the expectation that
women must "control themselves and be controlled by others during pregnancy
lest they miscarry."

11. Another useful comparison with surrogacy concerns the value and meaning ac-
corded "intent." In surrogacy, Ragoné tells us, the women involved (surrogate
and adoptive mothers) have developed a rhetoric of pregnancy that distinguishes between social and biological conception. The surrogate mother is credited with biological conception and the would-be adoptive mother is credited
with social conception—her desire for the child results in "conception in the
heart." The bereaved mothers who join pregnancy-loss support groups often
talk about and value both forms of conception.

12. For example, Janis Keyser (2001) writes, "I do know I am glad I carried her
within for nine months, even though she died."

    In the context of surrogacy, feminists tend to highlight the importance of
gestation whereas in the case of pregnancy loss no such recognition is forthcoming.

13. Rothman (1982:30–31) makes the useful distinction between "natural childbirth" and what she calls "prepared childbirth," noting that what are often
called natural childbirth classes typically serve to "prepare" women for medically managed childbirth. For example, with "the Lamaze technique of 'childbirth without pain' . . . women were encouraged to remain awake and aware,
working along with their doctors in the delivery of their babies. Doctors remained in charge" (1982:30).

14. My sense is that since so many pregnancy-loss support groups were founded by
hospital staff, more has been done to rethink the ways pregnancy losses are handled in hospitals than in OB/GYN offices (and that as a consequence, more
thought has been given to stillbirth and newborn deaths than to miscarriages).

Selected Bibliography

Abel, Hope. 1984. "A Father's Loss, Too." *UNITE Notes* 3(4):4.

Aizenberg, Isidoro (Rabbi). 1987a. "Treatment of the Loss of a Fetus Through a Miscarriage." Paper submitted to the Committee of Jewish Law and Standards.

———.1987b. "What Mourning Laws May Be Observed for a Child Who Died 30 Days Old?" Paper submitted to the Committee of Jewish Law and Standards.

Albom, Mitch. 1997. *Tuesdays with Morrie*. New York: Doubleday.

Allen, Marie and Shelly Marks. 1993. *Miscarriage: Women Sharing From the Heart*. New York: John Wiley & Sons.

Alvarado, Uncle Rick. 1995. "My Little Angel." *SHARE Newsletter* 4(6):11.

Amendolara, Phyllis. 1997. "Marissa's Story." *UNITE Notes* 15(3):1.

Anagnost, Ann. 1995. "A Surfeit of Bodies: Population and the Rationality of the State in Post-Mao China." Pp. 22–41 in *Conceiving the New World Order: The Global Politics of Reproduction*, edited by Faye D. Ginsburg and Rayna Rapp. Berkeley: University of California Press.

———.1997. "Scenes of Misrecognition: Maternal Citizenship in the Age of Transnational Adoption." *Positions: East Asia Cultures Critique* 8(2): 389–422.

Anonymous (M. for Mommy). 1995. "Because." *UNITE Notes* 14(4):5.

Antze, Paul. 1996. "Telling Stories, Making Selves: Memory and Identity in Multiple Personality Disorder." Pp. 3–24 in *Tense Past: Cultural Essays in Trauma and Memory*, edited by Paul Antze and Michael Lambek. New York: Routledge.

Antze, Paul and Michael Lambek, eds. 1996. *Tense Past: Cultural Essays in Trauma and Memory*. New York: Routledge.

Appadurai, Arjun. 1986. "Introduction: Commodities and the Politics of Value." Pp. 3–63 in *The Social Life of Things: Commodities in Cultural Perspective*, edited by Arjun Appadurai. Cambridge: Cambridge University Press.

Apple, Rima. 2001. "The Puzzle of Modern Motherhood," a review of *Transformative Motherhood* in *Feminist Collections* 22(1):9–11.

Arad, Gulie Ne'eman, ed. 1997. *Passing into History: Nazism and the Holocaust beyond Memory*. Special double issue of *History & Memory: Studies in Representation of the Past* 9(1/2). Tel Aviv: Tel Aviv University.

Aries, Philippe. 1962. *Centuries of Childhood: A Social History of Family Life*. Translated by Robert Baldick. New York: Vintage.

————.1974. *Western Attitudes Toward Death from the Middle Ages to the Present*.
    Baltimore: Johns Hopkins University Press.
————.1975. "The Reversal of Death: Changes in Attitudes Toward Death in
    Western Societies." Pp. 134–158. in *Death in America*, edited by David
    Stannard. Philadelphia: University of Pennsylvania Press.
————.1985 *Images of Man and Death*. Cambridge: Harvard University Press.
Armstrong, David. 1985. "The Invention of Infant Mortality." *Sociology of Health
    and Illness*, pp. 211–232.
Arney, William Ray. 1982. *Power and the Profession of Obstetrics*. Chicago:
    University of Chicago Press.
Ashbaker, Susan S. 1993. "Small White Box." *UNITE Notes* 12(2):1.
————.1994. "What Will You Look Like in Heaven?" *UNITE Notes* 13(3):5.
————.2000. "Two-Two-Ninety-two." *UNITE Notes* 18(4):5.
Association for Recognizing the Life of Stillborns. 1992. "Recognition of Life
    Certificates." *SHARE Newsletter* 1(5):5.
Atkinson, Melissa. 1987. "No heartbeat: After a perfect pregnancy, losing a child at
    birth is almost too much for a mother to bear" *Parents* April, 134–135.
Atwood, Richard. 1990. "Finding the Way." *SHARE Newsletter* 13(5):1.
Aunt Debbie. 1991. "Dear Little One . . . " *UNITE Notes* 10(3):5.
Avery, Mary Ellen, M.D. and Georgia Litwack. 1983. *Born Early*. Boston: Little,
    Brown and Co.
Bachman, Ann. 1999. "Missing David." *SHARING* 8(5):1–2.
Baker, Elena. 1992. "Our Special Baby." *UNITE Notes* 11(2):4.
Baker, Robin and Sharon Woodrow. 1984. "The Clean, Light Image of the
    Electronics Industry: Miracle or Mirage?" Pp. 21–36 in *Double Exposure:
    Women's Health Hazards on the Job and at Home*, edited by Wendy Chavkin,
    M.D. New York: Monthly Review Press.
Baldick, Chris, compiler. 1990a. "Paradox." *The Concise Oxford Dictionary of
    Literary Terms*, pp. 159–160. Oxford: Oxford University Press.
————.1990b. "Irony." *The Concise Oxford Dictionary of Literary Terms*, p. 114.
    Oxford: Oxford University Press.
Baldwin, Paula. 1994. "Christmas 1994." *SHARE Newsletter* 3(6):5.
Balshem, Martha. 1993. *Cancer in the Community: Class and Medical Authority*.
    Washington, DC: Smithsonian Institution Press.
Bannon, Kathleen. 1999. "My Special Christmas Gift." *UNITE Notes* 17(3):5.
Barad, Karen. 1998. "Getting Real: Technoscientific Practices and the
    Materialization of Reality." *Differences: A Journal of Feminist Cultural Studies*
    10:2.
Barker-Benfield, G.J. 1992. *The Culture of Sensibility: Sex and Society in Eighteenth-
    Century Britain*. Chicago: University of Chicago Press.
Barthes, Roland. 1983. *The Fashion System*. Translated by Matthew Ward and
    Richard Howard. New York: Hill and Wang.
Baudrillard, Jean. 1983. *Simulations*. New York: Semiotext(e), Inc.

Beck, Melinda, with Mary Hager, Ingrid Wikelgren, Lisa Brown, Donna Foote, and Lynda Wright. 1988. "Miscarriages." *Newsweek* August 15, 46–52.

Becker, Gay. 1994. "Metaphors in Disrupted Lives: Infertility and Cultural Constructions of Continuity." *Medical Anthropology Quarterly* 8(4):383–410.

———.1997 *Disrupted Lives: How People Create Meaning in a Chaotic World.* Berkeley: University of California Press.

———.2000. *The Elusive Embryo: How Women and Men Approach New Reproductive Technolgies.* Berkeley: University of California Press.

Belk, Russell W. 1993. "Materialism and the Making of the Modern American Christmas." Pp. 75–104 in *Unwrapping Christmas*, edited by D. Miller. Oxford: Clarendon Press.

Benjamin, Walter. [1955] 1989. "The Work of Art in the Age of Mechanical Reproduction." Pp. 571–588 in *The Critical Tradition*, edited by David H. Richter. New York: St. Martin's Press.

Berezin, Nancy. 1982. *After a Loss in Pregnancy: Help for Families Affected by a Miscarriage, a Stillbirth or the Loss of a Newborn.* New York: Simon and Schuster.

Bergels, Jacki. 1989. "Untitled." *UNITE Notes* 8(4):3.

Bergum, Vangie. 1989. *Woman to Mother: A Transformation.* Granby, MA: Bergin & Garvey.

Berman, Michael R., M.D. 2001. *Parenthood Lost: Healing the Pain after Miscarriage, Stillbirth, and Infant Death.* Westport, CT: Bergin & Garvey.

Bertell, Rosalie, Dr. 1985. *No Immediate Danger: Prognosis for a Radioactive Earth.* London: The Women's Press.

Best, Elizabeth Kirkley. 1981. *Grief in Response to Prenatal Loss: An Argument for the Earliest Maternal Attachment.* Unpublished doctoral dissertation. Department of Developmental Psychology. The University of Florida.

Bittman, Sam and Sue Rosenberg Zalk. 1978. *Expectant Fathers.* New York: Ballantine Books

Blair, Lynne. 1990. "An Empty Room." *UNITE Notes* 9(2):2.

Blake, William. [1863] 1970. "Auguries of Innocence." Pp. 31–35 in *A Choice of Blake's Verse*, edited by Kathleen Raine. London: Faber and Faber.

Bledsoe, Caroline. 1990a. "The Politics of Children: Fosterage and the Social Management of Fertility Among the Mende of Sierra Leone." Pp. in *Births and Power: Social Change and the Politics of Reproduction*, edited by W. P. Handwerker. Boulder: Westview Press.

———.1990b. "Strategies of Child-Fosterage Among Mende Grannies in Sierra Leone." Pp. 442–474 in *Reproduction and Social Organization in Sub-Saharan Africa*, edited by Ron Lesthaeghe. Berkeley: University of California Press.

———.1999. "'No Success Without Struggle': Social Mobility and Hardship for Foster Children in Sierra Leone." *Man* (N.S.) 25:70–88.

Bledsoe, Caroline, Fatoumatta Banja, and Anthony Carter. 2002. *The Contingent Lives: Fertility, Time, and Aging in West Africa.* Chicago: University of Chicago Press.

Blizzard, Deborah. 2000. "Situating Fetoscopy within Medical Literature and Lived Experience: An Opening for Social Analysis" Pp. 410–443 in *Bodies of Technology: Women's Involvement with Reproductive Medicine*, edited by A. Saetnan, N. Oudshoorn, and M Kirejczyk. Columbus: Ohio State University Press.

————.In press. *Looking Within: A Sociocultural Examination of Fetoscopy*. Cambridge: MIT Press.

Bloch, Maurice and Jonathan Parry, eds. 1982. *Death and the Regeneration of Life*. Cambridge: Cambridge University Press.

Boddy, Janice. 1998. "Remembering Amal: On Birth and the British in Northern Sudan." Pp. 28–57 in *Pragmatic Women and Body Politics*, edited by Margaret Lock and Patricia A. Kaufert. Cambridge: Cambridge University Press.

Bodenhorn, Barbara, ed. Forthcoming. *Names and Naming: New Views from Anthropology*. Cambridge: Cambridge University Press.

Bodenhorn, Barbara and Gabriele vom Bruck. In prep. "Converting anybodies to somebodies or how to do things with names." *Introduction to Tropes of Entanglement: Towards an Anthropology of Names and Naming*, edited by Gabriele vom Bruck and Barbara Bodenhorn.

Bogdan, Robert. 1988. *Freak Show: Presenting Human Oddities for Amusement and Profit*. Chicago: University of Chicago Press.

Boggs, Darlene. 1988. "The Funeral." Section 4, p. 54 in *Bittersweet . . . hellogoodbye: A Resource in Planning Farewell Rituals When a Baby Dies*, edited by Sister Jane Marie Lamb. Belleville, IL: Charis Communications.

Boling, Patricia, ed. 1995. *Expecting Trouble: Surrogacy, Fetal Abuse & New Reproductive Technologies*. Boulder: Westview Press.

Bolton, Michele Morgan. 2001. "A Quiet Service Recalls a Fallen Rider." *Times Union* July 17, 2001, pp. F-1,8.

Bongaarts, John and Robert G. Potter. 1983. *Fertility, Biology and Behavior: An Analysis of the Proximate Determinants*. New York: Academic Press.

Booth, Wayne C. 1974. *A Rhetoric of Irony*. Chicago: University of Chicago Press.

Bordo, Susan. 1993. *Unbearable Weight: Feminism, Western Culture, and the Body*. Berkeley: University of California Press.

Borg, Susan and Judith Lasker. 1981. *When Pregnancy Fails: Families Coping with Miscarriage, Stillbirth and Infant Death*. Boston: Beacon Press.

Boston Women's Health Book Collective. 1976. *Our Bodies, Ourselves: A Book By and For Women*. New York: Simon and Schuster.

————.1998. *Our Bodies, Ourselves For the New Century: A Book By and For Women*. New York: Simon and Schuster.

Bourdieu, Pierre. 1984. *Distinction: A Social Critique of the Judgement of Taste*. Translated by Richard Nic. Cambridge: Harvard University Press.

Bourne, Gordon, M.D., and David N. Danforth, M.D. 1975. *Pregnancy*. New York: Harper and Row.

Bowlby, R. 1987. "Modes of Modern Shopping: Mallarmé and the Bon Marche." Pp. 195–205 in *The Ideology of Conduct: Essays in Literature and the History of Sexuality*, edited by N. Armstrong and L. Tennenhouse. London: Methuen.

Bowman, Marion. 1999. "A Provincial City Shows Respect: Shopping and Mourning in Bath." Pp. 215–226 in *The Mourning for Diana*, edited by Tony Walter. Oxford: Berg.

Bowser, Kent Norman. 1983. *An Examination of 19th Century American Post-Mortem Photography*. Thesis, Department of Photography and Cinema, Ohio State University, Columbus, OH.

Boyd, Meghan. 1999. "A Letter to Riley." *SHARING* 8(4):14.

Boyer, Julie. 1986. "Am I a Mother?" *SHARE Newsletter* 9(3):3.

Boyette, Kathy. 1996. " No Vacation." *SHARE Newsletter* 5(3):15.

Boyte, Harry C. 1980. *The Backyard Revolution*. Philadelphia: Temple University Press.

Bricker, Stacy. 2000. "It's Mother's Day." *UNITE Notes* 19(1):1.

Brison, Susan J. 1997. "Outliving Oneself: Trauma, Memory, and Personal Identity." Pp. 12–39 in *Feminists Rethink the Self*, edited by Diana Tietjens Meyers. Boulder, CO: Westview Press.

Brody, Jane E. 1992a. "The Price of Ignorance Can Be Another Miscarriage." *The New York Times* December 12, C16.

———.1992b. "Researchers Discover New Therapies to Avert Repeated Miscarriages." *The New York Times* December 15, C3.

Broner, E.M. 1982. "Honor and Ceremony in Women's Rituals." Pp. 234–244 in *The Politics of Women's Spirituality*, edited by Charlene Spretnak. Garden City, NY: Anchor Books.

Bronzino, Joseph D., Vincent H. Smith, and Maurice L. Wade. 1990. *Medical Technology and Society: An Interdisciplinary Perspective*. Cambridge, MA: Massachusetts Institute of Technology Press.

Brown, Dotti. 1988. "Photographs of a Funeral." *UNITE Notes* 7(4):1.

Brown, Laura A. 1985. "Grief." *SHARING* 8(5):2.

Brown, Phil. 1993. "When the Pubic Knows Better: Popular Epidemiology." *Environment* 35(8):17–20, 32–41.

Browne, Ray B. 1981. "Introduction." Pp. 1–3 in *Objects of Special Devotion: Fetishism in Popular Culture*, edited by Ray B. Browne. Bowling Green, OH: Bowling Green University Popular Press.

Brunner, Donna L. 1992. "Me? Guilty?" *UNITE Notes* 11(2):3.

Buck-Morss, Susan. 1989. *The Dialectics of Seeing: Walter Benjamin and the Arcades Project*. Cambridge: MIT Press.

Burgan, Renee M. 1988. "To My Son, William Randolph Burgan." *UNITE Notes* 7(2):4.

Burns, Stanley B., M.D. 1990. *Sleeping Beauty: Memorial Photography in America*. Twelvetrees Press.

Burton, Karen. 1996. "On Being a Mother This Mother's Day." *SHARE Newsletter* 5(3):10.

Caiola, Julie. 2000. "To Angel." *UNITE Notes* 18(3):4.

Callon, Michel. 1998. "Markets and Externalities." Paper presented at the annual meeting of the Society for Social Studies of Science, October, Halifax, Nova Scotia.

Campbell, Hannah. 1990. "The Green Lollipop." *UNITE Notes* 9(3):3.

———.1991a. "Is My Baby Dead?" *UNITE Notes* 10(4):2–3.

———.1991b. "On Top of Our Tree at Christmastime." *UNITE Notes* 10(4):3.

———.1992. "The Picnic Basket." *UNITE Notes* 11(1):5.

———.1993. "Going Back and Giving Back to Group Meetings." *UNITE Notes* 11(4):3.

Campbell, Nancy D. 2000. *Using Women: Gender, Drug Policy, and Social Justice.* New York: Routledge.

Cantrell, Keith. 1987. "To Justin." *SHARE Newsletter* 10(6):1.

Caplan, Eric. 1998. *Mind Games: American Culture and the Birth of Psychotherapy.* Berkeley: University of California Press.

Caplan, Frank. 1973. *The First Twelve Months of Life: Your Baby's Growth Month by Month.* New York: Perigee Books.

Caplan, G. 1960. "Patterns of Parental Response to the Crisis of Premature Birth." *Psychiatry* 23:365–374.

Caplow, Theodore. 1982. "Christmas Gifts and Kin Networks." *American Sociological Review* 47:383–392.

Capps, Carson D. 1999. "A Dream." *UNITE Notes* 17(3):1.

Cardin, Nina Beth, Rabbi. 1999. *Tears of Sorrow, Seeds of Hope: A Jewish Spiritual Companion for Infertility and Pregnancy Loss.* Woodstock, VT: Jewish Lights Publishing.

Carlson, A. Cherre and John E. Hocking. 1988. "Strategies of Redemption at the Vietnam Veterans' Memorial." *Western Journal of Speech* 52:203–215.

Carrier, James. 1991. "Gifts, Commodities, and Social Relations: A Maussian View of Exchange." *Sociological Forum* 6(1):119–136.

———.1993. "The Rituals of Christmas Giving." Pp. 55–74 in *Unwrapping Christmas*, edited by Daniel Miller. Oxford: Clarendon Press.

———.1995. *Gifts and Commodities: Exchange and Western Capitalism since 1700.* London: Routledge.

Carrithers, Michael, Steven Collins and Steven Lukes, eds. 1985. *The Category of the Person: Anthropology, Philosophy, History.* Cambridge: Cambridge University Press.

Cartwright, Lisa. 1993. "Gender Artifacts in Medical Imaging: Ultrasound, Sex Identification, and Interpretive Ambiguity in Fetal Medicine." Paper delivered at the American Anthropological Association's annual meeting.

———.1995. *Screening the Body: Tracing Medicine's Visual Culture.* Minneapolis: University of Minnesota Press.

Casey, Kathy. 1995. "I Was Chosen." *SHARE Newsletter* 4(4):6.

———.1997. "How Early Is Too Early? Mourning a Baby Lost Through Miscarriage" *SHARING* 8(2):1.

———.1999. "I Choose to Remember." *Sharing* 8(2):2

Casimer, Lisa A. 1987. "Sarah's Story—with Love." *SHARE Newsletter* 10(3):11–13.

Casper, Monica. 1998. *The Making of the Unborn Patient: A Social Anatomy of Fetal Surgery*. New Brunswick: Rutgers University Press.

Castricano, Kathryn. 1985. "Dear Parents." Pp. 6–7 in *When Hello Means Goodbye: A Guide for Parents Whose Child Dies Before Birth, At Birth or Shortly After Birth*, edited by Pat Schwiebert and Paul Kirk. Portland, OR: Perinatal Loss.

Caywood, Sonya. 1997. "Our Shattered Dreams." *SHARING* 6(4):1–2.

Cecil, Rosanne, ed. 1996. *The Anthropology of Pregnancy Loss: Comparative Studies in Miscarriage, Stillbirth and Neonatal Death*. Oxford: Berg Publishers.

Centering Corporation. 1985. "Fathers Grieve, Too." Omaha, NE: Centering Corporation.

Chaidez, Sue. 1985. "Lacy." P. 16 in *When Hello Means Goodbye: A Guide for Parents Whose Child Dies Before Birth, At Birth or Shortly After Birth*, edited by Pat Schwiebert and Paul Kirk. Portland, OR: Perinatal Loss.

Charmaz, Kathy. 1980. *The Social Reality of Death: Death in Contemporary America*. New York: Random House.

Chase, Susan E. and Mary F. Rogers, eds. 2001. *Mothers & Children: Feminist Analyses and Personal Narratives*. New Brunswick: Rutgers University Press.

Chavkin, Wendy, M.D., ed. 1979. "Occupational Hazards to Reproduction: A Review Essay and Annotated Bibliography." *Feminist Studies* 5(2):310–325.

———.1984. *Double Exposure: Women's Health Hazards on the Job and at Home*. New York: Monthly Review Press.

Cheal, David. 1988. *The Gift Economy*. London: Routledge.

Chelouche, Adina, M.D. 2001. "Molar Pregnancy: Gestational Trophoblastic Disease." Pp. 138–140 in *Parenthood Lost: Healing the Pain after Miscarriage, Stillbirth, and Infant Death*, edited by Berman. Westport, CT: Bergin & Garvey.

Chiffens, Michell. 1991a. "I'm Here, Daddy." *UNITE Notes* 10(4):1.

———.1991b. "Sorrow and Hope." *UNITE Notes* 10(2):1.

Church, Martha Jo, Helene Chazin, and Faith Ewald. 1981. *When a Baby Dies*. Oak Brook, IL: The Compassionate Friends.

Ciany, Anne. 1999. "I'm a Mother Too." *SHARING* 8(3):6.

Clancy, Lisa. 1995. "Angels Always Come Early." *UNITE Notes* 14(1):6.

Clark, Chuck. 1984. "Winter Vow." *SHARE Newsletter* 7(3):1.

Clark, Leonard. 1985. "Stillborn." P. 5 in *When Hello Means Goodbye: A Guide for Parents Whose Child Dies Before Birth, At Birth or Shortly After Birth*, edited by Pat Schwiebert and Paul Kirk. Portland, OR: Perinatal Loss.

Clark, Martha Bittle. 1987. *Are You Weeping with Me, God?* Nashville: Broadman Press.

Clarke, Adele E. 1998. *Disciplining Reproduction: Modernity, American Life Sciences, and The Problems of Sex*. Berkeley: University of California Press.

Claybrook, Joan and the Staff of *Public Citizen*. 1984. *Retreat from Safety: Reagan's Attack on America's Health*. New York: Pantheon Books.

Cocke, Shelley. 1986. "Closure." *UNITE Notes* 6(1):5.

Coggins, Chrissy. 2000. "God Doesn't Make Mistakes." *UNITE Notes* 18(4):7.

Cohen, Elizabeth. 1997. "The Ghost Baby." *New York Times Magazine*, May 4, p. 84.

Cohen, Marion Deutsch. 1981a. "Bereavement and Growth." *UNITE Notes* 1(1):2.

———.1981b. "Funeral Poem #1." *UNITE Notes* 1(1):4.

———.1983a. "Funeral Poems." P. 9 in *She Was Born She Died: A Collection of Poems Following the Death of an Infant*. Omaha, NE: Centering Corporation.

———.1983b. "Trying to Conceive." P. 21 in *She Was Born She Died: A Collection of Poems Following the Death of an Infant*. Omaha, NE: Centering Corporation.

———.1983c. *She Was Born She Died: A Collection of Poems Following the Death of an Infant*. Omaha, NE: The Centering Corporation.

———.1983d. *An Ambitious Sort of Grief: Woman, Reproduction and Neo-natal Loss*. Mesquite, TX: Ide House.

———.1983e. "Intensive Care #1" in *She Was Born She Died: A Collection of Poems Following the Death of an Infant*, P. 5. Omaha, NE: Centering Corporation.

———.1986. *The Shadow of an Angel: A Diary of a Subsequent Pregnancy Following Neo-Natal Loss*. Las Colinas, TX: The Liberal Press.

———.1988. *Counting to Zero: Poems on Repeated Miscarriages*. The Center for Thanatology Research and Education.

Colburn, Jeanette. 1984. "Precious Feet." *SHARE Newsletter* 7(1):3.

Coleman, Linda and Cindy Dickinson. 1984. "The Risks of Healing: The Hazards of the Nursing Profession." Pp. 37–56 in *Double Exposure: Women's Health Hazards on the Job and at Home*, edited by Chavkin. New York: Monthly Review Press.

Comaroff, Jean. 1977. "Conflicting Paradigms of Pregnancy: Managing Ambiguity in Ante-Natal Encounters." Pp. 115–134 in *Medical Encounters: The Experience of Illness and Treatment*, edited by Alan Davis and Gordon Horobin. New York: St. Martin's Press.

Combes, Lisa Walsh. 1999. "The Daniel Flame." *SHARING* 8(4):8.

Condit, Celeste Michelle. 1990. *Decoding Abortion Rhetoric*. Urbana: University of Illinois Press.

Conklin, Beth A. and Lynn M. Morgan. 1996. "Babies, Bodies, and the Production of Personhood in North American and a Native Amazonian Society." *Ethos* 24(4):657–694.

Connolly, Deborah. 2000. "Mythical Mothers and Dichotomies of Good and Evil: Homeless Mothers in the United States." Pp. 263–294 in *Ideologies and Technologies of Motherhood*, edited by Helena Ragoné and Winddance Twine. New York: Routledge.

Connors, Kathy. 1992. "Letters." *UNITE Notes* 11(3):3–5.

Cook, Daniel. 1998. "The Commoditization of Childhood: Personhood, the Children's Wear Industry and the Moral Dimensions of Consumption 1917–1969." Unpublished Ph.D. dissertation, Department of Sociology, University of Chicago.

Cook, Judith A. 1988. "Dad's Double Binds: Rethinking Fathers' Bereavement from a Men's Studies Perspective." *Journal of Contemporary Ethnography* 17(3):285–308.

Cooksey, Thomas L. 1992. "The Aesthetics of Natural Theology: Charles Bucke and the Sublimities of Nature." Paper presented at the Society for Literature and Science's annual meeting, Atlanta, GA.

Cordes, Renee. 1993. "Miscarriage Rate High for Workers Who Fabricate Computer Chips." *Trial* February, pp. 96–97.

Cornell-Drury, Peter. 2000. "There's No Solution to This." *SHARING* 9(3):3.

Cote-Arsenault, Denise. 2000. "One Foot In–One Foot Out: Weathering the Storm of Pregnancy After Perinatal Loss." *Research in Nursing & Health* 23:473–485.

Cote-Arsenault, Denise, Deborah Bidlack and Ashley Humm. 2001. "Women's Emotions and Concerns During Pregnancy Following Perinatal Loss." *The American Journal of Maternal Child Nursing* 26(3):128–134.

Cote-Arsenault, Denise and Mary-T. B. Dombeck. 2001. "Maternal Assignment of Fetal Personhood to a Previous Pregnancy Loss: Relationship to Anxiety in the Current Pregnancy." *Health Care for Women International.* 22:649–665.

Cote-Arsenault, Denise and Nomvuyo Mahlangu. 1999. "Impact of Perinatal Loss on the Subsequent Pregnancy and Self: Women's Experiences." *Journal of Obstetric, Gynecologic, and Neonatal Nursing* 23:274–282.

Cote-Arsenault, Denise and Dianne Morrison-Beedy. 2001. "Women's Voices Reflecting Changed Expectations for Pregnancy after Perinatal Loss." *Journal of Nursing Scholarship* (3)239–244.

Craig, Karen. 1999. "Why?" *UNITE Notes* 18(1):6.

Crapanzano, Vincent. 1981. "Rite of Return: Circumcision in Morocco." Pp. 15–36 in *The Psychoanalytic Study of Society*, edited by Warner Muensterberger and L. Bryce Boyer. New York: Library of Psychological Anthropology.

Csordas, Thomas J. 1997. *Language, Charisma, and Creativity: The Ritual Life of a Religious Movement.* Berkeley: University of California Press.

Cuce, Barbara. 1998. "Somewhere You Haven't Been." *UNITE Notes* 17(2):6.

Cummings, Cindy. 1984. "From Mommy with Love." *SHARE Newsletter* 7(5):1.

Cunningham, F. Gary, et al. 1993. *Williams Obstetrics.* Nineteenth edition. Norwalk, Conn.: Appleton & Lange.

Cunningham, F. Gary, Norman F. Gant, Kenneth J. Leveno, Larry C. Gilstrap III, John C. Hauth, and Katharine D. Wenstrom. 2001. *Williams Obstetrics 21st Edition.* New York: McGraw-Hill.

Dalton, Diana. 2000. "Nonbiological Mothers and the Legal Boundaries of Motherhood: An Analysis of California Law." Pp. 191–232 in *Ideologies and*

Technologies of Motherhood, edited by Helena Ragoné and Winddance Twine.
New York: Routledge.

Daniels, Barbara A. 1988a. "Dead, Instead." Section 4, p. 29 in *Bittersweet . . .
hellogoodbye: A Resource in Planning Farewell Rituals When a Baby Dies*, edited
by Sister Jane Marie Lamb. Belleville, IL: Charis Communications.

———.1988b. "When My Baby Died." Section 1, p. 15 in *Bittersweet . . .
hellogoodbye: A Resource in Planning Farewell Rituals When a Baby Dies*. Sister
Jane Marie Lamb, ed. Belleville, IL: Charis Communications.

———.1988c. "Dream." *SHARE Newsletter* 11(5):2.

Daniels, Cynthia R. 1993. *At Women's Expense: State Power and the Politics of Fetal
Rights*. Cambridge: Harvard University Press.

D'Asaro, Andrea. 1996. "What I Learned from Baby Adam." *UNITE Notes*
15(2):3.

Davenport, Lisa. 1993. "The Shoebox." *SHARE Newsletter* 2(4):3.

Davidson, Arnold I. 1991. "The Horror of Monsters." Pp. 36–67 in *The Boundaries
of Humanity: Humans, Animals, Machines*, edited by James J. Sheehan and
Morton Sosna. Berkeley: University of California Press.

Davies, Douglas. 1988. "The Evocative Symbolism of Trees." Pp. 32–42 in *The
Iconography of Landscape: Essays on the Symbolic Representation, Design and Use
of Past Environments*, edited by Cosgrove and Daniels. Cambridge: Cambridge
University Press.

Davis, Deborah L. 1991. *Empty Cradle, Broken Heart: Surviving the Death of Your
Baby*. Golden, CO: Fulcrum Publishing.

Davis, Mary. 1988. "Miscarriage: Remnants of a Life." Section 1, pp. 24–25 in
*Bittersweet . . . hellogoodbye: A Resource in Planning Farewell Rituals When a
Baby Dies*, edited by Sister Marie Lamb. Belleville, IL: Charis Communications.

Davis, Natalie Zemon and Randolph Starn. 1989. "Introduction." Special issue of
Representations on "Memory and Counter Memory" 26:1–6.

Davis-Floyd, Robbie E. 1992. *Birth as an American Rite of Passage*. Berkeley:
University of California Press.

———.2002. "Home Birth Emergencies in the U.S. and Mexico: The Trouble
with Transport." In *Reproduction Gone Awry*, a special issue of *Social Science
and Medicine*, edited by Gwynne Jenkins and Marcia Inhorn.

———.In prep. "Consuming Childbirth: The Qualified Commodification of
Midwifery Care." In *Consuming Motherhood* (working title), edited by Janelle
Taylor, Danielle Wozniak, and Linda Layne.

Davis-Floyd, Robbie and Carolyn Sargent, eds. 1996. "The Social Production of
Authoritative Knowledge in Pregnancy and Childbirth." *Medical Anthropology
Quarterly* 10(2).

Deane, Margaret and Shanna H. Swan, John A. Harris, David M. Epstein, and
Raymond R. Neutra. 1992. "Adverse Pregnancy Outcomes in Relation to Water
Consumption: A Re-analysis of Data from the Original Santa Clara County
Study, California, 1980–1981." *Epidemiology* 3(2):94–97.

de Certeau, Michel. 1984. *The Practice of Everyday Life*. Berkeley: University of California Press.

DeLuca, Michael A. and Paul W. Leslie. 1996. "Variation in Risk of Pregnancy Loss." Pp. 113–130 in *The Anthropology of Pregnancy Loss: Comparative Studies in Miscarriage, Stillbirth and Neonatal Death*, edited by Rosanne Cecil. Oxford: Berg Publishers.

Dent, Elizabeth. 2000. "Remembering." *UNITE Notes* 18(3):2.

Dettwyler, Katherine A. 1993. *Dancing Skeletons: Life and Death in West Africa*. Prospect Heights, IL: Waveland.

Diaz, Raye. 2001. "Forever in Our Hearts." *SHARING* 10(2)8.

Dickinson, Debbi. 1995. "I Will Bring You Flowers." *SHARE Newsletter* 4(3):13.

———.1996. "The Struggle to Survive with No Living Children." *SHARE Newsletter* 5(4):11.

DiFabio, Jacqueline Pirrie. 1997. "Honor My Babies' Lives." *SHARE Newsletter* 7(1):1.

Dirks, Jane. 1988. "Her Picture." *SHARE Newsletter* 11(3):12.

Di'Saro, Andrea. 1998. "Swimming Towards Gabriel." *UNITE Notes* 17(2):4–5.

Doerr, Maribeth Wilder. 1992. "Memorializing Our Precious Babies." *UNITE Notes* 11(1):3.

Doherty, Mary Cushing. 1988. "At the Foot of the Cross." *UNITE Notes* 7(3):1.

———.1991a. "The Keepers of the Flame." *UNITE Notes* 10(3):1.

———.1991b. "Please." *UNITE Notes* 10(2):5.

Doman, Glenn. 1988. *How to Teach Your Baby to Be Physically Superb: More Gentle Revolution*. Philadelphia: The Better Baby Press.

Donato, Margaret. 1988. Untitled letter. Section 1, Pp. 32–33 in *Bittersweet . . . hellogoodbye: A Resource in Planning Farewell Rituals When a Baby Dies*, edited by Sister Jane Marie Lamb. Belleville, IL: Charis Communications.

Douglas, Ann. 1975. "Heaven Our Home: Consolation Literature in the Northern United States, 1830–1880." Pp. 49–68 in *Death in America*, edited by David Stannard. Philadelphia: University of Pennsylvania Press.

———.1977. *The Feminization of American Culture*. New York: Avon Books.

Douglas, Mary. 1966. *Purity and Danger: An Analysis of the Concepts of Pollution and Taboo*. London: Routledge and Kegan Paul.

Douglas, Mary and Baron Isherwood. 1979. *The World of Goods*. New York: Basic Books.

Down, Martyn Langdon. 1986. *Some Babies Die: An Exploration of Stillbirth and Neonatal Death*. (Film). Australia.

Downey, Gary Lee and Joseph Dumit. 1997. "Locating and Intervening: An Introduction." Pp. 5–30 in *Cyborgs & Citadels: Anthropological Interventions in Emerging Sciences and Technologies*, edited by Downey and Dumit. Sante Fe, NM: School of American Research.

Dubin, Lois C. 1994. "Fullness and Emptiness, Fertility and Loss: Meditations on Naomi's Tale in the Book of Ruth." Pp. 131–144 in *Reading Ruth: Contemporary*

Women Reclaim a Sacred Story, edited by Judith A. Kates and Gail Twersky Reimer. New York: Ballantine Books.

————.1995/6. "A Ceremony of Remembering, Mourning, and Healing After Miscarriage." *Kerem: Creative Explorations in Judaism* 4:67–79.

Duden, Barbara. 1991. *The Woman Beneath the Skin: A Doctor's Patients in Eighteenth-Century Germany.* Translated by Thomas Dunlop. Cambridge, MA: Harvard University Press.

————.1993. *Disembodying Women: Perspectives on Pregnancy and the Unborn.* Cambridge, MA: Harvard University Press.

Dumit, Joseph with Sylvia Sensiper. 1998. "Living with the 'Truths' of DES: Toward an Anthropology of Facts." Pp. 212–239 in *Cyborg Babies: From Techno-Sex to Techno-Tots.* edited by Robbie Davis-Floyd and Joseph Dumit. New York: Routledge.

Dunham, Charles. 1986. "From Ray with Love." *SHARE Newsletter* 9(4):1.

Dykstra, Lauri. 1991. "Forever Baby." *UNITE Notes* 10(4):5.

Eastman, Nicholson J. 1956. *Williams Obstetrics.* Eleventh Edition. New York: D. Appleton-Century-Crofts, Inc.

Eberly, Rosa. 2001. "Making Memory Public: Teaching 'The UT Tower Shootings and Public Memory.'" Paper delivered at the conference "Framing Public Memory," Syracuse University, September.

Eddy, Mary Lou. 1986. "A Letter to SHARE" 9(1):3–4.

Edelman, Helen S. 1995. "Safe to Talk: Abortion Narratives as a Rite of Return." Doctoral Dissertation Proposal, Department of Anthropology, SUNY Albany.

Ellberg, Amy, Rabbi. 1989. "Halachic Mourning Practices for Pregnancy Loss." Paper submitted to the Committee of Jewish Law and Standards.

Erikson, Kai T. 1976. *Every Thing in Its Path: Destruction of Community in the Buffalo Creek Flood.* New York: Simon and Schuster.

Erling, Susan. 1984. "Just 10 Weeks." *SHARE Newsletter* 7(2):1.

————.1988. "Change in Self—After the Loss of a Baby." *UNITE Notes* 8(1):2.

Evans-Smith, Heather Gail. 1999. "That Date." *UNITE Notes* 18(2):3.

Fadako, Rita. 1997. "Pictures of an Angel." *UNITE Notes* 16(1):1.

————.2000. "A Special Gift in the Little White Box." *UNITE Notes* 18(3):1.

Faldet, Rachel and Karen Fitton, eds. 1996. *Our Stories of Miscarriage: Healing with Words.* Minneapolis: Fairview Press.

Familyborn. 1985. "Familyborn . . . An idea whose time has come." Brochure.

Farrell, Angie. 1992. "My Missed Baby." *SHARE Newsletter* 1(4):2.

Fasolo, Gail. 2000. "A Mother Always Remembers." *SHARING* 9(3):15.

Fei, Hsiao-Tung. 1946. *Peasant Life in China.* New York: Oxford University Press.

Fein, Ester B. 1998. "For Lost Pregnancies, New Rites of Mourning." *New York Times,* January 15.

Feldman, George B., M.D., with Anne Felshman. 1984. *The Complete Handbook of Pregnancy: A Step-by-Step Guide from Preconception to the First Weeks following Birth.* New York: B. P. Putnam's Sons.

Fenlon, Arlene and N. Fenlon. 1986. *Getting Ready for Childbirth: A Guide for Expectant Parents.* New York: Prentice Hall.

Fenlon, Arlene, Ellen Oakes, and Lovell Dorchak. 1986. *Getting Ready for Child Birth: A Guide for Expectant Parents.* Boston: Little, Brown and Co.

Fernandez, James. 1986a. "Edification by Puzzlement." Pp. 172–187 in *Persuasions and Performances: The Play of Tropes in Culture.* Bloomington, IN: Indiana University Press.

———.1986b. "Returning to the Whole." Pp. 188–213 in *Persuasions and Performances: The Play of Tropes in Culture.* Bloomington, IN: Indiana University Press.

Fernandez, James and Mary Taylor Huber. 2001. "Introduction: The Anthropology of Irony." Pp. 1–40 in *Irony in Action: Anthropology, Practice, and the Moral Imagination*, edited by James W. Fernandez and Mary Taylor Huber. Chicago: University of Chicago Press.

Fetal Greetings. 2001. "Greetings from the . . . womb? Whoa, baby!" An advertisement appearing in *Self*, September, p. 96.

Feuchtwang, Stephan. 2000. "Reinscriptions: Commemoration, Restoration and the Interpersonal Transmission of Histories and Memories under Modern States in Asia and Europe." Pp. 59–78 in *Memory and Methodology*, edited by Susannah Radstone. Oxford: Berg.

Fiedler, Leslie A. 1978. *Freaks: Myths and Images of the Secret Self.* New York: Simon and Schuster.

Fillion, Kate. 1994. "Fertility Rights, Fertility Wrongs." Pp. 33–55 in *Misconceptions: The Social Construction of Choice and the New Reproductive Technologies, Volume Two*, edited by Gwynne Basen, Margrit Eichler, Abby Lippman. Ontario: Voyageur Publishing.

Finch, Robert and John Elder. 1990. *The Norton Book of Nature Writing.* New York: W.W. Norton & Company.

Fiske, John. 1989a. *Understanding Popular Culture.* Boston: Unwin Hyman.

———.1989b. *Reading the Popular.* Boston: Unwin Hyman.

Fitzgerald, Donna. 1988. "To My Special Friend." Section 1, p. 23 in *Bittersweet . . . hellogoodbye: A Resource in Planning Farewell Rituals When a Baby Dies*, edited by Sister Jane Marie Lamb. Belleville, IL: Charis Communications.

Fleming, Anne Taylor. 1994. "Sperm in a Jar: Entering the Sisterhood of the Infertile, Hoping to Reverse Time, Cheat Fate, Get My Hands on an Embryo, a Baby, a Life." *The New York Times Sunday Magazine*, June 12, pp. 52–55.

Fletcher, John and Mark Evans. 1983. "Maternal Bonding in Early Fetal Ultrasound Examinations." *New England Journal of Medicine* 308(7):392–393.

Florman, Samuel C. 1997. "Technology and the Tragic View." Pp. 93–103 in *Technology and the Future, Seventh Edition*, edited by Albert H. Teich. New York: St. Martin's Press.

Foley, Bernadette. 1985. "Our Grandpaernts' Day—Grief and Memories." *UNITE Notes* 4(3):1–3.

Forbes, Cheryl. 1971. "Beruryah." *Encyclopaedia Judaica*, p. 702. Jerusalem: The Macmillan Company.

————.1997. "Coffee, Mrs. Cowman, and the Devotional Life of Women Reading in the Desert: Toward a History of Practice." Pp. 116–132 in *Lived Religion in America*, edited by David D. Hall. Princeton: Princeton University Press.

Forsyth, Jane L. 1983. *Miscarriage: A Psychosocial Perspective of Women's Experience.* Unpublished doctoral dissertation. Boston University School of Education.

Fortes, Meyer. 1976. "An Introductory Commentary." In *Ancestors* edited by William H. Newell ed., pp. 1–16. The Hague: Mouton Publishers.

Forty, Adrian. 1999. "Introduction." *The Art of Forgetting*, edited by Adrian Forty and Susanne Kuchler, eds. pp. 1–18. Oxford: Berg.

Forty, Adrian and Susanne Kuchler, eds. 1999. *The Art of Forgetting*. Oxford: Berg.

Foster, Cindy Lee. 1985a. "Baby Things." *SHARE Newsletter* 8(5):1.

————.1985b. "Christmas Angel." *SHARE Newsletter* 8(6):1.

Foster, Nancy and Robert. 1994. "Learning Fetishism? Boys' Consumption Work with Marvel Super Heroes Trading Cards." Paper presented at the annual meeting of the American Anthropological Association, Atlanta, GA.

Foucault, Michel. 1978. *History of Sexuality. Volume I: An Introduction.* New York: Vintage.

Frank, Erica. 1999. "My Precious Angels." *SHARING* 8(1):7.

Franklin, Sarah. 1991. "Fetal Fascinations: New Dimensions to the Medical-Scientific Construction of Fetal Personhood." Pp. 190–205 in *Off-Centre: Feminism and Cultural Studies*, edited by Franklin, Lury, & Stacey.

————.1992. "Making Sense of Missed Conceptions: Anthropological Perspectives on Unexplained Infertility." Pp. 75–91 in *Changing Human Reproduction: Social Science Perspectives*, edited by Meg Stacey. London: Sage.

————.1997. *Embodied Progress: A Cultural Account of Assisted Conception.* New York: Routledge.

French, Stanley. 1975. "The Cemetery as Cultural Institution: The Establishment of Mount Auburn and the 'Rural Cemetery' Movement." Pp. 69–91 in *Death in America*, edited by David E. Stannard. Philadelphia: University of Pennsylvania Press.

Friedman, Rochelle and Bonnie Gradstein. 1982. *Surviving Pregnancy Loss.* Waltham, Mass.: Little, Brown and Co.

Friedeck, Jim. 1984. "Reflections Without Mirrors." *SHARE Newsletter* 7(3):2.

Friedeck, Sue. 1995a. "When Remembering Becomes More Sweet than Bitter . . . " *SHARE Newsletter* 4(4):1–2.

————.1995b. "Milestone or Millstone . . . " *SHARE Newsletter* 4(5):5.

————.1995c. "As Seasons Change . . . " *SHARE Newsletter* 4(6):5.

————.1995d. "Caring for Those Special Photos . . . " *SHARE Newsletter* 4(4):11.

————.1999. "When Remembering Becomes More Sweet than Bitter . . . " *SHARING* 8(4):4–5.

Frye, Northrop. [1957] 1973. *Anatomy of Criticism: Four Essays*. Princeton: Princeton University Press.

Fuchs, John. 1987. "Our Littlest Angel." *SHARE Newsletter* 10(3):1.

Fuller, Peter. 1988. "The Geography of Mother Nature." Pp. 11–31 in *The Iconography of Landscape: Essays on the Symbolic Representation, Design and Use of Past Environments*, edited by Cosgrove and Daniels. Cambridge: Cambridge University Press.

Fussell, Paul. 1975. *The Great War and Modern Memory*. London: Oxford University Press.

———.1983. *Class*. New York: Ballantine Books.

Gainer, Julie. 2000. "My Beautiful Aidy." *SHARING* 9(2):7.

Gamman, Lorraine and Merja Makinen. 1994. *Female Fetishism: A New Look*. London: Lawrence & Wishart.

Gana, Kathleen Rosso. 1982/3. "Letter to Miranda . . . and Lukas, Too." *UNITE Notes* 2(2):3.

———.1984. "Recoil . . . and Growth" *UNITE Notes* 4(1):3.

———.1985. "As the Wounds Heal." *UNITE Notes* 5(1):2–3.

———.1986. "Limbo." *UNITE Notes* 5(5):4.

———.1998. "Sleep in Heavenly Peace." *UNITE Notes* 16(3):7.

Gardner, Karen. 1986. "Time." *SHARE Newsletter* 9(4):3.

Gartner, Audrey. 1982. "Self-Help/Self-Care: A Cost-Effective Health Strategy." *Social Policy* 12(4):64.

Geertz, Clifford. 1983. "'From the Native's Point of View': On the Nature of Anthropological Understanding." Pp. 55–72 in *Local Knowledge: Further Essays in Interpretive Anthropology*. New York: Basic Books.

Gelis, Jacques. 1991. *History of Childbirth*. Translated by Rosemary Morris. Boston: Northeastern University Press.

Geordan's Grandmother. 1986. "Geordan's Answer." *SHARE Newsletter* 9(5):3.

Georges, Eugenia. 1995. "Fetal Ultrasound Imaging and the Production of Authoritative Knowledge in Greece." Special issue of *Medical Anthropology Quarterly*, edited by R. Davis-Floyd and C. Sargent, 10(2):157–175.

Gergen, Mary M. and Kenneth J. 1993. "Narratives of the Gendered Body in Popular Autobiography." Pp. 219–224 in *The Narrative Study of Lives*, edited by Josselson and Lieblich. Newbury Park, CA: Sage.

Gibson, Thomas. 1994. "Childhood, Colonialism and Fieldwork Among the Buid of the Philippines and the Konjo of Indonesia." in *Enfants Et Societes D'Asie Du Sud-Est*, edited by Jeannine Koubi and Josiane Massard-Vincent. Paris: Editions L'Harmattan.

———.1995. "Having Your House and Eating it: Houses and Siblings in Ara, South Sulawesi." in *About the House: Levi-Strauss and Beyond*, edited by Janet Carsten and Stephen Hugh-Jones. Cambridge: Cambridge University Press.

Gilbert, Kathleen R. and Laura S. Smart. 1992. *Coping with Infant or Fetal Loss: The Couple's Healing Process*. New York: Brunner/Mazel Publishers.

Gillis, John R. 1994. "Memory and Identity: The History of a Relationship." Pp. 3–26 in *Commemoration: The Politics of National Identity*, edited by John R. Gillis. Princeton: Princeton University Press.

Gimmi, Julie. 2001. "Zoe: Vignettes." *UNITE Notes* 20(3):3.

Ginsburg, Faye D. 1989. *Contested Lives: The Abortion Debate in an American Community*. Berkeley: University of California Press.

Ginsburg, Faye D. and Rayna Rapp, eds. 1995. *Conceiving the New World Order: The Global Politics of Reproduction*. Berkeley: University of California Press.

Ginsburg, Faye D. and Rayna Rapp. 1999. "Fetal Reflections: Confessions of Two Feminist Anthropologists as Mutual Informants." Pp. 279–295 in *Fetal Subjects, Feminist Positions*, edited by Lynn Morgan and Meridith Michaels. Philadelphia: University of Pennsylvania Press.

Glading, Jo Astrid. 1988. "Fetal Rights before High Court: Lawsuit over Stillbirth Poses Legal Dilemma of Personhood." *Daily Record*, Northwest NJ, May 8.

Glaser, B. G. and A. L. Strauss. 1965. *Awareness of Dying*. Chicago: Aldine.

———.1968. *Time for Dying*. Chicago: Aldine.

Godelier, Maurice. 1999. *The Enigma of the Gift*. Chicago: University of Chicago Press.

Goffman, Erving. 1963. *Stigma*. New York: Simon & Schuster.

Golden, Carol. 1994. "Faraway Flower." *UNITE Notes* 12(3):1.

Goldstein, Judith L. 1987. "Lifestyles of the Rich and Tyrannical." *The American Scholar*, pp. 235–247.

Gonzalez, Kelly J. 1988a. "Tears for Alycia" *UNITE Notes* 7(4):4.

———.1988b. "My Second Pregnancy." *UNITE Notes* 7(4):7.

———.1995. "Birthdays and Anniversaries." *SHARE Newsletter* 4(5):8–9.

———.1996. "Am I Really a Parent?" *SHARE Newsletter* 5(3):11.

Goodrich, Lawrence J. 1990. "US Religious Life Holds Steady." *Christian Science Monitor*, January 2:12.

Goody, Ester. 1970. "Kinship Fostering in Gonja: Deprivation or Advantage?" Pp. 51–74 in *Socialization: The Approach from Social Anthropology*, edited by Philip Mayer. London: Tavistock Publications.

———.1971. "Forms of Pro-Parenthood: The Sharing and Substitution of Parental Roles." Pp. 331–345 in *Kinship: Selected Readings*, edited by Jack Goody. Baltimore: Penguin Books.

Gorenstein, Shirley. 1996. "Introduction: Material Culture." In "Research in Science and Technology Studies: Material Culture," edited by Shirley Gorenstein, *Knowledge and Society* 10:1–18. Greenwich, CT: JAI Press.

Greenberg, Martin. 1985. *The Birth of a Father*. New York: Avon Books.

Gregory, C. A. 1980. "Gifts to Men and Gifts to God: Gift Exchange and Capital Accumulation in Contemporary Papua." *Man* 15(4):626–652.

———.1982. *Gifts and Commodities*. London: Academic Press.

Gryte, Marilyn. 1988. *No New Baby*. Omaha, NE: Centering Corporation.

Guenther, Debbie, ed. 1991. "Recognition of Life Certificates." *SHARE Newsletter* 14(1):7–8.

Guillemin, Jeanne Harley and Lynda Lytle Holmstrom. 1986. *Mixed Blessings: Intensive Care for Newborns.* Oxford: Oxford University Press.

Guralnik, David B., editor in chief. 1970. "Precious." P. 1120 in *Webster's New World Dictionary of the American Language, Second Edition.* New York: The World Publishing Company.

Guterson, David. 1994. *Snow Falling on Cedars.* New York: Harcourt Brace.

Habercorn, Jennifer. 1996. "Two More Angels." *SHARE Newsletter* 5(3):2.

Hacking, Ian. 1996. "Memory Sciences, Memory Politics." Pp. 67–87 in *Tense Past: Cultural Essays in Trauma and Memory,* edited by Antze and Lambek. New York: Routledge.

Hagley, Norman. 1985. *Comfort Us, Lord—Our Baby Died.* Omaha, NE: Centering Corporation.

———.1988. "A Father's Prayer for Inner Strength." Section 4, p. 31 in *Bittersweet . . . hellogoodbye: A Resource in Planning Farewell Rituals When a Baby Dies,* edited by Sister Jane Marie Lamb. Belleville, IL: Charis Communications.

Hahn, Robert A. 1995. "Divisions of Labor: Obstetrician, Woman, and Society in *Williams Obstetrics,* 1903–1989." Pp. 209–233 in *Sickness and Healing: An Anthropological Perspective.* New Haven: Yale University Press.

Hall, David D., ed. 1997. *Lived Religion in America.* Princeton: Princeton University Press.

Halloran, S. Michael. 1993. "The Rhetoric of Picturesque Scenery: A Nineteenth-Century Epideictic." Pp. 226–246 in *Oratorical Culture in Nineteenth-Century America: Transformations in the Theory and Practice of Rhetoric,* edited by Gregory Clarke and S. Michael Halloran. Carbondale, IL: Southern Illinois University Press.

Hamilton, Alice. 1925. *Industrial Poisons in the United States.* New York: The Macmillan Company.

Handler, Richard. 1988. *Nationalism and the Politics of Culture in Quebec.* Madison: The University of Wisconsin Press.

Haney, C. Allen and Dell Davis. 1999. "America Responds to Diana's Death: Spontaneous Memorials." Pp. 227–240 in *The Mourning for Diana,* edited by Tony Walter. Oxford: Berg.

Hardacre, Helen. 1997. *Marketing the Menacing Fetus in Japan.* Berkeley: Universit of California Press.

Harding, Susan. 1987. "Convicted by the Holy Spirit: The Rhetoric of Fundamental Baptist Conversion." *American Ethnologist* 14(1):167–181.

———.1992. "The Afterlife of Stories: Genesis of a Man of God." Pp. 60-75 in *Storied Lives: The Cultural Politics of Self-Understanding,* edited by George Rosenwald and Richard Ochberg. New Haven: Yale University Press.

Harrison, Michael R. 1982. "Unborn: Historical Perspective of the Fetus as a Patient." Pp. 19–24 in *The Pharos,* Winter.

Hartigan, Patti. 2002. "The Kindness of Strangers." *The Boston Globe Magazine* August 4. Pp. 10–11, 19–24.

Hartouni, Valeri. 1991. "Containing Women: Reproductive Discourse in the
    1980s." Pp. 27–56 in *Technoculture*, edited by Constance Penley and Andrew
    Ross. Minneapolis: University of Minnesota Press.
———.1996. "Fetal Exposures: Abortion Politics and the Optics of Allusion."
    Camera Obscura 29:131–149.
———.1997. *Cultural Conceptions: Of Reproductive Technologies and the Remaking
    of Life*. Minneapolis: University of Minnesota Press.
Hartzoge, Scarlett. 1990. "A Mother's Pain." *SHARE Newsletter* 13(6):8.
Hass, Kristin Ann. 1998. *Carried to the Wall: American Memory and the Vietnam
    Veterans Memorial*. Berkeley: University of California.
Hathaway, Marjie, Susan Jay, and James Jay, eds. 1989. *The Bradley Method
    Student Workbook*. Sherman Oaks, CA: American Academy of Husband-
    Coached Childbirth.
Hawkins, Anne Hunsaker. 1993. *Reconstructing Illness: Studies in Pathography*. West
    Lafayette, IN: Purdue University Press.
Hayashi, Kenji and Michael B. Bracken. 1984. "Hydatidiform Mole." In *Perinatal
    Epidemiology*. Oxford: Oxford University Press.
Heath, Deborah. 1998. "Locating Genetic Knowledge: Picturing Marfan Syndrome
    and Its Traveling Constituencies." Special issue of *Science, Technology and
    Human Values*, edited by Layne. 23(1):71–97.
Heil, Janis. 1981a. "Sharing Experiences." *UNITE Notes* 1(1):5.
———.1981b. "Jessica." *UNITE Notes* 1(1):5.
———.1982. "Giving Birth to Death." *UNITE Notes* 2(1):2.
———.1982/3. "Your Gift to Me." *UNITE Notes* 2(2):2.
———.1984. "A Prayer for Spring." *UNITE Notes* 3(3):1.
———.1985/6. "A Gift of Meaning." *UNITE Notes* 5(2):3.
———.1986. "Grief and Spring." *UNITE Notes* 5(3):5.
———.1989. "My Journey." *UNITE Notes* 9(1):3.
Heilberg, Marty. 2001. "Out of Place." *UNITE Notes* 20(3):4.
Heimer, Carol. 1999. "Conceiving Children: How Documents Support Case vs
    Biographical Analyses." Paper delivered at conference on "Documents: Artifacts
    of Modern Knowledge." Center for Law, Culture, and Social Thought,
    Northwestern University.
Hein, Debbie. 1984. "A Special Dad." *UNITE Notes* 3(4):1–2.
Helsinger, Elizabeth K. 1982. *Ruskin and the Art of the Beholder*. Cambridge:
    Harvard University Press.
Hely, Laura, RN, BSN. 1994a. "Remember Your Baby." *SHARE Newsletter* 3(7):10.
———.1994b. "The Baby Who Should Have Been." *SHARE Newsletter* 3(7):12.
Hemminki, K. E. Franssila, and H. Vainio. 1980. "Spontaneous Abortions Among
    Female Chemical Workers in Finland." *International Archives of Occupational
    and Environmental Health* 45:123–126.
Hendon, Julia A. 2000. "Having and Holding: Storage, Memory, Knowledge, and
    Social Relations." *American Anthropologist* 102(1):42–53.
Herda, Don or Donna. 1989. "Keepsakes." *SHARE Newsletter* 12(3):7.

Herr, Ron. 1984. "A Letter to My Son." *SHARE Newsletter* 7(3):2.

Hertz, Robert. 1960. "A Contribution to the study of the collective representation of death." In *Death and the Right Hand.* Translated by R. & C. Needham. London: Cohen and West.

Hess, Audrey. 1991. "In Memory of Nathan Allan who was born and died on March 26, 1990." *SHARE Newsletter* 14(5):2.

Hess, David. 1977. *Science Studies: An Advanced Introduction.* New York: New York University Press.

———.1995. *Science and Technology in a Multicultural World.* New York: Columbia University Press.

Hess, David J. 1992. "Introduction: The New Ethnography and the Anthropology of Science and Technology." In *Knowledge and Society: The Anthropology of Science and Technology,* 9:1–28. Greenwich, CT: JAI Press.

Hess, David and Linda Layne, eds. 1992. *Knowledge and Society: The Anthropology of Science and Technology.* Volume 9. Greenwich, CT: JAI Press.

Hickman, Nancy. 1992. "If Only Anne." *UNITE Notes* 11(1):1.

Hintz, Cathy. 1988. "Rainbows." *UNITE Notes* 7(3):3.

Hirsch, Julia. 1981. *Family Photographs: Content, Meaning, and Effect.* New York: Oxford University Press.

Hoch, Mickey. 1987a. "A Letter for Francis." *UNITE Notes* 6(4):5.

———.1987b. "Time." *UNITE Notes* 7(1):2.

———.1987c. "What Is Christmas?" *UNITE Notes* Holiday Supplement, December:4.

———.1988a. "Winter." *UNITE Notes* 7(4):5.

———.1988b. "A Miscarriage Hurts, Too." *UNITE Notes* 8(1):3.

———.1988c. "Two Years." *UNITE Notes* 7(3):4.

Hoffert, Sylvia D. 1989. *Private Matters: American Attitudes toward Childbearing and Infant Nurture in the Urban North, 1800–1860.* Urbana: University of Illinois Press.

Holper, Laurie. 1991a. "Marni." *UNITE Notes* 10(4):5.

———.1991b. "Josh." *UNITE Notes* 10(4):3.

Holthaus, Cathy. 1999. "Healing and Hope." *SHARING* 8(3):11.

Hood Museum of Art. 1991. *The Age of the Marvelous.* Exhibition Catalogue. Dartmouth College.

Horning, Anita. 1997. "Eight Priceless Days." *SHARE Newsletter* 6(2):15.

Hoyert, Donna L. 1995. "Perinatal Mortality in the United States: 1985–91." *Vital Health Statistics* series 20, number 26. Hyattsville, MD: U.S. Department of Health and Human Services.

Hubbard, Ruth. 1990. *The Politics of Women's Biology.* New Brunswick: Rutgers University Press.

Huber, Mary Taylor. 1988. *The Bishop's Progress: A Historical Ethnography of Catholic Missionary Experience on the Sepik Frontier.* Washington: Smithsonian Institution Press.

————.2001. "Irony and Paradox in the 'Conntact Sone': Missionary Discourse in Northern Papua New Guinea." Pp. 188–208 in *Irony in Action: Anthropology, Practice, and the Moral Imagination*, edited by James W. Fernandex and Mary Taylor Huber. Chicago: University of Chicago Press.

Hunn, Cindy. 1995. "Forever Gone." *UNITE Notes* 14(1):1.

Huntington, Richard and Peter Metcalf. 1979. *Celebrations of Death: The Anthropology of Mortuary Ritual*. Cambridge: Cambridge University Press.

Hutcheon, Linda. 1994 *Irony's Edge: The Theory and Politics of Irony*. London: Routledge.

Hyde, Lewis. 1979. *The Gift: Imagination and the Erotic Life of Property*. New York: Random House.

Hyneman, Nanci. 1988. "Ideas for Remembrance." *SHARE Newsletter* 11(3):6.

Iacono, Linda. 1982. "Faith." *UNITE Notes* 2(1):4–6.

Illich, Ivan. 1976. *Medical Nemesis: The Expropriation of Health*. New York: Pantheon Books.

Ilse, Sherokee. 1982. *Empty Arms: Coping After Miscarriage, Stillbirth and Infant Death*. Long Lake, MN: Wintergreen Press.

————.1989. *Presenting Unexpected Outcomes: A Childbirth Educator's Guide*. Long Lake, MN: Wintergreen Press.

————.1995. "Am I a Mother? Am I a Father? Preparing for Mother's and Father's Day After the Death of a Child." *SHARE Newsletter* 4(3):1.

Ilse, Sherokee and Linda HammerBurns. 1985. *Miscarriage: A Shattered Dream*. Long Lake, MN: Wintergreen Press.

Ingle, Kristen. 1981/2a. "Pink Blankets." *UNITE Notes* 1(2):2.

————.1981/2b. "For Elizabeth at Christmas." *UNITE Notes* 1(2):1.

————.1982/3. "Christmas Thoughts." *UNITE Notes* 2(2):1. Reprinted in *SHARE Newsletter* 10(6):1.

————.1986/7a. "10 Weeks Gestation." *UNITE Notes* 6(2):4.

————.1986/7b. "Subsequent pregnancy." *UNITE Notes* 6(2):4–5.

————.1992. "For Elizabeth at Christmas." *UNITE Notes* 1(2):1.

Inhorn, Marcia C. 1994. *Quest for Conception: Gender, Infertility and Egyptian Medical Traditions*. Philadelphia: University of Pennsylvania Press.

Irvine, Leslie. 1999. *Codependent Forevermore: The Invention of Self in a Twelve Step Group*. Chicago: University of Chicago Press.

Jackson, Charles O., ed. 1977. *Passing: The Vision of Death in America*. Westport, CT: Greenwood.

Jackson, Jean. 1994. "Mind and Matter: Chronic Pain's Challenge to Subject/ Object and Mind/Body Dualism." In *Embodiment and Experience: The Existential Ground of Culture and Self*, edited by Thomas J. Csordas. Cambridge: Cambridge University Press.

Jeffries, Lisa M. 1998. "We've Lost." *UNITE Notes* 17(2):1.

Johansson, Margit A. and Louise D. Bickman. 1982. *The Availability of Social Supports for Women Who Miscarry: A Statistical Report*. Unpublished final report to NIMH.

Johnson, Elizabeth. 1988. "An Untitled Poem." Section 4, p. 45 in *Bittersweet . . . hellogoodbye: A Resource in Planning Farewell Rituals When a Baby Dies*, edited by Sister Jane Marie Lamb. Belleville, IL: Charis Communications.

Johnson, Joy and Dr. S. Marvin Johnson. 1983. *Miscarriage: A Book for Parents Experiencing Fetal Death*. Omaha, NE: Centering Corporation.

Johnson, Joy, Dr. S. Marvin Johnson, Chaplain James H. Cunningham, and Irwin J. Weinfeld, M.D. 1985. *A Most Important Picture: A Very Tender Manual for Taking Pictures of Stillborn Babies and Infants Who Die*. Omaha, NE: Centering Corportation.

Jones, Bethan. 1999. "Books of Condolence." Pp. 203–214 in *The Mourning for Diana*, edited by Tony Walter. Oxford: Berg.

Jones, Carl. 1987. "A Fiery Tale." *SHARE Newsletter* 10(2):3.

Jones, Janet. 1992. "Family Portraits." *UNITE Notes* 11(2):4.

———.1991. "He Was Still Born." *UNITE Notes* 10(3):7.

Jones, Lori. 1989. "Another Angel." *UNITE Notes* 8(2):4.

Jordan, Brigitte. 1993. *Birth in Four Cultures: A Crosscultural Investigation of Childbirth in Yucatan, Holland, Sweden, and the United States*. Fourth edition, revised and expanded by Robbie Davis-Floyd. Prospect Heights: IL: Waveland Press.

Jordan, Todd. 1988. "Mary Catherine." Section 4, p. 54 in *Bittersweet . . . hellogoodbye: A Resource in Planning Farewell Rituals When a Baby Dies*, edited by Sister Jane Marie Lamb. Belleville, IL: Charis Communications.

Jorgensen, Julia, George A. Miller, and Dan Sperber. 1984. "Test of the Mention Theory of Irony." *Journal of Experimental Psychology* 113(1):112–120.

Joyce (Aunt). 1982/3. "An Ode to Billy." *UNITE Notes* 2(2):4.

Kaiser Daily Reproductive Health Report. 2001. "Colorado State Lawmaker Introduces Bill to Allow Women Option of Funeral for Fetal Death." www.kaisernetwork.org/dailyl_reports/ rep_repro.cfm, February 8.

Kalb, Claudia. 2001. "Should You Have Your   by Now?" *Newsweek*. August 13. pp. 40–47.

Karlin, Lori. 1996. "Dear Kelly Ann, Summer and Adeline." *UNITE Notes* 15(2):5.

"Kathie's Mom." 1983. "A Father's Grief." *UNITE Notes* 2(4):1.

Katz, Alfred H. 1993. *Self-Help in America: A Social Movement Perspective*. New York: Twayne Publishers.

Keeling, Marie. 1987. "To Laura." *UNITE Notes* 7(1):1.

Keener, Helen. 1981/2. "Tiny Pink Rosebuds." *UNITE Notes* 1(2):2–3.

Kelly, Mary and Emily Apter. 1993. "The Smell of Money: Mary Kelly in Conversation with Emily Apter." Pp. 352–362 in *Fetishism as Cultural Discourse*, edited by Emily Apter and William Pietz. Ithaca: Cornell University Press.

Kennedy, Kathleen. 1990. "The Moving Wall: Construction of Ephemeral Place." Paper delivered at the annual meeting of the American Ethnological Association.

Kennell, John H., Howard Slyter and Marshall H. Klaus. 1970. "The Mourning Response of Parents to the Death of a Newborn Infant." *The New England Journal of Medicine*, August 13:344–349.

Kermode, Frank. 1987. "Matthew." Pp. 387–401 in *The Literary Guide to the Bible*, edited by Robert Alter and Frank Kermode. Cambridge, MA: Harvard University Press.

Kevin. 1985/6. "A Baby's Gift." *UNITE Notes* 5(2):6.

Keyser (formerly Heil), Janis L. 1992. "The grief recovery process after the death of a baby: Inner experiences and personal meanings." Unpublished dissertation, Department Psychoeducational Processes, Temple University.

————.1999. "Death at Birth: Inner Experiences and Personal Meanings." in *Understanding and Treating Complicated Grief*, edited by Robert Stevenson and Gerry Cox. London: King's College, London.

————.2000. "Children of Trauma and Loss: Their Treatment in Group Psychotherapy." in *The Healing Circle: Group Psychotherapy for Trauma*, edited by Victor Schermer and Robert Klein. New York: Guilford.

————.2001. "Thoughts on New Years Eve." *UNITE Notes* 10(3):1.

King, Alex. 1999. "Remembering and Forgetting in the Public Memorials of the Great War." Pp. 147–169 in *The Art of Forgetting*, edited by Forty and Kuchler. Oxford: Berg.

Kirmayer, Laurence J. 1996. "Landscapes of Memory: Trauma, Narrative, and Dissociation." Pp. 173–198 in *Tense Past: Cultural Essays in Trauma and Memory*, edited by Antze and Lambek. New York: Routledge.

Klar, Beverly Ann. 1988. "Elizabeth." Section 4, P. 45 in *Bittersweet . . . hellogoodbye: A Resource in Planning Farewell Rituals When a Baby Dies*, edited by Sister Jane Marie Lamb. Belleville, IL: Charis Communications.

Klassen, Pamela E. In prep. "Dilemmas of Consuption in the Spiritualizing of Home Birth." In *Consuming Motherhood* (working title), edited by Janelle Taylor, Danielle Wozniak, Linda Layne, eds.

Klaus, Marshall H. and John H. Kennell. 1976. *Maternal-Infant Bonding: The Impact of Early Separation or Loss on Family Development*. St. Louis: Mosby Co.

Klaus, Marshall H., John H. Kennell, Nancy Plumb, and Steven Zuehlke. 1970. "Human Maternal Behavior at the First Contact with Her Young." *Pediatrics* 46(2):187–192.

Klaus, Marshall H., Richard Jerauld, Nancy C. Kreger, Willie McAlpine, Meredith Steffa, and John H. Kennell. 1972. "Maternal Attachment: Importance of the First Post-Partum Days." *The New England Journal of Medicine*, March 2:460–463.

Kleinman, Arthur. 1988. *The Illness Narratives: Suffering, Healing and the Human Condition*. New York: Basic Books.

————.1995. *Writing at the Margin: Discourse Between Anthropology and Medicine*. Berkeley: University of California Press.

Kleinman, Arthur and Joan Kleinman. 1997. "The Appeal of Experience; The Dismay of Images: Cultural Appropriations of Suffering in Our Times" in *Social Suffering*, edited by Kleinman, Arthur, Veena Das, and Margaret Lock. Berkeley: University of California Press. pp. 1–24.

Kleinman, Arthur, Veena Das, and Margaret Lock, eds. 1997. *Social Suffering*. Berkeley: University of California Press.

Knight, Carolyn. 1986. "Healing." *SHARE Newsletter* 9(1):1.

Knopf, Barb. 1999. "My Journey . . . My Memories . . . " *SHARING* 8(4):1.

Knorr, Vicki and Albert. 1988. "In Our Minds and Hearts." *UNITE Notes* 8(1):5.

Kocan, Ron. 1984. "My Life Starts as the Suffering Ends." *SHARE Newsletter* 7(3):4–5.

Kociscin, Peggy. 1993. "A Blossom in the Wind." *UNITE Notes* 11(4):1.

Kohn, Ingrid and Perry-Lynn Moffitt with Isabelle A. Wilkins. 2000. *A Silent Sorrow: Pregnancy Loss Guidance and Support for You and Your Family*. Second edition. New York: Routledge.

Kopytoff, Igor. 1986. "The Cultural Biography of Things: Commoditization as Process." Pp. 64–94 in *The Social Life of Things: Commodities in Cultural Perspective*, edited by Appadurai. Cambridge: Cambridge University Press.

Kovacik, Karen. 2001. "Between L=A=N=G=U=A=G=E and Lyric: The Poetry of Pink-Collar Resistance." *NWSA Journal* 13(1):22–39.

Kozak, Jody. 1987. "Stillbirth in Winter." *SHARE Newsletter* 10(4):3.

Kravet, Ginette. 1994. "Chanukah Is Here." *SHARE Newsletter* 3(6):7.

Kubler-Ross, Elizabeth. 1969. *On Death and Dying*. New York: Macmillan.

———.1985. *On Children and Death*. New York: Macmillan.

Kuhn, Kathy.1984. "Dear Brian." *SHARE Newsletter* 7(4):2.

Kushner, Harold S. 1981. *When Bad Things Happen to Good People*. New York: Avon.

Ladd-Taylor, Molly and Lauri Umaansky, eds. 1998. *'Bad' Mothers: The Politics of Blame in Twentieth-Century America*. New York: New York University Press.

Laderman, Carol. 1983. *Wives and Midwives: Childbirth and Nutrition in Rural Malaysia*. Berkeley: University of California Press.

Laderman, Gary.1996. *The Sacred Remains: American Attitudes Toward Death, 1799–1883*. New Haven: Yale University Press.

LaFleur, William R. 1992. *Liquid Life: Abortion and Buddhism in Japan*. Princeton: Princeton University Press.

Lahiri, Jhumpa. 1999. "A Temporary Matter." In *Interpreter of Maladies: Stories*. Boston: Houghton Mifflin Company.

Lamb, Michael E. 1982. "Early Contact and Maternal-Infant Bonding: One Decade Later." *Pediatrics* 70(5):763–768.

Lamb, Sister Jane Marie, ed. 1984. "Precious Feet." *SHARE Newsletter* 7(2):3.

———.1986. "A New Year's Message from Sister Jane Marie." *SHARE Newsletter* 9(1):4.

———.1988a. *Bittersweet . . . hellogoodbye: A Resource in Planning Farewell Rituals When a Baby Dies*. Belleville, IL: Charis Communications.

———.1988b. "Symbolism of the Tree." Section 3, p. 7 in *Bittersweet . . . hellogoodbye: A Resource in Planning Farewell Rituals When a Baby Dies*, edited by Sister Jane Marie Lamb. Belleville, IL: Charis Communications.

————.1988c. "A Blessing and Dedication of the Tree." Section 3, p. 8 in
*Bittersweet . . . hellogoodbye: A Resource in Planning Farewell Rituals When a Baby
Dies*, edited by Sister Jane Marie Lamb. Belleville, IL: Charis Communications.

————.1990. "Message from Sister Jane Marie." *SHARE Newsletter* 12(2):13.

————.1997. "The Beginning Years of SHARE 1977–1992." *SHARING* 6(5):6.

Lambek, Michael. 1996. "The Past Imperfect: Remembering as Moral Practice."
Pp. 235–254 in *Tense Past: Cultural Essays in Trauma and Memory*, edited by
Antze and Lambek. New York: Routledge.

Lammert, Catherine A. 1995. Book review of *Notes from Baby Angel Grace*. *SHARE
Newsletter* 4(6):8.

————.1995. "Dear Friends." *SHARE Newsletter* 4(6):7.

————.1996. Letter from the Editor. *SHARE Newsletter* 5(3):3.

————.1997. *Angelic Presence: Short Stories of Solace and Hope After the Loss of a
Baby*.

Lammert, Cathi. 1992. "The Christmas Tree." *SHARE Newsletter* 1(5):5.

————.1999a. "Dear Friends." 8(4):3.

————.1999b. "Dear Friends." 8(5):3.

————.2000. "Picking Up the Pieces—Finding Hope in the Puzzle." *SHARING*
9(4):1–2.

Lammert, Cathi and Sue Friedeck, eds. 1997. *Angelic Presence: Short Stories of
Solace and Hope After the Loss of a Baby*.

Landers, Ann. 1998a. "IRS Doesn't Consider the Stillborn a Person." *Albany, NY,
Times Union*, April 6, C2.

————.1998b. "Support Is Out There for Those Who Need It." *Albany, NY,
Times Union*, November 17, D2.

Landsman, Gail. 1998. "Reconstructing Motherhood in the Age of 'Perfect' Babies:
Mothers of Infants and Toddlers with Disabilities." *Signs* 24(1):69–99.

————.1999. "Does God Give Special Kids to Special Parents? Personhood and
the Child with Disablities as Gift and as Giver." Pp. 133–166 in *Transformative
Motherhood: On Giving and Getting in a Consumer Culture*, edited by Layne. New
York: New York University Press.

————.2000. "'Real' Motherhood, Class, and Children with Disabilities."
Pp. 169–190 in *Ideologies and Technologies of Motherhood*, edited by Helena
Ragoné and Winddance Twine. New York: Routledge.

————.In prep. "'Too Bad You Got a Lemon': Peter Singer, Mothers of Children
with Disablities, and the Critique of Consumer Culture." In *Consuming Motherhood*
(working title), edited by Janelle Taylor, Danielle Wozniak, Linda Layne.

Langer, Lawrence L. 1997. "The Alarmed Vision: Social Suffering and Holocaust
Atrocity" Pp. 47–66. In *Social Suffering*. Edited by Kleinman, Das, and Lock.
Berkeley: University of California Press.

Laqueur, Thomas W. 1994. "Memory and Naming in the Great War." Pp. 150–167
in *Commemoration: The Politics of National Identity*, edited by John Gillis.
Princeton: Princeton University Press.

Larson, Erik. 1992. *The Naked Consumer: How Our Private Lives Become Public Commodities.* New York: Henry Holt and Co.

Lasch, Christopher. 1991. *The True and Only Heaven: Progress and Its Critics.* New York: W.W. Norton & Co.

Lasker, Judith N. and Susan Borg. 1987. *In Search of Parenthood: Coping with Infertility and High-Tech Conception.* Boston: Beacon Press.

Launslager, Donna. 1994. "From 1–5: Multiple Births and the Family." Pp. 117–126 in *Misconceptions: The Social Construction of Choice and the New Reproductive Technologies*, vol. 2, edited by Gwynne Basen, Margrit Eichler, and Abby Lippman. Ontario: Voyageur Publishing.

Laux, Jana. 1985. Untitled. *SHARE Newsletter* 8(4):1.

———.1988a. "SHARE Baby Pictures Questionnaire—Part I." *SHARE Newsletter* 11(3):10–13.

———.1988b. "Baby Questionnaire—Part II." *SHARE Newsletter* 11(4):10–12.

Lawrence, Tim. 1991. "Funeral Rite or Wrong?: A Hospital Chaplain Is Cremating Foetuses without the Patients' Consent." *New Statesman* 4:22, April 19.

Layne, Linda L. 1988. Review of *Some Babies Die.* A film by Martyn Langdon Down, 1986. *Visual Anthropology* 1(3):491–497.

———.1990. "Motherhood Lost: Cultural Dimensions of Miscarriage and Stillbirth in America." *Women and Health* 16(3):75–104.

———.1992. "Of Fetuses and Angels: Fragmentation and Integration in Narratives of Pregnancy Loss." In *Knowledge and Society: The Anthropology of Science and Technology*, edited by Hess and Layne, 9:29–58. Greenwich, CT: JAI Press.

———.1994. *Home and Homeland: The Dialogics of Tribal and National Identities in Jordan.* Princeton: Princeton University Press.

———.1995. "'Bad Luck Genes': Fate and (Mis)fortune in Genetic Understandings of Pregnancy Loss." Paper delivered at the Society for Social Studies of Science's annual meeting, Charlottesville and the American Anthropology Association's annual meeting, Washington, DC.

———.1996a. "'How's the Baby Doing?': Struggling with Narratives of Progress in a Neonatal Intensive Care Unit." *Medical Anthropology Quarterly* 10(4):624–656.

———.1996b. "'Never Such Innocence Again': Irony, Nature and Technoscience in Narratives of Pregnancy Loss." Pp. 131–152 in *The Anthropology of Pregnancy Loss: Comparative Studies in Miscarriage, Stillbirth and Neonatal Death*, edited by Rosanne Cecil. Oxford: Berg Publishers.

———.1997a."Breaking the Silence: An Agenda for a Feminist Discourse of Pregnancy Loss." Invited submission to a special issue of *Feminist Studies* 23(2):289–315.

———.1997b. "Mother Nature/Freaks of Nature." Paper presented at the Electronic Conference "Cultures & Environments: On Cultural Environmental Studies." Washington State University American Studies Website.

———.1998. "Introduction." *Anthropological Approaches in Science and Technology Studies.* Special Issue of *Science, Technology and Human Values* 23(1):4–23.

————.1999a. *Transformative Motherhood: On Giving and Getting in a Consumer Culture*, edited by Layne. New York: New York University Press.

————.1999b. "'I Remember the Day I Shopped for your Layette': Goods, Fetuses and Feminism in the Context of Pregnancy Loss." Pp. 251-278 in *Fetal Subjects, Feminist Positions*, edited by Lynn Morgan and Meridith Michaels. Philadelphia: University of Pennsylvania Press. Reprinted in *Consumption*, edited by Daniel Miller, (2001) London: Routledge.

————.1999c. "Introduction: New Directions in EuroAmerican Gift Exchange." Pp. 1–27 in *Transformative Motherhood: On Giving and Getting in a Consumer Culture*, edited by Layne. New York: New York University Press.

————.1999d. "'True Gifts from God': Of Motherhood, Sacrifice, and Enrichment in the Context of Pregnancy Loss." Pp. 167–214 in *Transformative Motherhood: On Givning and Getting in a Consumer Culture*, edited by Layne. New York: New York University Press.

————.1999e. "Fertility, Gender, and Healing: Contributions Toward a Comparative Anthropology of Reproduction." *Reviews in Anthropology* 28:33–52.

————.2000a. "Baby Things as Fetishes?: Memorial Goods, Simulacra, and the 'Realness' Problem of Pregnancy Loss." Pp. 111–138 in *Ideologies and Technologies of Motherhood*, edited by Helena Ragoné and Frances Winddance Twine. New York: Routledge.

————.2000b. "'He was a Real Baby with Baby Things': A Material Culture Analysis of Personhood and Pregnancy Loss." *Journal of Material Culture* 5(3):321–345.

————.2000c. "'The Cultural Fix': An Anthropological Contribution to Science and Technology Studies." *Science, Technology and Human Values* 25(3):352–377.

————.2001. "The Search for Community: Tales of Pregnancy Loss in Three Toxically-Assaulted Communities in the US." Special issue of *Women's Studies Quarterly* on Women and the Environment, edited by Diane Hope and Vandana Shiva, Spring/Summer 2001, pp. 25–50.

————.2002. "Unhappy Endings: A Feminist Reappraisal of the Natural Childbirth Movement from the Vantage of Pregnancy Loss." In special issue edited by Marcia Inhorn and Gwynne Jenkins "Reproduction Gone Awry" of *Social Science and Medicine*.

————.In prep a. "'Your Child Deserves a Name': Names, Naming, and the Memeropolitics of Pregnancy Loss." In *Tropes of Entanglement: Towards an Anthropology of Names and Naming* edited by Gabriele vom Bruck and Barbara Bodenhorn.

————.In prep b. "Making Memories: Trauma, Choice, and Consumer Culture in the Case of Pregnancy Loss." In *Consuming Motherhood* (working title), edited by Janelle Taylor, Danielle Wozniak, and Linda Layne.

Lazarus, Ellen S. 1988. "Poor Women, Poor Outcomes: Social Class and Reproductive Health." Pp. 39–54 in *Childbirth in America: Anthropological Perspectives*, edited by Michaelson. South Hadley, MA: Bergin & Garvey.

Leach, Edmund. 1976. *Culture and Communication: The Logic by Which Symbols Are Connected*. Cambridge: Cambridge University Press.

Leather, Tami. 1995. "A Loving Support." *UNITE Notes* 14(1):7.

Leather, John. 2001. "Dear UNITE" 19(4):7.

Lee, Dorothy. 1959. "Are Basic Needs Ultimate?" Pp. 70–77 in *Freedom and Culture*. Englewood Cliffs, NJ: Prentice Hall.

Leon, Warren and Roy Rosenzweig. 1989. "Introduction." Pp. xi–xxvi in *History Museums in the United States: A Critical Assessment*, edited by Leon and Rosenzweig. Urbana: University of Illinois Press.

Levesque, Jeri. 1993. "Play It Again, Sam." *SHARE Newsletter* 2(2):1, 4.

Lewin, Ellen. 1993. *Lesbian Mothers: Accounts of Gender in American Culture*. Ithaca: Cornell University Press.

Lewis, Aliene. 1991. "Untitled." *SHARE Newsletter* 14(6):6.

Lewis, Charles J. 2001. "D-Day Memorial's Home Where Heart Is." *Times Union*, Albany, NY, June 4, A1.

Leys, Ruth. 1996. "Traumatic Cures: Shell Shock, Janet, and the Question of Memory." Pp. 103–150 in *Tense Past: Cultural Essays in Trauma and Memory*, edited by Paul Antze and Michael Lambek. New York: Routledge.

Lindbohm, Marja-Lisa and Markku Sallmen, Ahti Anttila, Helena Taskinen, and Kari Hamminki. 1991. "Paternal Occupational Lead Exposure and Spontaneous Abortion." *Scandinavian Journal of Work, Environment and Health* 17:95–103.

Liss, Andrea. 1998. *Trespassing through Shadows: Memory, Photography, and the Holocaust*. Minneapolis: University of Minnesota Press.

Lloyd, Jillian. 2000. "Causing a Miscarriage—An Act of Murder?" *The Christian Science Monitor*, February 15, p. 3.

Lock, Margaret. 1997. "Displacing Suffering: The Reconstruction of Death in Japan and North America." Pp. 207–244 in *Social Suffering*, edited by Kleinman, Das, and Lock. Berkeley: University of California Press.

———.1998. "Perfecting Society: Reproductive Technologies, Genetic Testing, and the Planned Family in Japan." Pp. 206–239 in *Pragmatic Women and Body Politics*, edited by Margaret Lock and Patricia A. Kaufert. Cambridge: Cambridge University Press.

———.2002. *Twice Dead: Organ Transplants and the Reinvention of Death*. Berkeley: University of California Press.

Lohr, Denise. 1986. "In Memory of Daniel Lohr Elbling." *SHARE Newsletter* 9(2):3.

Lovell, Alice. 1983. "Some Questions of Identity: Late Miscarriage, Stillbirth and Perinatal Loss." *Social Science and Medicine* 17:755–761.

Lowenthal, David. 1999. "Preface." Pp. xi–xii in *The Art of Forgetting*, edited by Forty and Kuchler. Oxford: Berg.

Luker, Kristin. 1975. *Taking Chances: Abortion and the Decision Not to Contracept*. Berkeley: University of California Press.

———.1984. *Abortion and the Politics of Motherhood*. Berkeley: University of California Press.

Lykens, Dawn. 2001. "From Her Wings, With Love . . . " *SHARING* 10(2)5.

MacCauley, Pat. 1982. "The Longest Sixteen Days." *UNITE Notes* 1(3):6–8.

MacCormack, Carol and Marilyn Strathern. 1980. *Nature, Culture and Gender.* Cambridge: Cambridge University Press.

MacFarlane, Alison and Miranda Mugford. 1984. *Birth Counts: Statistics of Pregnancy and Childbirth.* National Perinatal Epidemiology Unit (in collaboration with Office of Population Censuses and Surveys). London: Her Majesty's Stationery Office.

MacPherson, C. B. 1962. *The Political Theory of Possessive Individualism.* Oxford: Oxford University Press.

Madelyn Company. 1996. "Keepsake Pendants." *SHARE Newsletter* 5(4):10.

Makela, Klaus, et al. 1996. *Alcoholics Anonymous as a Mutual-Help Movement: A Study in Eight Societies.* Madison: University of Wisconsin Press.

Malinowski, Bronislaw. [1929] 1987. *The Sexual Life of Savages.* Boston: Beacon Press.

Mallock, D. 1985. "Untitled." *SHARE Pregnancy and Infant Loss Support Newsletter* 8(3):1.

Manning, Peter K. and Betsy Cullum-Swan. 1994. "Narrative, Content, and Semiotic Analysis" Pp. 463–477 in *Handbook of Qualitative Research*, edited by Norman K. Denzin and Yvonna S. Lincoln. Thousand Oaks, CA: Sage.

Maranto, Gina. 1995. "Delayed Childbearing." *The Atlantic Monthly* June 55–66.

March, Kathryn. 2001. "Childbirth with Fear." Pp. 168–173 in *Mothers & Children: Feminist Analyses and Personal Narratives*, edited by Susan E. Chase and Mary F. Rogers. New Brunswick, NJ: Rutgers University Press.

Marcus, George E. 1994. "What Comes (Just) After "Post"?: The Case of Ethnography." Pp. 563–574 in *Handbook of Qualitative Research*, edited by Norman K. Denzin and Yvonna S. Lincoln. Thousand Oaks, CA: Sage.

————.1998. *Ethnography Through Thick and Thin.* Princeton: Princeton University Press.

Markens, Susan, C. H. Browner, and Nancy Press. 1997. "Feeding the Fetus: On Interrogating the Notion of Maternal-Fetal Conflict." *Feminist Studies* 23(2):351–372.

Markoff, John. 1992. "Miscarriage Risk for Chip Workers: Widely Used Chemical Creates Hazards for Some Women an Industry Study Says." *New York Times*, December 4.

Marone, Joseph and Edward Woodhouse. 1986. *Averting Catastrophe: Strategies for Regulating Risky Technologies.* Berkeley: University of California Press.

————.1989. *The Demise of Nuclear Energy?: Lessons fro Democratic Control of Technology.* New Haven: Yale University Press.

Marsh, Margaret and Wanda Ronner. 1996. *The Empty Cradle: Infertility in America from Colonial Times to the Present.* Baltimore: The Johns Hopkins University Press.

Marshall Editions. 1985. *Growth and Development: The Span of Life.* New York: Torstar Books.

Martin, Bonita. 1995. "I'm Still a Mother." *UNITE Notes* 14(1):2.

Martin, Bonita and David Martin. 1995a. "When We Cry." *UNITE Notes* 14(1):3.

———.1995b. "Circle of Love." *SHARE Newsletter* 4(2):3.

Martin, Emily. 1987. *Woman in the Body: A Cultural Analysis of Reproduction*. Boston: Beacon Press.

———.1990. "The Ideology of Reproduction: The Reproduction of Ideology." Pp. 300–314 in *Uncertain Terms: Negotiation Gender in American Culture*, edited by F. Ginsburg and A. L. Tsing. Boston: Beacon Press.

———.1994. *Flexible Bodies: Tracking Immunity in American Culture from the Days of Polio to the Age of AIDS*. Boston: Beacon Press.

———.1998. "The Fetus as Intruder: Mother's Bodies and Medical Metaphors." Pp. 125–142 in *Cyborg Babies: From Techno-Sex to Techno-Tots*, edited by Robbie Davis-Floyd and Joseph Dumit. New York: Routledge.

Mauss, Marcel. 1969. *The Gift: Forms and Functions of Exchange in Archaic Societies*. New York: Routledge Kegan & Paul.

Maycock, Kim. 1999. "A Mother's Day Poem." *SHARING* 8(3):11.

McCann, Linda. 1984. "For Patricia." *UNITE Notes* 3(3):1.

———.1985. "A Love Letter to My Baby Girl." *UNITE Notes* 4(4):7.

McCann, Pat. 1984. "Growth Through Pain." *UNITE Notes* 3(3):5.

McCauley, Bernadette. 1986. " . . . Only a Miscarriage." UNITE Notes 5(4):4.

McClain, Dawn. 1984. "My Little One." *SHARE Newsletter* 7(4):1.

McClure, Nicola and Jovanka Bach. 1986. *The Rodale Book of Pregnancy and Birth*. Emmaus, PA: Rodale Press.

McCook, Leslie I. 1987. "A Study of the Relationship Between Pregnancy Identity and Motherhood Identity and the Perception of Loss in Women Who Have a Miscarriage." Doctoral dissertation proposal. Psychoeducational Processes, Temple University, Philadelphia.

McCracken, Grant. 1988. *Culture and Consumption: New Approaches to the Symbolic Character of Consumer Goods and Activities*. Bloomington: Indiana University Press.

McCrumb, Sharyn. 1992. *The Hangman's Beautiful Daughter*. New York: Charles Scribner's Sons.

McDonald-Grandin, Merrilyn. 1983. *Will I Ever Be a Mother?* Portland, OR: Celeste Books.

McDonnell, Jane Taylor. 2001. "On Being a 'Bad' Mother of an Autistic Child." Pp. 52–59 in *Mothers & Children: Feminist Analyses and Personal Narratives*, edited by Susan E. Chase and Mary F. Rogers. New Brunswick, NJ: Rutgers University Press.

McFaul, Traci. 1996. "Happy Birthday Sarah." *SHARE Newsletter* 5(3):13.

McGinness, Patty. 1988. "Refections & Regrets." Section 1, pp. 27–28 in *Bittersweet . . . hellogoodbye: A Resource in Planning Farewell Rituals When a Baby Dies*, edited by Sister Jane Marie Lamb. Belleville, IL: Charis Communications.

———.1988b. "Missing You." *SHARE Newsletter* 11(7):1.

McKinley, Robert. 1981. "Cain and Abel on the Malay Peninsula." in *Siblingship in Oceania*, edited by M. Marshall. Ann Arbor: University of Michigan Press.

McLeod, Carolyn. 2001. "Does Gift Language Elevate Devalued Forms of Motherhood?" Review of *Transformative Motherhood* in *Medical Humanities Review*, spring: 67–70.

McMillen, Sally G. 1990. *Motherhood in the Old South: Pregnancy, Childbirth, and Infant Rearing*. Baton Rouge: Louisiana State University Press.

McVeigh, Brian. 1996. "Commodifying Affection, Authority and Gender in the Everyday Objects of Japan." *Journal of Material Culture* 1(3):291–312.

Meinwald, Dan. 1990. *Memento Mori: Death in 19th Century Photography*. California Museum of Photography Bulletin 9(4). University of California at Riverside #92521.

Mellon, Emma. 1992. "A Ritual to Grieve Pregnancy Loss." *UNITE Notes* 11(1):2.

———.1999. "Zachary David." *UNITE Notes* 17(4):7.

Melucci, Alberto. 1996. *Challenging Codes: Collective Action in the Information Age*. Cambridge: Cambridge University Press.

———.1989. *Nomads of the Present: Social Movements and Individual Needs in Contemporary Society*. Philadelphia: Temple University Press.

Memories Unlimited. 1994. "The Memory Box for Personal Loss." *SHARE Newsletter* 3(5):13.

Merchant, Carolyn. 1980. *The Death of Nature: Women, Ecology and the Scientific Revolution*. New York: Harper & Row.

Meredith, Joann. 1988. "God's Will." *SHARE Newsletter* 11(2):2.

Merriott, Dionne. 1995. "Victoria's Lesson." *SHARE Newsletter* 4(5):15.

Mesthene, Emmanual G. 1997. "The Role of Technology in Society." Pp. 65–76 in *Technology and the Future*, 7th edition, edited by Albert H. Teich. New York: St. Martin's Press.

Metropolitan Museum of Art. 1978. *Baby's Journal*. New York: Charles Scribner's Sons.

Michaels, Meredith and Lynn M. Morgan. 1999. "Introduction." Pp. 251–278 in *Fetal Subjects, Feminist Positions*, edited by Morgan and Michaels. Philadelphia: University of Pennsylvania Press.

Miller, Daniel. 1993. "A Theory of Christmas." *Unwrapping Christmas*, edited by D. Miller. Oxford: Clarendon Press.

———.1997. "How Infants Grow Mothers in North London." *Theory, Culture & Society* 14(4):67–88.

———.1998. *A Theory of Shopping*. Ithaca: Cornell University Press.

Miller, Jim. 1984. "You're Not Here." *SHARE Newsletter* 7(4):1.

Miller, Pamela. 1981. "Hair Jewelry as Fetish." Pp. 89–106 in *Objects of Special Devotion: Fetishism in Popular Culture*, edited by Ray B. Browne. Bowling Green, OH: Bowling Green University Popular Press.

Mills, Gloria. 1988. "Baby's Breath Lapel Pin & Pendant." *SHARE Newsletter* 11(3):6.

Mitchell, Lisa M. 1994. "The Routinization of the Other: Ultrasound, Women and the Fetus." Pp. 146–160 in *Misconceptions: The Social Construction of Choice and the New Reproductive Technologies*, vol. 2, edited by Gwynne Basen, Margrit Eichler, and Abby Lippman. Ontario: Voyageur Publishing.

Mitchell, Lisa M. and Eugenia Georges. 1998. "Baby's First Picture: The Cyborg Fetus of Ultrasound Imaging." Pp. 105–124 in *Cyborg Babies: From Techno-Sex to Techno-Tots*, edited by Robbie Davis-Floyd and Joseph Dumit. New York: Routledge.

Mitford, Jessica. 1963. *The American Way of Death*. New York: Simon and Schuster.

Modell, Judith S. 1986. "In Search: The Purported Biological Basis of Parenthood." *American Ethnologist* 13(4):646–661.

———.1994. *Kinship with Strangers: Adoption and Interpretations of Kinship in American Culture*. Berkeley: University of California Press.

———.1996. "Rights to the Children: Foster Care and Social Reproduction in Hawai'i." Pp. 156–172 in *Reproducing Reproduction: Kinship, Power, and Technological Innovation*, edited by Ragoné and Franklin. Philadelphia: University of Pennsylvania Press.

———.1999. "Given Freely: Open Adoption and the Rhetoric of the Gift." Pp. 29–64 in *Transformative Motherhood: On Giving and Getting in a Consumer Culture*, edited by Layne. New York: New York University Press.

Moffitt, Perry-Lynn. 1987. "Miscarriage: Pregnancy is an exciting, happy time. The last thing you're prepared to do is grieve." *Parents*, April, pp. 133–135, 214–217.

———.1994. "Miscarriage: The Most Silent of Sorrows." *SHARE Newsletter* 3(7):1–2.

Mom. 1985. "Hello, Little Son." Pp. 22–23 in *When Hello Means Goodbye: A Guide for Parents Whose Child Dies Before Birth, At Birth or Shortly After Birth*, edited by Pat Schwiebert and Paul Kirk. Portland, OR: Perinatal Loss.

Mommy. 2000. "A Special Gift in the Little White Box." *UNITE Notes* 18(3):1.

Mommy and Daddy. 1995. "Happy 2nd Birthday Sherri Maria Porter." *UNITE Notes* 14(1):3.

Morgan, Chuck. 1995. "A Small Light That Shined Brightly." *SHARE Newsletter* 4(5):2.

Morgan, Lynn M. 1996a. "Fetal Relationality in Feminist Philosophy: An Anthropological Critique." *Hypatia: A Journal of Feminist Philosophy* 11(3):47–70.

———.1996b. "When Does Life Begin? A Cross-Cultural Perspective on the Personhood of Fetuses and Young Children." Pp. 24–34 in *Talking About People*, Second Edition, edited by Haviland and Gordon, Mountain View, CA: Mayfield Publishing Co.

———.2002. "'Properly Disposed of': A History of Embryo Disposal and the Changing Claims on Fetal Remains." *Medical Anthropology* 21(3–4):247–74.

Morgan, Lynn M. and Meredith W. Michaels. 1999. *Fetal Subjects, Feminist Positions*. Philadelphia: University of Pennsylvania Press.

Morgan, Marla. 1995. "Today Is Our Son's First Birthday." *SHARE Newsletter* 4(5):1–2.

Morgan, Rev. Terry. 1985. "Telling Emily Goodbye." *SHARE Newsletter* 8(3):9–10.

Morhardt, Beth. 1999. "It's My Mother's Day, Too?" *SHARING* 8(3):1.

Morley, John. 1971. *Death, Heaven and the Victorians*. Pittsburgh: University of Pittsburgh Press.

Morris, David B. 1997. "About Suffering: Voice, Genre, and Moral Community." Pp. 25–46 in *Social Suffering*, edited by Arthur Kleinman, Veena Das, and Margaret Lock. Berkeley: University of California Press.

Morton, Peggy A. 1996. "Perinatal Loss and the Replacement Child: The Emotional Limits of Reproductive Technology." Unpublished dissertation, Social Welfare, City University of New York.

Mountain, Corinna. 1996. "Easter Time." *SHARE Newsletter* 5(3):15.

Muecke, D.C. 1969. *The Compass of Irony*. London: Methuen.

Murphy, Joanne. 1991. "Remembering . . . Looking Forward." *UNITE Notes* 10(2):2–3.

Murphy, Robert F. and Jessica Scheer, Yolanda Murphy, and Richard Mack. 1988. "Physical Disablity and Social Liminality: A Study in the Rituals of Adversity." *Social Science and Medicine* 26(2):235–242.

Muschamp, Herbert. 1995. "If They Built a Memorial to the War in the Streets: Seven Proposals to Honor the Urban Dead." *The New York Times Magazine*, April 9, pp. 56–61.

Nagele, David F. 1986a. "For Jonathan." *UNITE Notes* 6(1):3.

———.1986b. "Private Lessons." *UNITE Notes* 6(1):4.

Narayan, Uma. 1995. "The 'Gift' of a Child: Commercial Surrogacy, Gift Surrogacy, and Motherhood." Pp. 177–202 in *Expecting Trouble: Surrogacy, Fetal Abuse & New Reproductive Technologies*, edited by Patricia Boling. Boulder, CO: Westview Press.

Nash, Roderick Fazier. 1982. *Wilderness and the American Mind*. Third Edition. New Haven: Yale University Press.

Neugebauer, Richard. 1987. "The Psychiatric Effects of Miscarriage: Research Design and Preliminary Findings." Pp. 136–149 in *Psychiatric Epidemiology: Progress and Prospects*, edited by Brian Cooper. London: Croom Helm.

Neugebauer, Richard, Kline, J., O'Connor, P., Shrout, P., Johnson, J., Skodol, A., Wicks, J., and Susser, M. 1992a. "Depressive Symptoms in Women in the Six Months after Miscarriage." *American Journal of Obstetrics and Gynecology* 166:104–109.

———.1992b. "Determinants of Depressive Symptoms in the Early Weeks after Miscarriage." *American Journal of Public Health* 82:1332–1339.

Neugebauer, Richard, Kline, J., Shrout, P., Skodol, A., O'Connor, P., Geller, P.A., Stein, Z., and Susser, M. 1997. "Major Depressive Disorder in the Six Months after Miscarriage." *Journal of the American Medical Association* 227:383–388.

Newman, Karen. 1996. *Fetal Positions: Individualism, Science, Visuality*. Stanford: Stanford University Press.

Newman, Katherine S. 1988. *Falling from Grace: The Experience of Downward Mobility in the American Middle Class.* New York: Vintage Books.

Newman, Lucille. 1969. "Folklore of Pregnancy." *Western Folklore* 28:112–35.

Niehoff, Michael L., PA-C, MS(R). 1994. "Healing Memories." *SHARE Newsletter* 2(4):1, 4.

———.1996. "Holiday Help for the Bereaved." *SHARE Newsletter* 4(6):3.

Niles, Tara. 1996. "The Missing Piece in Our Three Piece Puzzle." *SHARE Newsletter* 5(1):8.

Nisbet, Robert. 1980. *History of the Idea of Progress.* New York: Basic Books, Inc.

Nolan, Lynn Ann. 1991. "To My Baby." *UNITE Notes* 10(1):5.

Nora, Pierre. 1989. "Between Memory and History: Les Lieux de Memoire." In special issue of *Representations* on "Memory and Counter Memory," edited by Natalie Zemon Davis and Randolph Starn. 26:7–25.

Nucitelli, Linda. 1997. "David's Visit." *UNITE Notes* 15(4):1.

———.1999. "One Tiny Baby." *UNITE Notes* 17(3):3.

Oakley, Ann. 1984. *The Captured Womb: History of the Medical Care of Pregnant Women.* Oxford: Basil Blackwell.

Oaks, Laury. 1998. *Expert and Everyday Perceptions of Prenatal Health Risks: An Ethnography of Cigarette Smoking and Fetal Politics in the U.S.* Doctoral Dissertation, Departments of Anthropology and Population Dynamics, Johns Hopkins University.

———.2001. *Smoking and Pregnancy: The Politics of Fetal Protection.* New Brunswick, NJ: Rutgers University Press.

Ochs, Donovan J. 1993. *Consolatory Rhetoric: Grief, Symbol, and Ritual in the Greco-Roman Era.* Columbia, SC: University of South Carolina Press.

Ochs, Elinor and Bambi B. Schieffelin. 1984. "Language Acquisition and Socialization: Three Developmental Stories and Their Implications. Pp. 276–320 in *Culture Theory: Essays on Mind, Self, and Emotion,* edited by Shweder and LeVine. Cambridge: Cambridge University Press.

Office of Technology Assessment. 1988. *Infertility: Medical and Social Choices.* Washington, DC: Congress of the United States.

Ohnuki-Tierney, Emiko. 1994. "Brain Death and Organ Transplantation: Cultural Bases of Medical Technology." *Current Anthropology* 34(3):233–242.

Orenstein, Peggy. 2002. "Mourning My Miscarriage." *The New York Times Magazine,* April 21, pp. 38–41.

Oudshoorn, Nelly. 1994. *Beyond the Natural Body: An Archaeology of Sex Hormones.* New York: Routledge.

Page, Teresa. 1986. "Miscarried Joy." *SHARE Newsletter* 9(3):4.

———.1987. "Robins and Rainbows." *SHARE Pregnancy and Infant Loss Support Newsletter* 10(6):3.

Paget, Marianne A. 1988. *The Unity of Mistakes: A Phenomenological Interpretation of Medical Work.* Philadelphia: Temple University Press.

Paige, Karen Ericksen and Jeffery M. Paige. 1981. *The Politics of Reproductive Ritual.* Berkeley: University of California Press.

Palekar, April. 1988. "John Charles." *UNITE Notes* 7(2):3.

Panuthos, Claudia. 1984. *Transformation Through Birth: A Woman's Guide*. South Hadley, MA: Bergin & Garvey Publishers, Inc.

Panuthos, Claudia and Katherine Romero. 1984. *Ended Beginnings: Healing Childbearing Losses*. South Hadley, MA: Bergin and Garvey Publishers, Inc.

Paoletti, Jo B. and Carol L. Kregloh. 1989. "The Children's Department." Pp. 22–41 in *Men and Women: Dressing the Part*, edited by Claudia Brush Kidwell and Valerie Steele. Washington, DC: Smithsonian Institution Press.

Paré, Ambroise. [1573] 1982. *On Monsters and Marvels*. Translated by Janis L. Pallister. Chicago: University of Chicago Press.

Park, Katharine and Lorraine J. Daston. 1981. "Unnatural Conceptions: The Study of Monsters in France and England." *Past & Present* 92:20–54.

Parry, Jonathan. 1986. "The Gift, The Indian Gift and the 'Indian Gift.'" *Man* 21:453–473.

Pavlak, Frank. 1984. "Sarah's Secret Life." *SHARE Newsletter* 7(3):3.

Pellegrino, Edmund D. 1976. "The Sociocultural Impact of Twentieth-Century Therapeutics." Pp. 245–266 in *The Therapeutic Revolution: Essays in the Social History of American Medicine*, edited by Morris J. Vogel and Charles E. Rosenberg. Philadelphia: University of Pennsylvania Press.

Peppers, Larry and Ronald Knapp. 1980. *Motherhood and Mourning: Perinatal Death*. New York: Praeger.

Perin, Constance. 1998. "Operating as Experimenting: Synthesizing Engineering and Scientific Values in Nuclear Power Production." *Science, Technology and Human Values*, edited by Layne. 23(1):98–128.

Perrow, Charles. 1984. *Normal Accidents: Living with High-Risk Technologies*. New York: Basic Books.

Petchesky, Rosalind. 1987. "Fetal Images: The Power of Visual Culture in the Politics of Reproduction." *Feminist Studies* 13(2):263–292.

Pfeffer, Naomi. 1993. *The Stork and the Syringe: A Political History of Reproductive Medicine*. Cambridge: Polity Press.

Phillips, Laura. 1995. "Angel Children." *SHARE Newsletter* 4(3):7.

Piehler, G. Kurt. 1994. "The War Dead and the Gold Star: American Commemoration of the First World War." Pp. 168–185 in *Commemoration: The Politics of National Identity*, edited by John Gillis. Princeton: Princeton University Press.

Pinch, Trevor J. and Wiebe E. Bijker. 1989. "The Social Construction of Facts and Artifacts: Or How the Sociology of Science and the Sociology of Technology Might Benefit Each Other." Pp. 17–50 in *The Social Construction of Technological Systems: New Directions in the Sociology and History of Technology*, edited by Wiebe E. Bijker, Thomas P. Hughes, and Trevor Pinch. Cambridge, MA: The MIT Press.

Pines, Heather. 2001. "My Little Pink Cloud." *SHARING* 10(2)3.

Pizer, Hank and Christine O'Brien Palinski. 1980. *Coping with a Miscarriage: Why It Happens and How to Deal with Its Impact on Your Family*. New York: Signet.

Pointon, Marcia. 1999. "Materializing Mourning: Hair, Jewellery and the Body" Pp. 39–98 in *Material Memories: Design and Evocation* edited by Marius Kwint, Christopher Breward, Jeremy Aynsley.

Poirier, Suzanne and Lorie Rosenblum, Lioness Ayres, Daniel J. Brauner, Barbara F. Sharf, and Ann Folwell Stanford. 1992. "Charting the Chart—An Exercise in Interpretation(s)." *Literature and Medicine* 11(1):1–22.

Precious Parents.1987. "Precious Parents Philosophy." *SHARE Newsletter* 10(6):2.

Pregnancy Loss Support Program of the NCJWNYS and Mount Sinai Medical Center. 1999. "Understanding Your Pregnancy Loss: Coping With Miscarriage, Stillbirth or Newborn Death." New York City.

Preston, Brian. 1994. "Robbing the Cradle: Two Months After his Girlfriend's Miscarriage, Brian Preston Contemplates His Fatherhood Lost." *Details* April: 80–82.

Rabinbach, Anson. 1997. "From Explosion to Erosion: Holocaust Memorialization in America since Bitburg." Pp. 226–255 in "Passing into History: Nazism and the Holocaust beyond Memory." Special double issue of *History & Memory: Studies in Representation of the Past*, edited by Arad, Gulie Ne'eman. Vol. 9 (1/2). Tel Aviv: Tel Aviv University.

Rabinowitz, Linda. 1983. "One Mother's Feelings on Subsequent Pregnancy." *UNITE Notes* 3(1):4.

Radstone, Susannah. 2000a. "Screening Trauma: Forrest Gump, Film and Memory." Pp. 79–110 in *Memory and Methodology*, edited by Susannah Radstone. Oxford: Berg.

———.2000b. "Working with Memory: An Introduction." Pp. 1–24 in *Memory and Methodology*, edited by Susannah Radstone. Oxford: Berg.

Radway, Janice A. 1984. *Reading the Romance: Women, Patriarchy, and Popular Literature*. Chapel Hill: The University of North Carolina Press.

Ragoné, Helena. 1994. *Surrogate Motherhood: Conception in the Heart*. Boulder, CO: Westview Press.

———.1999. "The Gift of Life: Surrogate Motherhood, Gamete Donation, and Constructions of Altruism." Pp. 65–88 in *Transformative Motherhood: On Giving and Getting in a Consumer Culture*, edited by Layne. New York: New York University Press.

———.2000. "Of Likeness and Difference: How Race Is Being Transfigured by Gestational Surrogacy." Pp. 56–75 in *Ideologies and Technologies of Motherhood*, edited by Helena Ragoné and Winddance Twine. New York: Routledge.

Rapp, Rayna. 1997. "Real-Time Fetus: The Role of the Sonogram in the Age of Monitored Reproduction." Pp. 31–48 in *Cyborgs & Citadels: Anthropological Interventions in Emerging Sciences and Technologies*, edited by Downey and Dumit. Sante Fe, NM: School of American Research.

————.1999. *Testing Women, Testing the Fetus: The Social Impact of Amniocentesis in America*. New York: Routledge.

————.2001. "Gender, Body, Biomedicine: How Some Feminist Concerns Dragged Reproduction to the Center of Social Theory." *Medical Anthropology Quarterly* 15(4):466–477.

Rapp, Rayna, Deborah Heath, and Karen Sue Taussig. 2000. "Geneological Dis-ease: Where Hereditary Abnormality, Biomedical Explanation, and Family Responsibility Meet." in *Relative Matters: The Anthropology of the New Kinship*, edited by Sarah Franklin and Susan MacKinnon. Berkeley: University of California Press.

Rasmussen, Knud. 1975. "A Shaman's Journey to the Sea Spirit Takanakapsaluk." Pp. 13–19 in *Teachings from the American Earth: Indian Religion and Philosophy*, edited by Dennis Tedlock and Barbara Tedlock. New York: Liveright Publishing Company.

Reddy, Maureen T., Martha Roth, and Amy Sheldon. 1994. *Mother Journeys: Feminists Write about Mothering*. Spinsters Ink.

Reed, Richard. 1997. "Knaves-in-Waiting: The Exclusion of Fathers from Medical Birthing." Photocopy.

Regis, Helen A. 2001. "Blackness and the Politics of Memory in the New Orleans Second Line." *American Ethnologist* 28(4):752–777.

Reinharz, Shulamit. 1987. "The Social Psychology of a Miscarriage: An Application of Symbolic Interaction Theory and Method." Pp. 229–249 in *Women and Symbolic Interaction*, edited by Deegan and Hill. Boston: Allen & Unwin.

————.1988a. "Controlling Women's Lives: A Cross-Cultural Interpretation of Miscarriage Accounts." *Research in the Sociology of Health Care* 7:3–37.

————.1988b. "What's Missing in Miscarriage?" *Journal of Community Psychology* 16:84–103.

————.1988c. "Definitions in Context and Culture: The Experience of Miscarriage." Pp. 54–55 in *Sociology*. Third Edition, edited by B. Hess, E. Markson, P. Stein. New York: Macmillan.

————.1992. *Feminist Methods in Social Research*. New York: Oxford.

Reissman, Frank. 1982. "The Self-Help Ethos." *Social Policy* summer pp. 42–43.

Rich, Laurie A. 1991. *When Pregnancy Isn't Perfect: A Layperson's Guide to Complications in Pregnancy*. New York: Penguin Books.

Riessman, Catherine Kohler. 1990. *Divorce Talk: Women and Men Make Sense of Personal Relationships*. New Brunswick, NJ: Rutgers University Press.

————.1993. *Narrative Analysis*. Qualitative Research Methods, Vol 30. Newbury Park, CA: Sage.

Roan, Shari. 1990. "Childless Couples: New Hope." *Los Angeles Times*, October 29, A1, 19.

Rochlin, Gene I. 1997. *Trapped in the Net: The Unanticipated Consequences of Computerization*. Princeton: Princeton University Press.

Rodgers, Sarai. 1987. "A Letter to SHARE." *SHARE Newsletter* 10(2):4.

Rook, Dennis W. 1985. "The Ritual Dimension of Consumer Behavior." *Journal of Consumer Research* 12:251–263.

Rosaldo, Renato. 1993. "Grief and a Headhunter's Rage." Pp. 1–21 in *Culture & Truth: The Remaking of Social Analysis*. Boston: Beacon Press.

Rose, Colene. 1984. "To My Darling Erin, On Her Birthday." *SHARE Newsletter* 7(5):4.

Rose, Hilary. 1994. "Feminism and the Genetic Turn: Challenging Reproductive Technoscience." Pp. 171–207 in *Love, Power and Knowledge: Towards a Feminist Transformation of the Sciences*, edited by Hilary Rose and Anne Fausto-Sterling. Bloomington: Indiana University Press.

Rosenberg, John D. 1961. *The Darkening Glass: A Portrait of Ruskin's Genius*. New York: Columbia University Press.

Rosenblatt, Paul C., R. Patricia Walsh, and Douglas A. Jackson. 1976. *Grief and Mourning in Cross-Cultural Perspective*. USA: Human Relations Area Files.

Ross, Ellen. 1993. *Love & Toil: Motherhood in Outcast London, 1870–1918*. New York: Oxford University Press.

———.1999. "The Gift of a Child." *Reproductive Health Matters*, Vol. 7, no. 13.

Roth, Mom Mom and Pop-Pop. 1996. "Dear Baby Dominic Durante, III." *UNITE Notes* 14(4):2.

Rothman, Barbara Katz. 1982. *In Labor: Women and Power in the Birthplace*. New York: W.W. Norton & Co.

———.1986. *The Tentative Pregnancy: Prenatal Diagnosis and the Future of Motherhood*. New York: Penguin Books.

———.1989. *Recreating Motherhood: Ideology and Technology in a Patriarchal Society*. New York: W.W. Norton & Co.

Rowe, Deborah. 1993. "For the Best." *UNITE Notes* 12(2):3.

Rowlands, Michael. 1999. "Remembering to Forget: Sublimation as Sacrifice in War Memorials." Pp. 129–145 in *The Art of Forgetting*, edited by Forty and Kuchler. Oxford: Berg.

Royer, Debbie. 1985. "The Memory of Wade Allen." *SHARE Newsletter* 8(3):1.

RPI-Sage Hillel. 2000. Script from Yom Hashoah Commemoration on Holocaust Remembrance Day, "Remembering the Children" May 1, 2000, Troy, NY. Photocopy.

Rubinstein, Iris. 2001. "Storytelling With Our Hearts." *UNITE Notes* 19(4):3.

Ruby, Jay. 1995. *Secure in the Shadow: Death and Photography in America*. Cambridge, MA: MIT Press.

Ryan, Jennifer. 1999. "Memories." *SHARE Newsletter* 8(4):9.

Sahlins, Marshall. 1972a. "The Spirit of the Gift." Pp. 149–183 in *Stone Age Economics*. London: Tavistock Publications.

———.1972b. "On the Sociology of Primitive Exchange." Pp. 185–275 in *Stone Age Economics*. London: Tavistock Publications.

———.1976. *Culture and Practical Reason*. Chicago: University of Chicago Press.

Sandelowski, Margarete. 1993. *With Child in Mind: Studies of the Personal Encounter with Infertility*. Philadelphia: University of Pennsylvania Press.

Sandve, Jacki and Larry. 1984. "A Special Request." *UNITE Notes* 4(1):5–6.

Sariego, Lauren. 1996. "They Never Forget." *UNITE Notes* 14(4):2.

Sault, Nicole. 1994. "How the Body Shapes Parenthood: 'Surrogate' Mothers in the United States and Godmothers in Mexico." Pp. 292–318 in *Many Mirrors: Body Image and Social Relations*, edited by Sault. New Brunswick, NJ: Rutgers University Press.

Saum, Lewis O. 1975. "Death in the Popular Mind of Pre-Civil War America." Pp. 30–48 in *Death in America*, edited by David Stannard. Philadelphia: University of Pennsylvania Press.

Savageau, Jacqueline. 1991. "Amanda Leigh's Story." *SHARE Newsletter* 7(3):10.

Sawyer, Malinda. 1983. "Certificate of Baptism." *SHARE Newsletter* 9(3):10.

Schattschneider, Ellen. 2001. "'Buy Me a Bride'": Death and Exchange in Northern Japanese Bride-Doll Marriage." *American Ethnologist* 28(4):854–880.

Schatz, William H. 1984. *Healing a Father's Grief*. Redmond, WA: Medic Publishing Co.

Schauer, Gail M., Dagmar K. Kalouwek and J. Fergall Magee. 1992. "Genetic Causes of Stillbirth." *Seminars in Perinatology* 16(6):341–351.

Scheper-Hughes, Nancy. 1992. *Death Without Weeping: The Violence of Everyday Life in Brazil*. Berkeley: University of California Press.

Schmidt, Leigh Eric. 1997. "Practices of Exchange: From Market Culture to Gift Economy in the Interpretation of American Religion." Pp. 69–91 in *Lived Religion in America: Toward a History of Practice*, edited by David D. Hall. Princeton: Princeton University Press.

———.1995. *Consumer Rites: The Buying and Selling of American Holidays*. Princeton: Princeton University Press.

Schneider, David M. 1980. *American Kinship: A Cultural Account*. 2nd Edition. Chicago: University of Chicago Press.

Schneider, Jane and Annette B. Weiner. 1989. "Introduction." Pp. 1–29 in *Cloth and Human Experience*, edited by Annette B. Weiner and Jane Schneider. Washington, DC: Smithsonian Institution Press.

Schneider, Judi (Alexander's Grammy). 1995. "Grammy's Grief." *SHARE Newsletter* 5(2):6–8.

Schneider, Shawna. 1995. "My Angel Alexander." *SHARE Newsletter* 4(5):4.

Scholten, Catherine M. 1985. *Childbearing in American Society: 1650–1850*. New York: New York University Press.

Schorsch, Anita. 1976. *Mourning Becomes America: Mourning Art in the New Nation*. Catalogue of the William Penn Memorial Museum. Harrisburg, PA: Pennsylvania Historical and Museum Commission.

Schrift, Alan D. 1997. *The Logic of the Gift: Toward an Ethic of Generosity*. New York: Routledge.

Schroedel, Jean Reith and Paul Peretz. 1995. "A Gender Analysis of Policy Formation: The Case of Fetal Abuse." Pp. 85–108 in *Expecting Trouble:*

Surrogacy, Fetal Abuse & New Reproductive Technologies, edited by Patricia Boling. Boulder, CO: Westview Press.

Schwarcz, Vera. 1997. "The Pane of Sorrow: Public Uses of Personal Grief in Modern China." Pp. 119–148 in *Social Suffering*, edited by Kleinman, Arthur, Veena Das, and Margaret Lock. Berkeley: University of California Press.

Schwabe, Jean. 1984. "Joyful Subsequent Child." *SHARE Newsletter* 7(5):3.

Schwaegler, Susan D. 1989. "Pink Roses." *SHARE Newsletter* 12(1):1.

Schwartz, Barry. 1967. "The Social Psychology of the Gift." *The American Journal of Sociology* 73(1):1–11.

Schweibert, Pat. 1985. "Please Don't Tell Them You Never Got to Know Me." P. 14 in *When Hello Means Goodbye: A Guide for Parents Whose Child Dies Before Birth, At birth or Shortly After Birth*, edited by Pat Schwiebert, RN, and Paul Kirk, MD. Portland, OR: Perinatal Loss.

Schwiebert, Pat and Paul Kirk. 1985. *When Hello Means Goodbye: A Guide For Parents Whose Child Dies Before Birth, At Birth or Shortly After Birth*. Portland, OR: Perinatal Loss.

Seale, Clive. 1998. *Constructing Death: The Sociology of Dying and Bereavement*. Cambridge: Cambridge University Press.

Seatenan, Ann Rudinow. 1996. "Ultrasonic Discourse: Contested Meanings of Gender and Technology in the Norwegian Ultrasound Debate." *The European Journal of Women's Studies* 3(1):55–75.

———.2000. "Thirteen Women's Narratives of Pregnancy, Ultrasound and Self." in *Bodies of Technology: Women's Involvement with Reproductive Medicine*, edited by A. Saetnan, N. Oudshoorn, and M. Kirejczyk. Columbus: Ohio State University Press.

Seiter, Ellen. 1995. *Sold Separately: Children and Parents in Consumer Culture*. New Brunswick, NJ: Rutgers University Press.

Seriego, Lauren. 1996. "They Never Forget." *UNITE Notes* 14(4):2.

Sha, Janet L. 1990. *Mothers of Thyme: Customs and Rituals of Infertility and Miscarriage*. Ann Arbor, MI: Lida Rose Press.

Shapiro, Michael J. 1988. "The Political Rhetoric of Photography." Pp. 124–178 in *The Politics of Representation: Writing Practices in Biography, Photography, and Policy Analysis*, Madison: University of Wisconsin Press.

SHARE Newsletter. 1991. "Recognition of Life Certificates." *SHARE Newsletter* 14(6):7.

SHARE Newsletter. 1993. *International Perinatal Support Groups*. Belleville, IL: St. Elizabeth's Hospital.

Sharp, Lesley A. 2001. "Commodified Kin: Death, Mourning, and Competing Claims on the Bodies of Organ Donors in the United States." *American Anthropologist* 103(1):112–133.

Shaw, W. David. 1994. *Elegy & Paradox: Testing the Conventions*. Baltimore: The Johns Hopkins University Press.

Sheehan, Charles. 2001. "Mementos Mark Flight 93 Site." *Times Union*. Albany, NY, September 18. A4.

Sheehan, Melanie. 1996. "The Things I Grieve." *SHARE Newsletter* 5(4):1–2.

Sheppard, Grandma Jane. 1990. "To Keith—Our Brief Incandescent Flame." *UNITE Notes* 9(3):4.

Sherman, Daniel J. 1994. "Art, Commemoration, and the Production of Memory In France after World War I." Pp. 186–214 in *Commemoration: The Politics of National Identity*, edited by John Gillis. Princeton: Princeton University Press.

————.1999. *The Construction of Memory in Interwar France*. Chicago: University of Chicago Press.

Sherman, Edmund and Evelyn S. Newman. 1977. "The Meaning of Cherished Personal Possessions for the Elderly." *Journal of Aging and Human Development* 8(2):181–192.

Sheumaker, Helen. 1997. "'This Lock You See': Nineteenth Century Hair Work as the Commodified Self." *Fashion Theory* 1(4):421–446.

Shore, Brad. 1989. "Mana and Tapu." Pp. 137–174 in *Developments in Polynesian Ethnology*, edited by Alan Howard and Robert Borofsky. Honolulu: University of Hawaii Press.

Shumaker, Karen. 1990. "Forever Mine." *SHARE Newsletter* 13(4):1.

Shute, Patricia. 1988. "Six Days." *UNITE Notes* 7(3):5.

Simmel, Georg. 1950. "Adornment." Pp. 338–344 in *The Sociology of Georg Simmel*. Translated and edited by Kurt H. Wolff. New York: The Free Press.

Simonds, Wendy. 1992. *Women and Self-Help Culture: Reading between the Lines*. New Brunswick, NJ: Rutgers University Press.

Simonds, Wendy and Barbara Katz Rothman. 1992. *Centuries of Solace: Expressions of Maternal Grief in Popular Literature*. Philadelphia: Temple University Press.

Simons, Cari. 1995. "The Anniversary." *SHARE Newsletter* 4(5):7.

Simons, Robin. 1987. *After the Tears: Parents Talk about Raising a Child with a Disability*. San Diego: Harcourt Brace Jovanovich.

Singer, Isodore, ed. 1901. "Beruriah." Pp. 109–110 in *The Jewish Encyclopedia*. New York: Funk and Wagnalls.

Singer, Milton. 1978. "For a Semiotic Anthropology." Pp. 202–231 in *Sight, Sound and Sense*, edited by Thomas A. Sebeok. Bloomington: Indiana University Press.

Slater, Peter Gregg. 1977. *Children in the New England Mind: In Death and in Life*. Camden, CO: Archon.

Smith, Anthony. 1986. "The Last Hour." *SHARE Newsletter* 9(3):2.

Smith, Bardwell. 1988. "Buddhism and Abortion in Contemporary Japan: Mizuku Kuyo and the Confrontation with Death." *Japanese Journal of Religious Studies* 15(1):3–24.

————.1992. "The Social Contest of healing: Research on Abortion and Grieving in Japan" Pp. 285–317 in *Innovation in Religious Traditions*, edited by Michael A. Williams, Collette Cox, and Martin S. Jaffee. Berlin: Mouton de Gruyter.

Smith, Brad. 1986. "My Emily." *SHARE Newsletter* 9(3):1–2.

Smith, Julie Boyer. 1986. "Am I a Mother?" *SHARE Newsletter* 9(3):3.

Smith, Judy M. 1997. "We Wanted a Baby." *SHARING* 6(2):7.

Smith, Margaret Charles and Linda Janet Holmes. 1996. *Listen to Me Good: The Life Story of an Alabama Midwife*. Columbus: Ohio State University Press.

Smith, Sandy. 2000. "Chester County UNITE Group Celebrates Memorial Service." *UNITE Notes* 19(1):3.

Sontag, Susan. 1966. "The Death of Tragedy." Pp. 132–139 in *Against Interpretation and Other Essays*. New York: Anchor Books.

———.1973. *On Photography*. New York: Dell Publishing.

Soto, I. M. 1987. "West Indian Child Fostering: Its Role in Migrant Exchanges." Pp. 131–149 in *Caribbean Life in New York City*, edited by Elsa M. Chaney. New York: Center for Migration Studies.

Spallone, Patricia. 1989. *Beyond Conception: The New Politics of Reproduction*. Granby, MA: Bergin & Garvey.

Spigel, Lynn. 2001. *Welcome to the Dreamhouse: Popular Media and Postwar Suburbs*. Durham, NC: Duke University Press.

Squire, Susan Merrill. 1994. *Babies in Bottles: Twentieth-Century Visions of Reproductive Technology*. New Brunswick, NJ: Rutgers University Press.

———.2001. "Transplant Medicine and Transformative Narrative, or Is Science Fiction Rubbish?" Paper presented at the annual meeting of the Society for Literature and Science, Buffalo, NY.

Stabile, Carol. 1998. "Shooting the Mother: Fetal Photography and the Politics of Disappearance." Pp. 171–197 in *The Visible Woman: Imaging Technologies, Gender and Science*, edited by Paula A. Treichler, Lisa Cartwright, and Constance Penley. New York: New York University Press.

Stacey, Jackie. 1997. *Teratologies: A Cultural Study of Cancer*. London: Routledge.

Stacey, Judith. 1984. "Are Feminists Afraid to Leave Home? The Emergence of Profamily Feminism." Paper delivered at the Western Social Science Association's Annual Meeting, San Diego.

Stagoski, Michael. 1995. "Open Arms." *SHARE Newsletter* 4(3):7.

Stallybrass, Peter. 1993. "Worn Worlds: Clothes, Mourning, and the Life of Things." *The Yale Review* 81:35–50.

———.1998. "Marx's Coat." Pp. 183–207 in *Border Fetishes: Material Objects in Unstable Spaces*, edited by Patricia Spyer. New York: Routledge.

Stander, Henricus J. 1935. *Williams Obstetrics: A Textbook for the Use of Students and Practitioners*. Seventh Edition. New York: D. Appleton-Century Company.

Stannard, David E., ed. 1975. *Death in America*. Philadelphia: University of Pennsylvania Press.

Stark, Rodney and Charles Y. Glock. 1974. *American Piety: The Nature of Religious Commitment*. Berkeley: University of California Press.

Starkman, Monica N., MD. 1976. "Psychological Responses to the Use of Fetal Monitor During Labor." *Psychosomatic Medicine* 38(4):269–277.

Stearns, Peter N. 1999. *Battleground of Desire: The Struggle for Self-Control in Modern America*. New York: New York University Press.

Steffgan, Kim. 1999. "The Brown Star Story." Reprinted in *SHARING* 8(4):7 from *When Hello Means Goodby*.

Stevens, William K. 1994. "Experts Say Pesticides May Damage Fertility." *Albany Times Union*, August 23, pp. C-4.

Stewart, Nancy. 1986. "Women's Views of Ultrasonography in Obstetrics." *Birth* 13(1):39–43.

Stewart, Susan. 1984. *On Longing: Narratives of the Miniature, the Gigantic, the Souvenir, the Collection*. Baltimore: Johns Hopkins University Press.

Stone, Lawrence. 1979. *The Family, Sex and Marriage in England 1500–1800*. Abridged edition. New York: Harper and Row.

Stover, Jennifer Lynn. 1989. "To My Brother—Robert Joseph." *UNITE Notes* 8(2):4.

Strathern, Marilyn. 1988. *The Gender of the Gift: Problems with Women and Problems with Society in Melanesia*. Berkeley: University of California Press.

Stratton, Jon. 1996. *The Desirable Body: Cultural Fetishism and the Erotics of Consumption*. Manchester: Manchester University Press.

Strozzieri, Gia Kathleen. 1996. "My Little Girl." *UNITE Notes* 15(2):1.

Sudnow, David. 1967. *Passing On: The Social Organization of Dying*. Englewood Cliffs, NJ: Prentice-Hall.

Sutton-Smith, Brian. 1986. *Toys as Culture*. New York: Gardner Press.

Swanson, Kristen M. 1999a. "Effects of Caring, Measurement, and Time on Miscarriage Impact and Women's Well Being." *Nursing Research* 4(6):288–298.

———.1999b. "Research-based Practice with Women Who Have Had Miscarriages." *Image: Journal of Nursing Scholarship* 31(4):339–345.

———.2000. "Predicting Depressive Symptoms after Miscarriage: A Path Analysis Based on the Lazarus Paradigm." *Journal of Women's Health & Gender-based Medicine* 9(2):191–206.

Swanson-Kauffman, Kristen M. 1983. "The Unborn One: A Profile of the Human Experience of Miscarriage." Unpublished doctoral dissertation. Health Sciences Center, University of Colorado.

———.1986. "Caring in the Instance of Unexpected Early Pregnancy Loss." *Topics in Clinical Nursing* 8(2):37–46.

Swanton, Peggy. 1985. "Micaelee." P. 21 in *When Hello Means Goodbye: A Guide for Parents Whose Child Dies Before Birth, At Birth or Shortly After Birth*, edited by Pat Schwiebert and Paul Kirk. Portland, OR: Perinatal Loss.

Swett, Barb. 1987. "A Prayer for Kent." *SHARE Newsletter* 10(2):2.

Swora, Maria Gabrielle. 1999. "Commemoration and the Healing of Memories in Alcoholics Anonymous." Xerox.

Tangir, Jacob, M.D. 2001. "Infection and Pregnancy Loss." Pp. 168–179 in *Parenthood Lost: Healing the Pain after Miscarriage, Stillbirth, and Infant Death*, edited by Berman. Westport, CT: Bergin & Garvey.

Tatkon-Coker, Andrea. 1988. "Neonatal Loss: Nursing Implications and Ethnic Considerations." Paper presented at the annual meeting of the American Anthropological Association, Phoenix, AZ.

Taussig, Karen Sue, Deborah Heath, Rayna Rapp. 1999. "Soft Eugenics: Discourses of Perfectibility in Late 20th Century America." Anthropology in the Age of Genetics. Paper presented at Terresopolis, Brazil: Wenner-Gren Foundation.

Taylor, Emilie. 1993. "A Little Flower." *UNITE Notes* 12(2):1.

Taylor, Janelle S. 1992. "The Public Fetus and the Family Car: From Abortion Politics to a Volvo Advertisement." *Public Culture* 4(2):67–80.

————.1998. "Image of Contradiction: Obstetrical Ultrasound in American Culture." Pp. 15–45 in *Reproducing Reproduction: Kinship, Power, and Technological Innovation*, edited by Sarah Franklin and Helena Ragoné. Philadelphia: University of Pennsylvania Press.

————.2000a. "An All-Consuming Experience: Obstetrical Ultrasound and the Commodification of Pregnancy." Pp. 147–170 in *Biotechnology and Culture: Bodies, Anxieties, Ethics*, edited by Paul Brodwin. Bloomington: Indiana University Press.

————.2000b. "Of Sonograms and Baby Prams: Prenatal Diagnosis, Pregnancy, and Consumption." *Feminist Studies* 26(2):391–418.

Taylor, Janelle S., Danielle Wozniak, and Linda L. Layne, eds. In prep. *Consuming Motherhood* (working title). Book manuscript under review.

Taylor, Lou. 1983. *Mourning Dress: A Costume and Social History*. London: George Allen and Unwin.

Taylor, Verta. 1996. *Rock-a-by Baby: Feminism, Self-help, and Postpartum Depression*. New York: Routledge.

Tennant, LouAnn. 1995. "Our Family Portrait." *SHARE Newsletter* 4(5):6.

Tenner, Edward. 1996. *Why Things Bite Back: Technology and the Revenge of Unintended Consequences*. New York: Alfred A. Knopf.

Terbush, Cheryl. 1992. "Memorial Bricks." *SHARE Newsletter* 1(5):7.

Thorne, Barrie. 1982. "Feminist Rethinking of the Family: An Overview." Pp. 1–24 in *Rethinking the Family: Some Feminist Questions*, edited by Barrie Thorne with Marilyn Yalom. New York: Longman.

Thorsen, Liv Emma. 1996. "Taming Nature with Things." Paper presented to the joint meeting of the Society for Social Studies of Science and the European Association for the Study of Science and Technology, Bielefeld.

Time Magazine. 1991. "How a Dazzling Array of Medical Breakthroughs Has Made Curing Infertility More than Just a Dream." *Time Magazine*, Sept. 30, pp. 56–63.

Todd, Dennis. 1995. *Imagining Monsters: Miscreations of the Self in Eighteenth Century England*. Chicago: University of Chicago Press.

Tompkins, Jane. 1986. "Sentimental Power: *Uncle Tom's Cabin* and the Politics of Literary History." in *Ideology and Classic American Literature*, edited by Myra Schein and Saevan Berovitch. Cambridge: Cambridge University Press.

Torres, Gabriel. 1997. *The Force of Irony: Power in the Everyday Life of Mexican Tomato Workers*. Oxford: Berg.

Townsend, Nicholas. 1988. "'Spirit Babies' and 'Blood Children': The Social Meaning of Paternity." Paper presented at the annual meeting of the American Anthropological Association, Phoenix, AZ.

Traweek, Sharon. 1993. "An Introduction to Cultural, Gender, and Social Studies of Science and Technologies." *Culture, Medicine and Psychiatry* 17:3–25.

Treichler, Paula A., Lisa Cartwright, and Constance Penley. 1998. "Introduction: Paradoxes of Visiblity." Pp. 1–17 in *The Visible Woman: Imaging Technologies, Gender and Science,* edited by Paula A. Treichler, Lisa Cartwright, and Constance Penley. New York: New York University Press.

Trethowan, W.H. 1965. "Expectant Fathers Toothache." *Mother and Child Care* 1:53.

Trevathan, Wenda R. 1988. "Childbirth in a Bicultural Community: Attitudinal and Behavioral Variation." Pp. 216–227 in *Childbirth in America: Anthropological Perspectives,* edited by Karen L. Michaelson. South Hadley, MA: Bergin & Garvey.

Tsing, Anna Lowenhaupt. 1990. "Monster Stories: Women Charged with Perinatal Endanger." Pp. 282–299 in *Uncertain Terms: Negotiating Gender in American Culture,* edited by Ginsburg and Tsing. Boston: Beacon Press.

Turner, Kay. 1982. "Contemporary Feminist Rituals." Pp. 219–233 in *The Politics of Women's Spirituality,* edited by Charlene Spretnak. Garden City, NY: Anchor Books.

Turner, Victor. 1967. *The Forest of Symbols: Aspects of Ndembu Ritual.* Ithaca: Cornell University Press.

———.1974. *Dreams, Fields and Metaphors.* Ithaca: Cornell University Press.

Twin to Twin Transfusion Syndrome Foundation. 1994. "Compassionate Deliveries: When Loss Occurs in a Multiple Pregnancy." Booklet.

Twine, France Winddance. 2000. "Bearing Blackness in Britain: The Meaning of Racial Difference for Whit Birth Mothers of African-Descent Children." Pp. 76–110 in *Ideologies and Technologies of Motherhood,* edited by Helena Ragoné and Winddance Twine. New York: Routledge.

Unknown. 1836. "A Striking and Beautiful Emblem of Immortality." *The Lady's Book* January, 12:45.

Unknown. 1988. "A Poem." Section 4, p. 60 in *Bittersweet . . . hellogoodbye: A Resource in Planning Farewell Rituals When a Baby Dies,* edited by Sister Jane Marie Lamb. Belleville, IL: Charis Communications.

U.S. Dept. of Health and Human Services. 1999. *Child Health USA 1999.* Washington, DC: U.S. Government Printing Office.

Valian, Virginia. 1998. *Why So Slow? The Advancement of Women.* Cambridge: MIT Press.

Van Buren, Abigail. 1999. "Dear Abby." *Albany Times Union,* January 26, D2.

VanDer Meer, Jami. 2001. "Signs." *SHARING* 10(2)7.

Van Gennep, Arnold. 1960 [1908]. *The Rites of Passage.* Chicago: University of Chicago Press.

Van Sant, Dorothy. 1986. "Farewell Rituals and Religion." *SHARE Newsletter* 9(4):9–10.

Ventura, Stephanie J., et al. 1995. "Trends in Pregnancies and Pregnancy Rates: Estimates for the United States, 1980–92." *Monthly Vital Statistics Report*

43(11) May 25. Centers for Disease Control and Prevention/National Center for Health Statistics.

Ventura, Stephanie J., William D. Mosher, Sally C. Curtin and Joyce C. Abma. 2001. "Trends in Pregnancy Rates for the United States, 1976–97: An Update." *National Vital Statistics Reports* 49(4).

Visconti, Linda R. 1994. "Autumn." *UNITE Notes* 13(2):1.

———.2001. "Winter's Beauty/Spring's Sustenance." *UNITE Notes* 19(4):6.

Voegele, Liz, ed. 1991. "Recognition of Life Certificates." *SHARE Newsletter* 14(6):7.

Volti, Rudi. 1988. *Society and Technological Change.* Second Edition. New York: St. Martin's Press.

———.1995. *Society and Technological Change.* Third Edition. New York: St. Martin's Press.

Voorhorst, Ginger. 1987. "Empty Womb Too Soon." *SHARE Newsletter* 10(2):2.

Wagner, Nanette. 1984. "Unanswered Questions." *SHARE Newsletter* 7(1):2.

Wallace, Mary. 1991. "Spring." *UNITE Notes* 10(2):1.

Walter, Tony, ed. 1999. *The Mourning for Diana.* Oxford: Berg.

Walther, Joe and Boyd. In press. "Attraction to Computer-Mediated Social Support." In *Communication Technology and Society: Audience Adoption and Uses of the New Media,* edited by C. A. Lin and D. Atkin. New York: Hampton Press.

Ward, Judy. 1987. "Our Angel, Tuler Michael Rossi." *SHARE Newsletter* 10(1):2.

Warren, Bambina. 1995. "Peace." *UNITE Notes* 14(1):3.

Watts, Dennis. 1985. "Message to God." *SHARE Newsletter* 8(3):2.

Weeden, Terry. 1985. "Sharing from Terry." *SHARE Newsletter* 7(4):2.

Weiner, Annette B. 1976. *Women of Value, Men of Renown: New Perspectives in Trobriand Exchange.* Austin: University of Texas Press.

———.1988. *The Trobrianders of Papua New Guinea.* New York: Holt, Rinehart and Winston.

———.1992. *Inalienable Possessions: The Paradox of Keeping-While-Giving.* Berkeley: University of California Press.

Westmoreland, April. 1995. "Future Hopes." *SHARE Newsletter* 4(3):9.

WGBH Educational Foundation. 1986. *The Miracle of Life.* Photography by Lennart Nilsson. Boston: Sveriges Television.

Whipple, D. Loren. 1995. "Please Understand: A Letter to Friends." *UNITE Notes* 14(1):5.

White, Geoffrey M. 1992. "'Remember Pearl Harbor': National Memory in the (Re)making." Paper delivered at the annual meeting of the American Anthropological Association.

White, Lynn Jr. 1967. "The Historical Roots of Our Ecologic Crisis." *Science* 155(3767):1203–07.

White, Tami. 2000. "Choices We Made." *SHARING* 9(2):1–2.

Whittier, John Greenleaf. 1995/6. "God's Promise." *UNITE Notes* 14(3):7.

Widell, Diana. 1995. "Holiday Greetings . . . " *SHARE Newsletter* 4(6):4.

Wilcox, Allen J., Clarice R. Weinberg, John F. O'Connor, Donna D. Baird, John P.
    Schlatterer, Robert E. Canfield, E. Glenn Armstrong, and Bruce C. Nisula.
    1988. "Incidence of Early Loss of Pregnancy." *The New England Journal of
    Medicine* 319(4):189–194.

Wiley, Kim Wright. 1987. "After Miscarriage: Healing the Hurt." *Health*, May,
    Pp. 80–84.

Williams, Linda. 1987. "'It's Gonna Work for Me': Women's Experience of the
    Failure of In Vitro Fertilization and Its Effect on Their Decision to Try IVF
    Again." Paper delivered at the Third International Women's Studies Congress,
    Dublin.

Williams, Raymond. 1973. *The Country and the City*. Oxford: Oxford University
    Press.

Williamson, Judith. 1994. "Family, Education, Photography." Pp. 236–244 in
    Culture / Power / History: A Reader in Contemporary Social Theory, edited by N.
    Birks, G. Eley, and S. Ortner. Princeton: Princeton University Press.

Willis, Susan. 1991. *A Primer for Daily Life*. New York: Routledge.

Winner, Langdon. 1977. *Autonomous Technology: Technics Out of Control as a Theme
    in Political Thought*. Cambridge: MIT Press.

———.1986. *The Whale and the Reactor: A Search for Limits in an Age of High
    Technology*. Chicago: University of Chicago Press.

———.1998. "Technology as 'Big Magic' and Other Myths." *IEEE Technology
    and Society Magazine*, fall, pp. 4–16.

Winter, Carol. 1996. "Footprints on Our Hearts." *SHARE Newsletter* 5(5):1–2.

Withorn, Ann. 1986. "Helping Ourselves." Pp. 416–424 in *The Sociology of Health
    and Illness: Critical Perspectives*, Second Edition, edited by Peter Conrad and
    Rocelle Kern. New York: St. Martin's Press.

Wojtowicz, Jeannie. 1987. "For Hope, with Love." *UNITE Notes* 6(4):3.

Wolf, Naomi. 1995. "Our Bodies, Our Souls: Rethinking Pro-choice Rhetoric." *The
    New Republic*, October 16:26–35.

Wood, Lori Jordan. 1988. "Kenneth Daniel Jordan." *UNITE Notes* 8(1):4.

Woody, Kathy. 1985. "A Star For Anna." *SHARE Newsletter* 8(4):1.

Wozniak, Danielle. 1999. "Gifts and Burdens: The Social and Familial Context of
    Foster Mothering." Pp. 89–132 in *Transformative Motherhood: On Giving and
    Getting in a Consumer Culture*, edited by Layne. New York: New York
    University Press.

———.2001. *They're All My Children: Foster Mothering in America*. New York:
    New York University Press.

———.In prep. "What Will I Do With All the Toys Now? Consumption and the
    Signification of Kinship in U.S. Fostering Relationships." In *Consuming
    Motherhood* (working title), edited by Janelle Taylor, Danielle Wozniak, and
    Linda Layne.

Wrensch, Margaret, and Shanna H. Swan, Jane Lipscomb, David M. Eptsein,
    Raymond R. Neurtra, and Laura Fenster. 1992. "Spontaneous Abortions and

Birth Defects Related to Tap and Bottled Water Use, San Jose, California 1980–1985." *Epidemiology* 3(2):98–103.

Wright, Elizabethada. 1997. *Fern Seeds: The Rhetorical Strategy of [Grata] Sara[h] Payson Willis Eldredge Farrington Parton, A.K.A. Fanny Fern*. Doctoral Dissertation in Rhetoric. Rensselaer Polytechnic Institute.

Wucherpfennig, Kathy. 1999. "Kristine's Garden." *SHARING* 8(1):1.

Wuthnow, Robert. 1994. *Sharing the Journey: Support Groups and America's New Quest for Community*. New York: Free Press.

Yingling, Rick. 1986b. "A Letter to Lisa." *SHARE Newsletter* 9(4):2.

Yingling, Susan. 1986a. "My Little Lisa Ann." *SHARE Newsletter* 9(4):2.

Yoder, Pam. 1985. "Untitled." *SHARE Newsletter* 8(2):1.

Young, Allan. 1996. "Bodily Memory and Traumatic Memory." Pp. 89–102 in *Tense Past: Cultural Essays in Trauma and Memory*, edited by Antze and Lambek. New York: Routledge.

Young, Frank W. 1965. *Initiation Ceremonies: A Cross-Cultural Study of Status Dramatization*. New York: Bobbs-Merrill.

Young, James E. 1993. *The Texture of Memory: Holocaust Memorials and Meaning*. New Haven: Yale University Press.

———.1997. "Suffering and the Origins of Traumatic Memory." Pp. 245-260 in *Social Suffering*. Edited by Kleinman, Das, and Lock. Berkeley: University of California Press.

Yoxen, Edward. 1989. "Seeing with Sound: A Study of the Development of Medical Images." Pp. 281–306 in *The Social Construction of Technological Systems: New Directions in the Sociology and History of Technology*, edited by Wiebe E. Bijker, Thomas P. Hughes, and Trevor Pinch. Cambridge, MA: The MIT Press.

Zeches, Mary. 1989. "Dustin Michael, Child of My Heart." *SHARE Newsletter* 12(1):2.

Zelizer, Viviana A. 1985. *Pricing the Priceless Child: The Changing Social Value of Children*. New York: Basic Books.

Zemichielli, Christine. 1999. "Dear UNITE." *UNITE Notes* 17(3):4.

Zerbel, Tom. 1987. "Burial Cradle." *SHARE Newsletter* 10(3):7.

Zorn, Carolynn L. 2001. "The Picture of Joseph." *SHARING* 10(1):9.

Index

CPSIA information can be obtained at www.ICGtesting.com
Printed in the USA
LVOW010344140911

246041LV00020BA/4/P

9 780415 911481